Summary Proceedings

of the Fifty-Fourth Annual Meeting of the Board of Governors

September 28–30, 1999

International Monetary Fund
Washington, D.C.

ISSN 0074-7025 • ISBN 1-55775-879-4

CONTENTS

Page

*Speaking on behalf of a group of countries.

*Speaking on behalf of a group of countries.

*Speaking on behalf of a group of countries.

SPEAKERS BY SESSION

*Speaking on behalf of a group of countries.

INTRODUCTORY NOTE

The Fifty-Fourth Annual Meeting of the Board of Governors of the International Monetary Fund was held in Washington, D.C., from September 28 through September 30, 1999, jointly with the Annual Meetings of the Board of Governors of the World Bank Group. The Honorable Mahesh Acharya, Governor of the Bank and the Fund for Nepal, served as Chairman.

These Proceedings include statements presented by Governors during the meetings; resolutions adopted by the Board of Governors of the Fund over the past year; reports, recommendations, or communiqués issued by the Committees of the Board of Governors at the time of the meetings; and other documents relating to the meetings.

Statements by the Governors are listed in alphabetical order by country on pages iii–iv, speakers are listed by session on pages vii–ix, and a list of abbreviations used in the statements and documents is given on pages 335–6.

SHAILENDRA J. ANJARIA
Secretary
International Monetary Fund

Washington, D.C.
November 1, 1999

ADDRESS BY THE PRESIDENT OF THE UNITED STATES[1]

William J. Clinton

Thank you very much, Secretary Summers, President Wolfensohn, Chairman Acharya, Director Camdessus, Vice President Fall, Secretary Anjaria. Let me begin by saying how very grateful I am to be here with all of you. I appreciate the generous introduction. Some of you may have heard me say this before, but the introduction that Secretary Summers just gave me is an illustration of one of my unbending laws of political life: whenever possible, be introduced by someone you have appointed to high office. It is much easier, because he has done such a superb job, and I thank him.

Let me say, all of you know that a year ago we were here in a time of crisis, perhaps the most severe financial crisis in the global economy since the end of the Second World War—a grave challenge to the Fund and the World Bank. Thanks to the hard work that you and your countries have done, economies that were sliding down are rising again.

We have also worked hard, as Secretary Summers said, in the wake of these crises to prevent future ones, to respond more quickly and effectively, to lessen the toll they take on ordinary citizens. We have intensified our efforts to construct a global financial architecture that is stable and strong in the new conditions of the new economy.

Still, those who were hit by this crisis were hit very hard. And many are still reeling. People lost jobs, businesses, and dreams. So this can only be considered a continuing challenge for us, certainly not a time for complacency. We have more to do to restore people's faith in the future and to restore their faith, frankly, in the global economy and in global markets. Therefore, we have more to do to reform the global financial foundation upon which the future will be built.

As we approach the twenty-first century, we must also ask ourselves, however: is it enough just to fix the market that is? Should we accept the fact that, at a time when the people in the United States are enjoying perhaps the strongest economy in their history, 1.3 billion of our fellow human beings survive on less than a dollar a day? Should we accept the fact that nearly 40 million people—after the Green revolution,

[1]Delivered at the opening Joint Session, September 28, 1999.

most of us discuss agriculture and food as a cause for international trade conflicts because we want to fight over who sells the most food, since there are so many places that can produce more than their own people need—are we supposed to face the fact that nearly 40 million people a year die of hunger? That is nearly equal to the number of all the people killed in World War II.

Are we supposed to accept the fact that, even though technology has changed the equation of the role of energy in the production of wealth; even though technology has changed the distances in time and space necessary for learning, and for business, as well as educational, interchanges—are we supposed to accept the fact that some people and nations are doomed to be left behind forever?

I hope that we will not accept that. I hope that we will start the new millennium with a new resolve: to give every person in the world—through trade and technology, through investments in education and health care—the chance to be part of a widely shared prosperity, in which all the peoples' potential can be developed more fully. This is the challenge of the second half-century of the life of the Fund and the World Bank. And for me it is a personal priority of the highest order.

Open trade already has improved the prospects of hundreds of millions by marketing the fruits of their labors and creativity beyond their borders. In this way, both the Fund and the World Bank have played a vital role in helping more nations to thrive. We need you to work with the World Trade Organization (WTO) to build a rules-based framework for global trade. We need you to help developing countries provide education and training to lift wages, and to establish social safety nets for tough transitions.

I applaud the strong commitment that you have made at these meetings for concrete manifestations of support. We all must work to keep the economies we have influence over open, and trade growing, for developing and industrial powers alike.

In two months, I want to launch a new type of trade round in Seattle, at the WTO ministerial meeting. I want this round to be about jobs and development. I want it to raise working conditions for all. I want it to advance our shared goal of sustainable development. By breaking down barriers to trade, leveling the playing field, we will give more workers and farmers in those countries that are struggling for tomorrow—and in leading industrial nations, as well—more opportunities to produce for the global marketplace.

In Seattle, I hope that we will pledge to keep cyberspace tariff-free, to help developing countries make better and wider use of technology—whether biotechnology or the Internet. I hope that we will pledge to open markets in agriculture, and industrial products and services, creating new activities for growth and development. I hope that we will also work to advance the admission of the 38 developing countries that have applied for WTO membership. And I hope that we will keep working to give the least developed countries greater access to global markets. Here in the United States, I am working hard to persuade our Congress to pass my trade proposals for Africa and the Caribbean Basin this year.

But the wealth of nations depends on more than trade. It also depends on the health of nations. Last week at the United Nations, I committed the United States to accelerating the development and delivery of vaccines for AIDS, tuberculosis, malaria, and other diseases that disproportionately afflict poor citizens in the developing world.

At the same time, we must help these nations avert the health cost and pollution of the Industrial Age—using clean technologies that not only improve the environment, but grow the economy. Institutions like the World Bank play a special role here. Your energy strategy is a very good start and I thank you for it. I urge the Bank to continue setting aggressive targets for lending that promotes clean energy. It is no longer necessary to have Industrial Age energy use patterns to grow a modern, powerful economy. In fact, those economies will emerge more quickly with more sustainable development strategies.

Some of you in this room—a minority still—are nodding your heads "yes" as I say this. If you believe it, we must work together to achieve it. These efforts must be part of a broader approach that ensures the integrity and openness of emerging economies. Last Saturday, the Group of Seven (G-7) finance ministers outlined specific safeguards for Russia and called for comprehensive review by the World Bank and the Fund, to make sure that funds are used appropriately in high-risk environments. The United States will continue to insist on such accountability.

For many developing countries, however, there is a greater obstacle in the path to progress. For many of them, excessive and completely unsustainable debt can halt progress, drag down growth, drain resources that are needed to meet the most basic human conditions, like clean water, shelter, health care, and education. Debt and debt relief are normally subjects for economists. But there is nothing academic about them. Simply put, unsustainable debt is helping to keep too many poor countries and poor people in poverty. That is clearly why the Pope and so many other world leaders from all walks of life have asked us all to do more to reduce the debt of the poorest nations as a gift to the new millennium—not just to them, but to all the rest of us, as well.

Personally, I do not believe that we can possibly agree to the idea that these nations that are so terribly poor should always be that way. I do not think we can, in good conscience, say we support the idea that they should choose between making interest payments on their debt and investing in their children's education. It is an economic and moral imperative that we use this moment of global consensus to do better. I will do everything I can to aid this trend. Any country committed to reforming its economy, to vaccinating and educating its children, should be able to make those kinds of commitments and keep them.

In June, at the Group of Seven summit in Cologne, the world's wealthiest nations made a historic pledge to help developing nations. The debt relief program we agreed upon is a big step in the right direction, dedicating faster and deeper debt relief to countries that dedicate themselves to fundamental reform. This initiative seeks to tie debt relief to poverty reduction and to make sure that savings are spent where they should be—on education, on fighting AIDS and preventing it, and on other critical needs. It will help heavily indebted poor countries to help themselves and help to build a framework to support similar and important efforts by the Fund, the World Bank, and international financial institutions.

More than 430 million people could benefit from this effort. In Bolivia, for example, debt relief could help the government nearly double the people's access to clean water by 2004. In Uganda, it could allow health and education spending to increase by 50 percent between 1998 and 2001. Rural development expenditures there would more than double. That is why we all must provide our fair share of financing to global debt relief.

Last week, to make good on America's commitment, I amended my budget request to Congress and asked for nearly $1 billion over four years for this purpose. We must keep adequate assistance flowing to the developing countries, especially through the International Development Association. I am encouraged by the financial commitments made by some of the other donor countries this past week. And I call on our Congress to respond to the moral and economic urgency of this issue, and see to it that America does its part. I have asked for the money and shown how it would be paid for, and I ask the Congress to keep our country shouldering its fair share of the responsibility.

Now, let me make one final commitment. Today, I am directing my administration to make it possible to forgive 100 percent of the debt these countries owe to the United States when—and this is quite important—when needed to help them finance basic human needs, and when the money will be used to do so. In this context, we will work closely with other countries to maximize the benefits of the debt reduction initiative.

We believe that the agreements reached this weekend will make it possible for three-fourths of the highly indebted poorest countries, committed to implementing poverty and growth strategies, to start receiving benefits sometime next year—actually receiving the benefits sometime next year.

If we do these things as nations, as international institutions, as a global community, then we can build a trading system that strengthens our economy and supports our values. We can build a global economy and a global society that leaves no one behind, that carries all countries into a new century that we hope will be marked by greater peace and greater prosperity for all people. We have before us perhaps as great an opportunity as the people of the world have ever seen. We will be judged—by our children and grandchildren—by whether we seize that opportunity. I hope, and believe, that we all will do so.

OPENING ADDRESS BY THE CHAIRMAN OF THE BOARDS OF GOVERNORS AND GOVERNOR OF THE BANK AND THE FUND FOR NEPAL[1]

Mahesh Acharya

I feel greatly honored to chair these important Annual Meetings of the World Bank Group and the Fund. At the outset, I, on behalf of people of the Kingdom of Nepal, wish to express our sincere gratitude to distinguished Governors for providing Nepal the opportunity to serve as Chair of the Boards of Governors of the World Bank Group and the Fund.

We are delighted to meet once again in this beautiful city of Washington, D.C. And, at this auspicious occasion, I would like to invite you all to join me in expressing our sincere appreciation to the President and the people of the United States of America for their warm hospitality.

Fellow Governors, as we are at the dawn of the next millennium with great hopes for humanity, we have a great responsibility to carry forward our institutions to fulfill our international obligations to help member countries attain prosperity and advancement. We cannot and must not forget that many millions of people in the world look to us for both finance and development wisdom. In that context, I will concentrate on two major challenges facing us in the period ahead.

One major challenge that will confront us is to distill lessons from the recent crises. It is imperative that the reform of the international financial system leads to early and sustained results to help us deal more effectively with future challenges and to raise living standards. Another major challenge is to address the pressing needs of our most disadvantaged members. Primary among these are substantial debt relief, a sustained poverty reduction effort, and other important social needs.

My fellow Governors, it has been two years since the financial crisis of the late 1990s started in East Asia. We applaud the effective response of the Bank and the Fund to support reform efforts in the crisis-affected countries. Although a number of countries have begun to recover, the aftershocks of the crisis continue to affect several countries. We also note that the crisis exposed serious weaknesses in the public, financial, and corporate sectors and—most notably—the critical need to protect the poor and the vulnerable.

[1]Delivered at the opening Joint Session, September 28, 1999.

Let me stress that the transfer of resources to developing countries should continue to be a major concern of the international community. The current trend of net long-term flows to developing countries, including from both private and official sources, is particularly worrisome. I am sure you all will agree that resource transfer is among the most important ingredients for the growth and prosperity of developing countries. Because private flows are falling, there is a greater responsibility on the part of industrial countries to enhance official flows to ensure the development of poor countries and support global peace. We also take note of the emergency and restructuring needs that have arisen from natural disasters, and humanitarian and reconstruction efforts in many regions. However, this must not divert money away from the poor in other parts of the developing world.

Global Issues

My fellow Governors, the world economy has undergone vast changes in the 1990s. We have witnessed a surge of democracy, and growth pyramids peaking and falling in a short span of time. We have observed the power of high economic growth to reduce poverty in many developing countries. But not all of us were fortunate enough to attain sufficient economic growth to address the issues of poverty, and many of us have been unable to improve income distribution, neither among the continents nor among nations nor within nations. We must ensure that all countries can benefit from globalization through an orderly and well-sequenced integration into the world economy. In this context, it is essential that any new round of multilateral trade negotiations be a "development round," with developing countries participating fully in the negotiations.

Since we met last year, the outlook for the world economy has improved. We are happy to witness these improvements, although we need to remain vigilant. One important lesson from the recent turmoil is the need to maintain policy flexibility when responding to crises. The growth of world output is expected to increase moderately next year, as the recovery in Asia's crisis-afflicted emerging market economies gains momentum, strong growth continues in the United States, and better performance in Europe and Japan takes hold. However, the continued uneven pattern of growth among the major industrial countries poses a worrisome risk to the outlook. Ensuring the continuation of the global expansion will require a significant rebalancing of growth and addressing the existing large external imbalances.

Sustaining the recovery in the crisis-hit economies and reducing the vulnerability of all developing countries to external shocks will require the continued vigorous pursuit of structural reform programs, focusing in particular on the banking and corporate sectors. There is no room for complacency. Indeed, this highlights another lesson from the recent experience, namely, the need to focus on high-quality broad-based growth to ensure that all levels of society benefit from reform programs.

Among other emerging market economies, the improved outlook for Brazil and Mexico is encouraging, but the economic challenges facing other countries in Latin America is a matter of concern. While the economic downturn in Russia was less severe than previously expected, the need for far-reaching structural reforms remains essential to support a sustained recovery. For China, India, and other South Asian economies, growth prospects appear favorable. However, broad structural reform and poverty reduction agendas need to be addressed. For the Middle East and Africa, the recent oil price increases will help improve the fiscal positions and external balances of several countries, although other primary producing countries continue to be negatively affected by persistent weaknesses in many other commodity prices. Continued adjustment efforts—particularly at diversifying production toward manufacturing and services—need to be encouraged. The challenges facing our African members are particularly difficult, and the Bank and the Fund need to build on our support for their adjustment and capacity building efforts.

Strengthening the Architecture of the International Financial System

My fellow Governors, we note the substantial progress achieved in strengthening the architecture of the international financial system. The ultimate aim of these efforts must be to protect living standards worldwide by preventing future crises.

One major development has been the recent creation of Contingent Credit Lines (CCL) by the Fund as a new crisis-prevention mechanism. And the Fund has just created a special temporary facility to help member countries that encounter temporary balance of payments difficulties as a result of the Year 2000 (Y2K) computer problem.

Another central focus has been on improving transparency, both at the national and international levels. We must recognize that, in order to work smoothly, markets require timely and comprehensive economic information. To that end, a number of initiatives have moved forward on improving the communication of Bank and Fund policies and programs to the public.

We note that progress has been made on the development, dissemination, and adoption of internationally accepted standards—or codes of good practice—for economic, financial, and business activities. The Fund has made considerable progress in developing and refining voluntary standards in its core areas of expertise, such as through the strengthening of the Special Data Dissemination Standard, notably with respect to international reserves and external debt. It has also developed codes of good practice in the fiscal, and monetary and financial areas. Collaboration between the staffs of the Bank and the Fund in working on financial sector issues has been substantially improved by the establishment of the Bank-Fund Financial Sector Liaison Committee.

A further focus has been on financial sector strengthening, where the Bank and the Fund are working together under the recently concluded Financial Sector Assessment Program. It is expected that this will strengthen their dialogue with member countries and help to highlight emerging areas of stress in national financial systems. The program will provide clients with diagnosis, advice, and assistance in developing strategies to improve financial sector stability, build institutional capacity, and assure broader access to financial services. Work has also progressed on improving the involvement of the private sector in forestalling and resolving crises. The aim is to help bring about a more orderly adjustment process, limit moral hazard, strengthen market discipline, and help emerging market borrowers protect themselves against volatility and contagion. We have also worked hard to continue to strengthen our institutions, and we welcome in particular the proposed transformation of the Interim Committee of the Fund into the International Monetary and Financial Committee.

In order to reinforce the activities of the Bank in the financial sector, it has created a "New Spending Authority" program to assist countries in crisis or vulnerable to crisis. Resources were allocated for social sector programs to reduce the impact of the crisis on the poor and vulnerable groups, and to facilitate corporate restructuring and improve corporate governance. My fellow Governors, closely related to such developments is the issue of the liberalization of capital movements, and the integration of global capital markets. The recent emerging market crisis underlined the need to ensure that countries wishing to gain and maintain access to capital markets could do so in a way that recognizes the importance of their stability and economic security. This means an orderly and well-sequenced approach on the part of both creditor and debtor nations. Appropriate lessons must be drawn from countries' recent experience with the liberalization of capital movements and the use of capital controls—particularly with respect to potentially volatile short-term flows.

Poverty Reduction and Challenges

My fellow Governors, we are all aware that global progress toward the critical goal of poverty reduction has not been satisfactory. Worldwide poverty trends are worsening, particularly as a result of the recent financial turmoil. We note some achievements in the fight against poverty, such as an increase in life expectancy, a drop in infant mortality, and a rise in school attendance of girls. However, progress on poverty reduction and sustainable development is lagging in many developing countries. In fact, the number of poor people in South Asia, sub-Saharan Africa, Europe, and Central Asia is on the rise, particularly in the regions most affected by crisis and conflict. Half of the world's 6 billion people are trapped in poverty and subsist on less than $2 a day.

My fellow Governors, we all are aware that the financial crisis threatened our endeavors to reduce poverty. We, the policymakers, must shape our strategies so that they do not inadvertently inflict long-term hardships on the poor by triggering lower investment in education and health. While cuts in government spending might be unavoidable in a crisis, we must ensure that the services that protect the poor and keep children in school are maintained.

Moreover, we are faced with enormous challenges in the areas of literacy and basic health, especially for women and girls. The HIV/AIDS epidemic has compounded these challenges and is reversing decades of progress in improving the quality of life in developing countries, especially in Africa and South Asia. Developing countries in particular urgently need an AIDS prevention vaccine to contribute to their prevention efforts. This will require a combined effort of all partners. We are pleased to note that the Bank will continue to invest in preventing HIV and in strengthening health systems in developing countries.

My fellow Governors, we will all have to redouble our efforts to achieve our agreed goal to cut in half the incidence of poverty by the year 2015 and to attain a better life for our children. I call on the World Bank and the Fund, as well as other agencies to continue to improve the quality and delivery of their assistance in order to address the challenges of poverty reduction and global development.

Over the past year, the Bank and the Fund have continued to support the adjustment and development efforts of our members. The Bank began piloting the Comprehensive Development Framework (CDF), which seeks a better balance in policymaking by highlighting the interdependence of many elements. It also emphasizes strong partnerships among donors, civil society, the private sector, and other development actors. We need to underline the importance of technical assistance to strengthen the capacities of our members to implement these programs. We look forward to drawing lessons from the pilot projects currently under way. We stress again that the needs, interests, concerns, and aspirations of the developing countries must be reflected in the CDF.

We note that the strong adjustment lending in 1999 reflects the continuing focus of the Bank on responding to the financial crisis, emphasizing the protection of social spending and the strengthening of the social safety nets to protect the poor and the vulnerable.

We also welcome the closer linking of the operations of the Bank, IFC, and MIGA in the country assistance strategies. These have been increasingly formulated in consultation with civil society and other stakeholders, and focused on poverty outcomes and social issues. The Bank has also continued to enhance its system for evaluating the development impact of its efforts on the ground. We are pleased to note the agreement on the twelfth replenishment of the International Development Association (IDA), which includes new donor funding. We are confident that this will strengthen the efforts of the Bank Group to reduce poverty.

The proposal to introduce Poverty Reduction Strategy Papers (PRSP) is a concrete example of a combined Bank/Fund initiative to improve the effectiveness of the efforts to reduce poverty. This new approach will focus on helping countries to develop their own strategies for reducing poverty. These tripartite documents of the authorities, the Bank, and the Fund should become an effective vehicle to enhance the poverty reduction impact of IDA and Enhanced Structural Adjustment Facility (ESAF) lending programs. They will also link heavily indebted poor country (HIPC) debt relief more closely to poverty reduction, and ensure ownership, transparency, and broad-based participation. This fits well with the aim of making poverty reduction a central focus of the ESAF. I stress here the importance of strengthening the institutional capacities of developing countries to implement this initiative.

My fellow Governors, the Fund has also been very active in support of the adjustment and reform efforts of the membership. Its surveillance work has continued at a rapid pace. I am also pleased to note that, in addition to its traditional attention to macroeconomic issues, the Fund has continued to focus increasingly on a broader range of structural, institutional, and social issues in its consultations with national authorities. In addition to the establishment of Contingent Credit Lines, the Fund also agreed on modifications to the policy on post-conflict emergency resources to provide more financial assistance for a longer period of time. In response to the financial crises, the demand for Fund resources remained extremely heavy over the past year. We are pleased that the successful implementation of the Eleventh Quota Review provided the necessary financial resources to support adjustment efforts of member countries.

Financial Assistance to Developing Countries

My fellow Governors, hundreds of millions of the world's poor live in countries where crushing debt stands in the way of lasting poverty reduction. The HIPC Initiative has already yielded some positive results.

There has been extensive international cooperation among all partners in implementing the initiative. Nevertheless, recent developments and experiences have highlighted the vulnerability of many HIPCs to exogenous shocks. It is our duty to reinforce and to enhance this program so as to provide faster, deeper, and broader debt relief. We appeal to contributors to make additional financial commitments to ensure success of the initiative.

We must ensure that debt relief under this initiative should not come at the expense of other aid and other deserving recipients. It must complement, not replace development assistance. We must ensure that debt relief becomes an integral part of efforts to help countries grow and reduce poverty. This must make a difference in the lives of the people in the debt-burdened poor countries. Also, the resources freed from debt service must be better directed for the development of the social sector.

Consideration must also be given to alleviating the debt burdens of a number of poor countries excluded from the HIPC Initiative. In this context, I would like to bring to your attention the case of Nepal. Despite our efforts, the incidence of poverty in Nepal is pervasive, the level of social services is very low, and the human development needs are enormous. Substantial revenues are allocated by Nepal for debt servicing. Indeed, Nepal is regarded as one of the poorest countries in the world, yet it is not eligible for this initiative.

My fellow Governors, we have witnessed an accelerating pace of globalization recently. However, not all countries have benefited from this process. As we enter the new millennium, we must ensure better cooperation between all development partners, including bilateral donors, multilateral agencies, and national authorities. Our aim must be to facilitate the integration of poor countries into the global economy and to realize the potential to improve living standards in all countries. When future generations look back at our deliberations at these meetings, let us hope they say that their better future began today.

Fellow Governors, we have every reason to be proud of our two institutions. No doubt, we have a mammoth agenda before us, but our common resolve will take us to the height of success. I am confident that our two institutions will be able to meet the formidable challenges of the next century. I hereby declare open the fifty-fourth Annual Meetings of the World Bank Group and the International Monetary Fund.

OPENING ADDRESS BY THE PRESIDENT OF THE WORLD BANK GROUP[1]

James D. Wolfensohn

I am very pleased to welcome you to these Annual Meetings of the World Bank Group and the International Monetary Fund. I would like to express my appreciation to Chairman Mahesh Acharya, whose work in Nepal shows a deep understanding of many of the issues I wish to address today—and to my colleague and friend Michel Camdessus. We work ever more closely together, and I salute the remarkable team he leads.

Mr. Chairman, I have had the privilege of addressing you on four previous occasions. In 1995, I spoke of the challenge of development, of the need to educate girls and address the burden of debt. I saw the need for the Bank to reorganize within and to embrace partnerships outside with a wholly new vigor; to form partnerships with other official aid and development institutions, with civil society, and the private sector; to listen to and work more closely with the governments and people of the countries we serve.

In 1996, I emphasized our role as a Knowledge Bank. I spoke, too, of the "cancer of corruption." The Bank committed itself to join concerned governments to fight corruption wherever we found it. And since that time, we have been pushing ahead vigorously with that agenda. Later in the year, with our partners in the Fund, we articulated our approach to debt forgiveness for the poorest countries. The HIPC Initiative has made a real difference, and, at these meetings following the changes suggested at the Cologne Summit, further progress has been made.

In 1997, I spoke of "The Challenge of Inclusion," of the need to think of development in human terms and to bring the weakest and the most vulnerable from the margins of society to the center stage. A year ago, with the Asian financial crisis dominating our concerns, I spoke of "The Other Crisis," the human crisis of those condemned to poverty as well as those who had found hope and seen it roughly snatched away. I spoke of the special role of our institution in dealing with the impact of the crisis on people and of the urgent need to look beyond financial solutions, to take the social and the structural together with the macroeconomic.

[1]Delivered at the opening Joint Session, September 28, 1999.

Today as we meet one year later, it is tempting to take comfort in thoughts of a financial crisis passed—though for millions that other crisis still lives. It is tempting to put off the needed reforms—though for millions those reforms still matter. It is tempting to talk of safe passage—though for millions of poor and unemployed there is still no sight of harbor.

We meet today on the threshold of a new millennium. We must take stock and ask ourselves some fundamental questions. Will we seize the moment to raise our sights for a better world? Will we begin to judge our efforts not by the prosperity of the few but by the needs of the many? Will we be prepared to hold ourselves accountable, to make the effort necessary to bring about change?

For what is the millennial world that we see? A world where over the last 40 years life expectancy has risen more than in the past 4,000 years. A world where the communications revolution holds out the promise of universal access to knowledge. A world where democratic culture has opened up opportunities for many. A world where 5.7 billion people live in a market economy compared with 2.9 billion only 20 years ago.

But look more closely and we see something else. Per capita incomes that will stagnate or decline this year in all regions except east and south Asia. In the developing world, with the exception of China, 100 million more people are living in poverty today than a decade ago. In at least 10 countries in Africa, the scourge of AIDS has reduced life expectancy by 17 years. We have more than 33 million cases of AIDS in the world, of which 22 million are in Africa; 1.5 billion people still lacking access to safe water; 2.4 million children who die each year of waterborne diseases; 125 million children still not in primary school; and 1.8 million people who die annually of indoor air pollution. It is a world where the information gap is widening and the forests are being destroyed at the rate of an acre a second.

The picture is mixed and the challenges are great. But this is a moment in history when we can set a new course to a world of greater peace, equity, and security. It is a time not just for review, but for action. Last year my colleagues and I decided that in order to map our own course for the future, we needed to know more about our clients as individuals. We launched a study entitled "Voices of the Poor" and spoke to them about their hopes, their aspirations, their realities. Teams from the Bank and from nongovernmental organizations have gathered the voices of 60,000 men and women in 60 countries. Let me share with you our findings.

Poverty is much more than a matter of income alone. The poor seek a sense of well-being that is peace of mind; it is good health, community, and safety. It is choice and freedom as well as a steady source of income.

Well-being is having the chance to grasp new economic opportunities; something the poor feel much less able to do than a decade ago. Well-being is personal security. More women are working outside the household now, trying to make ends meet. But gender inequity at home persists, and domestic violence is on the rise. And corruption is a daily fact of life as the poor try to access public services and make a living.

What is it that the poor reply when asked what might make the greatest difference to their lives? They say, organizations of their own so that they may negotiate with government, with traders and with nongovernmental organizations. Direct assistance through community driven programs so they may shape their own destinies. Local ownership of funds, so that they may put a stop to corruption. They want nongovernmental organizations and governments to be accountable to them.

Let me share with you their world in their own words. An old woman in Africa: "A better life for me is to be healthy, peaceful, and to live in love without hunger." A middle-aged man in Eastern Europe: "To be well is to know what will happen to me tomorrow." A young man in the Middle East: "Nobody is able to communicate our problems. Who represents us? Nobody." A woman in Latin America: I do not know whom to trust: the police or the criminals. Our public safety is ourselves. We work and hide indoors."

These are strong voices, voices of dignity. Many represent a new generation seeking control of their lives. These people are assets, not objects of charity. They can build their future if given opportunity and hope. They are talking about security, a better life for their children, peace, family, and freedom from anxiety and fear. As we sit comfortably here in Washington, we must hear their aspirations. For they are no different from our own.

No, the crisis is not over. The challenge has barely begun. Next month our global population will reach 6 billion. Based on current trends, we will not meet the International Development Goal of halving poverty by 2015, nor the goal of providing universal primary education by 2015, nor that of reversing the current loss of environmental resources both nationally and globally by that date. In 25 years, those 6 billion people on our planet will grow to 8 billion. Of the 6 billion today, 3 billion live under $2 a day and 1.3 billion live under $1 a day. I am concerned that these extraordinary statistics may rise to 4 billion and 1.8 billion, respectively. This is not a legacy to leave our children.

The number of conflicts seems likely to be higher, the quality of our environment will be worse, the disparities between rich and poor will be wider. The voices of the poor will be louder; but will they be heard? What have we learned about development? We have learned that development is possible but not inevitable. That growth is necessary but not sufficient to ensure poverty reduction. We have learned that we must put poverty front and center. We have learned that we must take the social and the structural hand in hand with the macroeconomic and the financial. We have learned that for development to be real and effective, we need local ownership and local participation. Gone are the days when development can be accomplished behind closed doors in Washington, or Western capitals, or any capital for that matter.

At a recent meeting in Stockholm to assess progress on the Comprehensive Development Framework, President Mkapa of Tanzania said: "Ownership of development policies and programs is not only an understandably nationalist yearning, an inherent and sovereign right, but it also creates the most fervent disposition and conditions for hard work and for self-development, both at the national and the local level. Our people must be encouraged and facilitated," he said, "to be owners of their development: not just beneficiaries, but doers of development."

We must heed this call as we plan our development agendas in the years ahead. But we must go further. We must recognize our own role in helping, not hindering, those *doers* of development by better coordinating our own activities. It is shameful that Tanzania must produce 2,400 reports each quarter for its donors. It is shameful that Tanzania must suffer 1,000 missions from donors a year. And Tanzania is by no means alone.

So how do we proceed? It was in recognition of the need to better coordinate our efforts, to recognize the holistic nature of development, and to put the country firmly in the driver's seat that we launched the Comprehensive Development Framework this year.

Our aim was simple: to bring the social and the structural aspects of development together with the macroeconomic and the financial so as to establish a much more balanced and effective approach; to bring the players together so as to leverage all our activities; and to work with the broad development community—the United Nations, the European Union, bilaterals, regional development banks, civil society, and the private sector to build a new generation of genuine partnerships.

What are the results so far? Together with our partners, the CDF is now being piloted in 13 countries. We are learning to cooperate and coordinate our work better at the local level. After discussions with many ministers, I believe that the approach of the CDF is now widely supported. Not as a blueprint but as a process through which we pursue long-term, results-driven development with the country in the driver's seat and in partnership with the broad development community. Very shortly, the Development Assistance Committee will report on its review of bilateral and multilateral initiatives along lines similar to those of the CDF. It will conclude that the need for partnership and more coordinated efforts is widely recognized and accepted.

I am delighted, too, that we have reached a historic agreement with the Fund to have a common Poverty Reduction Strategy developed with our client governments. We will take a balanced approach linking macroeconomic and financial parameters with the human, structural, and social aspects, in one document that will guide the programs of each institution.

However, in the course of the past 12 months, I believe that we have also learned something else. We have learned that the causes of financial crises and poverty are one and the same. Countries may come up with sound fiscal and monetary policy, but their development is fundamentally flawed and will not last if they do not have good governance, if they do not confront the issue of corruption, if they do not have a complete legal system that protects human rights, property rights, and contracts, that gives a framework for bankruptcy laws and a predictable tax system—and if they do not have an open and regulated financial system and appropriate regulation and behavior that is transparent.

What use is the law book if the judges are corrupt, if the poorest and most vulnerable expect only brutality from police? What use is constitutional protection if women face discrimination in the marketplace and violence at home? What use is the foreign investor, if there are no accounting standards and requirements for transparency, no contract laws, and no predictable and fair tax system? What use is privatization if there are neither social safety nets to deal with unemployment nor rules to protect the public from private monopolies? Holes in institutional development and governance and lack of adequate and fairly paid staff gnaw destructively at policymaking, service delivery, and accountability.

We have learned both from our general experience and from our pilot CDF programs that strengthening the organization, human capacity, and structure of the state—both at central and local levels—is the first priority in our challenge to reduce poverty. We have learned that when we sequence the steps of the CDF, we must give the greatest emphasis first to strengthening governance and to capacity building in government and civil society.

That decision is confirmed by a recent United Nations Development Program (UNDP) survey of 150 resident coordinators: over half gave top priority to the need to strengthen governance and build capacity. It is supported by a recent survey of over 3,600 private firms in 69 countries that identified the need for strong institutions and rule making. It is supported by our own consultations with the poor who repeated the same cries over and over: too much corruption, too much violence, and too much powerlessness and weakness. They long for a system that gives them equity and voice, and if they cannot have this through the ballot box or through government, they want it through informal organization outside government.

What would it really take to move from powerlessness to a democratic culture? What would it take to move from weakness to a capacity for action? What would it take to move from violence to peace and equity? First and foremost, it will take real commitment from the leadership of each country—both elected leaders and those with financial power and influence. It will take willingness to reform systems of government, regulations, and institutions. It will take strong support for building capacity. It will take having police forces that are no longer seen as agents of oppression rather than protection and security. It will take strong local institutions to bring government closer to the poor. It will take empowering local people to design and implement their own programs because far less is lost in corruption when a community manages its own resources.

Whether you look at the government or the community level; whether you look through the prism of financial crisis or human need; whether you speak to investors, bankers, or the dispossessed; governance and capacity are key. With poverty reduction front and center on our agenda, our work at the rock face must be governance, institutions, and capacity building.

Studies are already showing what we surely knew intuitively. That good governance is associated with higher GNP per capita, higher adult literacy, and lower infant mortality. That bad governance—lack of accountability and transparency, together with corruption and crime—is the number one impediment to development and poverty reduction. Weak governance threatens to undermine HIPC—which will only work if the resources that are freed are purposefully used for poverty reduction. With weak governance, there will be no progress in education, health, water, energy, or rural and urban development. Weak governance threatens to marginalize countries and whole peoples from the economic mainstream, and it will keep them on the margins—for if lending is only effective in countries with sound policies and sound institutions, who will lend to the poor performers?

At the Bank, we propose to give great emphasis in the years ahead to the question of working with governments to strengthen structure and governance. Do we have all the answers? No. Do we have all the expertise? Certainly not. We can only have success in partnership with others in the development community, including civil society and the private sector. Within the next few months we will join with UNDP, which has special skills and experience in this area, and with others to look at what each of us is doing on governance and capacity building. We will assess the strengths and experience that each of us brings and determine how we might all go forward together.

Such an agenda requires that we focus on the interrelatedness of the systems that work and that make societies function effectively. It requires that we focus on sound public governance systems with checks and balances, and that governments take up the fight against corruption. It requires building legal and judicial systems that protect the rights of citizens and their endeavors, going beyond big-ticket governments and business deals. Corruption is a core poverty issue, robbing from the poor the little they have. We must focus on financial and banking systems that inspire equal confidence in the global investor and the peasant farmer with small savings, especially women. We must have modern corporate procedures, including accounting, audit, and disclosure policies at the highest level. We must focus on micro-credit schemes and finance for small and medium enterprises that work in both times of crisis and ordinary times.

We must train well-organized and motivated civil servants and civic leaders who see the purpose of their jobs in delivery to the communities they serve—and we must remember that this training rests in turn on effective teaching and learning. We must concentrate on building strong local official and civil society institutions that inspire trust. For there can be no doubt that the local level is the real key to effective poverty reduction. It takes more than changing formal rules to build these institutions. It means changing the informal rules and norms, it means building people, building values, and building skills and incentives that can support people committed to change.

There is a new model emerging in Africa, the Partnership for Capacity Building. It has taken two years to move from concept to action. It is African-led and will be implemented by Africans. It involves the direct support and collaboration of the Bank, the Fund, the UNDP, and the African Development Bank and it is rooted in partnership with the private sector and civil society. We have pledged $150 million to a supporting fund. We will all join with our African colleagues to support them in a coordinated and urgent effort to achieve their objectives. However, we must remember President Mkapa's enjoinder. We must create doers of development. Too many capacity-building efforts have floundered in the past because they have not been rooted in local ownership.

I have spoken at length about the complexity of reaching our goals at the country level. But we know that nations are dependent on one another. We know that nations are no longer the sole masters of their destinies. We need global rules and global behavior. We need a new international development architecture to parallel the new global financial architecture.

What might such an international development architecture look like? First it would be a coalition built on the cooperation of all the players—the United Nations, governments, multilateral agencies, the private sector, and civil society. It would be a coalition between recipients, donors, and the citizens of donor countries—a coalition based on results. There must be effective performance in utilizing development assistance—corruption-free and reaching the poor. Voters want to see that their assistance makes a difference. The goodwill exists—performance is what is needed. Second, it would be a coalition in which we recognize that, yes, we must break the chains of debt, but we must also have the resources to go much further and break the chains of poverty. The HIPC debt forgiveness that we have announced is the beginning of our challenge, not the end. Third, it would be a coalition that recognizes that we must have a trade system that works, with rules and norms that are fair, comprehensive, and inclusive—a Development Round for the twenty-first century. Fourth, it would be a coalition that recognizes that environment knows no borders. We need to implement international agreements on climate change, desertification, and biological diversity, just as we did with ozone depletion. We must move to action on these global conventions. We must ensure that the Global Environment Facility is fully funded to do its work. Fifth, it would be a coalition that recognizes the power of modern research to democratize health—to harness new vaccines to eradicate AIDS, malaria, tuberculosis, and polio. Sixth, it would be a coalition to make the information revolution truly universal—to bridge the growing knowledge gap, to connect all developing and transitional economies to the world and to each other, and to be a real vehicle for sharing and learning via satellite, email, and the Internet. For there is no doubt that the technological revolution will have an enormous impact on the substance of development.

Globalization can be more than the unleashed forces of the global market. It can also be the unleashing of our combined effort and expertise to reach global solutions. We need to build coalitions for change: coalitions with the private sector that will bring investment, create jobs, promote the transfer of technology and skills, and foster social responsibility; coalitions with civil society and communities to mobilize the kind of grassroots support we have seen behind the debt campaign—and to extend it to health, education for all, participation, and poverty reduction; coalitions with governments to assist them in taking charge of their own development agendas with the participation of their citizens; coalitions with each other to put an end to the turf battles, the wastage, and the duplication; coalitions with religions, with trade unions, and with foundations to benefit our common work; and coalitions of commitment to the seven United Nations pledges on sustainable development, gender, education, infant, child and maternal mortality, and reproductive health. I pledge to you our intention to work with all our partners to help build those coalitions for change, so that when we meet next year in Prague, we will have begun to put in place that new development architecture.

I have outlined a complex agenda. Is the Bank gearing up to meet this challenge? I believe unequivocally, yes. On governance, we are already spending over $5 billion a year—working on civil service reform, budget management, tax administration, decentralization, legal reform, judicial reform, and institution building. We are working with over two dozen countries on anticorruption programs. We help to train judges, and we run public national workshops that bring corruption into the bright glare of sunlight. We even train investigative journalists—conscious that a free and professional press is a society's voice.

On knowledge, we have made dramatic progress over the past four years. Our Knowledge Bank brings us closer together, through distance learning, using satellite connectivity. It also takes knowledge to far-away places by closing the information infrastructure gap—reaching students through the African Virtual University and through our WorldLinks program, which connects school children in the industrialized world with their brothers and sisters in the developing world.

We have a major project to clear slums with programs built on the efforts of the inhabitants with whom we work by introducing land titles and self-sustaining projects for infrastructure. With the World Wildlife Fund, we have built a powerful alliance to save our forests; with the private sector, the United Nations, and foundations, we are building a Global Alliance for Vaccines and Immunization, an AIDS Vaccine Task Force, and a malaria initiative. With over 140 different partners, we have already wrestled river blindness into submission. This stands as a marvelous example of what we can do together, and we are working with local communities building partnerships from the bottom up—through local democratic institutions, as in India. We have learned that the best and most effective projects we have are those that are locally based and close to our real clients, people in poverty in rural and urban communities. We have learned that local ownership and involvement must be central to our architecture.

Is the Bank up to the challenge? I believe that we have 10,000 extraordinarily gifted and committed staff in the Bank, IFC, and MIGA. It has been a tough year, and I want to thank them and their families for the contributions that they have made. We stand on the threshold of a new millennium. So much that is possible is within our grasp. Will we have the courage and the leadership to reach out and grasp it? Will we finally recognize that we live in one world? Look around. We are linked by financial systems, we are linked by communications, we are linked by environment, and we are linked by trade. Migration knows no borders;

crime knows no borders; and drugs, war, and peace know no borders. Only national budgets stop short at frontiers. Only national elections pay little heed to that larger world. We need leadership to explain to our peoples that our national interests are international. We cannot avoid the growth of our global population to 8 billion people in the next 30 years, nor the growth in trade, nor the growth in poverty.

From this understanding, we must reaffirm our commitment to development—a real commitment to each other—a real commitment to act on the generous statements made by so many of the leaders of industrialized countries toward the developing countries. We must find the commitment to meet the recommended level of 0.7 percent of GNP in official development assistance. And leaders of developing and transition economies must reaffirm their commitments to carry out their promises for good governance, equality, and growth.

These commitments need a human and moral aspect as well. There needs to be a passionate rededication to each other as we enter the next century. All of us have to assume a responsibility for global equity, which is the only assurance of peace. How can one not be moved by the comments of the poor to which I referred earlier?

A father from Eastern Europe said, "Poverty is humiliation, the sense of being dependent on them, and of being forced to accept rudeness, insults, and indifference when we seek help." And the voice of Bashiranbibi from South Asia said, "At first I was afraid of everyone and everything: my husband, the village, the police. Today I fear no one. I have my own bank account. I am the leader of my village's savings group. I tell my sisters about our movement."

We must look forward, we must commit ourselves to bring about the day when the poor of the world, the aged, the street children, the disabled, the rural workers, the slum dwellers, will all be able to cry out "Today I fear no one. Today I fear no one."

PRESENTATION OF THE FIFTY-FOURTH ANNUAL REPORT[1]

BY THE CHAIRMAN OF THE EXECUTIVE BOARD AND MANAGING DIRECTOR OF THE INTERNATIONAL MONETARY FUND

Michel Camdessus

"To the Excellencies and officials of Europe: We suffer enormously in Africa. Help us. We have problems in Africa. We lack rights as children. We have war and illness, we lack food.... We want to study, and we ask you to help us to study so we can be like you, in Africa."

(Message found on the bodies of Guinean teenagers, Yaguine Koita and Fode Tounkara, stowaways who died attempting to reach Europe in the landing gear of an airliner.)

Governors, ladies, and gentlemen, let me join Jim Wolfensohn in extending to you a heart-felt welcome to these Annual Meetings. I would like to extend special greetings to our new colleague in the International Labor Organization, Juan Somavia, and to broaden these greetings to include the heads of the many standard-setting and other agencies who are with us for these meetings. They all know how much we value their cooperation in reforming the international monetary and financial system.

Governors, the global economy has passed through a great ordeal. For a time, we faced the threat of the most extensive and harshest crisis since our institutions were established. Its human cost has been immense, and we may need a few more years to heal all the wounds. Remember our anxieties a year ago when the crisis was still ricocheting from one country to another. Now, the storm is abating, and the horizon is brightening, even though some risks remain. Several countries that were in the depths of crisis—Korea, Thailand, the Philippines, Brazil, and others—are advancing in their recovery.

This is, then, a good occasion to ask how this surprisingly quick, almost unprecedented, brightening of prospects is coming about. It is not by chance. It is evidence of the depth of globalization and a vivid illustration of the benefits of the market economy when supported by decisive,

[1]Delivered at the opening Joint Session, September 28, 1999.

flexible public policymaking. Above all, the recovery comes from the intense effort; the wisdom; and, most emphatically, the sense of cooperation of all concerned.

Specifically, it can be attributed:

- first and foremost, to the efforts of those countries most directly affected by the crisis. Far from abdicating their responsibility to pursue adjustment and reform, they seized the opportunity to lay the foundations for high-quality growth;
- to the efforts made by those countries at risk from contagion to bolster their defenses;
- to the solidarity shown by their financial and trading partners;
- to the efforts of the major industrial countries to maintain a favorable global environment, as reflected in the flexible approach to monetary policy in the United States and in Europe, as well as in Japan's determination to revive its economy;
- and last, but not least, to the efforts of the international institutions.

Governors, at the most demanding moments of this crisis, your cooperation has made all the difference. When we had to take unprecedented decisions under conditions of great urgency, you were there. When we were under storms of criticism contending that we were doing more harm than good, you were there. When essential programs had to be adopted for Thailand, for the Philippines, for Indonesia, for Korea, for Brazil, for Russia, and for others, you were there; we were together. You supported all decisions unanimously. At no time was a single vote missing at the Executive Board. For this support, for this cooperation, for this unanimity, at the time of the most severe test in our history, may I simply say: thank you. Let me add here that the work of the staff and its commitment to its tasks is also a crucial, indispensable, and important part of this success. To them also, I say a profound "thank you."

Beyond any doubt, this is a major lesson of this crisis: in the new world of globalization, cooperation is a must. A second lesson—a lesson of this very moment—is that we always run the risk, when economic prospects have improved, of moving too slowly to implement the reforms that are needed. There is still urgent need for action, for implementation of reforms decided. So I shall largely confine my remarks today to the two domains where I see a pressing need to move quickly to implementation: first, the reform of the international monetary and financial system; and second, the offensive to eradicate poverty and to humanize globalization.

But before proceeding, let me say a few words about IMF programs with two of our largest members, Russia and Indonesia. In Russia, the economy is recovering, and the program that began in July this year is on track. We look forward, as the program moves ahead, to Russia's advance in both structural reforms and improving governance. Amid all the recent controversy, we should not lose sight of the real progress that has been achieved during seven years of endless efforts to assist Russia in its journey toward a market economy. Nor should we ignore the fundamental decision, on which Russia has not wavered, to seek to develop a modern market economy and integrate itself into the international community. It would be the height of irresponsibility to turn our backs on this great nation. We will not do that.

In troubled Indonesia, with the vital support of the Fund as well as the World Bank, the Asian Development Bank, and bilateral donors, the government turned the economy around after taking office last year. Economic stability, in turn, helped make possible the freest elections in Indonesia's history. Now these achievements are threatened. But be sure we stand ready to resume our assistance as soon as the shadows hanging over the program are lifted. We expect to continue working with the next government of Indonesia to do our part in helping the country achieve its great potential, while we look forward to contributing, when the day comes, to the rebuilding and sustainable development of East Timor.

Now let me return to my two main themes: the work still to be done in the reform of the international financial system, and the pressing urgency of the war on poverty. In both these areas, the international community has taken important steps in the past few months, indeed in the past few days. But in reality, the hard work, the implementation, is only just beginning.

International Monetary and Financial Reform

First, architecture. Work is in progress. Sunday's communiqué of the Interim Committee contains an impressive catalog of significant steps. I do not need to dwell on them. Already remedies are beginning to address the deficiencies revealed by the challenges of globalization. Rightly, they focus on prevention; on the golden rule of transparency; on financial sector stability; and on the definition of global standards to underpin stable, fair, efficient, and transparent markets. An important step forward is the adoption by the Interim Committee of the Code of Good Practices on Transparency in Monetary and Financial Policies, which now joins the codes on fiscal transparency and data dissemination that are already in force. New facilities have been created: the Contingent Credit Lines, and the Y2K facility. Yes, the foundations are there of a safer, more robust, more adaptable architecture. But progress is slower in other areas where full consensus has yet to emerge. Let me briefly mention four of them.

First, we have begun a period of reflection on the scope and focus of surveillance. Several aspects are unquestionable:

- its central role in the work of the Fund;
- its priority in allocating our human and budgetary resources, since only the Fund has this mandate;
- its growing importance, in a new environment where early detection of emerging problems is of the essence; and
- its primary focus on matters that are the traditional mandate of the Fund—monetary stability, balance of payments sustainability, and growth-oriented economic policies.

But, as clearly indicated in your Declaration on Partnership for Sustainable Global Growth in 1996 and as the crisis has dramatically confirmed, major destabilizing factors can emerge anywhere. These risks call for robust banking and financial systems; sound, transparent, and participatory governance; arm's-length relationships among governments, banks, and enterprises; and supportive social policies. Now, the issue is how, and to what extent, to integrate these concerns into our surveillance and how to interact with the many other agencies. Of course, we have started. But how should the priorities be defined country by country? How can we avoid further stretching an already overloaded staff? What is the limit not to cross? And, lastly, how can we proceed with the monitoring and implementation of standards, particularly where they lie outside our traditional mandate?

We must clarify these issues. This will be a high priority in the coming months. You can be sure that a significant part of our response will rely on the arrangements we will set up with other agencies to share the task of disseminating and monitoring standards that lie outside the Fund's main areas of expertise: securities markets, accounting, auditing, insurance, corporate governance, and others. We have already made significant headway in developing a capacity to assess the soundness of financial sectors, working jointly with the World Bank, and collaborating with the Bank for International Settlements (BIS) in the development of principles for banking supervision.

Next, we have the problem of private sector involvement in crisis prevention and resolution. The volatility of private capital flows, as they swing from euphoria to panic, can and must be diminished by promoting a mature relationship between creditors and their sovereign clients, and between the financial community and the official sector. The involvement of the private sector is a matter of practical necessity, since the private sector will be increasingly important for financing the emerging market and developing countries. But it must be recognized that crises may arise that would benefit from closer cooperation and what we call "ex ante" approaches. We must now, drawing on the lessons of the actual cases that have arisen recently, try to distill a set of principles that could help to resolve crises at less cost than in the past. That being done, it will remain important, at least in my view, to have—for the protection of both creditors and debtors—a way of ensuring that countries are given time, in extreme circumstances, to seek orderly resolution with their creditors. One avenue consists of designing a mechanism that will permit a temporary stay of litigation; this could be achieved by an appropriate amendment or interpretation of the Fund's Article VIII(2)(b). Not all are yet convinced, I must confess!

Third, we have the debate on the relative merits of all-out liberalization of capital movements and the illusory virtues of exchange controls. This debate could, I think, soon be brought to a close. Consensus is achievable on the way to proceed with the orderly liberalization of capital movements; and in today's world of highly volatile capital flows, this consensus is all the more important. We have two core messages here: one is that, in the long term, liberal arrangements for capital movements are beneficial to global economic development. The other is that the process of liberalization should be an orderly one, tailored to individual countries' situations. Our recent proposal to introduce a gradual, country-specific approach reasserts the equal weight we attach to both goals and explicitly recognizes the great variety of country situations. I would urge you, Governors, to lend your personal attention to this important proposal, thereby bringing to completion the support you gave us in Hong Kong two years ago for an amendment to the purposes of the Fund and to extend our jurisdiction as needed.

Fourth, the question of exchange rate regimes. Here, mindful of the critical importance of an issue at the heart of the Fund's mandate, we have asked for a little more time to finalize our reflection. We know quite well that many of the problems of the so-called "casino economy" are related to the nature of exchange rate regimes and to the shortcomings of international cooperation in this field.

We have witnessed the effect of deficiencies in exchange systems or exchange rate management in triggering or amplifying crises, and their key role in transmitting domestically generated crises. And we know well the role played by the volatility of exchange rates in, what seems at times, the sheer irrationality of market developments. Clearly, for the time being, today's diversity of exchange rate regimes will continue. But, equally, the greater mobility of capital has made the maintenance of fixed exchange rates more demanding. In considering how to improve exchange stability we can be encouraged by:

- the widespread recognition of the essential role of the soundness of economic fundamentals; and
- the remarkable success of the introduction of the euro, with its potential to become a strong player in an orderly multipolar system.

Governors, as you see, we still face some difficult problems. They must be solved because the soundness of the new system is at stake in each of these instances. And the soundness of this system is a fundamental precondition for any sustainable worldwide progress in the human condition. This brings me to the imperative of eradicating poverty, since, as Angel Gurria put it yesterday, poverty is the ultimate systemic threat. Let me then turn to my second theme.

Humanizing Globalization

Sound finances clearly involve sophisticated instruments, standards, and smoothly working markets; but, ultimately, finances and markets are about people and for people. And it is the hard, the demanding, task—it is the honor—of the Fund, even if it is not a development institution, to try continuously to help governments to be responsive to the cries of the poor. The cries of the poor! I believe that we must keep in our minds and hearts the heartbreaking message of the two teenagers from Guinea, found dead in the landing gear bay of an airliner, a message to, I quote: "the Excellencies and officials of Europe." They said, "we suffer enormously in Africa. Help us. We have problems in Africa. We lack rights as children. We have war and illness, we lack food.... We want to study, and we ask you to help us to study so we can be like you, in Africa." This message, I presume, was also for each country and institution represented here today. It is a message from those in absolute poverty. It tells us that the extent of poverty still present at the end of a century of affluence is intolerable; and, of course, the degree of absolute poverty is absolutely intolerable. So it is time to respond.

But this is not new for you: social policies are central elements of government budgets, of donors' aid programs, and of international communiqués. Nor are these issues new to the Fund; for many years, IMF-supported programs have explicitly incorporated social policies. During the past decade, in most countries implementing IMF-supported programs, education and health care have significantly increased in real per capita terms. At the same time, there have been improvements in important social indices. But the voices of the poor around the world are telling us in no uncertain terms that this is not enough. The time has come for a new and more decisive start.

There are two dimensions in the war against poverty: one national, the other international. The first will remain predominant. As our friends, Mamadou Touré and Alassane Ouattara, have so frequently reminded us, the responsibility for alleviating poverty rests at home with each country, though this does not diminish the importance of the international community.

Poor countries themselves need to generate high-quality growth. We can learn from the positive experience of many African countries that, assisted by IMF-supported programs, have begun to reverse the sad cycle of one-and-a-half decades of declining per capita growth, high inflation, and external imbalances. We know the ingredients: a stable macroeconomic environment; an open, efficient market economy, a framework that fosters private investment; and, yes, transparency, financial sector soundness, and robust economic institutions. Good governance, of course! With all that entails: in particular, respect for the rule of law and an independent judicial system that recognizes property rights, enforces contracts, and protects basic citizens' rights. On all these aspects of development policies, I cannot but echo the thoughtful remarks made by Jim Wolfensohn this morning.

A fully articulated social dimension is of the essence. A vital interrelationship exists between growth and social development. This linkage has been too loose in our programs so far. The best route out of poverty is strong, sustainable high-quality growth. Strong social policies that address poverty at its roots lay the foundation for sustained economic growth. This is why we must aim—even if it is a long-run objective—at the eradication of poverty. But, for that, an international contribution is indispensable. I am delighted to tell you that an important set of measures the Executive Board has just endorsed aims precisely at that: a strong, concerted effort to reduce poverty.

A central element will be the transformation of the ESAF to the Poverty Reduction and Growth Facility, to incorporate the lessons of more than 10 years' experience; a new level of cooperation with the World Bank; new steps for debt reduction; and, above all, an explicit link with poverty reduction. A key feature will be the formulation by countries of their own comprehensive growth-oriented policies designed to reduce poverty. These policies will be articulated, after open discussion with civil society, in the form of Poverty Reduction Strategy Papers with IMF and World Bank support. And, since the Bank will base its IDA operations on the same policies laid out in these same papers, a far greater degree of synergy between the operations of the Fund and the Bank will be created. We look forward to the continued deepening of cooperation with the World Bank and the regional development banks to implement these changes and to tap their expertise. Equally, we believe this approach will foster more fruitful contacts with donors, official agencies, and civil society.

With the integration of social objectives at the heart of our programs; the deeper, faster, and broader debt relief provided by the new HIPC Initiative; the strong link established between debt relief and increased human development expenditure; all of this crowned by the adoption of the key principles of the new facility, the Fund is now well equipped to give a new impulse to the fight against poverty. Starting, of course, with the expeditious implementation of the new HIPC Initiative.

But, Governors, there is a price to pay for debt reduction. And for the Fund it is high. It has implied that we engage in exhaustive, indeed exhausting, negotiations to convince countries to contribute in one way or another to this effort. For their contributions, I thank all of them—on a preliminary count, 88 countries, of whom the large majority are developing or transition countries, including several who have used ESAF resources themselves. And I should beg their pardon for my, perhaps at times, intolerable persistence. On the part of the Fund itself, we have accepted that the Fund should almost triple, from 5 million ounces to as much as 14 million ounces, the stock of gold we will utilize to generate, through off-market transactions, the earnings needed to complete our contribution. Governors, for the Fund the job is done. The pledges that you have made, once they have been ratified by our members, will complete the Fund contribution to this initiative—a one-time truly exceptional operation in this most worthy of causes.

But, still more is needed for this strategy of poverty eradication to be credible. One important element is to boost trade as well as aid: for that, the industrial countries must make a bolder effort to open their economies to all the exports of the poorest countries. This small step need not await the so-called Millennium Round of trade negotiations to be launched in Seattle later this year, which, of course, we hope will bring major advances for the entire global economy. This is fundamental, but, at the same time, the trend of a decline in official development assistance must be reversed. In conference after conference, we—the industrial countries, developing and transition countries, and international agencies alike—have made pledges to promote human development. It is now imperative to put the financing in place. Remember the Copenhagen Declaration, which pledged to reduce by half the level of extreme poverty by the year 2015. In numerous other international gatherings, we have pledged to realize at least six other challenging targets in the next 15 years: universal primary education, a two-thirds reduction in infant and child mortality, a three-fourths reduction in maternal mortality, universal access to reproductive health services, together with the elimination of gender disparities in primary and secondary education by 2005.

Have a look at the small gray cards you have on your tables summarizing these seven pledges (see attachment), and let us imagine for one minute that they will be duly implemented: what a giant leap toward a better world, what a giant leap toward empowerment of the most disadvantaged among the poor: women, and children!

These commitments are a challenge to both developing countries and donor countries. For the poorest countries, the poverty reduction strategy I have just outlined should contribute significantly. On the donors' side, at a moment when we must, alas, recognize how far there is to go to meet the target of devoting 0.7 percent of GDP to development aid, let us stop merely lamenting this failure and see how to get back on target. A practical contribution to making sure that the pledges are implemented would be to monitor indicators that would allow us to check each year where we stand and to help us, if needed, to identify effective ways and means to transform pledges into action. Today I call all other relevant institutions to join with the Organization for Economic Cooperation and Development (OECD) Development Assistance Committee (DAC) in preparing these indicators and in sharing responsibility for this assessment. Governors, when preparing for all the celebrations of the millennium, let us decide to make the coming decades the decades of pledges fulfilled.

Finally, in this reflection on the use of our limited concessional resources, we cannot forget that repeated demands have been made for the alleviation of postconflict situations and that in many countries good policies have not survived the resurgence of armed conflict. We will, of course, continue to respond to these tragic situations, but we must be more proactive. That is why initiatives for peace are essential. And that is why I have no hesitation in repeating today some suggestions that have been made to restrain arms trade and military expenditures:

- restraining the sales of military equipment to sensitive regions;
- abolishing the provision of export credit for military purposes;
- adopting national maximum levels for military expenditure that should not exceed 1.5 percent of GDP in Africa, and might often be much lower;
- cooperating in the interdiction of the smuggling of raw materials and natural resources to finance armed conflict; and
- broadening the UN register to involve many more countries and to cover small arms and ammunition.

We must endorse them. Just think how many plowshares could be forged with such an oversupply of swords! Governors, before closing, let me underline the urgency of a number of tasks that must be addressed in the period immediately ahead:

- for the industrial countries: to take advantage of the recovery not only to achieve more balanced growth among themselves, but also to introduce flexibility to their structures and markets, and to consolidate their public finances;
- for countries emerging from crisis: to forge ahead with the major reforms still needed;
- for the HIPC countries: to adopt the policies needed to be counted among those reaching the decision point before the end of 2000;
- for all countries: to proceed with the possibly difficult budgetary choices that may be entailed in implementing the seven pledges on sustainable development I have recalled today; and
- for you, as Governors of the Fund: not only to make the Fund as modern as the markets, but also an institution that is even more responsive to the needs of the world, even more human centered and a better place for achieving a broader sense of world citizenship.

Governors, times of respite can be dangerous times, and they can be short lived; the temptation may not be, perhaps, to rest on our laurels, but to wait and see or to turn to different agendas. Governors, do not miss this opportunity to show the world that you—together—do not need the pressure of a crisis to do your collective job for the good of humanity. I say this with all my conviction: it is urgent! Next year, it could be just too late! As we look back at the past two years, we take pride in having worked with you and learned with you; we were saddened, as you were, at the difficulties facing your people and have rejoiced when your policies, with our support, have begun to show positive results:

- in the handful of countries at the center of the crisis;
- in more than 50 other countries—rarely caught in the glare of international attention—that are implementing IMF-supported programs; and
- in another 125 members with whom we are working through our surveillance, technical assistance, and training as they weathered this global crisis.

All these efforts have bought us time, not for celebration but for action to move the world economy from its present recovery to a path of high-quality sustainable growth and through that, through all our techniques and thoughts—as Pierre Teilhard de Chardin used to say—to full humanization. The need is there. The agenda is defined. The pledges have been made. Targets have been set. It is time for action. Let us go forward.

Annex

SEVEN PLEDGES ON SUSTAINABLE DEVELOPMENT[1]

Reducing extreme poverty: The proportion of people living in extreme poverty in developing countries should be reduced by at least one half by 2015. *(Copenhagen)*

Universal primary education: There should be universal primary education in all countries by 2015. *(Jomtien, Copenhagen, Beijing)*

Gender equality: Progress toward gender equality and the empowerment of women should be demonstrated by eliminating gender disparity in primary and secondary education by 2005. *(Cairo, Copenhagen, Beijing)*

Infant and child mortality: The death rates for infants and children under the age of five years should be reduced in each developing country by two-thirds of the 1990 level by 2015. *(Cairo)*

Maternal mortality: The rate of maternal mortality should be reduced by three-fourths between 1990 and 2015. *(Cairo, Beijing)*

Reproductive health: Access should be available through the primary health care system to reproductive health services for all individuals of appropriate ages, no later than 2015. *(Cairo)*

Environment: There should be a current national strategy for sustainable development in the process of implementation in every country by 2005, so as to ensure that current trends in the loss of environmental resources are effectively reversed at both global and national levels by 2015. *(Rio)*

[1]Pledges made in one or more of the following declarations:

Framework for Action to Meet Basic Learning Needs, World Conference on Education for All, Jomtien, Thailand, March 1990.

Rio Declaration on Environment and Development, UN Conference on Environment and Development, Rio de Janeiro, Brazil, June 1992.

Cairo Declaration and Program of Action, International Conference on Population and Development, Cairo, Egypt, September 1994.

The Copenhagen Declaration on Social Development and Program of Action, World Summit for Social Development, Copenhagen, Denmark, March 1995.

Beijing Declaration and Platform for Action, Fourth World Conference on Women, Beijing, China, September 1995.

REPORT TO THE BOARD OF GOVERNORS OF THE INTERNATIONAL MONETARY FUND BY THE CHAIRMAN OF THE INTERIM COMMITTEE OF THE BOARD OF GOVERNORS ON THE INTERNATIONAL MONETARY SYSTEM[1]

Gordon Brown

I am honored to report on the Interim Committee's discussions on the world economy and its new financial architecture. I report also on Sunday's first-ever joint meeting of the Interim and Development Committees, where together we entered into a historic commitment to deliver, in the year 2000, many of the world's poorest countries from burdens of unsustainable debt.

Since we met here in Washington last October, when turbulence threatened global stability, the world has taken decisive action. Our Committee observed that world growth prospects are now substantially better than they appeared even a few months ago, and the expectation is of recovery strengthening in 2000.

But as the Committee agreed, this is no time for complacency. The challenges ahead include ensuring that the sustained pickup in domestic demand in Europe and Japan, together with medium-term growth in the United States in line with potential, helps to achieve a more balanced pattern of growth. And the Committee urged the crisis-affected emerging market economies to press ahead vigorously with structural reforms that will accelerate their return to sustainable economic growth.

Last year our Committee concentrated on the design of a new framework for stability in the new global economy. This year we have been making important decisions, agreeing on a new design. In the coming year, we must translate our new consensus into effective implementation.

A New Framework for Global Stability

At its April meeting, the Committee noted that broad agreement had been reached on key aspects of a strengthened architecture. It called on the private sector, national authorities, the Fund, and other institutions and forums to carry forward their work in the months ahead. On Sunday, the Committee reviewed progress to date. I am pleased to report that significant progress has been made toward a new framework. Let me elaborate on the main elements.

[1]Delivered at the opening Joint Session, September 28, 1999.

Surveillance and Transparency

The first lesson we have learned from recent events is that stability is more likely where we have open and transparent procedures in fiscal and monetary policy—and in corporate standards—and where there are agreed objectives clearly and openly stated and regularly monitored.

The Committee underscored the importance of increasing transparency of national governments, the private sector, and the international financial institutions. I believe that, in today's global economy, governments need to set clear objectives for fiscal and monetary policies, and to follow open and transparent procedures. This is critical for their accountability and for investor confidence. Without transparency and proper procedures, investors may not make the long-term commitment so necessary for jobs, growth, and social progress.

Substantial progress has already been made in this area. The Fund has established the Special Data Dissemination Standard (SDDS), to which 47 countries have subscribed, and the General Data Dissemination System (GDDS), both of which will improve the quality, accuracy, and timeliness of data reporting, especially with regard to members' reserves and debt management policies.

The Fund adopted the Code of Fiscal Transparency in April 1998, and I am pleased to announce that the Committee on Sunday also adopted the Code of Good Practices on Transparency in Monetary and Financial Policies. These codes and standards are not incidental to the new architecture, they *are* the architecture.

The Committee encouraged the Fund, in cooperation with other standard-setting bodies, to continue to experiment with assessments of members' observance of international standards and codes of good practice. It asked the Executive Board to consider whether to integrate such assessments into the surveillance process.

The Committee also reiterated the importance of greater transparency in policymaking. It welcomed the widespread release of Public Information Notices, the public release of IMF policy papers and the associated summaries of Board discussions, and the release of the external evaluators' reports on IMF surveillance and economic research activities. The Committee reaffirmed the importance of independent evaluations of the Fund's operations and policies. The decision of 46 countries that have already volunteered to participate in the pilot program for the release of Article IV reports is particularly welcome, as is the Fund's agreement to establish a presumption in favor of publication of program documents. The Fund is encouraged to take further actions to make IMF practices and members' policies more transparent, while taking care that this does not compromise the role of the Fund as confidential advisor to governments.

Financial Sector Reform

In the financial area, governments must maintain strong internal financial controls and tighten supervision and regulation of domestic financial institutions and offshore banking centers, including measures to deter money laundering. The Committee urged the Fund to enhance its support for members' efforts in this area.

Because today's financial markets are global, we need not only provide proper national supervision but also better financial regulation worldwide. The Fund and the Bank are enhancing coordination on surveillance and their advice in the financial sector.

The Fund, the Bank, other international groups, and financial supervisors have also stepped up their efforts to develop and implement principles and good practices for sound financial systems, and to improve their capacity to make assessments of financial sector vulnerabilities. The Committee welcomed these efforts.

The Financial Stability Forum has now been established. This welcome initiative makes cooperation between the international financial institutions and the regulators a fact of life. The Forum has made a successful start by establishing working groups to coordinate the work of the international financial community on the implications of highly leveraged institutions, offshore centers, and short-term capital flows.

Considerable progress has been made by business, financial institutions, and government agencies around the world in preparing computer systems for the millennium date changeover—the Y2K computer problem. Nevertheless, the risk of possible Y2K-related problems exists. The decision by the Fund's Executive Board to introduce a temporary facility that would help members deal with unforeseen balance of payments problems that may arise in connection with Y2K is therefore welcome. But members must continue to press ahead and take the necessary steps to minimize Y2K-related disruptions in their financial systems.

Crisis Prevention and Resolution

There is a general consensus that prevention of crises remains the key. Analysis of members' vulnerability to crises should be strengthened, and the Fund and its members should focus, in the context of both surveillance and program design, on minimizing and managing this vulnerability. Here, the continued involvement of the private sector—in both forestalling and resolving crises—is critical.

The Committee noted the progress achieved in securing the involvement of the private sector in individual cases. It considered that the report by the G-7 Finance Ministers to the Cologne Economic Summit provides a helpful framework on which to build, and within which the international community can work to address individual cases. The Committee has asked the Executive Board to build on this framework and to report at its next meeting on the ways in which the broad principles have been implemented.

Choice of Exchange Rate Regimes

While it is up to members to decide what exchange rate regime to adopt, it should be borne in mind that individual members' choice of exchange rate regime has repercussions for the member itself, but also in some cases potentially for the world economy. The Committee noted that IMF surveillance and programs should further focus on the consistency of a member's macroeconomic policies, institutional arrangements, and exchange rate regime.

Transformation of the Interim Committee

To strengthen the policymaking process, the Committee endorsed the recommendation of the Executive Board to the Board of Governors that the Interim Committee be transformed into the International Monetary and Financial Committee, and that its advisory role be strengthened.

Poverty Reduction

It is important that, in building a strengthened financial system, we do not forget the plight of the poor. The low-income heavily indebted countries must also benefit from the new architecture. A critical need is to reduce poverty. There is a now general recognition that growth by itself is not necessarily sufficient for reducing poverty. Sustainability of growth requires rising incomes founded on durable productivity growth. This in turn entails policies, in areas such as health and education, that raise productivity and enhance employment opportunities, especially for the poor. Moreover, in fostering economic growth through prudent macroeconomic policies and structural reforms, it is critical that the burden of adjustment does not fall on the poorest and most vulnerable.

The reform of the Fund's ESAF into the Poverty Reduction and Growth Facility, which will make poverty reduction an explicit and overarching goal, is a major step forward. The Committee warmly welcomed this reform of the ESAF. The cornerstones of the new approach are (i) a comprehensive Poverty Reduction Strategy Paper that will be prepared by the country, with assistance from the World Bank and the Fund, to guide the design of programs; (ii) social and sectoral programs, aimed at poverty reduction, will be taken into account fully in the design of economic policies for promoting faster, sustainable growth; (iii) greater emphasis will be accorded to good governance, in particular in all government activities, through greater transparency, effective monitoring procedures, anticorruption initiatives, accountability, and the involvement of all sectors of society; and (iv) higher priority will be accorded to key measures critical to achieving governments' social goals.

The Committee recognized that a mountain of inherited and hitherto immovable debt stands in the way of economic development in the poorest countries: unsustainable debt that is a burden imposed from the past on the present generation, which is tragically depriving millions of their chance of a future. And it is in the spirit of those who founded the Fund and the Bank that all of us believe that we have obligations beyond our front doors, responsibilities beyond the city wall, duties to others beyond our national borders, that we are called to take decisive action.

So let it be said of the conclusions from the historic joint meeting of the Development and Interim Committees—that those to whom the world's greatest wealth has been given have joined with those burdened down by the world's greatest debt and destitution to form a new and worldwide alliance against poverty.

First, by endorsing the enhancements and reforms to the HIPC Initiative, we set ourselves a challenging target to move three quarters of eligible countries through the process and the remainder on the path to debt relief by end-2000.

Second, in seeking to establish a virtuous circle of debt relief, poverty reduction, and economic development, we endorsed a major and decisive shift in policy on poverty. The old approach underplayed the importance of social policy. The new approach is that countries will prepare reduction strategies in partnership with the Bank and Fund and that these will stress how together macroeconomic, structural, and social policies can generate growth and contribute to reducing poverty.

We agreed that poverty reduction strategies should be country-driven, engage the broad participation of civil society, and be explicitly linked to achieving agreed international development goals, the most pressing and challenging of which is to halve world poverty by 2015.

Third, financing our reforms—and in this area in particular I pay tribute, as in so many areas, to the work of Michel Camdessus, James Wolfensohn, and their staffs, without whom faster, deeper, and wider debt relief could not have been possible. The Interim Committee endorsed the decision of the Fund for off-market transactions of up to

14 million ounces of gold to fund the Fund contribution to the new enhanced HIPC framework. In the last week alone, an additional $1.5 billion has been promised or committed to the HIPC millennium trust fund. The challenge is for those countries in need of debt relief to secure that debt relief now, and I believe that the first country can now benefit from our enhanced debt relief not just in a year, or in months, but in weeks.

Concluding Remarks

So, in all our decisions, we are reaffirming the public purpose and high ideals that 54 years ago brought the Fund and the new international financial order into being; demonstrating our belief that prosperity is indivisible and that we cannot take refuge in absentee government; showing that, by the strong helping the weak, it makes us all strong; and by that public action, we can say from here in Washington, on the eve of a new century, we are determined to advance a new and worldwide prosperity for all.

REPORT TO THE BOARDS OF GOVERNORS OF THE BANK AND THE FUND BY THE CHAIRMAN OF THE JOINT MINISTERIAL COMMITTEE OF THE BOARDS OF GOVERNORS ON THE TRANSFER OF REAL RESOURCES TO DEVELOPING COUNTRIES (DEVELOPMENT COMMITTEE)

Tarrin Nimmanahaeminda

As Chairman of the Development Committee, I am pleased to report to you on the Committee's work during the two meetings held this year. The Committee's agenda in these meetings focused on three basic areas. These are:

- the enhancement of the HIPC Initiative; and
- strengthening the international system and architecture; and
- important World Bank developments and issues.

Let me address each one briefly.

HIPC Initiative

The HIPC Initiative began over three years ago in the Development Committee, and it has continued to be a major focus of our attention. In April we encouraged the institutions to develop options designed to make the debt relief "broader, deeper, and faster," and to establish a clear link between debt relief and poverty reduction. These goals served as the basis for the agreements reached two days ago at a joint meeting of the Interim and Development Committees, and yesterday at the Development Committee.

The HIPC Initiative was the ideal issue for this first-ever joint meeting of the two committees. The Executive Boards of both institutions have been deeply involved at every stage, and so it is appropriate that the far-reaching proposals for change were reviewed by the full membership of both Committees. The results were reflected in a joint statement issued by Chancellor Brown and myself after the meeting. We stated that "this joint meeting symbolizes the cooperation and high political commitment of all countries and institutions in this effort, and the new closer relationship between the Bank and Fund which will be crucial to achieving this goal."

We believe the Committee has contributed to a major strengthening of Bank-Fund collaboration in support of poverty reduction—increased cooperation that is likely to have an impact far beyond the HIPC Initiative. The enhanced initiative entails, of course, additional costs for all participants. The Development Committee and the Joint Meeting have built the political support and momentum needed for success. Central to achieving this political support has been the reaffirmation of several key principles that have guided the initiative from the start, including the additionality of debt relief, the maintenance of the financial integrity of multilateral financial institutions, and the importance of fair and equitable burden sharing. The Committee has also considered the special problems of countries in conflict, and the assistance provided by the Bank and the Fund to assist post-conflict countries. We stressed the need to link such efforts to preparing countries for eligibility in the HIPC Initiative. In short, we are very pleased with the leadership role played by the two institutions and their leaders in making this ambitious venture possible, of course with the generous support of many partners represented in this hall today.

Strengthening the International System and Architecture

The Committee has addressed a number of important subjects that directly or indirectly form part of the international architecture. In the past year we have explored the following areas:

Developing countries and the international trade agenda. We were pleased to have as a plenary speaker yesterday the new Director-General of the World Trade Organization, Mr. Mike Moore. He set the tone for important and supportive comments in our communiqué, which emphasized that the next round of trade negotiations needed to deliver "early and substantial benefits for developing and transition countries, in particular the least developed countries."

Principles and good practices in social policy. The Committee discussed this subject in the aftermath of the Asian crisis, stressing the importance of concerted action to help countries bolster their social policies and institutions. We concluded, however, that further development of basic principles in this area was best pursued with, and within, the framework of the United Nations, and leaving the Bank to concentrate on translating broad principles into practical country-specific results.

Strengthening international fora. The Committee discussed a number of options for strengthening the work of the Development Committee, including its links to the Interim Committee. Some of our members had advocated experimenting with a joint session of the two committees, and as a result of our experience two days ago we know that under certain circumstances it can work to good advantage. We are also seeking to ensure the minimum of overlap between the agendas of the two committees, so as to make the best use of members' time.

World Bank Issues

The Comprehensive Development Framework. During these two meetings the theme of the CDF has frequently arisen, as many ministers have stressed the valuable contribution the CDF can make to formulation of development programs. Its holistic approach, the central role played by the host government, and the emphasis on partnership have struck a strong and positive note among many Committee members. One aspect of partnership particularly emphasized by the Committee is the need to strengthen further the World Bank's cooperation with regional development banks.

Bank capital adequacy. The President has worked closely with the Executive Board in reviewing carefully the status of the Bank's financial capacity. Their conclusion, supported by the Development Committee, is that the Bank's finances remain sound, but that there are clear limits on what it can do to respond to future demands, especially if there is a deterioration in the global financial environment. We will be keeping the subject under review, based on regular reports from the Bank.

Conclusion

In conclusion, over a year ago, when I became Chairman of the Development Committee, there was great concern that Bank-Fund cooperation was insufficient on many important issues. Now I am pleased to report that such is no longer the case, as the Bank and the Fund have cooperated closely on many common institutional challenges facing them in this past year.

STATEMENT BY THE GOVERNOR OF THE FUND FOR THE REPUBLIC OF ARMENIA

Levon V. Barkhoudarian

I am pleased to participate at these Annual Meetings of the World Bank Group and the Fund and to be able to offer briefly Armenia's views on those policy directions for the year 2000 and beyond that will enhance global growth and development for my country and for those like us who seek to complete the difficult transition to a fully functioning market economy.

Overcoming financial crises this past year in parts of the world economy once again highlights for us all the importance and the necessity of continued joint efforts by the international financial community. At the same time, I believe that these financial failures also underscore the critical importance of creating and executing specific strategies that will address problems at the pre-crisis stage, before world markets are buffeted by events that may be avoidable.

While none of us can predict the future with absolute certainty, I believe that the Governors should affirm a forward-looking policy that states unequivocally that a country that has already demonstrated convincingly its commitment to tight monetary and fiscal policies shall have the backing of the international community. Without such mutual accord between country and community, agreed to and understood in advance, the world economy will continue to face similar shocks, a corresponding decrease in the level of trust of the people in countries seeking international integration, a resultant lowering of trade volumes, and a general decrease in the efficiency of the world economy.

It should go without saying that, during our discussions on world integration, special attention should be devoted to the equal treatment of all countries, which recognizes the necessity of financial support for transition economies—especially small and therefore comparably manageable ones—firmly following the path of establishing a market democracy.

The Republic of Armenia, together with many of the countries in the world, has been affected by the international, and especially the Russian, financial crisis. The impact of the latter was multiplied—a decrease of income flowing into Armenia, a contraction of gross demand and decrease in consumption volumes, with a corresponding reduction of fiscal revenues, a noticeable decline in both import and export volumes, and an outflow of capital from both the treasury bill market and important investment projects. Obviously, our government had to take corrective action swiftly to contain the impact of the crisis in Armenia. As evidence of the efficacy of the measures undertaken, I am pleased to state that the midterm review under the ESAF has just been concluded, and the documents have been presented for discussion by the Fund's Executive Board at the beginning of October.

Armenia attaches great importance to the attraction of foreign investments. As a factor in assuring the stability of the investment environment in our republic and, as important, in asserting our firm position with respect to our maximum integration into the world economy, I want to reaffirm Armenia's best efforts toward accession to the World Trade Organization. I hope and expect that our efforts will show results this year.

Perhaps the Governors will agree with me when I say that a situation where some two-thirds of all foreign direct investment flows to only a few countries cannot foster the level of development for all countries that we would desire. The problem in my country is made even more acute by the fact that almost all investment flow so far has been related to the privatization process. I would urge that the efforts of the international financial institutions in the new millennium be directed toward offering the full assistance required by emerging economies in gaining the knowledge, experience, and tools necessary to compete successfully in the global marketplace.

A fully integrated world economy is difficult to imagine without regional cooperation. The strengthening of such cooperation is one of Armenia's top priorities. International financial institutions could greatly facilitate regional cooperation in our region and in others by giving increased importance to those projects that benefit both the country and the region.

The financial crises that we have experienced appear to have contributed to an even greater appreciation of the importance of transparency, as reflected in the implementation of Bank and Fund programs. Transparency is the only means by which it is possible to reach an understanding within a society on the economic programs being implemented and, thus to ensure their success. Armenia, for one, participates in the pilot project of the Fund to guarantee greater transparency of projects being implemented, and I can tell you that it has been our experience that encouraging public discussions enhances the efficiency of these programs. As stated in the principles adopted by the Fund, monetary and fiscal policies benefit greatly when their goals and instruments are presented to and understood by the public.

We welcome the day-by-day increase in cooperation between international financial institutions, especially the Fund and the World Bank. I consider that in such areas as pensions, provision of satisfactory infrastructure for the development of the private sector, environmental protection, and fiscal federalism, the cooperation of sister organizations in a coordinated and efficient manner can bring major benefits to the economic prosperity of the countries involved. In such circumstances, the on-site study of projects and the initiation of public discussion on projects being implemented acquire greater importance than ever. And, in this regard, it is worth noting that both the Bank and the Fund have the possibility of associating their lending programs with nonlending activities, such as technical assistance, consulting services, and other such mechanisms that help develop efficient solutions to specific problems.

The topic of the Annual Meetings—"Setting the Agenda for Global Growth and Development on the Eve of the Millennium"—is designed to give us an opening to discuss the problems the world economy faces at the end of the millennium, and to identify coming tasks and new policy directions. I believe that the Governors should continue to focus their attention on the areas of greater transparency, crisis prevention, and regional and global integration. Next year in Prague, I hope that we will be able to affirm our progress in this regard and to continue our discussion on specific measures to reach these objectives.

STATEMENT BY THE GOVERNOR OF THE BANK AND THE FUND FOR AUSTRALIA

Peter Costello

In the past two years, beginning with events in Thailand in July 1997, we faced some of the greatest challenges to the international financial system ever. And in East Asia, financial crisis quickly led to economic recession and worse. The region that had been the world's strongest growth region for a decade or more suddenly reversed. Millions of people had their standards of living savaged and their opportunities shattered. But the situation has now stabilized. There are signs of strong growth in Korea, Japan shows signs of recovery, the United States is strong, Europe is picking up, and the world economy is likely to continue improving in the remainder of 1999 and into 2000.

However, optimism about the outlook needs to be tempered by a strong note of caution. Many economies still face substantial policy challenges. We remain concerned by economic developments in Indonesia and the very troubled state of affairs in East Timor. I call on the international community to lend its humanitarian hand to address the crisis in East Timor. In crisis-affected economies, there is a continuing need to push on with domestic structural reforms, and on the international front to address management challenges.

The Australian economy is expected to continue growing strongly, albeit at a more moderate pace than the 4.5 percent this past year. Sound macroeconomic policies have set the foundation for sustained low inflation outcomes, a low interest rate environment, and strong employment growth. The cornerstones of those policies have been a focus on transparency, in the conduct of both monetary and fiscal policies, and a commitment to ambitious medium-term goals.

The government has a medium-term fiscal strategy that includes maintaining budget surpluses while economic growth prospects remain sound and halving the Commonwealth general government's net debt to 10 percent of GDP by 2000–01. Australia is achieving both these fiscal objectives. With its privatization program, there is a real possibility that Commonwealth general government net debt might be completely eliminated within the next few years.

Ongoing structural reforms in both the product and financial markets have led to a leap in productivity. In the face of severe economic circumstances in our region, exporters were able to maintain export volumes by diverting to other markets. The flexibility of the economy and its performance through this crisis illustrate the benefits of policy reform. It is important to remember, however, that the task of reform is a continuing one. We must always look forward, anticipating problems before they arise and maintaining the momentum of reform to meet them.

That is why our country is tackling the difficult area of tax reform. This has been a huge area of work for the last two years. On July 1, we will introduce a value-added tax, major reductions in income tax, the abolition of a wide range of inefficient taxes, and the reform of a wide range of social security benefits. Building on that, this month, the government announced details of the reform of the business tax system in Australia. The new tax system will be more commercially focused and internationally competitive, while at the same time providing a sustainable revenue base. Company tax rates are being lowered and will be among the lowest in the Asian region. The new system will also improve incentives to save and invest by lowering capital gains taxes. Small business taxes will be simplified and lowered.

Reform is just as important at the international level. Recent economic difficulties exposed weakness in the operation of the international financial system, and in the traditional policy and surveillance frameworks used by international financial institutions, as well as structural weaknesses in the countries themselves. Australia is contributing to the work being undertaken by the international financial institutions to strengthen the international financial architecture, and I would now like to turn to a number of issues on this important agenda.

Highly Leveraged Institutions

Australia has concerns about the potential impact of destabilizing short-term capital flows and the role of highly leveraged institutions, particularly their potential ability to manipulate small to medium-sized foreign exchange markets. Steps are necessary to ensure adequate disclosure by hedge funds and other highly leveraged institutions and to ensure appropriate risk management on the part of creditors and counterparties in dealings with such entities. We are pleased with the Financial Stability Forum's work on highly leveraged institutions and strongly support the development of that work into concrete proposals for change.

Involving Private Sector in Forestalling and Resolving Financial Crises

We have also been pursuing the issue of the role of private sector borrowing in the international financial system, encouraging consideration of the issue in the Fund, as well as through Asia-Pacific Economic Cooperation (APEC) and the Manila Framework Group. It was also an area examined by a high-level Task Force that I chaired in 1998 to report on how Australia could contribute to international financial reform. I am pleased to see that a number of practical options that were raised in the report are now under consideration by the international financial institutions.

Australia welcomes the establishment of the Group of Twenty, which will be able to look at private sector involvement in the prevention and resolution of crises. We support a framework of guiding principles and tools that are not overly prescriptive. We are greatly encouraged by the agreement of the Interim Committee at these Meetings to ask the Executive Board to report at the Committee's next meeting on the ways in which the broad principles could be implemented.

We would encourage the Fund to extend the excellent work done to date—and develop ways on how the private sector involvement might be activated and negotiated in particular circumstances. We would expect there to be sufficient room for flexibility to allow common sense solutions to prevail and take into account the circumstances of individual cases. A set of practical "ground rules" that can shape expectations about the handling of a crisis would facilitate discussion between debtors and creditors and speed up the resolution of these extremely difficult situations.

Enhancing the Initiative for Heavily Indebted Poor Countries

The developments in the past few days that will lead to an enhanced HIPC Initiative hold the prospect of great benefit for indebted countries and their poverty-stricken peoples. Australia will more than double its contributions to this initiative, and I congratulate both the Bank and the Fund for their tireless work on financing the initiative. Write-offs offer new hope for countries crippled by debt. Economic policy to harness this opportunity will be required to build high hopes for a new start into reality. Economic growth is the best way of breaking poverty. High-quality growth and the conditions that promote it—honest institutions, accountable and transparent policy, declining trade barriers, open society, and respect for human rights and property—are the foundations for raising living standards, opening opportunity, hope, and achievement. And the achievement of policy in the face of crisis over the past two years should strengthen us to continue this work in the future.

STATEMENT BY THE GOVERNOR OF THE BANK FOR AUSTRIA

Wolfgang Ruttenstorfer

The Record of the Previous Year

When I had the honor and the pleasure of chairing this meeting last year, it was at an important crossroads for the stability of the global financial system. We were confronted with a difficult situation, which was considered by many to be a very serious threat to the stability and even viability of the worldwide financial system. Today we can say that we have lived up to this challenge. Starting from the deliberations we were then exploring, our common efforts have brought about the outline of a framework that is designed to make our common economic and financial world more stable and less fragile.

Today we are in the process of implementing this framework. Under the heading of "New Financial Architecture," we have devised a set of rules and guidelines consisting of three important blocks:

- *Rules to improve and strengthen each country's own economic policy and financial system.* In economic policy, we have identified areas of fragility and are still studying such important questions as the appropriate exchange rate regime. We are in a constant learning process, both for countries in an increasingly global economy and for the institutions that advise them. We continue to give this central question our best efforts. As for financial systems, we have seen the unfortunate effects of a fragile system on a country's ability to withstand market pressures, and we have also learned that special caution must be maintained when reforming such a system. We are pleased with the common efforts of the World Bank and the Fund to assist countries in their endeavor to strengthen their financial systems.

- *Rules to improve the relevant international institutions.* This central question has led us to the establishment of new structures, and some new forums have emerged, together with a stronger commitment toward better cooperation. These new structures are all linked to existing ones and reaffirm the central responsibility of the Bretton Woods institutions. I hope that these steps will stand the test of time and contribute to institutions that are efficient and effective while being representative of their universal membership.
- *Breaking new ground for the interaction of all segments involved, with special emphasis on the private sector.* Interaction with the private sector is a very challenging subject, as we all wish for a cooperative, balanced approach that does not resort to excessive regulation. Solutions should be found—as far as possible—in a voluntary discussion process. Still, we are all aware that public funds are limited and cannot be used to assume the risks while the private sector makes the profits.

We have now moved on from the first steps of exploring possible solutions toward the "nitty-gritty" of making these rules part of our legal and political daily reality. There is still much work to be done. The general direction of where we must go seems clear. There is widespread consensus about this path. We must clear up the remaining unsolved problem areas and move quickly toward the finalization of implementation.

Poverty Reduction

At the same time, as has been emphasized repeatedly over the past couple of years by the President of the World Bank, it is important to recognize the importance of the social dimension of crisis situations. Until recently, such crises had been seen primarily, if not exclusively, as financial crises. The recognition of the social dimension has brought to the surface new challenges to mitigate the effects on the most vulnerable, the poor people in our societies.

I would like to underline how important it is that the World Bank continue its work to help countries to address their structural and social problems. The Bank's strength is its focus on structures and projects and its engagement in long-term work rather than short-term emergency lending. It is in this context that I would caution the Bank not to increase its engagement in this direction, as this certainly would very quickly make it surpass its financial as well as its institutional capacity.

In the context of our continued efforts to fight poverty, the important work on HIPC must continue. I appreciate and fully support the enhancements to the HIPC Initiative framework as it has been discussed by the Interim and Development Committees. I do appreciate the progress made during the past few days on this framework. I am concerned, however, that while expectations have been raised in the countries concerned, at the same time there seems to be an inclination to bypass a number of important particulars and to leave them open for future agreements. Such an approach, in my view, could do substantial damage to the credibility of the initiative and should be avoided. I would like to emphasize here, that Austria stands ready to provide her fair share of financial support to the HIPC Initiative within an agreed framework of fair burden sharing.

Indeed, the principle of fair burden sharing has a variety of implications. Not only do we have to balance the burden among industrial countries; middle-income countries might also have to bear part of the burden because of the interrelationship between the services provided by international institutions and the implications of allocations of the net income of the institutions for various purposes. Therefore, while seeing some maneuvering room for additional contributions by the international financial institutions, I would argue that the demand for such contributions should not be overstretched, for the reasons mentioned and, moreover, in order to protect the financial integrity of the international financial institutions.

Another broadly accepted principle to be observed in the HIPC Initiative is additionality. It is all the more important that, from the outset, we have a viable concept about the overall financial requirements and a credible plan for how these requirements would be fulfilled. Countries benefiting from the initiative should be given a clear perspective of what they can expect in terms of new financial aid as well as in terms of debt reduction conditional upon implementation of the mutually agreed measures and programs, not only in the short term but also over an extended period of time. Part of such programs under consideration must include issues of governance, budget management, and the structure of public expenditures, including social sector spending and military expenditures.

It is clear that the programs to be implemented have to be observed to their full extent. We welcome the Poverty Reduction Strategy Plans to be developed by the countries concerned as particularly useful instruments. However, I urge both the Fund and the World Bank that programs be designed in a pragmatic fashion as far as the underlying economic thinking is concerned. They should take into consideration the lessons learned in the past from what has worked and what has not worked in previous programs. It is in this context that I view the concept of a Comprehensive Development Framework, as introduced by the World Bank earlier this year, as particularly helpful and important. At the same time, I fully support the Fund's intention to take into account consistently the social aspects and effects of its stabilization programs, and I welcome the steps to make the ESAF a program oriented toward poverty reduction as a central focus.

Middle-Income Countries Must Not Be Forgotten

However, in addition to our efforts to either stem crises or alleviate the harshest economic difficulties, we must not forget all those countries that are neither immediate victims of financial crises nor in extreme poverty, but are, nevertheless, very much in need of our assistance. There is "everyday business" for all of us that must not be forgotten because of the more extreme cases. Fortunately this has not been the case so far, though our collective focus was on the seemingly more pressing problems. I am talking, among others, of our middle-income neighbors and friends, with whom Austria is strongly linked, by virtue of its history, tradition, geography, and also its constituency in the Bretton Woods institutions.

The important long-term cooperation with many countries is a crucial feature of IMF and World Bank activities. Of course, we have to deal with crises when they occur, and of course we have to find solutions for our poorest member countries as well. But this must not happen at the expense of those who do not fall into either of these two categories. The increasing focus of both Bretton Woods institutions on a small group of debtors would be regrettable and may be dangerous in the long term. A broad outreach to the membership of the institutions is important, both in surveillance and in terms of appropriate assistance, and should reflect the universality of the institutions.

Let me give you one example: the work of the Fund and the World Bank in the countries now preparing for accession to the European Union is a very important and successful effort. It underlines the fact that sound policies and a clear, credibly pursued goal have been able to shelter these markets to a remarkable extent from the contagion effects of the financial crises felt in many parts of the world.

Furthermore, I would like to emphasize that we attach great importance to the fact that the cooperation between the World Bank and the European Union is functioning well. I would like to encourage both Bretton Woods institutions to continue to broaden this cooperation and, as appropriate, coordinate activities with the European Union. This should reflect the growing role and responsibilities of the European Union as one of the major players in the global economy.

Needless to say, the support of the World Bank is particularly important for the region of southeastern Europe. There we cannot just rely on time to heal the wounds of the conflicts between various population groups, but must undertake active efforts in order to plant the seeds for an eventual reconstruction and reconciliation within this troubled region. This is another important example for the deepening and broadening cooperation between the world community, the European Union and the Bretton Woods institutions, and a particularly crucial one. A good economic basis and a fair social structure will be essential ingredients in any concept for lasting peace in the region.

Let me say one word on the programs with the Russian Federation. For us, it is clear that, at this crucial time, the Bretton Woods institutions must continue to support the changeover to a market process in this large country. We urge the Fund, however, to put additional efforts into monitoring its Russia program effectively.

Permanent Adjustment to Change Is a Necessity for All Countries

These Annual Meetings serve to reaffirm our common goal of making our economies and our cooperation better, and of our continued determination to work well together and to find solutions to our common economic problems. It is encouraging to see that we have implemented—and are still implementing—many of the decisions we made last year.

This continuous implementation of new policies, this permanent renewal of our policies, is sometimes a difficult process, but unavoidable for all of us. No matter at which step on the ladder of economic and social development we stand, how large or small we are, in which region of the world we are located—all of us must continuously adjust to the changed circumstances with which an ever-changing world confronts us, in order to reap the greatest possible benefits from the globalized and integrated markets of today. Austria is no exception to this rule. Recent policy efforts were directed toward increasing the research, development, and technology potential for Austrian firms, to provide easier access to venture capital to Austria's small and medium-sized firms, and to strengthen business firms in general. A major tax reform to become effective as of January 2000 should be one vehicle to support these endeavors. Future activities all will have the goal of making Austrian business firms and the population more ready to accept change and to be able to profit from it.

To sum up, while I am very pleased to see that the financial crises of the past couple of years seems to be over, and that for a number of countries the macroeconomic situation looks quite promising, the real effects of the crises on the respective populations are far from over at this point in time. A lot remains to be done to ameliorate their situation, and to avoid—as far as possible—such dramatic social effects in the future.

Finally, there is a recent development that I find worrisome. We are gathered here because we are all members of the Bretton Woods institutions. We have all experienced, in different ways, the important positive contributions that these institutions can make to our common global goals. Therefore, I deeply regret to see how the credibility and reputation of these institutions are suffering right now from a less than fully constructive public debate.

While I believe that intense public debate about the best way to manage the difficult challenges our complex world presents to us is necessary, it would be highly regrettable if such a debate led to the weakening or loss of a credible and efficient international framework of cooperation in financial and development matters. Therefore, I call on all countries participating in these meetings to contribute to a more substantive debate about the Bretton Woods institutions and to help prevent these important institutions from being drawn into national party politics.

One possible way out of such situations might be to refocus the discussion on the tasks assigned to the institutions in their Articles of Agreement, thereby enabling them to maintain their independence from the day-to-day political interests of their shareholders, small or large.

In conclusion, I would like to take the opportunity to extend my congratulations to Mr. James Wolfensohn for his reappointment as President of the World Bank.

STATEMENT BY THE GOVERNOR OF THE BANK FOR BANGLADESH

Shah A.M.S. Kibria

It is an honor for me to address the 1999 Annual Meeting of the World Bank Group and the International Monetary Fund. I take this opportunity to extend to you, Mr. Chairman, my warmest felicitations on your election to the Chair. Let me also congratulate the Managing Director and the President for leadership through very difficult times.

We are only a few months away from the twenty-first century. Our hopes for the new century are driven by the accelerating pace of technological innovations and the spread of liberal pluralism in recent decades. The twenty-first century is likely to bring some fundamental shifts in global economic organization, international relations, and the pace and nature of economic development. Globalization and localization represent some of the most potent forces of change. The nation-state is envisaged to assume a new role in the emerging world: it will negotiate with the actors in the global arena, on the one hand, and with those in the local arena, on the other, to set up new institutions to pursue diverse goals. This process of change will necessarily be accompanied by greater instability and uncertainty, and we must ensure that international institutions are geared to meeting these new challenges. The existing institutions are the result of a series of "contracts" in which the whole international community participated, directly or indirectly, and these institutions have evolved through a process of continuous "negotiation," renewal, and reform. It seems to me that the challenge of the new century requires a degree of coordinated planning that only the governments of nations can provide. Civil society performs a key function in defining and articulating public interests, but it represents a collection of disparate causes and interests. Nations that embrace democratic values can play an effective role both in guiding the transition to the new era while expanding space for civil society and in the orderly resolution of divergent interests and attitudes in a plural society. Moreover, in preparing for the new century, we will be well advised to recognize the limitations of nations and the need to develop institutions that can deal effectively with challenges and problems that transcend national boundaries.

We note with some satisfaction that official development assistance (ODA) from DAC members rose to $51.5 billion in 1998, which is 0.23 percent of the aggregate GDP of the member countries—up from 0.22 percent, which was the lowest level ever reached. Though this is an improvement, regrettably it is about one-third of the goal of 0.7 percent of the GDP of the DAC countries set by the United Nations. We would urge the DAC members to reach the goal set unanimously by the developed and the developing countries.

In the context of official development assistance, I would like to draw your attention to the need for flow of adequate resources to the developing countries. There is a need for pragmatism and for the Bank and the Fund to take into account the local context and, in particular, the realities of democratic governance in designing institutional and policy reforms. More importantly, the recipient countries must have a greater role in diagnosing and designing their own reform programs. Adequate concessional funding is needed to sustain public investment programs geared toward private sector oriented growth. The Bank and the Fund should be working to ensure adequate availability of resources to the developing countries while continuing with efforts for better policy and institutional reforms. In this regard, special considerations should be given to countries that have avoided large-scale commercial borrowing, preferring to pursue cautious financial policies geared to maintenance of macroeconomic stability. Let me now briefly turn to the development initiatives of the government of Bangladesh taken under the leadership of Prime Minister Sheikh Hasina.

- We achieved a growth rate of over 5.2 percent in FY 1999, despite the floods of 1998—the worst in history. Macroeconomic stability was maintained against the backdrop of the Asian economic crisis.
- The government continued to make progress in structural reforms, despite the difficult macroeconomic situation.
- Reforms of state-owned enterprises, and particularly their divestiture, continued. The government has succeeded in building up a strong coalition of stakeholders in favor of reforms.
- The government has introduced a series of safety-net measures. Though modest in scale, these have given new hope to many groups largely bypassed by recent economic growth and development programs. These include old age allowance and allowances to widows with young children and distressed women abandoned by their husbands; shelters for the aged without family or community support; establishment of an Employment Bank and a Housing Fund. The last two schemes were financed entirely by the government and are directed toward helping the poor or the ultra-poor. The representatives of local government institutions, members of civil society, and nongovernmental organizations participate in selection of the

beneficiaries and administration of these social security schemes.

- Public expenditure on education and health, including nutrition, has increased. Emphasis is on primary education and literacy, primary health care, reproductive health, and HIV/AIDS. Expenditures on basic social services have risen steadily during 1990s to over 25 percent of government spending.
- The government has undertaken wide-ranging programs for mitigation of various environmental problems such as arsenic pollution, air pollution, and deforestation.
- The government supports a wide range of micro-credit and poverty alleviation programs and provides support to nongovernmental organizations implementing similar programs. Micro-credit programs of nongovernmental organizations are refinanced through the Palli Karma Shahayak Foundation (PKSF); in addition, the government has guaranteed bonds issued by Grameen Bank and makes grants to eligible nongovernmental organizations.
- In order to enhance accountability, the government has strengthened the role of the Parliament and the Standing Committees. Members of the Parliament—and not the Ministers—chair these committees.
- In order to broaden the scope of public participation and decentralization of governance, the government has initiated the process of establishing representative local self-government institutions at village, union, upazila, or subdistrict and district levels. Reservation of seats for direct election of women in all local government institutions enhances political empowerment of women. Furthermore, local government institutions are expected to enhance accountability and quality of services delivered at the local level.

The government of Bangladesh would like to thank the World Bank for its active help and cooperation in all our development efforts and the Fund for its timely assistance following the floods of last year. We look forward to working with both these institutions to deal with the daunting development challenges that we face.

Statement by the Governor of the Bank for the Republic of Belarus

Gennady V. Novitsky

First of all, let me express my gratitude to the management and staff of the World Bank Group and the International Monetary Fund for the excellent organization of the meetings.

Noting the highly important role of international financial organizations in reforming transition economies, we support a number of principled trends in the World Bank's activities in recent years, which were initiated and are implemented under the leadership of Mr. Wolfensohn, President of the World Bank. What we mean is a more clear account by the Bank of its clients' specific features and needs, having the aim to improve living standards and ensure conditions for economic growth. We also welcome the expanded presence of the Bank in its member countries, particularly in transition economies. At the same time, we stress our concern about the problem of the Bank's net income. We would like its solution not to harm the borrowing countries.

Taking into account and supporting new trends in World Bank strategy, aimed at a better account of specific features and conditions of its member countries, let me briefly outline the economic situation in Belarus at this stage. The unsustainability of the general economic position, caused by a number of negative factors affecting the national economy, has been a characteristic feature of the social and economic situation in the republic in 1998–99. It is connected both with the continuing effects of distortions and deep crisis phenomena in the Belarussian economy in 1992–94 and with new emerging destabilization processes of external origin. From 1991 through 1994, Belarus, like most countries of the former Soviet Union, survived a period of hyperinflation and deep recession. At times, the pace of price upswing exceeded 30 percent a month. During that period GDP dropped two times. In those circumstances, the first and foremost priority of the governmental economic policy was to encourage economic growth.

From 1996 through 1998, the implementation of stabilization measures to curb an overall output reduction, resume economic growth, and increase living standards produced positive results. According to the 1997–98 outcomes, real GDP grew by 20.6 percent in comparison to the 1996 level (average annual growth pace was 9.8 percent), industrial output increased by 33 percent, and real money incomes of the population went up by 25 percent.

At the same time, the measures conducted for financial improvement of the economy appeared to be not as fully fruitful as expected due to the remaining unsatisfactory inflation environment. All that badly affected the competitiveness of domestic products and led to accumulation of a trade balance deficit and reduction in external reserves.

These as well as other negative trends grew under the predominant influence of the financial and economic crisis in Russia, which is our major neighbor and one of the most important trade partners. Its impact was most appreciable for the country's foreign exchange market, the condition and level of domestic prices, and foreign trade.

It is enough to mention that since the second half of 1998, the pace of economic growth has slowed down considerably, and the financial position of domestic enterprises has deteriorated. Starting from August 1998, there has been a substantial increase in the pace of inflation in the economic system of Belarus. From January through August 1998, inflation growth was 3.4 percent in average monthly terms, while from September through December it reached 21.3 percent. As a result, real profitability of most enterprises turned negative. The share of loss-making enterprises in their total number rose from 12.3 percent in early 1998 to 14.2 percent by early 1999. The Belarussian rubel devalued, further widening the disparity between the official and market rates.

Affected by the crisis processes, the demand on internal markets of Russia and other Commonwealth of Independent States (CIS) countries went down. Owing to that, in 1998 Belarussian foreign trade turnover shrank by 2.3 percent compared with the 1997 level, including a reduction in exports and imports by 3.2 percent and 1.6 percent respectively. However, among the noted difficulties in the country's economy, it was possible to achieve some positive results on most major macroeconomic indicators in 1998. Comparing with the 1997 level, GDP grew by 8.3 percent, industrial output—12 percent, fixed capital investment—16 percent, and real money incomes—19 percent. Despite a hard financial situation in the country, the external debt remained unchanged, and the state budget deficit was maintained at a level lower than previously planned.

As for the performance of the country's economy in 1999, it should be first of all noted that a proceeding recession and instability in the economy, as well as extremely unfavorable weather conditions in Belarus, continue to exert their influence on the social and economic development of the Republic of Belarus. According to the results of economic development for January–August 1999, actual GDP has grown only 1.5 percent in comparison to the same period of 1998, agricultural output has been 10.2 percent less than the last year's level, and fixed capital investment has decreased by 3 percent. Industry was the only stable working economic sector with growth at 106.6 percent.

The results for January–July 1999 show that given the same period of 1998, foreign trade turnover has shrunk by 26.9 percent, including a decline in exports and imports by 21.6 percent and 31.3 percent, respectively. Along with it, the share of barter operations has grown in both exports and imports. Changes in export structure were determined by an unfavorable situation on world markets, instability and low solvency of markets in Russia and other CIS countries, increased competition on non-CIS markets with regard to many kinds of Belarus-made export products, as well as by inefficient foreign exchange controls and preserved multiple exchange rate of the Belarussian rubel. Changes in import structure were mostly conditioned by financial instability and unsustainability of enterprise importers, the general situation on the foreign exchange market, and low solvency of both population and enterprises. At the same time, we should note a "spontaneous" reorientation of foreign economic flows to the West: for seven months of 1999, exports to Russia have dropped by 39.5 percent while those to the western countries have risen by 33.1 percent. The process of transition in Belarus is aimed at the creation of a "socially oriented market economy"—that is, an economy that combines the social and economic criteria of development, the advantages of market competition and efficient social security system, and the ideas of market self-control and state regulation.

The government is satisfied that in the prevailing circumstances this approach has led to better results than have been obtained in other countries. For the last three years, output growth in the republic has been significantly higher than in other CIS countries. The 1999 UNDP *Human Development Report* confirms this progress: its Human Development Index of 174 countries shows that Belarus has moved up from sixty-eighth place to sixtieth.

Belarus is interested in economic reforms including public assets restructuring. It is evidenced by the fact that the current share of nonpublic enterprises in total industrial output is about 41 percent. Over 40 percent of the employed in the republic's economy work in the nonpublic sector. At the same time, we adhere to reasonable restructuring of public and leasing enterprises with the attraction of external investments. The main objective of the ongoing state property reform is to increase production efficiency. This will be the basis for our activities in the forthcoming period.

Now I would like to characterize the relations of the government of the Republic of Belarus with the Fund and the Bank. In our view, neither the government of the Republic of Belarus nor the Fund or the Bank are satisfied with their status. Resumed discussions on possible financial support from the Fund under the Stand-By Arrangement have not been productive so far. The Fund refrains from extending a loan to the republic within the Compensatory and Contingency Financing Facility (CCFF) to compensate for the losses resulting from the decline in exports to Russia and poor grain crops in 1998. This year we have thus far failed to bring export deliveries to Russia up to the 1998 level, and as for the grain crops, the preliminary data show that we have harvested 12.5 percent less than in 1998, which was a poor harvest year as well.

We have reached the awareness that the republic requires to comprehensively revise the basic principles of the existing monetary and credit policy. The government has approved the finalized Monetary and Credit Policy Concept of the Republic of Belarus for 1999–2000. Its key points (targets and terms of implementation) will be reflected in a social and economic development forecast and the 2000 budget of the Republic of Belarus, which are being worked out and will be based on a national currency stabilization program. With such a program, we are ready to initiate another negotiation with the Fund regarding elaboration of a joint economic program to qualify for Fund financial support under a Stand-By Arrangement.

I avail myself of the opportunity to note that the World Bank also promotes, to a certain extent, the economic development in Belarus. We highly esteem the Bank's support of the forestry and energy sectors and its technical assistance. At the same time, the general character of the World Bank Country Assistance Strategy for Belarus effective since 1999 is, in our view, excessively tight and constrains the attraction of external credit resources to the country's economy. The main lending criteria, when applied to Belarus, are extremely strict and prevent us from full utilization of the Bank's resources. The Bank's overcautious approach often hits the target quite opposite to one of the Bank's main objectives, to promote market reforms in its member countries through rapid and adequate response to their needs and economic changes. Unfortunately, the Bank's practical approach to Belarus lacks due attention to the regional features. We believe that a lending possibility assessment should be better based on the level of project efficiency, its recoupment, and its role for the regional development in specific country conditions.

In this regard, allow me to express my hope that the Bank's priorities will change and the Bank will define a more flexible strategy, which would take into account the necessity of complex development in the regions that are at different stages of transition to the market economy. The Bank's financial support of social and environmental projects, and private and energy sector development, is of prior interest to the Republic of Belarus.

On our part, we will be insistent in improving general operation conditions and investment climate in our country and seek more intensive, open, and comprehensive cooperation with the Bank on issues of mutual interest. Today, we are ready to start a dialogue with the Bank on preparation of a full-fledged Country Assistance Strategy, including ramified scenarios of cooperation between Belarus and the World Bank. In conclusion, I would like to express my hope for the Bank and Fund's understanding of our problems on the way to the "socially oriented market economy" and concrete support in their solution.

STATEMENT BY THE GOVERNOR OF THE BANK FOR BELGIUM

Didier Reynders

It is a great pleasure for me to address the Annual Meetings of the International Monetary Fund and the World Bank today. As Belgium's new Minister of Finance, I have had my first opportunity over the past several days to follow the deliberations at the various meetings of the two institutions, and I have done so with great interest. I have taken due note of the major role that the Bretton Woods institutions play in the pursuit of sustainable development, and of their constant and determined efforts to combat poverty and underdevelopment. Both of these missions make the two institutions crucial participants in the work of analyzing and resolving the major economic problems of our era.

Belgium's Implementation of Essential Structural Adjustments

This year again, the United States will experience significantly greater economic growth than the European Union, particularly the euro zone. This gap, which has been discernible over most of the past decade, suggests that there is a genuine "output gap" between the United States and Europe. One explanation for this may lie in the rigidities of the European labor market, elimination of which has been the focus of a number of economic policy measures. Belgium has always advocated a coordinated approach to the issue.

The policy of the new Belgian government, which took office in July 1999, has resolutely reflected this approach. The government is therefore determined to develop an active welfare state through training and employment policy designed to increase the labor-force participation rate, which is low in Belgium, compared with that of the other European countries. Various measures are planned, including a significant reduction in employer social security contributions and payroll taxes, the introduction of a youth employment program to enable all young persons to enter the labor market within six months of leaving school, steps to increase participation in the labor force by persons over 50 years of age, and similar measures.

The government of Belgium will introduce far-reaching reforms to reduce taxes on earned income. The reforms will reduce the number of tax brackets, raise the minimum taxable income, and regroup deductions in a limited number of flat-rate categories. The government has already confirmed the redefinition of all personal income tax brackets, and plans to eliminate the emergency surtax. The government also wishes to alter the income tax structure so that it will be possible to pursue our national objectives with respect to employment and sustainable development more effectively. This shift will depend on progress on the European tax harmonization front. All these reforms will be the subject of legislation introduced during this government's term of office, in a move toward ongoing reductions in tax and parafiscal pressures. By implementing this policy, the Belgian government expects to achieve the following two objectives, which it was advised to pursue by the Fund during their last series of consultation discussions:

- Tax reform will make it possible to reduce the tax wedge existing between individuals' gross and net income. In Belgium, the difference between these two is very large, and this will eventually become a serious competitive handicap within the euro zone.
- The government's policy will also serve to eliminate employment traps. In the case of the lowest levels of earned income, net disposable income will be higher, with the result that the differential between this and replacement income will increase. This will inevitably increase incentives to seek employment.

Some might fear that an innovative policy such as this could jeopardize Belgium's recent macroeconomic achievements, in particular, its improved fiscal position. However, this is by no means the case. Belgium will comply with the budget objectives set forth in its 1999–2002 stabilization program. Over the medium term, the planned measures for reducing employer social security contributions and payroll taxes should produce favorable effects on employment, and this in turn will improve the budgetary position. Belgium's new economic policy is therefore moving close to the optimum mix of measures advocated by the Fund during the most recent Article IV consultation discussions. Long-term simulations have indicated that strict control of public spending, combined with structural reform, including reduction of the tax wedge and introduction of employment incentives, should provide the most rapid means by which Belgium's indebtedness can be reduced.

Strengthening of the International Monetary and Financial System

The debate on the future role of the International Financial and Monetary Committee should continue. It would be wrong to believe that the international monetary and financial architecture is an unimportant matter, and that the main focus should be on dealing with more substantive issues, rather than on determining in what forums they are to be discussed. We consider the following to be fundamental objectives:

- the preservation of a multilateral approach, as embodied by institutions such as the Fund;
- acknowledgment of democratic legitimacy in decision making and increased emphasis on the need to provide justification for decisions; and
- the need to reconcile flexibility in examining certain types of problems with the absolute need for an overall coordinating body to deal with financial and monetary issues.

Consequently, the International Financial and Monetary Committee should—ideally—become a forum for decision making on Fund matters, and for coordination and consultation on related financial issues. The preparatory meetings of Alternates should continue, so that the Committee's plenary sessions can be more effective. Systematic use should be made of working groups, so that the Committee's central role will be preserved, and particular issues can be dealt with by groups with the necessary ad hoc membership. I would also emphasize that the International Financial and Monetary Committee should be given an enhanced role in the auditing of operations. This would be a way of ensuring that all financing provided is being properly used, monitoring that would go beyond mere enforcement of the macroeconomic criteria normally applied.

Initiatives for Poverty Reduction and the Promotion of Sustained Growth

I am pleased to note that the policies of the Bretton Woods institutions have been modified so as to meet the need for finding lasting solutions to the debt problems of the poorest countries. The Belgian government has always been receptive to the wishes of civil society, including the call for an intensification of the struggle against poverty. Consequently, I wish to indicate here today that the government will support the initiatives for promoting goods manufactured by socially equitable methods, its purpose being to promote balanced global trade. I therefore advocate the establishment of links between programs such as ESAF and HIPC and efforts to reduce poverty in the poorest countries.

At present, the most important consideration is to ensure that these programs receive the necessary financing. Belgium's contribution to this financing is substantial, and the country stands ready to participate in any additional joint efforts, provided that the costs are shared equitably. In addition, the use of Fund-based approaches—and in particular the revaluing of a portion of the Fund's gold reserves—seems fully justified in the present circumstances. While focusing on the heavily indebted poor countries, we cannot forget the specific problems that other countries face, and so we particularly support the program of assistance for Turkey, which suffered a devastating earthquake on August 17.

Central Africa

Belgium has historic links with Central Africa and believes that the time has come to take the political initiative in this part of the world, promoting peace and restoring trade and economic activity. This will open the way to a renewal of economic assistance for the region, made available through a number of different channels. Such assistance should be provided through procedures that are flexible, adaptable over time, and tailored to meet the needs of the individual countries in the region. I call upon the Bretton Woods institutions to increase their assistance for these countries in the very near future by contributing to an in-depth study of their problems and proposing special technical assistance programs. Such initiatives will confirm that the vocation of these institutions is truly universal.

Conclusion

I believe that the phase we have just passed through, during which we enhanced our initiatives for providing debt relief for the poorest countries, has been most important. We must now strengthen the activities of the Bretton Woods institutions by giving them a more clearly defined social focus, and by incorporating education and health programs into these activities, since these have a considerable impact on the poorest communities. Finally, we must ensure that, over the coming years, development remains a prime concern when the new rules governing world trade are formulated, and that there is closer coordination of the activities of organizations as different as the WTO, the United Nations (UN), the Fund, and the World Bank.

STATEMENT BY THE GOVERNOR OF THE FUND FOR BELIZE

Ralph Fonseca

It is Belize's honor to speak on behalf of the Caribbean Community countries. We wish to join colleagues in expressing appreciation to the managements of the Bank and Fund for the excellent arrangements that have been made for these meetings.

We are living in interesting times. Our last two meetings were dominated by the financial markets crisis and by uncertainty over the potential consequences of that crisis for global economic activity in general and for developing countries in particular. Recent events have shown clearly that there is no place for dogma in the management of the international financial system; and that, particularly with respect to small countries, staff of international financial institutions must approach the business of policy advice carefully in the full realization that small countries can ill afford policy errors. Orderly institutional development and the proper sequencing of reforms will always be important steps in the attainment of policy objectives.

We have an ongoing concern about the relative roles of the Bank and the Fund in the emergency response to the financial crisis. We see a primary role for the Fund in the initial response to balance of payments crises, where quick-disbursing assistance is required; while the primary role for the Bank is in addressing underlying structural issues, in promoting long-term development, and in fighting poverty. We are uncomfortable with recent funding responses by the Bank, which appear to be indistinguishable from emergency balance of payments support, not least because of the effects on the Bank's ability to discharge its core functions and the effects on financing costs for noncrisis borrowers. We therefore call on the Bank's management and its other members to take the necessary action to ensure that the core responsibilities of the two institutions are not blurred, and to ensure that sufficient resources are available for the proper discharge of the respective mandates.

We are not satisfied with the results so far of the Bank's work in helping small states identify and deal with their peculiar problems. There is a need for assistance for the longer-term development effort, for the medium-term effort to cope with rapid liberalization and globalization, and for the associated rapid change in trading arrangements. These developments have been driven from within the developed countries. What we expect, and what we wish to see, is a comprehensive analysis of the situation and prospects of small states, together with an appropriate set of recommendations both to guide domestic policies, and to refocus the operations of the international institutions to the peculiar circumstances of these small states. We wish to emphasize the need for broad and deep consultation with these small states during the course of the review process to ensure full ownership of the analyses and recommendations by all parties. We also feel that there may be a need for consultation with the main trading partners of these small states. We recognize that this process may take some time, and we in the Caribbean do feel that the time should be spent in the interest of producing a meaningful and functional report, which would have had the benefit of extensive consultation.

We are very concerned about this issue, because of a recent experience with the Fund on a study to review adjustment policies in the Caribbean. We must express our disappointment that the Fund was unable to be fully engaged on this project despite assurances from management to our heads of government. Given the critical importance of trade to our economies and the difficulties a number of our Community members face as a result of the dramatic changes in the international trade regime, we warmly welcome the arrangements being proposed by the Bank to assist developing countries in evaluating and restructuring their situations. With the Bank's assistance, we will be able to take advantage—on a continuing basis—of the opportunities to make representation in international trade forums. It is no secret that equal access does not always mean fair access. The extent of economic openness of Caribbean economies is such that any change in trade has immediate and significant impact on fiscal performance and on every other aspect of economic activity. Unlike developing countries with large domestic markets, the issue for us does not involve the appropriate arrangements for opening the domestic economy; we are already highly open. The issue is how to develop and maintain the domestic flexibility to cope with compressed product cycles and increased global competition, and how to reduce public sector reliance on trade for revenue while maintaining, and perhaps even increasing, our openness. However, we are happy with the recent changes within the Fund's Western Hemisphere Department to facilitate a more meaningful focus on the Caribbean, and we are also happy with the arrangements that have been proposed for more meaningful dialogue with the Caribbean Community and its institutions as a region.

We look forward with great expectation to the first steps in this process, and to the completion of the restructuring arrangements in order to bring the Fund's work on all of our small countries more effectively together. We welcome the Bank's work on the Comprehensive Development Framework, with its implications for a new relationship between the Bank and developing countries and its emphasis on governance and capacity building.

The implications for the Caribbean of the WTO ruling on bananas and the response thereto continue to be a matter of great concern to our governments and people and will have a gravely negative impact on the strength and vibrancy of the regional economy. We urge the international community to recognize the considerable effort that we have made to restructure this industry to face competition. Simply put, any settlement arrived at that does not provide an adequate transition period is unacceptable. At a minimum, we expect that there will be a tariff rate quota and appropriate licensing system. We should note in this connection that the OECD's response to our efforts to exercise our very limited diversification options and to develop an international business sector has caused us great consternation and alarm. The potential consequences of the OECD Report on Harmful Tax Competition are particularly troubling, as services, including financial services, were seen by the Caribbean as a feasible alternative.

Our governments have previously been encouraged by the international financial institutions to diversify out of commodities and import-substituting manufacturing because of adverse terms of trade effects and the small size of the domestic market, respectively. The destruction of our international financial services sector would have not only dire direct income and employment effects, but also severe social consequences. In addition, we are forced to ask the question: what would the developed countries have us do for a living?

Tax competition needs to be viewed holistically, involving all sectors, activities, incentives, and subsidies, including policy actions at all levels of government, both federal and state. Without relinquishing any sovereignty, the Caribbean will continue to cooperate with genuine attempts to strengthen the international financial system. However, the process needs to be fair, taking into account the special circumstances of small economies.

On the issue of debt relief, we generally welcome the G-7 initiative and the enhanced HIPC to assist countries where development and poverty eradication efforts are severely hampered by high debt-service obligations. However, we need to point out that in the Caribbean Community and Common Market, members are both creditors and debtors. In this regard, we would urge that consideration be given to this fact in the deliberations regarding relief to members to ensure that relief granted to any one country should not be to the detriment of another. As far as possible, appropriate safeguards should be considered to cushion any negative impacts. We also need to point out that there are countries that, while not qualifying for debt relief under HIPC, also carry significant debt burdens that adversely affect their poverty reduction efforts. We would like to see a mechanism designed to assist those countries' efforts as well.

We want to conclude by saying that we have little to be complacent about. Recovery from the emerging market crisis is fragile in some countries, and is yet to start in others—and in many countries, including those in the Caribbean, there is significant and growing poverty. It is clear that an urgent and major task still lies ahead, work that will tax our capacities and inventiveness to the limit. It is important therefore, that the relationships between the Bank and Fund staffs and the Caribbean be strengthened and reinvigorated in order to deal with the challenges ahead. Finally, let us rededicate ourselves to the work of development—to economic growth with a human face that will redound to the benefit of so many of our people who face the daily reality of hardship and suffering.

STATEMENT BY THE GOVERNOR OF THE BANK FOR BOSNIA AND HERZEGOVINA

Mirsad Kurtovic

(Delivered by the Hon. Jadranko Prlic, Alternate Governor of the Fund)

Less than four years since the war in Bosnia and Herzegovina ended, remarkable progress can be seen throughout the country.

- People are living peacefully and normally.
- Improvements in infrastructure are visible everywhere.
- A stable macroeconomic framework and a convertible national currency have been instituted (convertible marka).
- An IMF Stand-By Arrangement is in the process of stable implementation and will be converted into an ESAF Arrangement in the coming months.
- The privatization process has started.
- Relations with the majority of international financial institutions are being normalized.
- Total foreign debt has been consolidated and has been serviced on a regular basis.

- A number of basic laws adopted will lead Bosnia and Herzegovina toward democratization and a market-oriented economy.
- The process of mobilizing international assistance through donors' conferences has been successfully undertaken, and now we expect faster disbursement of these pledges.

We have achieved this progress with the generous support of the World Bank, the International Monetary Fund, the Office of the High Representative, the European Union, the United States, Japan, and many other donors. I would like to take this opportunity to express our sincere appreciation and gratitude. Thanks to donors' generous assistance, the first post-war phase of reconstruction and development, primarily focused on rehabilitation of infrastructure, has come to the final stage. Unfortunately, there has not been significant progress in economic recovery or an increase in the level of employment. We expect, however, that in the next phase of international assistance, the focus will be on these needs, with the aim of building a self-sustainable economy.

Our recent tragic history and today's rapidly changing world urge for the creation of a new strategy, not only for reconstruction, but also for the comprehensive development of Bosnia and Herzegovina. It should include security, the economy, health care, the environment, ethics, the judiciary, philosophy, and religion, since all of these areas are interconnected. In particular, Bosnia and Herzegovina may serve as an example for the application of the Comprehensive Development Framework. With the assistance of the World Bank, the Fund, and the European Union, we plan to develop a new strategy for midterm development and to present it to our donors at the next Donor Conference.

Our unemployment, with a rate of 40 percent, is just one of the many consequences of the war that should be eliminated through accelerated economic growth. That is why we hope that our donors will support the implementation of ongoing economic reforms, especially those pertaining to property rights transformation—that is, the privatization process. Our goal is to transfer the biggest part of state-owned properties into private ownership. Further development of the financial and banking sector and, above all, the recovery of trust in domestic commercial banks, as well as the greater presence of the foreign-based bank branches in the country, are necessary preconditions.

Another important structural change that is being implemented is the introduction of market-oriented criteria in economic judgment and decision making. We seek to develop an economic environment based primarily on the market as the main regulator of economic activities, with very limited state intervention. Finally, we are also facing the very important task of building a sustainable system of social services. Our comparative advantages are the basis for optimistic forecasts of our economic growth. One of them is the highly skilled labor force. Due to our well-developed prewar educational system, our workers' skill levels are still very high and evenly spread throughout the country.

Second is land, a primary asset in rural areas, which is in private ownership, and is generally distributed evenly throughout the country. This shows that Bosnia and Herzegovina's society rests on a sufficiently stable socioeconomic basis. Therefore, the privatization process of the remaining state property must be lawful, nondiscriminatory, and transparent, and must not reflect war conquests.

Geopolitically, strategically, and economically, Bosnia and Herzegovina belongs to Europe and should become part of the European integration processes. We welcome establishing the Stability Pact for Southeastern Europe as a first step toward this goal, as demonstrated during the Sarajevo Summit this July.

Membership in the WTO is also one of our highest priorities, and we do expect that the accession process will be successfully finished in the short period. Our small economy urgently needs an enhancement of trade relations with other markets and stable cash inflows.

Our commitment to conduct all necessary economic reforms is very resolute and indisputable. As we seek to realize this goal, we have encountered many obstacles that are the aftermath of the recent war, including huge numbers of refugees and displaced persons, outdated technology, physical destruction of plants, war victims and disabled persons, a lack of adequate government structures, uncontrolled and unregulated borders, and an increase in the elderly population. Therefore, we need continued international assistance in the coming months. We hope that the international community and the World Bank will continue to support the reconstruction of Bosnia and Herzegovina, at least for the support of those activities that would lead to accelerated economic growth and increased employment.

Future additional IDA funds are of extreme importance, especially for supporting the continuing implementation of economic reforms and budget support, including the payment of foreign sovereign debt. We should use the new cycle of donors' conferences primarily to obtain favorable credits to stimulate economic growth in Bosnia and Herzegovina, rather than for reconstruction of the infrastructure. This will enable us to build a self-sustainable economy and integrate with the EU and the rest of Europe.

Without these reforms, we will be faced with growing social and economic problems, and our citizens will continue to seek refuge and a better future in other countries. (Therefore, the problem of Bosnian refugees may multiply.)

We will continue to implement economic reforms and other facets relating to the democratic transition of our society. We are fully aware that our future development depends on our ability to attract foreign investment. But a main precondition for these reforms is stability in Bosnia and Herzegovina and the whole region. To this end, further strong and strict implementation of the Dayton Agreement is necessary. With the assistance of the donor community, we must do everything in our power to provide for the return of all refugees. This is no longer just a humanitarian issue, but also a stability issue. Unfortunately, the stability of the entire region, owing to the ongoing political crisis in the Federal Republic of Yugoslavia (Serbia/Montenegro), has not yet been provided.

Since lately there has been increasing concern among donors, caused by some alarming reports of corruption in Bosnia and Herzegovina, on this occasion we want to reiterate and assure the donor community that, for the most part, donor assistance and financial contributions of the World Bank, the IMF, the EU, the U.S. Agency for International Development, and all other donors have been effectively utilized without corruption or misuse. Independent audit institutions and control agencies have already confirmed this.

This is not to suggest that corruption and other forms of criminal behavior do not exist. Corruption is mostly present in the area of public funds, owing to the malfunctioning and absence of the institutions envisioned under the Dayton and Washington agreements. We are eager to fight corruption and to establish a system to prevent corruption through regulatory and educational measures. This is not a simple task, and we need foreign assistance. An independent analysis of the origins and causes of corruption is a first step in our fight against this social and moral disease. Bosnia and Herzegovina therefore asks for assistance from the World Bank in order to establish anticorruption mechanisms. Indeed, we would ask that the World Bank lead in this undertaking. We are also very grateful for the help that the EU and the United States are providing to Bosnia and Herzegovina in its fight against corruption. We appeal them to continue in this important endeavor.

The international community, the World Bank, and other donors have made an enormous and valuable contribution toward improving the political, economic, and social situation in Bosnia and Herzegovina. Hundreds of thousands of citizens have been saved, and a better standard of living has been provided through internationally funded projects in housing, schools, medical centers, electricity, road networks, the water supply, social services, and other sectors.

The basic prerequisites for the improvement of living standards have been achieved. Yet, an additional effort has to be made, in order to create conditions for the citizens of Bosnia and Herzegovina to become self-supporting. We do hope that the international donor community will continue to be our partner, as it used to be in previous years.

STATEMENT BY THE GOVERNOR OF THE BANK FOR CAMBODIA AND BY THE GOVERNOR OF THE FUND FOR CAMBODIA

Keat Chhon and Chea Chan To

It is indeed a great honor and privilege for us to address the fifty-fourth Annual Meetings of the World Bank and the International Monetary Fund. Let us take this opportunity to congratulate James Wolfensohn and Michel Camdessus for the tremendous efforts they are making through the World Bank and the Fund to deal with the serious financial cataclysm confronting Asia and the world economy in 1997 and 1998.

These Annual Meetings of the World Bank Group and the International Monetary Fund take place when the world economy has better prospects for a resumption of speedy growth. Some of the Asian economies that have suffered from the financial crisis and experienced economic downturn seem to have seen signs of restored confidence and recovery. Positive indicators include the return of stability in the foreign exchange markets; rising current account surpluses and a buildup of reserves; the substantial decline in domestic interest rates; the easing of inflationary pressures; the recovery in the stock markets; the improvement in consumer sentiment; and the positive growth of the real economy. This has happened because of the determination undertaken by these countries in pursuing decisively adequate policies and measures with the assistance of the international community and especially of the two Bretton Woods institutions. Both the Bank and the Fund have responded with commendable resolve to this crisis and help countries in the region to implement reform measures to address its causes and impact.

To prevent the recurrence of the crisis and to cope with the fast-changing global environment caused by the force of globalization, Cambodia has expressed its full support for the "common Association of South East Asian Nations (ASEAN) position in reforming the international financial architecture," which includes equal application of standards of transparency and disclosure to the public and private sectors, closer and more coordinated monitoring of short-term capital flows, closer collaboration and information sharing among national and international regulators, an orderly and well-sequenced approach to capital account liberalization in tandem with the degree of development of the domestic financial sector and supervisory regime, and sound, consistent, and credible macroeconomic policies to support exchange rates. We have attached serious importance to the ASEAN Surveillance Process, which is aimed at providing an early warning on a possible crisis to member countries.

On the front of economic integration, Cambodia is well prepared to take an active part in the ASEAN Free Trade Area (AFTA) and other ASEAN economic initiatives. Attention is given to the establishment in the next century of the ASEAN Economic Region in which there is a free flow of goods and services, a freer flow of capital, equitable economic development, and reduced poverty and socioeconomic disparities. We are committed to ensuring close cooperation in strengthening the open, multilateral trading system, and reinforcing the role of the business sector as the engine of growth.

Let us take this opportunity to appraise this distinguished forum of the recent development in Cambodia. A general election was organized in July 1998 on our own last year and was pronounced by the international community as free and fair. A new coalition government was established based on a common platform to serve the people of Cambodia. Peace, so elusive in the past many decades, now finally prevails all over the country. Cambodia has regained its seat at the UN, joined ASEAN, and is determined to play its responsible role in the regional and international affairs.

The new royal government of Cambodia, established in November 1998, continues its reform policies with the ultimate goal of accelerating economic growth and alleviating poverty. Landmark, wide-ranging reform measures were unveiled to build up a strong foundation for long-term economic growth and sustainable development. The key areas of the reforms include public sector restructuring aimed at strengthening democracy; improving and increasing the efficiency of the public administration; military and police demobilization; sustainable forestry management; and fiscal, financial, and banking reforms. We clearly recognize that the key to success of this reform program is good governance. For us, this means aiming at improving the efficiency and effectiveness of the public sector, on one hand, and fighting corruption, on the other. We have asked the Bank for technical assistance for capacity building in this important endeavor.

Based on the macroeconomic performance in the first half of 1999, we are confident that the Cambodian economy has rebounded and real GDP growth will be 4 percent as forecast. Therefore, 1999 is the year of a return to economic growth and macroeconomic stability. The annual inflation is expected to decrease from 12.6 percent in 1998 to 6.5 percent in 1999, and the exchange rate will be kept under control. Net foreign assets and liquidity of the banking sector, in particular the foreign currency deposits, continued to grow, compared with end-1998. This is a testimony to the confidence of the public and investors alike in Cambodia's economy and its banking system. The gross foreign reserves of the banking system are projected to increase by 9 percent in 1999.

The objectives of macroeconomic and structural policies are to raise economic growth and per capital income, and reduce poverty. The key elements of the strategy are stepped-up efforts to strengthen revenue collection and enhance the transparency of fiscal operations, combined with reforms of the civil service and military. Cambodia is strongly determined to continue the implementation of the fiscal reform programs with a view to enhancing revenue and improving the management of public expenditure. We are committed to vigorously implement new measures aimed at improving the tax and budget system—strict implementation of the value-added tax, a policy of avoiding tax exemptions, tightening incentives granted to investment projects, enhancing the collection of nontax revenue and direct transfer of revenue to the treasury, and recovery of arrears from the private sector. The fiscal agenda aims at strengthening the role of the budget for economic management, and generating the resources needed to fund increased spending in priority areas. The main goals are to raise government saving to finance the public investment program and to avoid bank financing. The main focus of revenue mobilization is on the strengthening of tax and customs administration, and on full collection of nontax revenues, including arrears. Administration and enforcement of tax compliance will be enhanced through the exchange of taxpayer information between government departments and intensified on-site tax audits.

Efforts are being undertaken to strengthen Cambodia's banking system. The banking supervision capacity of the National Bank of Cambodia has to a certain extent already been upgraded and is being further strengthened, notably with the Fund technical assistance. Further improvements are being made to overhaul prudential regulations and to better assess the quality of banks' assets. A new modern financial institution law is expected to be approved by the National Assembly and the Senate by mid-October this year that would provide a better legal basis for both regulation and supervision. Moreover, so as to create a true market discipline, the National Bank of Cambodia is firmly promoting internationally accepted standards in the areas of accounting and public disclosures for both the national bank and commercial banks. Under the above-mentioned legal framework, many microfinancial institutions will be established to provide savings and credit facilities in the rural areas.

Investment in human capital is another priority of our policy platform. We believe that a highly educated labor force is one of the most crucial factors contributing to the country's economic growth in the next century. Therefore, the royal government of Cambodia has begun shifting budgetary resources from defense and security to health and education, as well as to other economic sectors, such as agriculture and rural development.

We are in the process of finalizing negotiations with the Fund to resume the ESAF. We also recently held discussions with the World Bank on the Structural Adjustment Credit (SAC). We would like to inform you that we achieved a positive result in these endeavors and are optimistic that we will be able to conclude the programs with both the Fund and the World Bank in the future. There is no doubt that these programs will contribute to the furtherance of our reform process and ensure a sound foundation for our future growth.

We welcome the coalition between the Bank and the Fund, which have departed from the traditional macroeconomic framework to a combination of efforts in linking structural adjustments with a poverty reduction agenda. In this regard, Cambodia supports efforts being made to relieve the burden of unsustainable debt in the poor countries through a new HIPC Initiative that links debt relief to the efforts to eradicate poverty. While supporting the Bank policy on focusing investment in the social sector, we still believe, however, that in a least-developed country, such as Cambodia, investment in economic and physical infrastructure is crucial to economic growth, only with which poverty could be alleviated on a sustainable basis.

In conclusion, we would like to take this opportunity to express our sincere gratitude to the World Bank and the Fund, as well as other international financial institutions and Cambodia's bilateral partners, for their support and assistance in our endeavors to engineer economic development and alleviate the poverty of our people. We are looking forward to enhancing our cooperation with the Fund and the Bank in the pursuit of ameliorating the social and economic conditions in Cambodia.

Statement by the Temporary Alternate Governor of the Bank and the Fund for Canada

James Peterson

Last year at this time, we were facing a very tenuous situation. You may recall that the World Economic Outlook document characterized the economic situation at the time as "unusually fragile." Fortunately for most of the world—though not all—the risks outlined in the document have not materialized. After the global financial turbulence of the past two years, and its devastating impact on economic activity and living standards in a wide range of countries, there are signs that the world economy is on the mend.

Economic Performance and Prospects in Canada

Developments in the Canadian economy have been more favorable than expected a year ago. In large measure, this reflects the government's commitment to sound economic and financial policies—low and stable inflation and balanced budgets or better. Growth in Canada slowed significantly in the middle of 1998, owing in part to the global financial uncertainty and turmoil of the time. As the effects of this and other disturbances have passed, growth has strengthened, averaging an annual rate of 4.0 percent over the past three quarters. As a result, the most recent consensus of private sector forecasters has real GDP growth upgraded to 3.5 percent in 1999 and 2.6 percent in 2000. The most recent Fund staff projections are consistent with the private-sector consensus.

Policy Challenges

In part, this year's more favorable global economic outlook reflects a number of policy steps taken over the past year, by both advanced and emerging market countries, to foster greater financial market stability and promote sustainable growth. Clearly, however, significant policy challenges remain. Perhaps the most serious risk is that we might not succeed in implementing the necessary reforms to make our own financial systems and the international system less vulnerable to crisis. There are at least two reasons why our efforts could fall short. The first is complacency. We will be making a grave error if we let the return of relative calm in financial markets and the improvement in world growth prospects lead us to believe that further reforms are not necessary. The second danger is that we could get caught up in a flurry of activity that, while giving the appearance of achievement, leaves critical issues or gaps unaddressed. Although a lot has been started over the past two years, some fundamental questions remain about where we are going with reforms to the international financial architecture.

Consultative Fora

Asking the right questions is only one of the challenges. Another is to have the proper institutional infrastructure to deal with them. This is an area where we are making progress; for example, by giving a revitalized Interim Committee permanent standing as the International Monetary and Financial Committee and by creating the Financial Stability Forum.

Private Sector Involvement in Crisis Resolution

The work plans of the existing and new fora should be dictated by our vision of how we want to see the international financial system evolve. One of the key questions for us in this regard is how to ensure an adequate framework so that the private sector can be productively involved when a crisis does break out.

Canada believes that we need to develop mechanisms that enable an orderly workout of debts. The role of the official sector should essentially be that of a neutral broker in the negotiation of a debt workout. The provision of large-scale official finance should be a rare occurrence.

To have the private sector involved in crisis prevention and resolution, however, we are going to have to establish a framework that will enable private investors to know in advance their responsibilities in the event of a crisis. And, we are going to have to ensure the mechanisms that operate within this framework balance the rights of creditors and the responsibilities of debtors, to ensure that both sides have an incentive to achieve a cooperative solution with adequate financing supplied at an appropriate price. Each crisis, however, will be unique. Each will have elements that we may not have encountered before. For this reason, we are going to have to be flexible and ready to adjust to specific sets of circumstances.

Debt Relief and Poverty Reduction

So far, I have devoted most of my remarks to the problems and issues facing the international financial system. I would also like to address a few remarks to the equally important issues of debt relief and poverty reduction. At the Group of Seven Summit this year, Canada pressed for faster and more generous debt relief for more countries and further action on poverty reduction. Canada fully endorses the two significant outcomes of the summit in these areas. Debt relief under the new initiative will more than double. Combined with relief under current mechanisms and forgiveness of aid-related claims, this could release significant resources for poverty reduction programs.

Ensuring that the HIPC Initiative is adequately financed is an important priority. While significant progress has been made to date in identifying financing, much more needs to be done. We would urge the international financial institutions to redouble their efforts to identify resources for this purpose. For its part, Canada will do its share and has fully paid in the $40 million it committed to the HIPC Trust Fund and has also pledged some $24 million from its refund on the Fund's second Special Contingent Account (SCA-2). Canada has also recognized the burden that new debt would represent for HIPCs, and so, in addition to forgiving all its official development assistance loans from HIPCs, Canada now provides all its bilateral ODA on a grant-only basis. As well, Canada is committed to writing off 100 percent of the commercial debt of the least developed nations. To prevent debt crises from becoming a recurring problem for developing countries, Canada also calls on lenders to adopt more transparent lending practices.

Canada's Export Development Corporation has already taken steps to increase the transparency of its lending operations in developing countries, including making available a country-by-country breakdown of its loans. Canada calls on other creditors to join in developing common standards in this regard to help prevent future debt crises.

Expanding the HIPC Initiative by itself, however, will not be sufficient to meet the challenge of poverty reduction. The HIPC Initiative can only form one element of what must be a much broader attack on global poverty. Collectively, we have a good sense of the key causes of poverty and where our efforts should be directed. In this regard, the education of women, in particular girls, is critically important, because educating women means educating families. This should form the cornerstone of our efforts in education—expanding opportunity to all segments of our societies. We need to recognize as well that all too often families and individuals are poor because they are ill. Relatively modest investments in health care and pharmaceutical research targeted at the diseases of the poor could potentially yield enormous dividends.

In countries where governance is strong, a radical shift is needed in the culture of development. One that places the developing country—its government and its people—in the driver's seat. We are encouraged that steps in this direction are being taken by various players, with leadership emanating from the World Bank through its proposal for a more holistic approach to development under a CDF. However, the shift in development thinking must go further. Experience has shown that, to be truly effective, development assistance needs to be targeted to countries whose governments pursue good policies and which are committed to developing and maintaining strong institutions. Governance has been a dominant theme of development assistance work over the past few years, and it must remain at the top of the policy agenda. In fact, good governance has become the essential building block for solid gains in poverty reduction and effective development assistance.

Effective multilateral institutions must also be a strong pillar of our development assistance efforts. We, as shareholders, have looked to the Bank to play a significant role in addressing the emerging markets' financial crises over the last two years and we, therefore, have to acknowledge that this has created pressures on the institution. Canada remains open to supporting a capital increase for the IBRD as an option for reinforcing the institution's lending capacity. However, our support for this option would be predicated on a strong link between Bank lending and development effectiveness, as well as to performance on governance issues.

The Challenges for Small States

Canada views with particular concern the development challenges faced by the world's smallest states. We welcome the World Bank's joint involvement with the Commonwealth Secretariat as well as the Fund's commitment to further research and policy work to assist small states in a rapidly changing world environment.

Our constituent members in the Caribbean are clearly facing a difficult transition period with the changes to existing trade preferences, the decline in development assistance, and the need for increased participation in the global economy. These changes would be a formidable challenge for any developing economy. But for the small states of the Caribbean, many of which are at the mercy of potentially devastating hurricanes, these changes can appear overwhelming at times. Their vulnerability to a single event that can have disastrous economic and social effects magnifies the adjustment challenge they face. Small states have a vulnerability that large states do not have. External trade shocks and natural disasters can easily eliminate hard-won gains in economic and social development. Their vulnerability is a fundamental differential that must be acknowledged.

Development, trade, and finance institutions must recognize the impact of the phase-out of the Lomé preferences on small states and help smooth the transition. Financial and technical assistance, and time, are needed in support of small states' efforts at restructuring their economies for the new external environment. Changes in global trade have made unsustainable some sectors that once accounted for a large portion of small states' gross domestic product.

The importance of this issue cannot be overemphasized. The research conclusions and policy prescriptions laid out will be used by international development players to sharpen their interactions in small states over the years to come. Furthermore, and potentially most important, this research will set the stage for small-state participation and treatment within the next round of WTO trade negotiations. We look forward to seeing the results of this work by the time of the spring meetings next year.

Conclusion

Although the crises of the past two years have receded, we are still faced with important challenges. We must make headway while the waters are relatively calm, putting in place the conditions for a stable international financial system and improved living standards for all. Only then will we be able to focus more on the opportunities that the world economy presents, and less on its challenges.

STATEMENT BY THE GOVERNOR OF THE BANK FOR THE PEOPLE'S REPUBLIC OF CHINA

Xiang Huaicheng

At this time, when we meet here, the economies of some crisis-hit countries in Asia and elsewhere have begun to bottom out and gradually regain growth. The currency and stock market situations have basically stabilized. Investor confidence has been restored, and global economic and financial prospects have improved. This has not come easily. It is a result achieved by the former crisis countries through their strong reform and adjustment efforts. It is also a result of enhanced international cooperation.

However, we should not be overly optimistic. The global economic environment, though improved, has not stabilized completely. The recovery of the formerly crisis-hit countries has just started. Their economic fundamentals are still fragile, and many deep-rooted issues remain to be addressed. There are still many uncertainties in today's world economy. Regional trade protectionism has been on the rise recently. The exchange rates between major currencies have seen wide fluctuations. The commodity price level is still unstable. The external environment faced by developing countries has not been improved fundamentally. To further consolidate the recovery and stabilize the world economy is a challenging task before the governments around the world. Developing countries need to continue their economic restructuring. At the same time, we call upon developed countries to increase resource transfer to and import from developing countries. We also urge them to implement proactive and responsible fiscal and monetary policies, and coordinate their interest and exchange rates policies, so as to create a better environment for the healthy development of the world economy.

The international community needs to draw lessons from the crisis in a serious manner. In order to prevent any future crisis, it is all the more important to strengthen the international financial cooperation and promote the trouble-free and smooth operation of the international financial market. To this end, the international community should, on the one hand, help developing countries improve their financial supervision and risk-prevention capacity, and on the other hand, strengthen the supervision of short-term capital flows and contain the excessive speculation of cross-border hot money.

The formidable shocks of the financial crisis have prompted a reassessment of the costs and benefits of globalization. Globalization has created opportunities as well as challenges and risks. While deepening market liberalization, enhancing competition, and raising efficiency, globalization also put forward to countries, and particularly those in the developing world, an issue of how to protect their economic security. We are of the view that economic globalization and financial integration should be based on equity and aimed at prosperity for all. The law of the jungle must be abandoned. Globalization and integration will not be sustainable if they benefit only a few. Therefore, in the process of reforming the international financial architecture and establishing a new international financial order, the developing countries' full participation is essential, and their interests and demands must be reflected. At the same time, the policy choices made by the affected countries or regions to overcome the crisis must be respected, and no model should be imposed indiscriminately.

The financial crisis also caused serious difficulties to China's economy, but the Chinese government has taken effective measures based on China's own circumstances and maintained the rapid growth of the economy. At the same time, the Chinese government, taking into account the need to maintain a healthy development for the Asian and the global economy, has adopted a highly responsible policy stance and made tremendous sacrifice by keeping the Chinese currency stable, thereby contributing to the recovery of the Asian economy. The economy of the Hong Kong Special Administrative Region has shown strong signs of recovery since the second quarter and is expected to realize positive growth for the whole year.

During the past year, the Chinese government further enhanced the macroeconomic regulation. In order to cushion the negative effects of the deteriorating external environment, weakening consumption, inadequate investment, and the slowing down of exports, China continued to implement a proactive fiscal and monetary policy by increasing the issuance of treasury bonds, cutting interest rates, and increasing the money supply moderately. These measures succeeded in expanding the domestic demand and stimulating investment, particularly in infrastructure. Meanwhile, in order to stimulate consumption, the Chinese government also took steps to increase the income of civil servants, the unemployed, laid-off workers from state-owned enterprises, and the urban poor. In addition, the Chinese government made special efforts to increase exports by optimizing the product mix and diversifying markets. On top of a 7.8 percent growth for 1998, China's economy grew by 7.6 percent for the first half of 1999. By the end of August, the fixed asset investment increased by 10.4 percent, compared with the same period last year. Consumption grew by 6.3 percent. The financial situation remained stable, and the growth rate of the money supply began to pick up. The total foreign trade rose by 7.3 percent, reaching $220.8 billion, with a trade surplus of $16 billion. The export volume amounted to $118.4 billion, and the decline in exports has been basically arrested. The foreign direct investment commitment reached $59.8 billion. The foreign exchange reserve exceeded $150 billion, and the Chinese currency, the renminbi, remains stable. The Chinese government is fully confident of achieving this year's growth targets.

Since the beginning of this year, the Chinese government has further accelerated the pace of reforms. In the area of state-owned enterprise reform, we are pressing ahead more vigorously with merger and acquisition, liquidation, downsizing, and redeployment of displaced workers. At the same time, the Chinese government is encouraging the development of the nonstate sector in various forms. In March of this year, the National People's Congress approved an amendment to the constitution to the effect that the nonstate sector is affirmed as an important component of the socialist market economy. As regards the financial sector reform, the central bank's independence and its role in macroeconomic regulation and financial supervision have been further strengthened. A system of regulating the banking, insurance, and securities industries separately has been established. Drawing on the international experience, the state commercial banks have set up asset management companies, respectively, to process their nonperforming loans. The asset management companies are also engaged in debt-equity swaps for the related state-owned enterprises to reactivate their stock assets and reduce their debt ratios, thereby advancing state-owned enterprise reform and preventing financial risks. In addition, the Chinese government is also making efforts to establish and improve the nationwide social security system suited to the socialist market economy.

The Chinese government has opened more sectors to the outside world, especially the service sectors, including banking, insurance, foreign trade, retail, tourism, and accounting, legal, and consulting services. As China's reform and opening progresses further and the socialist market economy takes shape, China's economy will achieve greater success in the twenty-first century.

For many years, the World Bank has made important contributions to poverty reduction and sustainable development in its member countries. At present when the economy of crisis-affected countries has generally restored stability, the Bank should shift its focus back to addressing the long-term development issues still facing developing countries, particularly poverty reduction. We hope that the Bank, as the largest development finance institution, will build upon its comparative advantages to provide more concessional funds and further promote the capital flow to its developing country members. We also hope that the Bank will strictly maintain its political neutrality in the conduct of its business and resist any attempts to politicize the Bank. We urge all the member countries, and the major shareholders in particular, to respect and protect the Bank's Articles of Agreement with a view to creating a better environment for the Bank to fulfill its development mandate.

We support the efforts by the Bank and the Fund in strengthening debt reduction for the heavily indebted poor countries and poverty alleviation in low-income countries. We have also noted the increased emphasis placed on social sector issues by the two institutions. We believe that economic development is a precondition to solutions to poverty alleviation and social issues. The two institutions should help developing countries achieve stable and steady growth, which in turn will help reduce poverty and resolve social issues. In this connection, we support the Fund's plan to increase gold sales in a nonmarket form with reasonable cost sharing.

In supporting the Fund's efforts to lend more to the HIPCs and strengthen the financing for the ESAF, China, as a low-income developing country, has decided to deposit its funds from SCA-2, free of interest, in the Fund's trust fund account.

We endorse the proposal to change the name of the Interim Committee to the "International Monetary and Financial Committee." We strongly request that the representation of developing countries be safeguarded. We hope the committee will do a better job in coordinating the major proposals for reforming the international monetary and financial system. Increasing the transparency of all market participants will help raise efficiency and prevent crisis. However, a lack of transparency is not the main cause of the financial crisis. We are not in favor of mandatory enforcement in any form, and Article IV consultations should not be linked with a transparency assessment.

The Fund's role in promoting capital account liberalization should be helping developing countries put in place the necessary conditions for liberalizing capital accounts, rather than pushing only the speed of liberalization. The international community should encourage the private sector to participate in preventing and finding solutions to financial crises, and there should be concrete actions as soon as possible. At the same time, the cooperation between debtors and creditors should be strengthened, and a balance maintained between their short-term and long-term interests.

Statement by the Governor of the Fund for the Republic of Croatia

Marko Skreb

One year after the wake-up call for concerted action on the part of the international financial community aimed at containing the financial crisis and facing the challenges of globalization, one can observe with pleasure that steps to create positive changes in the international financial system have been taken and have made gains.

Like most countries, Croatia has also been touched by effects of the financial crisis, and unfortunately, not only a financial but also a political one—that in Kosovo. That happened in the moment when, after four years of fast growth of GDP of around 6 percent, accompanied by reconstruction and an increase in the standard of living, the expansion of domestic demand exhausted its potential. So we had to contend with an increasingly difficult external environment, while experiencing a slowdown in domestic demand. These conditions resulted in a sharp contraction of economic activity followed by disturbances in the banking system.

Despite these circumstances, Croatia has been able to maintain price stability, keeping inflation at 4 percent throughout 1999. The policy of the Croatian National Bank will continue to be uncompromising and steadfast adherence to the principle of low inflation.

An area of great concern to us has been our external current account deficit. However, although Croatia had a very high deficit in 1997 (12.6 percent of GDP), it has been steadily going down. In 1998 it was 7.8 percent of GDP, and it would have gone down to 6.5 percent of GDP had it not been for the Kosovo crisis in 1999. We expect the deficit of current account to remain at around 7 to 7.5 percent of GDP this year, and to decrease at least one percentage point further in 2000, thereafter falling well below 5 percent in 2002–03, a level that we believe to be both sustainable and necessary at this point in the transition. Therefore, we have not only avoided the worst-case scenario in the past few years, but we have also successfully brought the deficit down by 5 percentage points of GDP in only three years. Unfortunately, there are no quick fixes. The external current account deficit has many deeper, structural reasons, and stimulating depreciation of the kuna would surely exacerbate it.

It is our belief that our export performance cannot be buttressed by superficial measures such as exchange rate changes; rather, exports' ability to compete has to be enhanced. That, in turn, can only be achieved by increasing foreign direct investment (FDI) and by swift and full integration of Croatia into the various levels of regional integration. Let me develop both points.

If we compare ourselves to other transition economies, those of Hungary and Poland for example, we will see that Croatia has received only a fraction of their FDI: $2.5 billion. Both Hungary and Poland have received well in excess of $20 billion, although both countries have already gone through the phase of "privatization-related FDI" that is still in front of Croatia. The export performance of the sectors that received the FDI improved markedly, yet the export performance of the sectors that did not remains bedeviled by the same worries as Croatian export sectors—loss of market share in the European Union, and generally losing out in the battle for competitiveness. Apart from that, the Central European Free Trade Agreement (CEFTA) and the Association Agreement with the European Union are considered to be the main prerequisites of the investors' interest. The fact that we are still not in CEFTA makes our exports more expensive in that market from the outset. That remains the goal of the Croatian government and the Croatian National Bank in particular. Only with significant increase in export sector efficiency can we improve our current account balance.

In terms of economic policies, the government further encourages adjustment to continuously changing circumstances. As already emphasized by many distinguished colleagues, responsible policymakers cannot imagine withstanding the pressure from defense of the peg in the present world of a globalized economy and high capital mobility, without having sound economic and financial structures. This would be just one reason more for enhancing structural reforms, continuing with sound fiscal policy and with consolidation of financial system. These will continue to have a salient position in the agenda for the Croatian economy.

Allow me to brief you on what have we done from this point of view in order to prepare us for the future. In terms of structural reforms, a lot of work has been done (privatization of telecommunications, the establishment of the related regulatory framework, the restructuring of some other public enterprises so as to prepare the basis for their further privatization, etc.), but there are still some deep-seated problems to be resolved. From this point of view, significant steps have been taken to implement a program of measures encompassing: amendments to legislation regarding bankruptcy and the execution of court decisions (collaboration with the World Bank is under way); measures for enhancing the independence of the judicial system to prevent abuses and crime in the economy and social system; measures to further encourage the honoring of contracts; and more. The successful implementation of these measures (along with the reform of the pension and health care system) is a keystone for maintenance of macroeconomic stability at this stage. In addition, fiscal consolidation is at the top of priority tasks. So far, fiscal policy has been carefully managed.

After the successful introduction of the value-added tax, with enhanced collection efforts and despite the drop in revenues because of the economic slowdown, the central government overall balance has been kept within the limits of Maastricht criteria. But (one has to be honest) the existing level of public spending is unsustainable in the long run. Serious measures have been therefore endorsed.

The health care and pension system reforms, supported by World Bank expertise and resources, are continuing—but they take time. So as to be able to get through this transitional period, government has vigorously started with measures to improve administration and financial management as well as to increase transparency (the introduction of a single treasury account system is expected at the very beginning of 2000). Recommendations stated in the Code of Good Practices in Transparency of Fiscal Policy and the accompanying—revised—manual, are a helpful reference from this point of view.

Monetary policy has been characterized by a high degree of consistency throughout past years, consistency of both goals and instruments. That will be the case, I assure you, in the future as well. No surprise will come from monetary policy, and we will maintain our conservative position, both in the goals (low inflation, stable exchange rate) and in the instruments.

With respect to fiscal policy, there is no news either. The central budget can borrow from the Croatian National Bank only to bridge its gaps between receivables and expenditures and up to a limit, which is predetermined by the Law on Croatian National Bank. The central budget is currently indebted 1.3 billion kuna or less than $0.2 billion to the central bank; and this will be returned by the end of this year. There will be no monetary relaxation in important matters such as financing of the budget.

The progress achieved in the banking system consolidation (the banking industry still prevails in the Croatian financial system) is an example. Work has still not been completed but much has been done. After a generally successful restructuring of some major—at the time—state-owned banks, addressing problems inherited from the former socialist system, in 1998 we were suddenly faced by severe disturbances in the banking industry, especially in some of the newly established banks. At the end of 1998, the first problems in the banking sector started to surface and became apparent. Much before that, the central bank, aware of the irregularities in some of the banks, had started to initiate the procedure to have a new Banking Law adopted. Under the old law, the maneuvering space for the central bank was very limited, and powers to deal with the problematic banks hardly existed. The new law was adopted in December 1998, after a relatively quick parliamentary procedure. Immediately after that, the central bank exercised the powers granted to it by the new law by installing temporary administrators in the banks that were suspected to be in a serious trouble.

The causes of the banking crises are well known. After two years of very rapid economic growth and credit expansion, during which the credits to domestic sectors grew 44 percent in 1997 and 22 percent in 1998, there was a general slowdown of the economy. The credit supply diminished, and some big private companies went bankrupt, dragging down the banks that were connected to them. Needless to say, the bankrupt banks had high amounts of connected lending, and their asset portfolios were not healthy, so they were vulnerable to the collapse of their connected enterprises. The effect was confined only to a handful of banks, connected further among themselves. There was very little systemic damage beyond this particular group of the banks.

Public perception is very important, because although we continually maintained that the troubles were confined to a smaller group of banks and that the rest of the banking sector is healthy, and in better shape than a few years ago, it was important that public choices prove this to be the case. Today, we have a group of big and medium-size banks that are doing very well, we have some banks with the substantial foreign participation, we have rehabilitated big banks that are going to be privatized in the course of the next two years, and we have an important number of the foreign branches and one subsidiary. The situation is certainly much better than it was before.

This year, it became more than evident that the general recommendations of the international financial community had to be applied quickly and become reality for the Croatian banking system. The adoption of internationally accepted standards and their internal development and dissemination, enhancement of transparency, closer monitoring of banking system soundness through effective supervision (supported by an adequate legislative framework), in relation with macroeconomic policy as well, have to be our priority. Besides, a number of rules have been set or are going to be established in the near future as to enhance market discipline, owner control, and supervisory effectiveness. Precious advice in this respect has been received from the World Bank and IMF staff through technical assistance missions. Needless to say, in the design and implementation of the above-mentioned measures, provisions of the Basel Core Principles for Effective Banking Supervision and other internationally accepted standards have been duly respected. By increasing transparency in this way, we have tried to facilitate foreign entry in order to increase the competition.

As everything is mutually related, one change so as to achieve an aim leads to another. The recently experienced turbulence in our economy taught us that close communication with all market participants (domestic or foreign) is a prerequisite for having an effective macroeconomic policy transmission mechanism. Transparency in one area by itself does not suffice. The Fund initiative in terms of the Code of Good Practices on Transparency in Monetary and Financial Policy and its further elaboration through the manual will be of utmost help. Once again, tasks at the micro level (that is, country level, regardless the size of the country) are identical to global prerequisites. Our adherence to the SDDS is already well established, as is our openness to IMF policies and advice. Croatia, that is, made public its Letter of Intent five years ago. Therefore it is needless to say that we support the release of the Article IV staff report.

A larger integration of the Croatian economy into the world economy remains one of the main goals in the future, although the growth of foreign trade and foreign direct investment has been evidenced in the last year (1998). As the process of negotiation is approaching its end, it is expected that Croatia will become a full member of the World Trade Organization at the end of this year. We truly hope that this is going to open the doors for Croatia in other international and regional organizations and associations.

In a small, open economy at the advanced stage of transition as the Croatian economy is, we cannot allow ourselves not to be up to date with (above all) recent discussions, opinions, and experiences related to capital account liberalization. It is beyond any doubt that capital account liberalization is necessary as a part of financial integration. But so as to use all the benefits from liberalization, it should be carefully managed and adjusted to the strength of the financial system of the country concerned (especially, in transition countries). If financial disturbances are to be avoided, this fact must be taken into account by all international institutions that try to monitor or regulate capital account liberalization. In this respect, the Fund study on the use and effectiveness of specific capital controls is going to be of invaluable help to us.

Consequently, we support all the efforts of the international financial institutions in searching for mechanisms for the prevention and resolution of crises by securing private sector involvement. It is essential to limit moral hazards, strengthen market discipline, and ensure orderly adjustment processes, while maintaining international financial flows. The only thing I would like to stress in this regard is that, independently of the approach taken, the equality of treatment should be ensured.

Further, we believe that IMF readiness to place more emphasis on social issues in developing programs will be broadly welcomed. This will undoubtedly increase public support for the Fund programs, and make implementation of them easier, especially in recipient countries.

Throughout the year we have reached out continuously (more or less successfully) for help from the Fund and the World Bank—our friends and critics alike—to obtain appropriate solutions in banking, financial, and social sectors, as well as to mitigate the effects of regional spillovers associated with the Kosovo crisis.

And now allow me to express our thanks to the management and the entire staff of the Fund and the World Bank for their valuable assistance and unselfishly shared expertise and knowledge.

STATEMENT BY THE GOVERNOR OF THE BANK FOR CYPRUS

Takis Klerides

It is encouraging to note that the world economic situation is now distinctly better than it was 12 months ago and that the global growth momentum during 1999 has been improving. There are still considerable downward risks for the world economy, especially if the expected deceleration in the growth of the U.S. economy is not offset by faster growth in the other major industrial economies. It is important that this momentum be sustained, so as to enable significant improvements in the living standards of the population of the poorer developing countries.

The experience of the past two years has demonstrated the vital role that international financial institutions can play in resolving and helping countries recover from financial crises. Indeed, the enhancement of the resources and facilities of the Fund, including its new Contingent Credit Line should help the Fund to prevent and contain future financial crises. However, we are concerned that some of these enhanced facilities, such as the strengthened HIPC Initiative, will require further large funding in order to provide timely financing and debt relief to deserving countries. In this vein, Cyprus would urge that early agreement be reached on the full financing and equitable burden sharing for the enhanced HIPC Initiative. And in view of the rapid increase in the World Bank Group's lending portfolio and its higher degree of concentration, as well as the downgrading of a number of borrowing countries, we believe that consideration could also be given to capital replenishment for the Group, including the International Finance Corporation.

With respect to the "New International Financial Architecture" and "Strengthening Global Economic Governance," we would support the view that the Fund must continue to perform the role of a crisis manager on the global financial stage, but that public resources be used more prudently and only with strong conditionality so as to avoid moral hazard. New mechanisms must be developed and implemented to strengthen the involvement of the private sector in forestalling and resolving financial crises, a process that would make imprudent creditors and investors bear part of the burden and losses associated with financial crises.

The recovery and resumption of strong economic growth in East Asian countries that were most directly affected by the recent financial crises is encouraging. However, we are concerned that countries hurt by the indirect effects of the East Asian crisis, mainly through sharply falling primary commodity prices, will continue to experience irretrievable losses in income and will remain vulnerable to further price fluctuations. In this context, we would welcome the creation of the commodity price risk insurance scheme for developing countries that has recently been proposed by the World Bank. We trust also that, in the development of new trading arrangements at the forthcoming World Trade Organization meeting in Seattle and those to follow the Lomé Convention for the African, Caribbean, and Pacific (ACP) Group with the European Union, sufficient priority be given to assuring that developing countries have continued access for their main export commodities to the markets of the European Union and other industrial countries.

In Cyprus we are well aware of the vulnerability of small open economies to fluctuations in export prices and volumes. In 1999, a considerable fall has been recorded in the international prices of our main commodity export, namely potatoes, but fortunately our largest foreign exchange earner, tourism, has experienced substantial rises in both the number of tourists and their average expenditure. The continued pegging of the Cyprus pound to the euro has contributed to improving export competitiveness in 1999, especially for tourists from the United Kingdom, while permitting the importing of low inflation from the countries of the European Monetary Union. For 1999, the real GDP of Cyprus is expected to increase by about 4.5 percent, the annual rise in the consumer price index is forecast to average 1.5 percent, and the unemployment rate will remain at about 3.4 percent.

Despite these favorable macroeconomic indicators we are concerned that we have not been able to reduce the fiscal deficit to below 5½ percent of GDP in 1999. For the first time, in conjunction with the tabling of the government budgets for 2000 at our House of Representatives, the government will propose a detailed and substantive package of tax measures aimed at bringing about a sizable reduction in the fiscal deficit. As the magnitude of the budgetary allocations is dependent on securing revenue from the new tax measures, any failure by the House to agree on a significant package of tax measures will mean that budgeted expenditures for 2000 will have to be reduced.

In concluding, I will emphasize that Cyprus continues to support and cooperate with the Fund and the Bank in their efforts to foster a stable economic and financial environment conducive to healthy growth and development. Also, I would take this opportunity to thank the management and staff of the Fund and the Bank for the constructive advice they have rendered to Cyprus.

STATEMENT BY THE GOVERNOR OF THE FUND FOR FIJI

Jone Yavala Kubuabola

It is an honor to attend the fifty-fourth joint Annual Meeting of the Boards of Governors of the International Monetary Fund and the World Bank Group. My delegation and I wish to thank Mr. Camdessus and

Mr. Wolfensohn and their staff for the support and advice to countries during these testing times and for their initiatives to promote a more stable financial environment. Allow me also to congratulate the President of the World Bank, Mr. Wolfensohn, for his reappointment for another term.

Global economic conditions look more favorable than they did 12 months ago. The U.S. economy continues to provide good support for the world economy, growth in the European economies looks to be picking up, and the Japanese economy appears to have steadied. In the developing countries, economic conditions have generally stabilized, and in some cases are showing considerable improvement. Against this improving global backdrop, Fiji's economy is also looking to pick up by over 7 percent this year, as the economy returns to more normal conditions following the debilitating effects of the drought and the weaker global conditions over the past couple of years. Despite these positive developments in global economic and financial conditions, many downside risks remain. Great care will now be necessary to nurture the fragile global recovery and guard against some of the potential hazards that lie ahead.

The global economy has faced setbacks in the past two years—indeed we have come through the most severe worldwide economic crisis of the past 50 years. These events have been caused by a combination of factors; in particular, problems with macroeconomic management, deficiencies in domestic financial systems, and weaknesses in the international financial system. The Fund and the World Bank have played an important role in stabilizing conditions during this period and putting in place policies to foster sustained recovery. The opportunity has also been taken to look at ways of strengthening the international financial architecture to help guard against financial crises in the future.

The events of the past two years, while painful, have also provided us with a number of valuable lessons. Many of these lessons are not new, but they reinforce thinking that is broadly accepted but often less enthusiastically applied. Let me touch on a few of these.

- The first issue is liberalization. We all know that financial sector liberalization can spur economic growth and development but liberalization also entails risks if reforms are not appropriately designed and implemented. The recent crises in Asia, Russia, and Latin America have demonstrated the urgency of finding ways to achieve orderly liberalization. In Fiji, we have proceeded cautiously with liberalization, opening up the capital account progressively over the past decade as conditions allowed.
- Second, the need for strong financial structures and institutions that are able to withstand the types of shocks that affect more

open economies. The lesson is now very clear—as part of the reform process, policymakers should work toward developing systems, institutions, and financial markets that are strong enough to withstand potential shocks to the economy. Strong domestic financial sector regulation and prudential oversight are important ingredients for weathering financial storms.

- Third, sound macroeconomic management, which include strong fiscal positions that provide governments some cushion to withstand unfavorable shocks. Appropriate monetary policy is also important to maintain stability and confidence in the financial system.
- The fourth major lesson that comes from the experiences of the past couple of years is the need for greater transparency, by both the public and private sectors. Better and timely information allows better risk assessment and decision making by policymakers and the private sector. The recent codes of good practices on transparency in monetary and fiscal policies are good examples of recent initiatives in this area. I understand the SDDS have now been adopted by some member countries. Fiji has been involved in the GDDS pilot in the Pacific region.

The events of the past two years have focused attention on building the international financial architecture and reviewing the multilateral institutions' policy prescriptions. The new financial order will no doubt take into account the lessons learned, in particular, the need to encourage transparency and accountability. Higher and volatile capital flows ought to be properly managed to minimize their disruptive impact on domestic markets.

This new financial system calls for closer consultation and better burden sharing. We therefore welcome recent discussions at the Fund and the Bank about better ways to involve the private sector in preventing and managing financial crises. This is a complex issue, but one of utmost importance. In practice, it involves finding ways of getting creditors and debtors to come together in a collaborative manner to assess problem situations and arrive at mutually beneficial processes for recovery.

We are also pleased with other recent Fund and World Bank initiatives. On the Fund side, we welcome the introduction of two new facilities—the Contingency Credit Line and Y2K facilities. These facilities will provide a useful complement for existing techniques and may help member countries respond quickly to financial crises.

On the Bank side, we would like to reaffirm our support for the Comprehensive Development Framework. We certainly look forward to further developments on the framework, particularly the dissemination of lessons learned, which we could draw upon to help us refine and strengthen our development strategies. Undoubtedly, the CDF will allow us to look at our development strategy in a coherent manner with the appropriate balance between macroeconomic and financial concerns on the one hand, and social and structural issues on the other. Furthermore, the emphasis on country ownership and partnership, with the required longer-term foresight, are fundamental principles that will ensure effective policy building and implementation in developing countries.

Fiji's overriding goal to improve living standards through sustainable and equitable growth is very much in line with the CDF approach. Our government is strongly committed to addressing the social and structural imbalances we currently face. Broadly, these involve increasing employment opportunities in areas where we have comparative advantages, increasing and improving the delivery of social services, protecting the poor, and effecting social transfers to reduce the cost of living for low-income earners. From the lessons learned from the international experience over the past two years, we definitely see the need to cushion the economically vulnerable from income fluctuations.

As a small state, we are optimistic that the CDF principles of ownership and effective collaboration with development partners should bring about more sensitivity to the special problems of our economies. We welcome the small states' strategy jointly developed by the World Bank and Commonwealth Secretariat. In our view, the strategy for such an initiative should concentrate on the vulnerabilities of small states. For Fiji, as a small South Pacific Island state, our major challenges are our isolation from major markets, meager resources, and susceptibility to natural disasters, such as hurricanes and droughts. We eagerly look forward to the finalization of the strategy for small states after full consultation with the relevant member countries.

Let me comment on another of the Fund and the Bank's recent initiatives—the proposed debt relief for highly indebted poor countries. This is a very worthwhile initiative and commands wide support. We are heartened by the Fund's decision to undertake off-market transactions, rather than open market sales of gold to fund this initiative, which would avoid the disruptive effects on gold-producing countries such as Fiji.

On a final note, let me just touch on one other issue that is on everyone's minds at the moment—the Y2K problem. Dealing with the issue has become quite complex—as you are aware the issue is not just about fixing a computer problem—as policymakers we must recognize that the Y2K issue involves managing risk. In Fiji, we have been taking the necessary steps to minimize Y2K-related problems in our financial system. We applaud the decision by the Fund to introduce a temporary facility that will help members deal with unforeseen balance of payments problems that may arise in connection with the Y2K problem.

I conclude by thanking the Bank and the Fund for their assistance and support to Fiji and the Pacific region. As always, we will continue to look to the Fund and the Bank for assistance in infrastructure, human resource development, institutional strengthening, and economic and financial policy advice. We commend the services of the Pacific Financial Technical Assistance Center and thank the Fund, the United Nations Development Program, and other donor countries for their continued support in this and other areas. I would like to wish the Fund and the World Bank well in their future endeavors.

STATEMENT BY THE ALTERNATE GOVERNOR OF THE FUND FOR FRANCE

Jean-Claude Trichet

The latest forecasts established by the Fund confirm the dynamism of world growth. This favorable situation does not dispense us from reflecting upon new kinds of regulations for a more effective and equitable world. To do so, we must identify the ways to achieve long-term, balanced growth and to define the framework that will enhance this dynamic movement. The international financial community has a considerable responsibility in this regard. It is in this spirit that we have made several proposals. The improvement in the general situation now allows us to focus on the most pressing problems of the poorest countries.

Mobilization for Long-Term, Balanced Growth

Nine months after the successful creation of the euro, the economic recovery in the European Union and the euro area is confirmed and the conditions for a robust and sustainable growth are present. Prospects for industry have been improving for the past few months, households' confidence is strong, their purchasing power remains well oriented, and exports are on the upswing. The French economy is contributing substantially to the European growth.

So, we are confident in our economic prospects, but of course we should also remain vigilant so that the more robust growth that we currently enjoy lasts as long as possible. We particularly should take into account incipient short-term pressures on consumer prices related to the higher oil prices observed over the past months and the lagging effects of the evolution of the euro. With a view to extending the period of noninflationary recovery and to significantly reduce unemployment, it is also necessary to continue implementing structural reforms.

In Japan, self-sustained growth is not yet guaranteed, despite recent more favorable indicators. I welcome the commitment of the Japanese authorities to continue policy aimed at avoiding any further growth weakening. External demand can play an important role on the condition that the value of the yen ceases to rise: this analysis is shared by the Group of Seven countries.

Strong growth in the United States remains impressive. In this regard, I welcome the fact that fiscal policy is contributing to reducing the national saving deficit: lowering taxes would only increase existing imbalances. Yet, household saving remains insufficient.

The emerging and developing economies are gradually recovering, after having experienced a very difficult and uncertain period as a result of the financial crises and of the 1998 decline in commodity prices. But improvement remains uneven. The positive signs that have appeared in the last several months, especially in Asia, should not lead to underestimating the vulnerability of these economies to external shocks or the scope of the structural reforms still to be undertaken. In most Latin American countries, courageous adjustments have taken place. But activity in the region continues to be sluggish, or even losing some ground.

A year ago, our meeting opened in an atmosphere of anxiety. The sound economic policies followed in Europe and the United States, the determined action of the Bretton Woods institutions—I wish to pay special tribute to their heads—the courage of the governments and people of countries affected by the crisis in the emerging world, made it possible to avoid the worst. Current prospects for world growth are such as to inspire new optimism. We should now consolidate these results.

For This Renewed Growth, We Need a Better Framework in Support of Good Governance and Against Money Laundering and Corruption.

We need a better framework for banking and tax havens, especially for combating money laundering and corruption. To meet the challenge of globalization, we must define new regulations. In international trade, fair competition is crucial for efficient international competition. For the past two years, encouraged notably by France, initiatives have been launched within the relevant international fora. These should rapidly result in concrete reforms. If not, these scourges will continue to develop. It is in this spirit that France has made the following proposals in favor of the following:

- more specific and stringent rules, especially as concerns a ban on underregulated legal entities (shield companies) and strengthening legislation against money laundering and bribery;
- strengthening our power to act through the rapid establishment by the Financial Action Task Force and prudential authorities of a list of noncooperative states and territories and engaging reinforced technical cooperation with those states and territories to implement international standards according to a defined timetable;
- identifying drifts more effectively by an increased mobilization of the international financial institutions in the fight against money laundering and corruption. These institutions, especially the Fund, could adopt a "Governance Charter," which could review good governance in the context of assessing a country's economic situation (Article IV). This could also be a precondition for providing financial support; and
- graduated sanctions going from incentives to sanctions within the multilateral framework and, in bilateral relationships, up to and including measures to progressively restrict capital movements with offshore centers to be implemented under the aegis of the prudential authorities.

The next step: toward a better international financial architecture. The transformation of the Interim Committee is an important step toward reinforcing the governance of the Fund and improving its functioning. The Fund would thus become all the more effective. We have made a very positive step today, but it is still only a step. For France, the arguments for a "Council" of the Fund remain valid, and a more ambitious reform is perceived as both necessary and inevitable.

The reform of the international monetary and financial system that we launched over a year ago has made real progress. Working out the different codes, strengthening the Fund's surveillance mechanism for assessing potential economic vulnerability, and defining an orderly strategy for liberalizing capital flows are all essential building blocks.

There are nevertheless three issues that deserve more progress: exchange rates regimes, regulation of financial activities, and private sector involvement in crisis resolution. In the context of financial globalization, they are essential for a more efficient regulation.

First, we need more transparency and consistency as regards exchange rates regimes. Exchange rate systems and policies have played a crucial role in the recent crises. In conformity with its mission, the Fund must develop a global strategy. But we should remain pragmatic. Pure floating or currency boards are not the only available alternatives. Had only a polar approach prevailed, the euro would not have become the

European currency and would not be a magnet for many European countries. Room should be left for regional cooperation.

Transparency and consistency should prevail: in adopting a particular exchange rate regime, a country should make clear the objectives it is pursuing. The Fund should continue to reflect on this, taking into account the policy choices of each country.

The experience of the 1990s demonstrates that, in countries where capital account liberalization has been completed, consistent macroeconomic policies are a prerequisite for appropriately managing or pegging exchange rates. Nonetheless, financial crises in various emerging economies have highlighted that macroeconomic discipline alone does not suffice to sustain pegs and must be accompanied by sound and robust financial systems, effective regulation and supervision, good corporate governance, as well as greater transparency in the conduct of monetary and financial policies.

In regulating financial activities, the issue of hedge funds must be addressed. Traditionally limited to protecting savings, it is now recognized that prudential regulation impacts the macroeconomy. The creation of the Financial Stability Forum, which unites the Bretton Woods institutions and the financial oversight organizations, illustrates this point.

In the context of the Forum's activities, I wish that the will to act would prevail. For example, a large commercial bank whose potential difficulties could have a systemic impact on markets must be subject to prudential regulation to limit its leverage, its liquidity risks, and its exposure concentration. In my view, it is not inconceivable to submit an investment bank or a hedge fund to similar regulations. These institutions can harbor exactly the same systemic risks. For this reason, it seems indispensable to develop regulations applicable to these funds and as a first step to request more transparency in their operations vis-à-vis both their financial counterparts and the market.

Finally, the private sector must be involved in resolving crises. The principle of private sector involvement in crisis management is a given. But recent examples of negotiation with the private sector have demonstrated the limits of a strictly cooperative approach. We must be prepared to disseminate an agreed framework to facilitate private sector involvement. I would like the Fund, along with other interested institutions, to work as quickly as possible on the basis of the principles proposed by the G-7 at the Cologne Summit, and with the intent to achieve equitable treatment for all private creditors.

With the Paris Club principle of comparability of treatment, we have at our disposal a preliminary response. I would ask that in other cases, the international community be sure that all categories of creditors be involved equitably, no matter what the nature of the debts at stake. We must also be ready, in situations where the cooperative approach upon which we have based our procedures reaches its limits, to have recourse to more forceful solutions.

The Way Is Open for Dealing Quickly with the Heavily Indebted Poor Countries.

The debt burden in the poorest countries represents a major obstacle to their development. When a country's debt service is greater than its education or health budgets, it is impossible to envisage steady development progress. France has always fought in favor of debt cancellation. It will now be necessary to go much farther to free the poorest countries from debt overhang. We must be watchful that this goal is achieved in full accordance with three fundamental principles that France has put forward from the outset:

- solidarity, which should lead us to concede the most favorable possible treatment to the poorest countries;
- equity, which is the basis of fair burden sharing between all bilateral and multilateral creditors; and
- responsibility, which justifies that these exceptional measures support the social sectors of countries with irreproachable public management.

This new impetus must be equitably financed. France has not stalled, waiting for others to pay in our place. France is definitively in the front ranks of funding the initiative. We are waiting for other developed countries to commit to a comparable effort. Countries like France that make large bilateral efforts have a right to expect equal effort from the multilateral institutions and their shareholders. The credibility of our multilateral system depends on equitable burden sharing.

I warmly thank Michel Camdessus and James Wolfensohn for the efforts they have made to come to a solution. I know that it was not without sacrifice. It will allow us to take advantage of a global solution, which directs additional resources to the institutions whose situation is critical, thanks to the efforts realized by the Fund and the World Bank to mobilize to the maximum of their internal resources.

Dealing with debt must lead to an effective fight against poverty provided by debt cancellation. The dose of oxygen should, by priority, be targeted at the most vulnerable populations and should allow eligible countries to establish basic public services: education for all, access to health care, and the provision of basic infrastructure. For this, it will be up to the developing country governments to adopt economically and socially coherent development policies and to improve governance.

Our consistent action in support of development must also go forward. France has increasingly affirmed that, in view of the constant reduction in public aid flows, simply dealing with debt and private investment flows in a few emerging countries will not alone suffice to resolve the problems of development.

Maintaining a sufficient flow of public aid is vital. The concessional loan funds, principally the International Development Association and the African Development Fund, at the multilateral banks must in fact receive the resources committed during the recent replenishments.

At the moment when the World Trade Organization is opening a new cycle of commercial negotiations, it also behooves each of our governments to reflect on how they will affect development in poor countries. The new cycle of negotiations should be an opportunity for us to reaffirm the importance of developing country access to developed countries' markets. As you know, France and Europe have long ago incorporated this dimension into their relations with the developing countries, notably through the Lomé convention.

Regional integration is also a necessary step. Integration is a source of political stability, of convergence, and of peer pressure between governments. Integration gives regional economies critical mass in the global one. It is not a question of creating new regional fortresses, but of facilitating global integration.

To conclude, I would like to emphasize two points:

- First, the global economy is doing much better than it was a year ago. This calls for two *coups de chapeau*: one to some emerging economies, notably in Asia, that have demonstrated remarkable efforts to adjust in a very short lapse of time; the second, to the international financial institutions, and in particular the Fund and the World Bank, which have demonstrated—in the most difficult circumstances—lucidity, determination, and courage.
- Second, this is not the time for complacency. The global economy is in much better shape, but there remain risks and challenges. We must demonstrate that we can take advantage of a quieter and calmer period to embark resolutely on the reforms that are needed.

STATEMENT BY THE GOVERNOR OF THE FUND FOR GERMANY

Ernst Welteke

Two years on from the far-reaching currency and financial crises in Southeast Asia and the subsequent financial turmoil in other regions, we are now able to look to the future with some degree of optimism. The past few months have witnessed a considerable improvement in the world economic situation and its medium-term prospects in virtually all regions.

In many emerging economies, especially in Southeast Asia and Latin America, reforms are showing the first positive effects: the massive currency distortions have been largely overcome, and economic recovery has set in. The economic climate has continued to improve in industrial countries as well. All major economies can note continuing favorable growth trends or are in a recovery phase.

This also holds true for the countries that launched the euro as their common currency on January 1 of this year. The Fund expects growth of 2.8 percent for the euro area in the year 2000. This performance will contribute to a more balanced growth among major industrialized countries. At the same time, the euro has already become the second most important currency in the world. The countries making up the euro area are aware of the responsibility this imposes on them. With the continuation of fiscal policy consolidation and structural reform, the euro countries will create the conditions to promote sustained, vigorous growth and high employment.

But risks remain, despite the improvement in global prospects. Hence, it is vital to press ahead with the necessary reforms. We must also be prepared for the possible threats posed by the Y2K computer problem. The Fund has made preparations to offer temporary financial help to member countries encountering difficulties from the Y2K problem. However, it will be the foremost responsibility of all countries to prepare thoroughly and convincingly for the date change.

The positive results of the past few months should not distract us from further resolute action to reform the international financial architecture. Much has already been achieved in the course of the past months:

- The Fund and the World Bank have enhanced the transparency of their operations, providing the financial markets with an improved basis for decision making.
- The new Financial Stability Forum will bring together the international supervisory bodies and the Bretton Woods institutions

and create the opportunity to improve early identification of crises and strengthen global cooperation.

- Initial progress has also been made on involving the private sector in crisis prevention and resolution. Given the potential for a variety of situations on the part of debtors and creditors, it is reasonable to assume that the precise modalities for the involvement of the private sector can only be determined on a case-by-case basis. What is important, however, from the German perspective is that the financing role of the official sector will be determined a priori in a way that precludes a "bailout" of private creditors.

The Fund and the World Bank have done excellent work in reforming the international financial architecture. I expressly welcome the contribution by Michel Camdessus and Jim Wolfensohn and the work by the staffs of both institutions. But much remains to be done.

People in economically less-developed countries must also be enabled to benefit from the opportunities for lasting growth, innovation, and socially equitable, ecologically acceptable development provided by globalization. We must all work together to create the conditions for this.

In view of the continuing vulnerability of many highly indebted poor countries to exogenous shocks, Germany and other major industrial countries have proposed to enhance the HIPC Initiative, which was put into effect in 1996. The initiative of the Cologne Summit has been brought to a successful conclusion during these Annual Meetings.

The enhanced debt initiative presents major financial challenges to bilateral and multilateral donors. Many industrial economies are in the process of budget consolidation calling for cutbacks by the population as well. Yet, Germany will contribute to the World Bank Trust Fund and will cancel substantial amounts of bilateral debt. Within the Fund, Germany will make an appropriate contribution to financing the ESAF enhancement and the Fund contribution to the HIPC Initiative.

Other multilateral donors must now step up their efforts to secure financing for the HIPC Initiative as well. We must especially endeavor to ensure that the most efficient and broadest possible use is made of the institutions' own resources. However, debtor countries' enhanced scope for policy action offered by debt relief will only prove beneficial to them if they pursue sound economic policies and avoid unproductive expenditures to a higher extent than in the past.

The funds released through debt relief must—in the context of a comprehensive poverty-reduction strategy—be targeted at social improvement. Promoting health care and education, for example, is a crucial requirement to ensure lasting economic development and, hence, economic and political stability.

What is important is that the Fund and the World Bank participate in these tasks within the confines of their respective mandates. Poverty reduction strategies are the task of the countries concerned and the World Bank. The World Bank should concentrate on social and structural issues. The Fund should restrict itself to the macroeconomic issues.

Economic growth cannot achieve sustained development and overcome poverty unless it wears a human face. In the same vein, the efforts of the Fund and the World Bank, as well as the bilateral and other multilateral donors, will fail unless they are backed up by vigorous efforts on the part of the developing countries themselves. This would foster the creation of a political and economic environment within the country, which motivates individuals and allows them to put their capabilities to productive use. In this context, encouraging transparency and good governance is indispensable in securing the effective deployment of bilateral and multilateral assistance.

The importance of good governance is demonstrated not least by the problems of money laundering and corruption. In any case, recipient countries must always take all necessary actions to avoid a misuse of funds.

The Fund and the World Bank must stick to their respective mandates, but close cooperation between the two institutions, based on mutual trust, is vital. It is also vital for both institutions to retain their roles as the central forums of international cooperation. Ensuring this is the task to which we are all committed.

STATEMENT BY THE GOVERNOR OF THE BANK FOR GREECE

Yannos Papantoniou

When we last met here a year ago, the world financial markets were still in turbulence and we were reflecting on the causes of the crises, their expected effects, and the best ways to react. Since then world economic developments have turned more positive.

- World growth has picked up.

- We have started implementing the actions necessary to prevent and detect crises, and to improve the functioning of the international financial system.

It is generally accepted, however, that even if progress has been made, this is no time for complacency. Actions are needed in coordinating the surveillance process and in designing incentives so that the private and the public sector alike benefit from international financial stability.

The introduction of the euro in 1999 played a substantial part in fostering a climate of stability. Today, the sound macroeconomic policies pursued by the euro member states have led to an environment of low inflation and healthy public finances. Members of the euro area can now enjoy the benefits of stability and exploit the opportunities created by the Single Market. Stability in the euro area has led to a resumption of economic growth, while improved coordination of economic policies is expected to lead to higher efficiency and employment. Greece is about to join the Economic and Monetary Union, effective January 1, 2001, and to share in the advantages that it creates.

The case of Greece could serve to illustrate the benefits that arise from sound macroeconomic policies and a positive attitude toward reform. The Greek economy has shown resilience to the financial crises and is exhibiting high rates of growth.

The process of macroeconomic rationalization started in Greece later than in other European countries. With the 1994 convergence plan, we pursued policies designed to achieve the Maastricht Treaty criteria and have made substantial progress in achieving them. Indeed, from the middle of this year we satisfy four out of the five criteria, and we are confident that in the next few months we will be successful on all five.

- Following the devaluation of the drachma in March 1998, we participated in the exchange rate mechanism, and from January 1999 we are members of its successor, ERM2.

- We reduced the general government deficit from 13.8 percent of GDP in 1993 to 2.5 percent of GDP in 1998 and 1.5 percent of GDP this year. This is a reduction of over 12 percentage points of GDP and is almost three times as big as the improvement registered in the rest of the European Union in the same period. The lowering of the government deficit resulted from applying strict controls on public expenditure and from increases in the revenue side owing to a broadened tax base and an effective combating of tax evasion.

- Government debt was reduced from 111.8 percent of GDP in 1993 to 106.1 percent of GDP in 1998 and 105.1 percent by the end of this year. Privatization revenues contributed substantially to debt reduction.
- Increased credibility of the government policy has led to a substantial fall of government bond yields. The yield on the 10-year government bond was 10.7 percent in 1997, 562 basis points above the yield on the German 10-year government bond. At the middle of September of this year, the yield stood at 6.75 percent, about 160 points higher than the German 10-year government bond.
- The anti-inflationary incomes policy pursued in the public sector and the increased competition in a number of areas, such as telecommunications and transport, together with a reduction in inflation expectations, have led to a drastic drop in the annual rate of inflation. In 1993, the average annual rate of inflation was 14.4 percent. In August 1999, the annual rate of inflation was only 2 percent. These are rates of inflation last recorded in Greece more than three decades ago.

In the past few years, we have proceeded with structural reforms in the product, capital, services, and labor markets. Our privatization program has been intensified in the past two years; at present, 27 state corporations either have been privatized or are in the process of being privatized. Receipts from privatization in 1998 and 1999 have reached 7 billion dollars.

Economic reform, together with substantial public infrastructure investment, partly financed by the European Union, led to a substantial acceleration of real growth. In fact, 1999 will be the sixth consecutive year of substantial growth, while in the past three years, growth rates reached 3.5 percent, significantly higher than the European Union average.

The prospects point to further considerable growth in the next few years. The investment opportunities that arise from making Thessaloniki the center for the development of southeastern Europe, the direct and indirect productivity gains from faster investment and output growth itself, and the organization of the Olympic Games in Athens in 2004 are likely to introduce further dynamism in the growth process. At the moment, we are forecasting an increase of GDP of the order of 3.7 percent for the year 2000 and more than 4 percent in 2001.

The crises of the past few years have made it clear to all of us that transparency in corporate, financial, and state institutions is paramount in preventing and detecting nonviable situations. It is in the interest of transparency that Greece, one of the very first countries to do so, is participating in the two Fund initiatives in this direction—the release of the conclusions of Article IV consultations as well as the fiscal transparency exercise.

Our economy has been put to the test by the financial crises of the last few years. Our exchange rates, short-term interest rates, bond yields, stock market, and real economy remained unaffected in all but the very short run. Last year, Michel Camdessus noted in his concluding statement that programs work only if governments want them to. We have indeed been determined to succeed.

Last year the Meetings were sessions of reflection on how to go about preventing, detecting, and remedying crises. This year, we are in the more comfortable position of being able to evaluate our actions in these areas. Let us hope that we will carry on in this direction, so that next year we can appreciate the results in the form of accelerated growth, more employment, and improved welfare.

STATEMENT BY THE GOVERNOR OF THE BANK AND THE FUND FOR INDIA

Yashwant Sinha

Participation in the Bank and Fund Annual Meetings is always a source of great pleasure and inspiration for us. But this year, our happiness is even greater, because the meetings are being chaired by our neighbor and a member of the South Asian Association for Regional Cooperation (SAARC), Nepal. I have no doubt, Mr. Chairman, that the proceedings this year will greatly benefit from your rich experience and sagacity.

At the outset, let me congratulate both the Fund and the Bank for their active role in reviving global economic and financial prospects. Although the signs of recovery are visible, there is a need to temper the optimism with caution. The sustainability of the recovery is not yet assured, and a number of risks and uncertainties continue to cloud the outlook for the near future, especially for developing countries.

The economic crisis that began two years ago has pulled down the world growth rate in the 1990s to the lowest level in the past three decades. The crisis has impoverished millions in the developing world and blunted the aspirations of many more millions. We owe it to them to rectify this unfortunate situation in the first decade of the coming millennium. At this critical juncture, we need to go beyond short-term policy perspectives and seek a new mandate for the enduring goal of more rapid and sustained economic development. Toward this goal, this last Annual Meeting of the twentieth century provides an important opportunity.

The recent crises have underscored the critical role of multilateral public resources in calming exchange and financial markets and in paving the way for economic recovery. While there is every need to empower the Bretton Woods institutions, so as to enable them to effectively deal with the emerging challenges, we must not lose sight of the basic mandate of these organizations. The preoccupation with crisis management in some countries must not distract the Fund and the World Bank from their basic missions of providing temporary balance of payments support and long-term development finance in all developing countries, respectively. The recent upheavals have also sparked a debate on the approach to macroeconomic policy, capital flows, exchange rate regimes, fiscal and financial systems, and standards and codes. The debate is still on, and we must be prepared to reassess earlier positions.

We endorse the efforts currently under way to improve the international financial architecture. After the initial spurt of ideas on basic changes in the institutional framework, attention is now increasingly being focused on limited modifications to the existing system. While there is an imperative need for improvements in the present structure, there is also a risk that such efforts may not go far enough, especially if the long-standing concerns of developing countries do not receive their due attention.

I would like to remind this distinguished assembly that issues, such as the declining levels of aid, stagnation of other official flows, insufficient international liquidity at times of financial stress, low primary product prices, and the limited access of most developing countries to private capital flows, need to be brought to the forefront of the global agenda. Furthermore, we must ensure that political considerations are not injected into the programs and operations of the Bretton Woods institutions. We must consciously strive to protect the integrity and objectivity of these great international economic institutions from the encroachments of short-term national and foreign policy expediencies.

It is one of the ironies of the past 40 years that, although developing countries as a group have grown much faster than the developed countries over this period and their relative economic strength in terms of output and trade has increased substantially, their role in international economic governance has not expanded commensurately. This anomaly needs to be corrected in the next quota exercise in the Fund. In the decision-making structures of the "new" financial architecture that is taking shape, developing countries must also have due representation. This will enhance the strength and credibility of our international institutions.

While considerable progress has been achieved by developing countries over the past 50 years, it is amply clear that, in terms of poverty reduction, progress has been less than satisfactory. The international community cannot turn a blind eye to certain iniquitous aspects of global financial and economic developments during the recent past. In fact, while there is a lot of talk about the world being made smaller by the information technology revolution, for hundreds of millions of people who are outside the envelope of this technology, the emerging "cyber-based" world is getting more distant. We live in a world where the rich are enjoying the best-ever quality of life, while the poor continue to suffer from deprivation, sickness, and malnutrition. This is unacceptable. To my mind, equitable distribution of the enormous benefits of the new technological revolution is going to be one of the central issues for the new millennium.

An important sector where private initiative had been expected to play a much larger role is the provision of physical infrastructure. So far, the results have been mixed at best. Private provision of infrastructure has been characterized by long delays, considerable legal wrangling, and often intense politicization. The fact is that much of what constitutes infrastructure has a "public good" dimension and long gestation periods. The World Bank used to play a central role in financing the physical infrastructure needs of developing countries. It should reassert its leadership in this area.

I am happy that social sector issues have gained in prominence in the Fund-Bank agenda, and that the link between debt relief and poverty reduction has been emphasized. Larger HIPC funding should, of course, be effected on the principles of additionality and equitable burden sharing among developed countries without affecting the financial integrity of the Bretton Woods institutions. Moreover, it must be recognized that strategies for global poverty reduction will not be successful unless there is also an adequate flow of additional development assistance to those countries that have managed their economies prudently and have met their debt obligations despite difficulties.

The pressure on the World Bank's resources will be considerable if it is to respond effectively to the challenge of meeting the poverty reduction goals that have been established. This and other demands on the Bank's net income have meant that the financial strength and integrity of the World Bank could be weakened unless remedial steps are taken. Since we have already increased loan charges last year, I feel that a general capital increase will be more equitable. It would also send out a strong and clear message of shareholder support for the institution.

Let me take this opportunity to apprise this distinguished gathering of recent developments in the Indian economy. We are indeed happy that our program of economic reforms and commitment to macroeconomic stability continue to yield impressive rewards even against the background of a serious global slowdown. India improved its GDP growth rate from 5 percent in 1997–98 to 6 percent in 1998–99 and is expected to register a higher growth rate in 1999–2000. This makes India one of the 10 fastest-growing economies during the 1990s. Furthermore, this recent revival in India's growth has been accompanied by a welcome decline in the rate of inflation to below 2 percent, the lowest attained in 17 years.

Although world trade growth has remained anemic, our external sector continues to exhibit strength, with the current account deficit expected to be below 2 percent in 1999/2000, despite the sharp increase in world oil prices. The major indicators of external stability continue to improve. The debt-service ratio is expected to decline even further to less than 18 percent in 1999/2000. Foreign currency reserves have increased substantially in the last 18 months despite the slowdown in the world trade and the effects of the East Asian crisis. It has been our policy to ensure that short-term debt is kept within prudent limits, and it now constitutes less than 5 percent of our aggregate external debt.

As you are aware, our country is currently going through the largest democratic election ever held in the history of mankind. I am proud to say that our economic progress has been achieved within a vibrant democratic framework. We are fully conscious that in order to maintain and improve upon a strong economic record, we have to implement an ambitious agenda of second-generation reforms and continue to conduct vigilant macroeconomic management. The next wave of reforms will cover the entire spectrum, including revitalization of the rural economy, fiscal policy, the financial sector, trade, foreign investment, infrastructure, and industrial relations, as well as the right-sizing of government and the restructuring and privatization of public enterprises, as necessary. With these reforms, we are confident that the daunting task of lifting hundreds of millions of people out of poverty is attainable within the first decade of the new millennium.

STATEMENT BY THE ALTERNATE GOVERNOR OF THE BANK FOR INDONESIA

Boediono

It is reassuring to hear the recent news about the world economy. The U.S. economy continues to show strength, while Europe and Japan are transmitting positive signals. Meanwhile, emerging economies as a group are also faring better. Japan, in particular, deserves to be congratulated for its remarkable turnaround. Meanwhile, the proposed reform of the HIPC Framework would make not only good politics, but also good economics.

Turning to my country, Indonesia, it is clear that the better prospects of the world economy should provide a better environment for our recovery. Conversely, the world economy is bound to benefit from our quick recovery. Let me mention some recent facts about Indonesia.

One year ago, at the time of the last joint annual meetings, Indonesia's economic fortunes had reached a nadir. Inflation had risen to an annual rate of 82 percent, the rupiah had depreciated by some 75 percent and traded at Rp 10,000 per $1, one-month interest rates were at 64 percent, and real GDP had collapsed by 16 percent. At that time, no one knew whether things would get better or worse in the months to come. Significant political uncertainties lay ahead.

Today the Indonesian economy is in far better shape but, unfortunately, similar uncertainties remain. Inflation has almost been eradicated, with the annual rate falling to less than 6 percent in August. The one-month interest rates have dropped below 13 percent. By mid-July of this year the rupiah had strengthened to Rp 6,600 per $1, before it weakened again to the current level around Rp 8,400 per $1. Share prices on the Jakarta Stock Exchange have risen by more than 60 percent from their level one year ago. Consumer spending, agricultural production, and a few manufacturing activities are starting to look up. With oil prices having doubled from the beginning of the year and commodity prices beginning to stabilize, Indonesia's external payments position should improve in coming months.

In recent weeks, these clear signs of economic recovery have been blurred by uncertainties arising from the emergence of a bank scandal, events in East Timor and rising political temperature in the run-up to the Presidential election. There is a lesson to be learned here. The underlying message of this experience is that despite two years of unprecedented economic misfortune, the Indonesian economy remains alive and fundamentally strong. Given half a chance, it will bounce back. At the same time, it is also clear that the recovery remains fragile and requires constant nurturing by a steady and caring hand.

Much of the credit for the improved outlook is due to the implementation of a consistent economic stabilization and restructuring program, in support of which the international community has played a crucial role. We wish to express our appreciation for this support. Financial sector restructuring and corporate debt resolution have been key elements of this program. Over the past year, notable progress has been made on both fronts, which I shall not elaborate here.

However, recent events threaten to undo much of such progress. The restructuring program has been paralyzed by a banking scandal that strikes at the integrity of the institutions charged with recapitalizing and restructuring our banks. We consider it to be a very serious matter and we know that we need to resolve it in a transparent manner and in a manner that is consistent with Indonesian law. A judicial process for the case will start within a matter of days. I should add that the prevailing public sentiment ensures that only a transparent and complete resolution will meet the public's expectations. The upcoming presidential election is another source of uncertainty. It is our hope that the resolution of these two issues will allow us to regain the momentum that we had attained earlier this year.

Finally, I would like to express the deep regret of the people of Indonesia for the loss of life caused by events in East Timor. Let me reaffirm that the government of Indonesia is committed to taking the steps necessary to enable the fulfillment of the newly expressed will of the majority of East Timorese to seek a new destiny outside Indonesia.

STATEMENT BY THE GOVERNOR OF THE BANK FOR THE ISLAMIC REPUBLIC OF IRAN

Hossein Namazi

Global economic and financial conditions after the turbulence in emerging markets in 1997–98, which gave rise to fears of a widespread credit crunch and global recession, have now markedly improved, and most of the economies recently in crisis have begun to recover. Economic improvement in economies afflicted by the Asian crisis has been faster and more robust than expected earlier, and the further bouts of financial turbulence in other parts of the world have been effectively brought under control. Nevertheless, many challenges remain to be addressed to ensure that these recoveries are sustainable and that prerequisites for a stronger and more stable growth in the world economy in the next decade are in place.

Now, the concern over the collapse of the international financial system has given way to the need for better policy coordination among the industrial countries to maintain the continuity of orderly economic growth in the world. There are positive signs for the restoration of an atmosphere of trust and confidence in the international financial markets. Despite such a positive development and the relative improvement in global financial and economic conditions, those crises, mainly the Asian crisis, have made the international economic environment more difficult and uncertain for developing countries, and the financial flow from international capital markets to developing countries has been cut in half compared to the pre-crisis period. Moreover, access to these resources has become prohibitively costly and limited solely to creditworthy borrowers.

The developing countries are the essential partners of the industrial nations in the globalized world. It is, therefore, incumbent on the industrial countries to work closely with all developing countries, especially with the poorer nations, and to increase the volume of official development assistance in support of their efforts to eradicate poverty, launch effective policies for sustainable development, and build the economic capacity of their countries. Needless to say, the stability and integrity of the world economy depend on rational relationships between the industrial and developing countries and the political support for the efforts of every developing country that seeks to achieve sustainable development.

Our meeting is taking place at a time when the dawn of the new millennium approaches, and our world is facing pressing challenges in all areas of political, economic, financial, social, and cultural endeavors. Accordingly, the need to have a holistic and comprehensive approach toward development issues has become more critical, both at national and international levels. The significance of this comprehensive approach has been duly recognized by the Bretton Woods institutions. Many issues that are interlinked with comprehensive and multifaceted economic, social, and cultural development of human societies have made their way onto the agendas of these institutions. These issues are essential parts of human prosperity and well-being, such as debt reduction of heavily indebted poor countries, poverty alleviation, strengthening of the international financial architecture, management of social dimensions of crisis, and in particular, a multifaceted approach, under the theme of "Comprehensive Development Framework."

The comprehensive approach to development in the conceptual plan is welcomed. However, it should be ensured that this framework does not constitute an intrusion on national decision making. While supporting the need for such a comprehensive approach toward all economic, political, financial, social, and cultural issues, I wish to express my concern over any instrumentalization of this concept. Now that there is a clear recognition at the international level of the significance of this comprehensive approach, we need to pay attention to the following facts:

- The main objectives of the founders of the Bretton Woods institutions, according to their Articles of Agreements, were to assist the member countries in the reconstruction and development of their territories and to promote economic cooperation among them. To achieve these objectives, the Bretton Woods institutions offer advisory services that are of the utmost importance. The important point in these efforts lies in the distinction between offering advisory views and dictating a series of inflexible instructions to developing countries with a view to putting their economic house in order.
- The target audience for the rules and regulations of these institutions has consistently been a set group of member countries, while the issues dealt with by these institutions are very broad and universal, and should target, as a general rule, all members—industrialized or developing. Indeed, a one-sided and selective approach will not serve the above-mentioned purposes and objectives.
- The chief objectives of the founders of the Bretton Woods institutions were purely economic in their nature and character. It is imperative that these institutions adhere to principles clearly stated in their founding agreements and strive to achieve these concrete objectives. Tainting the decisions of these institutions with political considerations will inevitably lead to imposition of discrimination on certain members, which is neither desirable nor in line with the objectives of these institutions.
- Differences in the structure of economies and institutional capacities among countries with varying levels of development requires the Bretton Woods institutions to adopt a broader view in advising member countries, and to refrain from forging one-size-fits-all policies. As it has been increasingly realized, country-specific features play a greater role than previously envisaged in determining the set of appropriate macroeconomic policies toward stability and growth. This point should be truly recognized and fully appreciated in dealing with the member countries.

The most obvious policy recommendation that needs to be revisited in the light of recent experiences is the liberalization of the capital account. Recent experiences suggest that the liberalization process should be very cautious and orderly. The member countries should not be advised, let alone pressed, to liberalize their capital accounts in the absence of necessary financial structures and a supervisory and regulatory capacity. Structure and capacity development requires time, which itself varies with the social and cultural foundations of countries. It would also require a substantial amount of financial and technical support from the Fund and the Bank. I would like to reiterate that the Executive Board of the Fund must also carry on very careful deliberations in designing an effective and protective framework, allowing the members to undertake capital account liberalization at their own pace and with full confidence that appropriate safety nets are in place should their economies be subjected to shocks in the process. We welcome the international support for poverty reduction and commend the Fund and the World Bank for further progress being made in the initiative to assist heavily indebted poor countries and post-conflict societies. It is hoped that by broadening the scope for eligibility under the HIPC Initiative and by increasing financing, more substantial assistance to a larger number of poor countries will be made available. We also welcome the efforts made in ensuring adequate funding for the ESAF (the Poverty Reduction and Growth Facility).

In conclusion, I would like to present a general view of the economic condition in my country. The continuation of global recession and the declining trend in the oil market, particularly the sharper fall of oil prices in the second half of 1998, brought about heavy pressure on the balance of payments and resulted in a carryover of the budget deficit to the first months of 1999. Nevertheless, the available statistics indicate that, despite the shocks, the nation's economy managed to absorb to a large extent these pressures, and the negative effects of these shocks were much less than what we initially expected, mainly because of advance preparations and capacity building, and investments in the past decade. The preparation of the third five-year economic development plan, which will be implemented in the next fiscal year, is going through its final stages. Some of the main objectives of this plan are as follows:

- greater transparency in the macroeconomic system and regulatory frameworks;
- budget reforms;
- tax reforms;
- downsizing of the government's role in economic activities and privatization of government enterprises;

- promotion of the private sector;
- dismantling of monopolies and promotion of competition; and
- establishment of a comprehensive social safety net to protect the most vulnerable groups.

Once fully operational, the program will pave the way for the full integration of the Iranian economy into the global system.

STATEMENT BY THE GOVERNOR OF THE BANK FOR IRAQ

Issam Rashid Hwaish

Governors, ladies, and gentlemen, I am honored to greet you on behalf of the Iraqi delegation and to express our wishes for continued success to you, and to the Managing Director of the International Monetary Fund, the President of the World Bank Group, and the governors attending this meeting today, in your efforts to achieve the goals pursued by the international community, and by the Bretton Woods institutions in particular.

Over the past nine years, the Iraqi delegation has pointed out that the economic sanctions imposed on Iraq, along with the freezing of its assets and bank deposits, contradict one of the Fund's most important purposes set forth in Article I, paragraph (iv), of the Fund's Articles of Agreement: to eliminate restrictions that hamper the growth of world trade and to strive to achieve international economic stability and prosperity. This abnormal situation, which is in conflict with the Fund's philosophy and its Articles of Agreement, remains in effect after more than nine years. That is why I am requesting the Fund, in accordance with its objectives, to denounce the continuation of these long-standing economic sanctions against Iraq, one of the founding members that signed the Bretton Woods Agreement in 1945.

The suffering of the Iraqi people and humanitarian considerations require that the international community raise its voice to rectify the deteriorating situation in Iraq, which could lead to a great human tragedy if measures are not taken soon to lift sanctions. The Iraqi delegation has addressed this assembly on several occasions over the past years, describing in detail the economic and social effects of continued sanctions, including their direct adverse effects on the production of goods and services in all sectors of the economy, rising inflation rates and the concomitant deterioration of household incomes, the shortage of medicines and medical equipment, potable water, and sewerage facilities, resulting in significantly higher death rates in the various age groups and the spread of communicable diseases that had once been practically eliminated from Iraq, such as polio, cholera, hepatitis, etc., not to mention the contamination of the environment and its harmful effects on life in Iraq.

More than two years have elapsed since the initial implementation of the memorandum of understanding concerning the "Food for Oil" agreement signed by Iraq and the United Nations on March 20, 1996, whereby limited quantities of crude oil would be exported in order to import food, medicines and medical equipment, and other basic necessities of life. Yet Iraq continues to face a number of artificial obstacles to implementing contracts signed on the basis of this agreement, owing to the position taken by the United States and supported by the United Kingdom—alone in the international community—which contradicts the agreement's objective of relieving a small measure of the suffering and pain the Iraqi people are enduring as a result of these protracted sanctions, which are unprecedented in human history and in complete contradiction with the provisions of international law. Governors, I am speaking not only of the sanctions imposed upon the Iraqi people and their harmful effects upon an entire nation, a nation that had a pivotal role in advancing human civilization. I am also speaking of sanctions that are being used as a political weapon against particular countries, in conflict not only with the Articles of Agreement of the Bretton Woods institutions, but also with their principles and announced policies, and with the desires of the international community to promote development, fight poverty and hunger, and achieve a world in which justice and peace prevail.

Iraq has both rights and obligations with respect to the Fund and the Bank, and we wish to exercise these rights to meet our obligations. Therefore, Iraq requests the Fund's management to consider the possibilities for legally accommodating such a situation, whereby countries facing economic sanctions—on the basis of international legitimacy or other pretexts—would be allowed to exercise their rights and meet their obligations in accordance with the agreements signed with the international institutions concerned.

I stand before you today, asking the Fund and the Bank, in the spirit of their Articles of Agreement, to call for an end to the economic sanctions against Iraq and the release of its assets in international banks. I likewise call on the distinguished governors, ministers of finance, and central bank governors to spare no effort in urging their governments to help end the suffering of the Iraqi people, restore balance to our relations with the international community, and prevent the domination and coercion of Iraqi society carried out by certain countries today, with no guarantee that such domination will not be extended to other countries tomorrow. I call for a joint effort to end economic sanctions and airspace restrictions, which are unsupported by any Security Council resolution or international endorsement.

STATEMENT BY THE GOVERNOR OF THE BANK AND THE FUND FOR IRELAND

Charlie McCreevey

Ireland's general views on current issues are reflected in the statement made on behalf of the European Union. There are, however, a number of topics I would like to highlight that are of particular concern to Ireland.

International Financial Architecture

Considerable thought and debate has taken place in the past year about the appropriate structure for what is referred to as the international financial architecture. As a small, open economy, Ireland has a vital interest in a stable international economic and financial environment, and we strongly support current efforts to address the challenges posed by globalization. As recent crises have shown, various aspects of this process are interrelated, and it is important to develop a holistic approach, particularly in dealing with developing economies.

Role of Bretton Woods Institutions

The Bretton Woods institutions have a vital and central role in the international economic and financial area. To carry it out adequately, they will need to intensify cooperation among themselves, with other agencies in the economic, social, and political arenas, and with the various informal groupings. Cooperation will need to be intensified not only with member governments, but also with a wide range of civil society, particularly in program countries. Ownership of programs by stakeholders is a prerequisite for successful implementation. An implication of this is that, for example, Fund programs need to take on board, at the design stage, the social and civic implications of their implementation. This is not the same as saying that the Fund should engage directly in the social or developmental aspects, but that the macro-design of its programs should be able to fully integrate outside expertise.

Transparency

In keeping with evolving trends at the national level, the Bretton Woods institutions need to be more transparent. Such a trend has been quite marked in the past 12 months, not only with the publication of hitherto unpublished information, but also with its speedy publication in a widely accessible form over the Internet. This has enabled many interested parties to have easier and quicker access to the work of the institutions. This, in itself, constitutes a form of empowerment of stakeholders, which will become more evident as time goes on. Information is not, however, a substitute for active participation by stakeholders, and the current trend needs to be accompanied by positive efforts by the institutions to involve stakeholders more in their work, as the ultimate responsibility lies with the member governments representing their citizens.

HIPC Initiative

Debt relief is a vital element in a more broad-based development strategy aimed at growth and poverty alleviation. The HIPC Initiative, driven by the Bank and the Fund, is clearly at a crucial stage in its development. Although its beginnings were relatively modest, its ideals—or declared aims—were ambitious. It aims at both freeing the most heavily indebted poorest countries from the burden of the unpayable element of their debt, and offering them a definitive exit from the debt treadmill, which is seriously undermining their development.

We are all aware of the wide public support for a serious attack on the problem of unbearable debt, which is reflected in the extent of popular support for Jubilee 2000. This must be addressed, and the HIPC Initiative must be implemented in a way that achieves its basic aims. We must remain open to any further enhancements required for this to be achieved, in particular, taking greater account of human needs in determining eligibility and the extent of the relief required. I would, therefore, call on Governors to resolve any outstanding difficulties in implementing the enhanced HIPC Initiative at this stage, particularly in regard to its financing. Earlier this year, Ireland adopted legislation enabling it to participate in funding the enhanced initiative to a degree commensurate with its relative standing in the donor community.

Statement by the Governor of the Fund for Israel

Avraham B. Shochat

It is an honor and a privilege for me to address this distinguished assembly on the occasion of the Annual Meetings of the International Monetary Fund and the World Bank Group. Before I begin, I would first like to thank the staffs of both the Fund and the World Bank for all their hard work in organizing this conference, which holds great significance for the world economy and for Israel as an active participant in it.

The peacemaking process in which we are now involved is a historic one. When the late Prime Minister Rabin and Shimon Peres decided to conclude an agreement with the Palestinians after a hundred years of conflict, they understood that the matter would require painful compromises. The Oslo process marks the beginning of a complicated path to peace. This complex process is having an impact on the entire Middle East—peace with Jordan, economic conferences, reducing the intensity of the Arab boycott, and opening of Arab countries' diplomatic missions in Israel. For the Israeli people, the peace process will create an environment that stimulates economic growth.

The Health of Israel's Economy

The shocks of the world economic crisis last year did not pass over Israel; they did not leave permanent scars either. Israel's economy, like those of the industrial nations of Europe and North America, demonstrated resilience, stability, and strength. Our ability to weather the storm is based on strong fundamentals. The international investment community has recognized the inherent stability and health of the Israeli economy and, through its actions, has expressed confidence in it. In fact, foreign direct investment in Israel has grown steadily. There is good reason for the confidence of the international community in Israel's economy. Since the mid-1980s Israel has been undergoing a revolution, marked by two major features:

- the transition from an economy troubled by excessive government intervention to a free-market economy, driven by the private sector and open to competition both at home and from abroad; and
- the transition from an economy based on traditional industries to one based on information technologies and high-tech industries.

The public sector has played an important role in these developments. Responsible fiscal policy, control of inflation, liberalization of trade and foreign currency regimes, antitrust legislation, and capital market reform have contributed to the business-friendly environment in Israel. The primary credit for Israel's transformation, however, goes to the private sector. Our human capital—significantly boosted by the arrival of 1 million new immigrants who have blessed our shores since 1990—has once again proven to be our greatest resource. Know-how and entrepreneurial spirit has launched new enterprises, many of which today comprise some of Israel's largest companies.

- We will continue to control both inflation and the budget deficit through sound and responsible fiscal and monetary policies.
- We will mobilize resources to stimulate growth through renewed investments in infrastructure, education, human capital, and peace.
- Structural reform of the economy and privatization will continue, encouraging a competitive business environment.
- We will go forward with capital market reforms, with an eye to promoting international integration.
- We will continue to invest heavily in research and development.

Israel and the Region

The strategic location of the southeast Mediterranean as an axis between three continents and two oceans offers vast business opportunities for all economies in the region. The economic potential created in this simple geographic fact has been ignored far too long. Only through regional cooperation and partnership can we create an economic environment that favors peace. To encourage this process, international assistance is needed. While some groundwork toward establishing regional cooperation was laid in years past, the time has now come to vigorously move forward. On September 13, Israel and the Palestinian Authority began working on a final political settlement. Teams on both sides have started to negotiate a comprehensive agreement that will bring full reconciliation and create a new political and economic environment.

Israel as a Donor Nation

On the eve of the new millennium, Israel sees itself as a fully developed post-industrial economy and we are prepared to take our place in the global community as a donor nation, and joined the International Development Association. Finally, the new government is moving the peace process ahead, including sincere and genuine negotiations with Syria—negotiations that, among other things, will solve the Lebanon problem and eventually result in comprehensive peace in the Middle East. We are looking forward to an era of newly formed partnerships both inside and outside the Middle East for the benefit of all involved.

STATEMENT BY THE GOVERNOR OF THE FUND FOR ITALY

Giuliano Amato

International economic conditions have considerably improved since our last meeting. The U.S. economy continues to perform strongly. Economic activity in the euro area is accelerating. Signs of an upturn are coming from Japan. The financial and real instability that has recently characterized the emerging markets has been subdued. While the risks for the world economy seem to have diminished, steadier economic growth continues to be burdened both by the imbalances in the current account positions of the main industrial countries and by delays in structural reform and fiscal consolidation in several developing and transition countries. Action is certainly needed in the United States, to increase private savings while ensuring a soft landing of the economy; structural policies are needed in Europe, to improve the functioning of markets and increase the overall productivity of European economies, as well as in Japan, where the efforts to sustain aggregate demand and press ahead with structural reforms are key for the turnaround of the economy.

At the close of this decade, inflation has been driven to very low levels in almost all industrial countries. This is the result of appropriate monetary policies and of structural factors, including increased competition and technological advances. Somewhat paradoxically, though, price stability has been accompanied by more, not less, exchange rate volatility between the major currencies. We must be aware that such volatility produces repercussions on other countries' economies. This does not mean, however, that we should introduce forms of exchange rate rigidity between the three major currencies, which would only come at the expense of domestic stability.

Emerging market economies must be careful in choosing their exchange rate regimes. With increased capital mobility, countries should peg their exchange rate only if they can implement economic policies that are consistent with both domestic and external requirements. The Fund has the responsibility to assist countries in devising the most appropriate exchange rate regime and supporting policies.

Major challenges remain for achieving a stable international financial system. First, efforts should be renewed to preventing financial crises. Standards and codes of good practice have been designed by the Fund and the Bank, in collaboration with other standard-setting bodies in a number of areas. They should now be implemented by all countries on a voluntary basis, but according to an agreed-upon and transparent timetable. The Fund has a major responsibility in monitoring the implementation of these standards. In this endeavor, the Fund and the Bank must strengthen cooperation among themselves and with other relevant international organizations as well.

Second, progress has to be made in involving the private sector in crisis resolution. Building on existing experience, and on the broad principles that have been agreed upon, the Fund must now design the "rules of the game" for a consistent approach to crisis management.

Third, and most important, poverty reduction must come at the core of the activities of the international financial institutions. The enhanced HIPC Initiative provides deeper, faster, and broader debt relief and establishes a close link between debt relief and poverty reduction. The funding of the initiative needs to preserve the principles of additionality and the financial integrity of the international institutions. Multilateral institutions thus need additional support on a bilateral basis to cover the costs associated with the enhanced framework. Let me say that Italy has already made a substantial contribution to a stronger link between debt relief and poverty reduction by canceling all commercial and ODA debt to HIPC countries with a per capita income lower than 300 dollars. In addition, Italy has contributed its full share, around $60 million, to the ESAF-HIPC Trust of the Fund. Italy will contribute $70 million to the HIPC Trust managed by the World Bank.

Let me stress again, going toward my conclusion, that no economic progress and no social progress is attainable without a parallel process of poverty reduction. Priority must be given to assist countries affected by conflicts. Marginalization, social unrest, and external conflicts always have their roots in inadequate economic development and inequality. The World Bank, which is engaged in efforts to help countries that are in post-conflict transition, must use its resources to provide assistance for reconstruction, thereby reestablishing stability and growth in these countries.

These are ambitious tasks. And our task will have to be even more ambitious in the not-so-distant future, when many people will live in this world, and an increasing number of them may fall below the poverty line. The significant progress achieved in these days is the result of effective and meaningful cooperation among the member countries. It is a good promise for the future. In this respect, Italy fully supports the institutional changes proposed to the Board of Governors. They will strengthen the role of our institutions and make them better equipped to meet the challenges ahead.

STATEMENT BY THE ALTERNATE GOVERNOR OF THE BANK AND THE FUND FOR JAPAN

Masaru Hayami

Introduction

I am very happy to have this opportunity today to address the Annual Meetings of the World Bank Group and the International Monetary Fund as Alternate Governor for Japan.

First of all, I sincerely welcome the reappointment of Mr. Wolfensohn as President of the World Bank. Since his appointment in 1995, Mr. Wolfensohn has been taking the lead on bold reforms of the institution and strategy in the World Bank, and has been tackling many challenges, such as the response to the Asian crisis. I am confident that Mr. Wolfensohn will play, in his next term, an increasingly important role in addressing various development issues that the Bank Group will face.

The Post-Crisis World Economy

As I look back to our meeting last year, I am reminded of the grave sense of uncertainty and tension that gripped the international financial markets at that time. The negative impact of the Russian crisis that had erupted in August was spreading to Brazil and other Latin American countries, as well as to Asia's emerging market economies, which were just beginning to regain their footing after the previous year's crisis. The United States was shocked by the near collapse of Long-Term Capital Management, while in Japan, major banks were in dire difficulty. But what a difference a year can make. The Brazilian crisis has been brought under control through the assistance program led by the Fund, the United States has successfully calmed the market through a number of interest-rate cuts, and Japan has taken the necessary actions to strengthen its financial sector. These and other efforts by the international community have helped shake off the uncertainty in the international financial markets and reestablish a sense of stability in the world economy. It is particularly noteworthy that positive growth has been projected this year for almost all of the Asian emerging economies that were in crisis two years ago—Indonesia, Korea, Malaysia, the Philippines, and Thailand. Their growth is expected to accelerate next year, with the region enjoying a conspicuous upturn in economic activity.

Let me now turn to the Japanese economy. For the first time in nearly two years, we have experienced positive growth of real GDP in two consecutive quarters. The worst is now over, and economic activity is improving somewhat. The positive signs that we are beginning to see are the result of assiduous efforts with regard to macroeconomic and structural policy. Since last summer, the government has made economic recovery its main priority, while recognizing the eventual need to implement fiscal structural reform. We have also tackled the problems of the financial sector by recapitalizing banks with public funds on condition that they implement far-reaching restructuring plans. The financial sector is now regaining the confidence of the markets, and financial institutions are making dramatic moves that will facilitate the reform of this sector. We will continue to monitor carefully developments in the economy and to concentrate our efforts on the implementation of various measures to strengthen the foundations for recovery.

The Need for Global Response

As I mentioned, conditions in the international financial markets have improved significantly in the past year. However, we must consider preventive measures for the future, as we cannot completely avoid the risk of crisis, and be prepared to implement them swiftly when a crisis erupts. We have discussed the relevant issues from various perspectives, and now two years after the Asian crisis, a consensus has been established on a number of important matters. Based on this consensus, the Fund Executive Board is currently discussing various reform measures and moving toward their implementation. We must remember that no single reform measure can act as a panacea for reinforcing the international monetary system. All parties should be required to implement their share of reforms: emerging market economies, which are exposed to the risk of currency crises; private investors who are investing in these countries; developed countries, which are responsible for instituting prudential regulations covering their investors; and the Fund and other international financial institutions. I would like to present Japan's thinking on various points pertaining to these reforms.

Issues for the Emerging Market Economies—Responses of Capital Recipients. The massive inflow of foreign capital into the emerging market economies creates opportunities for accelerated economic growth in these countries. However, at the same time, it entails potential risks. In order to minimize these risks, it is essential for individual governments to pursue sound macroeconomic and structural policies. The Asian crisis has also impressed upon us the importance of reinforcing the financial system by instituting appropriate prudential regulations and strengthening the existing supervisory arrangements. In this context, we must not forget that when steps are being taken toward capital liberalization, it will be even more important than before to closely monitor private sector liabilities, including those of the financial sector. It is also necessary to improve debt management and liquidity management for countries as a whole. This issue is currently being considered by the Fund and the World Bank, and we look forward to seeing the results of these deliberations.

On the question of what type of exchange rate regime should be adopted by emerging market economies, we must remember that numerous crises have been caused by misguided efforts to maintain a de facto fixed exchange rate pegged to a single currency. Based on extensive past experience, the Fund should provide appropriate advice on this matter through the programs it supports and its surveillance activities.

Issues related to capital liberalization and restrictions on capital flows are of vital importance and require continued examination. In the course of recent IMF discussions, we have seen growing support for the view that, if combined with appropriate measures, such as a more flexible exchange rate system, restrictions on capital inflow can suppress the inflow of speculative short-term capital. Malaysia's recent use of restrictions on capital outflow was effective in drawing a line of defense against speculative attacks and stabilizing the foreign exchange market. We expect further discussions on the usefulness of restrictions on capital flows from a practical point of view. Possible effects include the reinforcement of appropriate macroeconomic policies and strengthening of the financial sector in some cases, especially the supplementing of prudential regulations.

Issues for Private Investors and the Developed Countries—Response of Capital Providers. To maintain stability in the international monetary system, improved risk management is needed on the part of investors. A particularly important issue, which is currently being discussed in the Financial Stability Forum, is the question of hedge funds and other highly leveraged institutions (HLIs). A consensus has been reached on the need to expand the scope of disclosure for all market participants, including HLIs, and to institute more thorough risk management by counterparties to transactions. As an initial step, it is important to translate this consensus into concrete action. At the same time, we believe that it is also necessary to further examine the following types of defensive actions by the emerging market economies. When there is a possibility of market manipulation, measures may be taken, such as requiring HLIs to report on their activities in the interest of maintaining market integrity. The use of nonstandard interventions like those recently made by the Hong Kong Special Administrative Region and Malaysian authorities—which are different from traditional policy responses, namely, intervention in foreign exchange market or the adjustment of interest rates—may be necessary in special circumstances.

Even more important on the investor side is to increase private-sector involvement in order to both prevent crises and help resolve those that do occur. The continued use of public funds to bail out private investors is not viable and invites moral hazard. We now have an international consensus that private creditors, including bond holders, must be asked to cooperate appropriately. However, it is true that the actual implementation of such a cooperative approach entails numerous difficulties. There are certain matters that must be borne in mind in promoting greater private sector involvement. It must be clarified that the objective is to promote appropriate burden sharing and cooperation between public sector and private sector creditors.

From this perspective, measures should be taken to promote dialogue with the private sector concerning conditions in borrowing countries and to improve ways and means to encourage private sector involvement. Moreover, a framework should be developed for cooperative action for individual country cases. It is important that the Fund lead the way in discussing specific measures in this area, and that the entire international community cooperate toward achieving appropriate private sector involvement.

IMF Reform. As the central institution in the international financial system, the Fund should strengthen its functions of providing assistance to countries in crisis—subject to proper terms and conditions—and providing appropriate policy advice to member countries. A decision has been reached to re-institute the Fund's Interim Committee as a standing committee to be renamed the "International Monetary and Financial Committee." We urge the new Committee to work toward enhancing the functions of the Fund and to play an important role in the international community's engagement in problems related to international finance. In this connection, I would also like to mention the Group of Seven's proposal for the first meeting of a new mechanism for informal dialogue, which would include the emerging market economies, to be convened at the end of this year. We hope that this forum will play a constructive role in reinforcing the international monetary system.

Finally, I should like to touch briefly upon some recent improvements in Fund procedures. We welcome the higher level of transparency achieved through the publication of Fund staff papers. This year has also seen Fund surveillance and research activities undergo external evaluation, yielding a number of positive recommendations. Let me reiterate a point made in this external evaluation process: Fund surveillance and programs should remain focused on the core areas of fiscal and monetary policies, exchange rate regimes, the financial sector and capital movements, and problems directly related to these core areas.

Regional Responses—Manila Framework and New Miyazawa Initiative

Today's international financial crises are both global and regional in nature: global in the sense that they are rooted in characteristics of an international financial system, regional in that, once started, they tend to spread very rapidly within specific regions. Therefore, intraregional cooperation among countries with close ties has proved particularly effective in coping with such crises. For example, in the case of the Asian crisis, Japan hosted a meeting of countries in the region to rescue Thailand, and the participating countries complemented the Fund's global action with a speedy and large-scale regional response. Based on the experience of the Thai currency crisis, the Manila Framework was created, and it has functioned effectively in complementing the actions of the Fund in terms of both surveillance and financing.

In addition to this, last October, Japan launched the New Miyazawa Initiative, which includes a $30 billion financial support package for the affected Asian countries. The urgent capital needs of each Asian country were met through funding via the New Miyazawa Initiative and other public assistance, and the economies in the region are bottoming out. It is now essential to mobilize domestic and foreign private sector funds to achieve a full-scale, vigorous recovery in these economies. With this purpose in mind, Japan announced the "Resource Mobilization Plan for Asia (Second Stage of the New Miyazawa Initiative)" on May 15, 1999 at the APEC Meeting of Finance Ministers. As part of this program, in line with the scheduled establishment of the Japan Bank for International Cooperation in October, we have enacted the necessary legislation to allow it to guarantee public sector bonds issued by the Asian countries. Japan has also contributed about $3 billion for the creation of the Asian Development Bank's "Asian Currency Crisis Support Facility," which is to be used to provide guarantees for raising of funds from the markets and for interest subsidies.

Recently, Japan called on various countries in the region to participate in cooperative efforts for the establishment and development of bond markets throughout the Asian region, and discussions are already under way. We will also increase our efforts to provide technical and personnel assistance for the establishment of a stable financial system in the region. I would like to reiterate that Japan is committed to implementing this initiative while maintaining close cooperation with related countries and international institutions.

Issues in Development

The World Bank's Response to Crises. During the past two years, the central issue in the area of development has also been how to respond to the crises in the emerging market economies. The World Bank and other multilateral development banks (MDBs) have responded to the crises by providing a wide range of assistance, which was beyond their traditional functions. At the outset of the crises, by utilizing their fund-raising functions from the markets, together with the Fund, they supplied funds expeditiously to the affected countries, and prevented the entire loss of the fruits of development for years. The New Miyazawa Initiative, Japan's bilateral assistance that responds to the sharp economic downturn, has been also implemented in close coordination with the World Bank and the Asian Development Bank.

The World Bank's swift and effective response to the crises should be highly appreciated now. Such a response was made possible by the World Bank's flexible management and financial soundness, and we must spare no effort in restoring and maintaining the World Bank's risk-bearing capacity.

As a recent example of such a swift response by the World Bank, I would like to point out the World Bank's announcement of its assistance to aid in the aftermath of the Marmara earthquake within 36 hours. As a country that has also suffered from earthquakes, Japan expresses its deepest sympathies to the victims of the earthquake in Turkey and will extend reconstruction support. At the same time, we fervently hope that as the core of the international community's assistance, the World Bank will contribute to the reconstruction in Turkey by providing timely and large-scale loans. Another important challenge is assistance for reconstruction and development from the recent turmoil and destruction in East Timor. We expect the World Bank to lead the reconstruction process, and Japan intends to play an important part in the reconstruction and development.

In a number of Asian countries, signs of recovery from the crisis are now discernible in economic dimension, although with regard to the social dimension the situation is still serious particularly in the poor and vulnerable groups. Those who had received the smallest fruits of economic growth are now being left behind. Moreover, this is not unique to directly crisis-hit countries, but also to those affected indirectly.

We call on the World Bank to challenge the new poverty generated by the crises as one of its top agenda items and to further strengthen its assistance in areas such as health, sanitation, education, and employment, underpinned by high standards of governance. In close coordination with MDBs, Japan will identify its support to meet these urgent needs by making new contributions to the World Bank and the Asian Development Bank.

The Enhanced HIPC Initiative. Assistance to heavily indebted poor countries represents another vital area in combating poverty. I welcome the fact that the enhanced framework of the initiative for "broader, deeper, and faster" debt relief was recently endorsed. Under the enhanced initiative, Japan will provide the largest-scale bilateral official development assistance for debt relief. The enhanced initiative is now expected to be implemented speedily.

In the implementation of the enhanced HIPC Initiative, it is necessary to identify financial resources to meet the increasing cost to international organizations. Maximizing the use of their internal resources should come first and then, bilateral contribution on the basis of the principle of fair burden sharing. I welcome the agreement on a financing plan that will permit the enhanced HIPC framework to be launched and the delivery of debt relief to begin for countries requiring retroactive relief and those expected to reach their decision points over the near term. I would like to express my appreciation for the efforts made by the managements of the Bank and the Fund.

It is also important to clearly identify the initiative as an integral part of the World Bank's poverty-reduction strategies and to ensure a link between debt relief and poverty reduction. It is essential to secure developing country governments' ownership and participation of civil society during implementation. We should fully recognize the necessity of tailoring assistance to reflect each country's poverty situations, available resources from debt relief, and implementation capacity.

A New Vision for the Asian Economies. It has been only six years since the World Bank published its highly acclaimed "East Asian Miracle," in which it analyzed the high growth of the Asian emerging market economies during the 1980s and presented the growth potential and policy issues in the region. The recent crisis in the region was not only an economic crisis, but also a challenge to our vision of the Asian economies. From this viewpoint, it would be meaningful for the World Bank as a "knowledge bank" to comprehensively analyze the unprecedented recent economic turmoil, to show its long- and medium-term prospects on the road to overcome poverty, and to indicate a direction on policy management for the region. I would like to propose that the World Bank undertake a comprehensive research project, under a title such as "Toward a New East Asia—Revisiting Its Miracle," and hereby announce that Japan will support this project.

Conclusion

Throughout the twentieth century, and particularly during the first half of the century, the global society repeatedly suffered the calamities of war and serious economic dislocation. However, when we look back at this century in its entirety from our current vantage point, we realize that this was a century in which mankind sought to liberate itself from the shackles of poverty, and growing numbers of people were in fact able to do so. It goes without saying that the Fund and the Bank have made extremely important contributions to the stability and development of the world economy during the second half of the century.

As we stand on the threshold of the twenty-first century, we have been made to witness and to realize that our globally integrated international financial system has a shadow side of putting national economies at risk of grave crisis through sudden and massive reversals in capital flows. Yet, in crisis, we have observed how the countries of the world, including those directly affected by the crisis, in earnest consultation with the Fund and the Bank, have been drawn together as a single international society to work toward the prevention and resolution of future crises. Herein lies our hope for the twenty-first century. Let us remember that we have overcome numerous difficult problems during the twentieth century. In the process, we have been able to develop a firm foundation for international cooperation and coordination, and have learned to bring together and share our knowledge and our wisdom. If we continue to apply these valuable global assets to the challenges and issues that lie ahead, I am certain that we will be able to overcome the problems of the twenty-first century as well.

STATEMENT BY THE GOVERNOR OF THE FUND FOR KOREA

Bong-Kyun Kang

It is a great pleasure and honor for me to represent the Republic of Korea at this fifty-fourth Annual Meeting of the Fund and the World Bank Group. I would like to take this opportunity to express my profound gratitude to the Fund and the World Bank, and to member countries for helping Korea to not only overcome the financial crisis, but also quickly restore economic vitality.

International Cooperation for Stable Global Economic Growth

I am pleased to see that most economies in Asia have recovered from financial crisis faster than expected, and that the instability in other regions of the world has largely abated. In this regard, international financial institutions have played an indispensable role in stopping the spread of financial crises. Indeed, they have done this in many ways, but most importantly, they have guided crisis-affected countries in the right direction by assisting them to set up and implement their own structural reform programs. I praise the World Bank and the Fund for their accomplishments.

Yet for structural reforms to become deep-rooted and effective, it is critical that the global economic environment remains stable. Specifically, we look to a soft landing for the U.S. economy and a sustained economic rebound in Japan and the EU member countries. By achieving stability in the global financial environment, we will all benefit from strengthened policy coordination among the world's major countries.

Korea's Economic Reform and Recovery

Since the onset of the crisis, Korea has spared no efforts in overcoming the crisis and reforming its economy. We have acted to reinvigorate our economy; we have continuously implemented structural reforms to build a foundation for sustainable growth; and we have greatly emphasized a social harmonization policy throughout the reform process.

Thanks to the strong leadership of President Kim Dae-jung and the resolve of the Korean people, Korea's economic recovery has been remarkable. GDP growth recorded 7.3 percent for the first half of this year and is expected to be around 7 percent for the year as a whole. Other major macroeconomic indicators show equally favorable developments, including a historically low inflation rate of 0.7 percent during the first eight months of this year.

Korea's foreign exchange reserves have reached record-high levels, rising dramatically from near depletion at the onset of the crisis to more than $65 billion. The large current account surpluses and the active capital inflows contributed to the rapid buildup of reserves. At the same time, foreign exchange markets have stabilized since the beginning of the year.

The total amount of external debt has continued to decline and its structure too has improved toward a much lower share of short-term debt. Based on these achievements, Korea was able to repay the entire amount of its Supplemental Reserve Facility (SRF) borrowings from the Fund—$13.5 billion—nine months ahead of schedule.

A significant improvement has also been achieved in Korea's financial markets, now equipped with greater capacity to absorb shocks. Interest rates have declined to the single-digit range for the first time ever, and the stock market index has nearly doubled this year, recovering above pre-crisis levels. These conditions have translated into an environment conducive for corporate sector reform, particularly for the rapid improvement of debt-equity ratios. The success of corporate restructuring is paramount for enhancing the overall competitiveness of the Korean economy and achieving international credibility.

Korea's strong reform drive proved to be painful to many of our people, especially those in the middle- and low-income class. Thus, following through on our conviction that the government's drastic structural reforms cannot succeed without strong social cohesion, we have greatly expanded the social safety net to provide adequate protection for those most vulnerable. The government has also strengthened its support programs for small- and medium-sized firms and venture capital enterprises to help contain unemployment problems.

Reforming the International Financial Architecture

I would now like to turn to the issue of reforming the international financial architecture. I welcome the international community's efforts to enhance transparency through the establishment of more stringent global information standards. Also, to promote an orderly financial integration, the international community should cooperate closely in strengthening regulations on short-term capital flows and devising safeguards that can be readily implemented during times of crisis. In this context, I urge stepped-up international efforts for improved monitoring and regulation of hedge funds to minimize their disruptive effects on emerging market economies.

In the spirit of a more balanced approach to improving the global financial system, I strongly support the expansion of the existing G-7 consultation framework to include so-called "systematically important countries" such as Korea.

Helping the Heavily Indebted Poor Countries

Before closing, I would like to take this opportunity to express Korea's support for the Fund-World Bank initiative to help heavily indebted poor countries. Korea is willing to contribute to the ESAF-HIPC trust fund on the basis of a fair burden-sharing principle.

Conclusion

This Annual Meeting takes place as we approach the turn of a century, at the time when the world economy is moving into a new era marked by challenges and opportunities. I can assure you that Korea is fully committed to playing an important role toward promoting global economic prosperity. To this end, Korea will push forward major reforms to achieve its historical goal of a simultaneous achievement of democracy and market economy.

STATEMENT BY THE GOVERNOR OF THE BANK FOR THE LAO PEOPLE'S DEMOCRATIC REPUBLIC

Boungnang Vorachith

I have the greatest honor to represent the government of the Lao People's Democratic Republic at the fifty-fourth Joint Annual Meetings of the World Bank and the International Monetary Fund. These Annual Meetings are being held in the midst of an improving global economy, compared with that of the past year. With assistance from the international financial institutions, especially the World Bank, the Fund, and developed countries, the economies of the countries encumbered with the financial crisis in Asia and other parts of the world have been able to restore the confidence of investors, enabling the economies of those countries to emerge from the recession. This is the preliminary achievement of the concerted efforts of the international financial institutions and developed countries toward resolving the adverse effects of the crisis. However, the challenge in the future is the maintenance of coordination and cooperation, so as to ensure that the global economy in the twenty-first century be truly rid of the recession trend. In my view, I think that it is the responsibility of this Joint Annual Meeting to consistently explore approaches and measures to guarantee the persistent efficiency of the international coordination, particularly ensuring that the concentration of efforts for solving problems in countries facing the economic crisis does not impede the needs of other groups of countries of the world.

The Lao People's Democratic Republic is one of the least developed countries in Asia that is being affected by the financial crisis in the region. During the 1998 Annual Meetings, the impact of the regional financial crisis on our economy were not clearly portrayed in our report to the Meetings. Even though macroeconomic problems had started to emerge, specifically the devaluation of the kip and the increase in the consumer price index, the annual growth rate of the economy of the Lao People's Democratic Republic was sustained at a level of about 7 percent—a level witnessed by the years during which the Lao People's Democratic Republic has embarked on an open-door policy in investment and cooperation with other countries. For 1998, the adverse effects of the regional financial crisis could be clearly seen, particularly in the decrease in the flows of foreign investments, which were reduced by 48 percent, compared with 1997. Moreover, owing to the rigidity of the conditionalities of the external assistance, disbursements of foreign loans were also diminished. Meanwhile the volume of Lao commodity exports was limited. This adverse situation caused the growth rate of the economy to be reduced to a level of 4 percent in 1998.

The growth of the economy in the Lao People's Democratic Republic could have dropped to even a lower level had it not been for the government's effort to concentrate public investment in the agricultural sector, the base of the Lao economy, by expanding the irrigation network. Agricultural production in 1998 increased by 3.7 percent, accompanied by the growth in hydropower production following the completion of the Theun Hinboun dam, which began producing in the second quarter of 1998. In addition, the recovery of the textile industry following the restoration of the Generalized System of Preferences given to garments made in the Lao People's Democratic Republic by the European Union has substantially contributed to the maintenance of the recorded level of economic growth in 1998.

Because the domestic production base has not expanded in recent years, society's demand for consumption and capital goods continues to depend heavily on imports. Public investments are largely dependent on domestic loans in the form of advances from the central bank, as a result of the shortfall of budget revenue collection owing to the slow growth of production in the economy. As a consequence, broad money increased by 113 percent by the end of 1998, compared with 65 percent at the end of 1997. This has resulted in increasing pressure on foreign exchange demand to finance imports, which, in turn, caused the kip to depreciate even further, resulting in a consumer price index increase to a three-digit level that continues to persist through the present days. With such high inflation, even the upward adjustment of public service salaries by 100 percent at the end of 1998 could not resolve the hardships in the living conditions of the poor and low-income public servants. The devaluation of kip and the increase in the consumer price index can be explained by the deterioration of balance of payments which witnessed the reduction in official foreign reserves from a level equivalent to 2.7 months of imports at the end of 1997 to only 2.2 months at the end of 1998.

The prevalent macroeconomic instability can be attributed to the lack of conduct of appropriate and prudent fiscal and monetary policies. In order to restore macroeconomic stability in the immediate and medium terms, the government of the Lao People's Democratic Republic has committed to implement more prudent fiscal and monetary policies, with an aim of bringing down the inflation to a two-digit level and confining the devaluation of kip within a limit acceptable to the society.

In this connection, the government, within the framework of 1999/2000 budget, will exert efforts toward fiscal consolidation, with a revenue collection target of about 12 percent of GDP. By adhering to a prudent and tight fiscal stance, the government expects to realize a budget deficit not exceeding 5–6 percent of GDP, while maintaining investments in the priority sectors within the range of 11–12 percent of GDP.

With respect to monetary policy, the Bank of the Lao People's Democratic Republic is determined to implement measures to curb inflation by limiting credits to all sectors. Furthermore, in view of limiting the devaluation of kip and supporting the exchange rate policy, a policy involving the use of the interest rate as a means to absorb excess liquidity into the banking system has been put in place. The structural adjustment, especially the reform of the banking system, will be steadfastly carried out. The newly merged state-owned commercial banks have set up the reserves for nonperforming loans to improve their financial situation. Concurrently, the process is ongoing to establish plans for recapitalization and to upgrade the knowledge and skills of managers of the newly merged state-owned commercial banks through the process of modern banking technology transfer training to be conducted by foreign experts. To enhance the confidence in the Lao banking system, the Bank of the Lao People's Democratic Republic has committed to improve its regulatory and supervisory role through the prudential regulations for commercial banks. In this connection, emphasis will be placed on the importance of external auditing and the publication of an annual report to increase transparency and promote public confidence in the Lao banking system.

In the area of international cooperation and trade, the government continues to implement the open door policy to foreign direct investment and to promote production of tradable goods and services. This is particularly important to enable the country to make greater benefits from the present era of globalization, especially after having integrated itself into the ASEAN. To promote trade as a means of attaining sustainable growth and poverty reduction, work is under way to prepare the ground for future involvement under the regional free trade agreement, the AFTA. Furthermore, preparation is ongoing for the purpose of accession to WTO membership in the near future.

Prior to the outbreak of the regional financial crisis, the Lao People's Democratic Republic was able to witness strong growth and thereby the improvement in the quality of life for the multi-ethnic people thanks to the strong foreign investment and assistance flows. The future efforts to sustain high growth and stability are highly dependent on the external environment, particularly the continuing recovery in the crisis-stricken countries in the Asian region. The speedy recovery of those economies becomes, therefore, imperative to enable the investment projects presently on hold to resume and the negotiation or implementation of new projects to be expedited. We, therefore, commend the authorities of the economies concerned for their remarkable progress made thus far and wish them all the best for their continuing endeavors.

The improved global economic environment is also very important for the purpose of ensuring the environment of a more balanced treatment among groups of countries of the world. In the recent past, we feel that the concentration of efforts by the international community to address the problems of the crisis-stricken emerging markets and large economies was made at a cost to other groups of countries. While appearing more accommodating to countries in crisis, the treatment given by the international community to other countries also suffering from the adverse impact of the crisis seemed to have become more rigidly orchestrated. Had a more flexible and balanced approach been followed in the recent past, the much needed financial aid flows would have been forthcoming to enable our authorities to stabilize the kip and thereby reduce inflation. As a consequence, our already poor population and low-income public servants would have been salvaged from the intense hardship caused by the long-lasting high inflation.

We strongly believe that any efforts toward macroeconomic stabilization without the availability of financial support and assistance from the international community would not be productive, particularly in the case of a least-developed economy in the process of transition, having a very small and fragile economic base and suffering from the contagion effects of the regional crisis, like the Lao People's Democratic Republic. However, we have been very encouraged by developments during the recent months and days leading to the present joint Annual Meetings. We welcome and fully endorse the proposals made by the Group of Twenty-Four (G-24) countries concerning the attenuation of conditionalities attached to assistance and loans provided by the international community to countries with low-level socioeconomic development. At the same time, we welcome the initiative made at the G-7 Summit in Cologne to further enhance the HIPC Initiative and the proposal to replace the ESAF with the new Poverty Reduction and Growth Facility. We congratulate those institutions, countries, and individuals concerned for their contribution to this very desirable and timely move to address the long-lasting problems of debt and poverty in the world and to an expeditious and successful realization thereof.

At this juncture, our government would like to thank countries, international financial institutions, international organizations, and nongovernmental organizations for their past financial and technical support, as well as for the investment flows that our country has received. We strongly hope that you will continue to give us your support and assistance in the future to enable people to exit from poverty and enjoy their share of the fruits of globalization in the next millennium. Allow me, on behalf of the Lao delegation, to wish the Chairman a glorious success in presiding over these historical joint Annual Meetings.

Statement by the Governor of the Bank for the Republic of Latvia

Roberts Zile

Let me address the honorable meeting on behalf of the three Baltic countries: Lithuania, Estonia, and Latvia. The year between the two Annual Meetings has once again reminded us that we all are an integral part of the world economy and subject to both regional and global turbulence. This has put extra challenges to the World Bank. This also has induced the Bank to think more in long-term categories about its own financial standing. Therefore, we fully support President's position on the issue of maintaining the financial strength of the Bank. Without this, the Bank will not be able to fulfill its core mission of fighting poverty.

We, the Baltic countries, would like to express our appreciation of the World Bank's flexibility in responding to the developments at the burning spots on the world map. We appreciate its readiness to step in with the most urgently needed and indispensable assistance. Yet, we hope that this will not cause the funds to flow away from the ongoing projects, or those in the pipeline. We hope this will not become an extra borrowing cost for the rank-and-file borrowers.

We suggest that both the Bank and the Fund develop strict criteria in order to evaluate countries' defaults. Natural disasters, business failures, and mistakes in management should be clearly distinguished from deliberate fraud and corruption. The latter deserves a very different handling and attitude. This is especially important now, when the Bank's long-term financial capacity is on the agenda.

I can say with pride that our three countries have been insistent and dedicated in pursuing the goals set by ourselves. Our own motivation, combined with the highly constructive macroeconomic monitoring and economic analysis carried out by the Bank and the Fund, has delivered good results. The financial sector vulnerability studies have helped us to focus the spotlight on the issues that need a closer analysis and care.

I believe that everybody will agree readily that the three Baltic countries are definitely in the most advanced group of the transition economies. Latvia was the first of the Baltic countries to be admitted to the World Trade Organization. Estonia has already been invited to the EU accession negotiations, to be followed eventually by Latvia and Lithuania. All three countries intend to join the North Atlantic Treaty Organization as well.

Our countries—Latvia, Estonia, and Lithuania—have attained macroeconomic stability. It is a precondition for any government to win the confidence and support of its own nation and of the international community. The investment grade credit ratings, repeatedly assigned to our countries, are evidence of our creditworthiness and reliability.

All the Baltic countries have demonstrated a sustainable growth over the past four to five years. However, one has to admit the impact of the global crisis. It started in Asia and extended to other regions, including the Russian Federation, and has caused certain, although limited, setbacks in the Baltic countries as well. During the past 12 months, growth has slowed down, but all three countries are still expecting a positive GDP in 1999. Long-term growth prospects continue to be optimistic. Our governments have adjusted the budgets for the remainder of 1999 to minimize deficits; the next year's budgets, under discussion right now, will be in compliance with the Fund criteria. The inflation rates are presently in the range of 2 to 4 percent. National currencies have retained stability over time. We can conclude that the external pressures have given a hard test to the durability of our structural reforms, and we are glad we have managed to pass this test.

The Baltic countries congratulate the Comprehensive Development Framework initiative launched by the Bank. We see this as an attempt to recognize the complexity and integrity of the world. An attempt to address all the factors—economic, financial, structural, and social—to support a balanced development of the countries. This matches perfectly with our intent to enhance social sector reforms and development. We believe that the local expertise on welfare, health, and education projects in the Baltic countries could be helpful to developing countries. We are ready to assist the World Bank in disseminating the lessons learned.

Our governments have always been encouraged that it is themselves, and not the World Bank, who—speaking in CDF metaphor—are sitting in the driver's seat and holding the wheel. The World Bank is only an instructor. Nor is it teaching the "ABC's" of driving—it is rather advising how to improve our driving habits and techniques. The decision of the Baltic states was a road leading to market economy and democracy, with the well-being of all people as the ultimate goal. And we have not deviated from this goal on any single occasion.

Statement by the Governor of the Bank for Lebanon

Georges Corm

It is my pleasure to address this distinguished audience in my capacity as a member of the new government of the Republic of Lebanon that came to office in December 1998 with a pledge to undertake a full reform of its public finance. This reform is targeting two main goals: establishing transparency and efficient governance in public spending and in the taxation system on the one hand, and addressing effectively the issue of ever-increasing public deficit that has plagued the Lebanese economy and led to an unbearable level of real interest rate, on the other.

As you may know, through its regular constitutional process, Lebanon elected a new president in October 1998. Our government that took office in December, within the framework established by President Emile Lahoud, is dedicated and committed to implementing all the basic elements of good governance and accountability. More specifically, we have pledged to abide by the rule of law, to reinforce the role of institutions, to introduce transparency in public accounts, and to ensure full disclosure of data and statistics. We are also addressing the issue of distributing fairly the tax burden among citizens, and we will attempt to stop the continuing damage to the environment.

It is our feeling that the issues of good governance and accountability, which are receiving more international support and focus, are key issues for the next century. We have to thank the Fund, the World Bank, and other UN institutions for promoting these issues and bringing them into the limelight, but more efforts have still to be made. The development of free market economies, the dismantling of cumbersome regulations, and the opening of markets to international trade and to financial flows have all created a new frontier for development but also with potential negative side effects. What has happened in certain parts of the world, in terms of economic instability, financial disruption, and abuse of public assets, shows that the global markets are indeed needing better governance and accountability to become more beneficial.

In fact, the transition to free market economies and the globalization of the international economy and financial markets constitute a difficult turning point. Neither all countries, nor all social groups inside each country, are taking advantage of global markets and more productive economic freedom. Social inequalities are on the increase in many parts of the world. Too often, globalization is associated with undue and unproductive windfall profits. State institutions are encountering many difficulties in adapting to the new role of impartial regulator of liberalized domestic markets. Low-paid and inadequately trained civil servants are not always able to resist being influenced by large private companies. However, corporate governance rules that are enforced in some countries are not being introduced or implemented in many other countries. Owing to this situation, privatization does not always yield the expected benefits for the consumer and the economy in general. This is why we believe that both the Fund and the World Bank, in their remarkable efforts to induce member states to fight corruption more efficiently, should put the same emphasis on corporate governance in the private sector as is being put on state and public sector governance, transparency, and accountability rules. In many emerging markets, private sector companies are resisting the introduction of corporate governance and business ethics rules. Legal rules and the judicial system are not being adequately modernized and made more efficient to secure the minimum level of corporate governance to the benefit of the economy as a whole.

We in Lebanon consider that putting economic growth on a sound and sustainable basis requires clear priorities to be addressed. This is why our government has devoted its first months to producing a five-year fiscal consolidation plan to address the need to reintroduce financial discipline in public finance. After 15 years of war and 8 years of high annual deficits and a huge pileup of domestic debt, we have developed a package of financial reforms to curb public deficits, reduce the very high and unsustainable level of domestic debt, and allow real interest rates to fall down from their very high level. This first priority is designed to allow for a comeback of private investment as the main engine of growth. During the reconstruction years, private investment has been oriented toward real estate and contracting, which has come to a stop after a few years. Oversupply in the real estate sector and the piling-up of state arrears to contractors have affected negatively the private sector, in addition to the crowding-out effect of the private sector on the credit market owing to the increasing need for public sector financing. An additional result of this situation has been the high costs of running the economy and a lack of competitiveness of domestic products, and thus an ever-increasing gap in our external current account balance.

This is why our package of financial reform is designed to cure the unhealthy situation prevailing in both the public and private sectors. We need to slim down the inflated role of the public sector in the economy and bring back domestic private investment in the various sectors of the economy at the forefront of economic development. Investment will have to be oriented toward increasing the competitiveness of the economy and diversifying its productive capacity.

Our financial reform package is based on two main components. The first is a comprehensive plan to review and modernize our outdated tax system, which is yielding only 14 percent of GDP as tax receipts, while our level of spending is above 35 percent. Our plan is to increase tax receipts to the level of 19 percent of GDP in five years while, at the same time, trimming down expenses to 25 percent of GDP.

The main components of our tax reform program are the following:

- the introduction of a value-added tax to replace most excise duties and reduce the very high dependence of tax receipts on custom duties that will have to be trimmed down in the future;
- the introduction of a global income tax system to replace the old system of scheduled income taxes that assess separately, and at different rates, the various sources of revenues of the tax payer;
- the modernization of the stamp duty;
- a package of tax incentives that will induce companies to invest and to upgrade their productive capacities, to open their share capital to foreign participation, and to register their capital stock on the local stock exchange; and
- the raising of the ceiling of income tax rates from the present low level of 10 percent for the higher tranches of revenues to 20 percent.

The changes in income tax rates have already been adopted by the Lebanese Parliament in the 1999 budget law. A draft law on the value-added tax will be presented to parliament before the end of the year.

The second main component of our financial reform package is privatization. Although Lebanon has never had a large number of public enterprises, there is a need to modernize public services and secure better-priced and more efficient services for the consumer, mainly in the areas of water, electricity, and telecommunications. However, in our privatization program, we want to avoid the mistakes that have been done elsewhere. It is extremely important for our government that we do not just transfer a public monopoly into the hands of a private monopoly consisting of a few large shareholders from the private sector. The aim of our privatization efforts will be to enhance competition to the benefit of the consumers, thus reducing prices and optimizing the flow of resources accruing to the State Treasury. In addition, we would like to see the largest distribution of shares among the Lebanese public so as to activate the domestic financial market and avoid any monopoly position.

To abide by transparency rules and fair competition principles, we have prepared a draft law that is now being discussed in parliament. The law states clear procedures to be implemented and requires that adequate regulatory authorities be created to supervise privatized sectors.

Our financial reform package has already produced very beneficial results on the domestic financial markets. The previous negative trends have been reverted, and interest rates on domestic treasury bills have declined by almost 2 percent. The budget deficit is being held below 40 percent, against an average of more than 50 percent in previous years, and the balance of payments has returned to a positive trend after last year's huge deficit of more than $400 million. In addition, our government has also recognized state and public sector unbudgeted arrears piled up by the former government to the private sector. The parliament has approved the government's request to pay these arrears and allowed the ministry of finance to issue three-year treasury bills to be delivered to the beneficiaries of the arrears as payment. But we still have a long way to go to establish proper governance and transparency. Our next steps will be the following:

- determining the exact amount of arrears inside the public sector and clearing them to suppress financial distortions and unfair situations between public entities, or between the state and public entities;
- establishing a fair and acceptable tax framework. In this context the ministry of finance intends to settle old unaudited taxpayers' files in an acceptable and fair way, to induce people unknown to

the tax authorities to register themselves with the concerned tax department, and to review and simplify all tax procedures and suppress sources of corruption;

- setting up an efficient, fair, and transparent system for the management of the public domain in Lebanon. As in many other Arab countries, this is a big issue in Lebanon. Too often, the public domain is being leased at very low rates—when it is not being illegally occupied;
- improving public procurement procedures to secure proper competition; and
- improving expenditure control procedures by shifting the emphasis from ex-ante control to ex-post control, so as to establish a real accountability in spending procedures instead of diluting responsibilities; creating effective cost control criteria; setting a transparent management system for non-privatizable public enterprises; and establishing an adequate social network to tackle enlarging social pain and help the poor to adapt to economic and financial structural adjustment.

In our endeavor, we are very grateful for all the assistance we are receiving from the Fund, the World Bank, and the IFC. We are developing a very fruitful dialogue with all three institutions and are trying to make the best use of their experience and advice. We are very glad that the World Bank is opening an office in Beirut, and we are looking forward to more cooperation with the Bretton Woods institutions.

We do hope that all the efforts that are being developed to reinforce the architecture of the international, financial, and monetary system, as well as efforts for poverty alleviation, will be successful in the near future. We need to enter into the next millennium with a more stable and more transparent world, and a much fairer and more equitable system for the distribution of chances within the new context of global markets.

STATEMENT BY THE GOVERNOR OF THE BANK FOR THE SOCIALIST PEOPLE'S LIBYAN ARAB JAMAHIRIYA

Mohamed A. Bait Elmal

It is a great pleasure to me, Mr. Chairman, to congratulate you, personally and on behalf of the delegation of the Great Libyan Arab Jamahiriya, for being chosen to chair the meeting of the Boards of Governors of the International Bank for Reconstruction and Development and the International Monetary Fund in its current session. We wish you all success in conducting these meetings and realizing results that will reflect the hopes that the peoples of the world pin on both of these institutions. I would also like to express gratitude and appreciation to Mr. Wolfensohn, President of the World Bank Group, for his efforts to push forward economic and social development in developing countries and for his skillful management of crises. I would also like to express gratitude and appreciation to Mr. Camdessus, Managing Director of the Fund. Despite the recent modest global economic growth, economic and financial crises still face us and their economic and social impacts still wreak havoc among numerous economies worldwide, albeit on different scales. The lesson learned from the financial crisis experienced by some countries of the world is the need to create a financial and banking system that operates under an effective and transparent oversight framework coupled with a framework of moral responsibility.

We believe that developing countries do not need capital that is intent on realizing quick profits, usually at the expense and for the detriment of the financial and economic stability of the countries involved. Developing countries need capital that is ready to contribute, along with national investments, to increased production and the development of national productive forces. Consequently, we believe that there is a need for developing and organizing means and instruments for the movement of capital among the various countries of the world. The challenges facing many countries worldwide as we approach the third millennium are reflected by escalating poverty, the spread of disease, mounting indebtedness, the ever-growing gap between developed and developing countries, as well as increased conflicts, civil war, and globalization. Such challenges make it incumbent on us to study and discuss such phenomena and their economic and social impacts on the world community at large, and on developing countries in particular. We need to find appropriate solutions and to mobilize adequate financial resources and proper technical assistance with a view to achieving development in such countries. Although the IBRD formulated, in recent years, programs aimed at eradicating poverty in developing countries, such programs have not been put under actual implementation so far. This will require that the IBRD take practical and urgent actions to combat such a phenomenon in the context of increasing the effectiveness of its efforts in this respect, thereby strengthening the world community's confidence in such efforts.

The concepts of globalization, partnership, cooperation, and liberal international trade—collective, bilateral, and multilateral—have led to extensive controversy between industrial and developing countries. Moreover, the promotion of globalization as the freedom of movement of goods, services, labor, capital, and information will lead to monopolization by a few countries and corporations of international trade in goods and services. It will also help giant international corporations to control global economy and to weaken the economies of developing nations in the absence of regulatory arrangements and controls. Unless such arrangements and controls materialize, developing countries will pay an exorbitant price, owing to a lack of ability to compete with developed nations. Developing countries will then be transformed into consumer markets for the products of advanced countries. From this forum, we stress the fact that the Fund and the World Bank operate, in their capacity as international institutions, in the framework of the respective Articles establishing each of them, to provide economic stability, and support development and progress opportunities in the various countries of the world. Consequently, their approach must be characterized by absolute professional objectivity removed from any political, racial, religious, or any other influences.

Experience has shown that the methods of using economic might, as exercised by some countries, in a coercive and arbitrary manner to achieve political objectives have failed. Besides being devoid of any moral justification, such methods are not in agreement with the requirements of economic freedom in the world. They have proved to be, in principle, detrimental to the interests of all the parties involved.

Finally, it is true that the economies of many countries—particularly developing countries—experienced crises in the decade. But my country, as you all know, depends entirely on a single and nonrenewable source of income (i.e., oil) whose prices fluctuate sharply from time to time. Yet, we have paid increased attention for a long time to the diversification of our country's income and the identification of alternative non-oil sources of income. In this respect, my country invested its oil revenues in implementing infrastructure projects, establishing numerous agricultural and industrial projects, providing public services, particularly in the education and health care sectors, and creating new job opportunities for residents.

Despite the major challenges that my country had to face over the recent years, we succeeded in maintaining an appropriate standard of living for our citizens and in achieving a remarkable rate of growth in GDP in the various non-oil economic sectors of activity. The achievements that my country accomplished in this respect would not have been realized had it not been for the desire to establish strong economic ties with various countries in the world, based on the principle of mutual and reciprocal respect and the achievement of benefits and interests in common among countries, in addition to continued cooperation with the various regional and international economic and financial institutions. In conclusion, allow me to express gratitude and appreciation to you again for providing this opportunity for me to address this honorable meeting. I wish you all success and good results. Peace be with you.

STATEMENT BY THE GOVERNOR OF THE FUND FOR MADAGASCAR

Tantely R.G. Andrianarivo

I have been given the honor and privilege of sharing with you, on behalf of my fellow African Governors, Africa's achievements in establishing macroeconomic stability and an appropriate environment for sustained growth as a necessary condition in its fight against poverty, which continue to be our priorities as we approach the new millennium. Africa is now at a crossroads in its history, and we must move forward resolutely toward its successful integration into the global economic and financial system. This is a joint responsibility that begins with the reform efforts of the African countries, to be complemented by the international community, if Africa is to make its rightful contribution to global prosperity. We are convinced that this approach to international cooperation will open the way to a peaceful, equitable, and stable world economic order.

On our part, our countries have been implementing deep economic and structural reforms with the support of the Fund and the World Bank. We have embarked on political pluralism, which is contributing to greater accountability and transparency, and the private sector has been given a pivotal role as the engine of growth. We are hopeful that the encouraging results achieved in recent years can be sustained and improved, with the help of the international community. Our economies face tremendous development challenges that will require strengthened cooperation with the international community. These include, inter alia, financing development and poverty reduction in the face of declining resource flows, the high instability of Africa's export earnings, the debt burden, Africa's marginal role in the international financial system, the threat of the HIV/AIDS epidemic, and weak human and institutional capacity.

Financing Development

In order to achieve a significant reduction in poverty, Africa requires an average annual real growth rate of at least 7 percent over a sustained period, which calls for a substantial increase in the investment rate. Given Africa's low level of savings and the reduction in official development assistance and in foreign direct investment, a major effort is needed to mobilize resources necessary to support this ambitious growth objective. Greater public savings can be mobilized through improved tax administration; prudent monetary policy and increased financial intermediation can also help promote private savings. However, much of the needed resources will still have to come from foreign savings.

Given the low level of income in most of our economies, external financing should be on concessional terms. In this context, we welcome the twelfth replenishment of the International Development Association (IDA-12), which has increased the association's capacity to respond to Africa's needs in the areas of poverty reduction, investment in human capital, the environment, and private sector development. Africa's current economic recovery—and its continued commitment to reform—should constitute grounds for increased development assistance. In this context, we urge the donor community to reach a timely agreement on the funding of the ESAF, so that it can focus more on growth and poverty reduction. We also call for adequate provision of international technical and financial assistance to post-conflict countries, including those in arrears to multilateral institutions.

In assuming greater ownership of our economic programs, we have given increased emphasis to transparency, accountability, poverty reduction, and social safety nets, as well as regional integration. We look forward to the continued support of the Bank and the Fund in this endeavor, and encourage them to play a catalytic role in the matter of resource mobilization. In this connection, we urge the Fund and the World Bank to increase their partnership with the donor community and to enhance collaboration in support of these objectives.

The increased uncertainty about emerging markets in general that has resulted from the recent financial crises has had an adverse effect on the ability of African countries to attract private capital. However, tremendous investment opportunities have been opened up through greater economic integration, continued economic and structural reforms, the establishment of an investment-friendly environment, and the consolidation of the rule of law. We therefore expect to attract greater flows of foreign private capital into Africa in the near future.

Export Diversification

The continuing decline in commodity prices has highlighted the vulnerability of our economies to external shocks, leading to significant losses of real income. So far, African economies have coped with the deterioration of the terms of trade and the international financial crisis by strengthening their adjustment effort. This has not been an easy task. In this connection, we welcome the International Task Force on Commodity Risk Management in Developing Countries, recently established by the Bank, to seek market-based hedging mechanisms that could reduce Africa's vulnerability to commodity price fluctuations and increase the predictability of export revenue flows.

If commodity prices were to remain depressed, domestic adjustment policies would reduce economic activity and dramatically increase poverty. We believe that our adjustment efforts need to be complemented by concessional external financing. However, the long-term solution for commodity-exporting economies lies in the diversification of exports and of export markets. This requires that industrial countries liberalize their markets for African exports in areas where our economies have a comparative advantage.

The Debt Problem

In addition to the development financing problems, the economic expansion of Africa faces a major handicap, namely, its heavy debt burden, which absorbs over 50 percent of government revenues in most countries. Most of the heavily indebted low-income countries are in Africa, which calls for special attention. Creative solutions need also to be found for the debt burden of middle-income countries. There is a danger that, unless debt cancellation or substantial debt relief is granted, any potential for high economic growth expansion in Africa will be further jeopardized.

The launching of the HIPC Initiative in 1996 by the Fund and the World Bank had raised hopes for a comprehensive solution to the debt problem. However, so far, only two African countries (Uganda and

Mozambique) have benefited from it. We reiterate our call for a fundamental change in its structure and for a relaxation of the eligibility criteria so as to include a larger number of countries. Funds released through debt reduction would enable our countries to allocate additional resources to the development of the social sectors and to poverty reduction. We welcome the recent initiatives to reduce further the debt burden of the poorest countries, so as to foster sustainable development. In particular, we welcome the recommendations of the Group of Seven in its recent Cologne Summit and the global consensus for reform. We therefore urge a rapid implementation of the modifications to the HIPC Initiative as approved by the Boards of the Fund and the World Bank. We are well aware that the proposed reforms would entail additional costs, and we support the ongoing efforts by the international community to secure financing in the context of an appropriate burden-sharing arrangement. We would like to emphasize that enhanced debt relief should not be provided at the expense of official development assistance funding or IDA operations.

Africa and the International Financial System

Since the Asian crisis—the repercussions of which appeared to threaten the stability of capital markets throughout the world—African countries have shared the view that, although the consequences of the crisis have been contained, the financial sector should be extensively reformed. Our efforts are being directed to crisis prevention through strengthened supervision, increased surveillance, improved transparency, and implementation of internationally recognized standards, so as to detect weaknesses in a timely manner and protect our economies against the adverse effects of any similar crises.

In this connection, we welcome the recent creation of the Financial Stability Forum (FSF), which should contribute to the establishment of a sound and stable international financial system. We call for an extension of the FSF's membership to include developing countries and urge the FSF to ensure that African countries and their views are suitably represented during its deliberations. Similarly, African governors insist that the relevant organs of the new international financial system maintain a constituency-based structure that is representative of member countries. This would increase the chances that solutions to crises will be reached through consensus.

We believe that the integration of our economies into the international financial market is a precondition for harmonious integration into the process of globalization. However, the liberalization of capital movements should be done within a sound macroeconomic framework and should go hand in hand with the development and strengthening of our financial systems.

The HIV/AIDS Epidemic

In Africa, as highlighted in the recent meeting in Lusaka, more than anywhere else in the world, the scourge of HIV/AIDS epidemic has spread with alarming speed. According to United Nations statistics, 22 million Africans are living with HIV/AIDS, and more than 11 million have died of AIDS. Last year alone, 4 million Africans were infected, and in at least four African countries one adult in every five is living with the HIV virus. At this rate, and given the fact that it is the young, and therefore the most productive, who are the most vulnerable, it is sadly obvious that the disease poses a threat to the continent's economic development.

In these circumstances, a concerted effort must be launched, both within and outside Africa, by the entire international development community to eradicate this scourge.

Capacity Building and Technical Assistance

Africa regards its human resources and institutional capacities as the basis for securing sustainable development. In this regard, we urge continued donor support for the recently established Partnership for Capacity Building in Africa (PACT); in particular, we call upon our development partners to contribute to the PACT Trust Fund.

Africa is reforming its policies, its structures, and its institutions. African countries are also willing to implement transparency codes and appropriate standards in the context of the new international financial architecture, and are preparing to deal with the Y2K computer problem. We are concerned that this Y2K problem could disrupt economic activity in a wide range of sectors. To this end, assistance from the Fund, the World Bank, and the international community in human and financial resources is desired. However, we are of the view that these new demands should not be addressed at the expense of traditional technical assistance.

Conclusion

Economic reform efforts of African countries have produced some positive results. However, much remains to be done to achieve sustainable development. We are determined to redouble our adjustment efforts and to strengthen our regional integration process, and, therefore, call for the coordination of economic policies at the international level so as to revive the global economic activity. We are confident that, as we enter the new millennium, Africa can start reaping the fruits of its economic, structural, and political reform efforts. However, sustained growth will require a steady development of our human resources, effective HIV/AIDS prevention and care programs, increased concessional and private capital flows, debt cancellation or substantial debt relief, and increased access to export markets. We trust that we can count on the continued support of the international community and thus ensure a successful integration of African countries into the global economic system.

STATEMENT BY THE GOVERNOR OF THE BANK AND THE FUND FOR MALAYSIA

Dato' Mustapa Mohamed

When we gathered here last year, the growth outlook for the crisis-affected East Asian economies was gloomy. Since then, economic conditions in these economies have improved markedly and there is greater optimism that the worst may finally be behind us. Reflecting this, there have been upward revisions in growth projections for East Asian economies. Similarly, prospects for world growth have also been revised upward.

In September of last year, Malaysia imposed selective exchange controls in order to prevent further internationalization of our currency, the ringgit, and restore stability in the financial market. In the past year we have used this window of opportunity to strengthen the fundamentals of the Malaysian economy. The banking and corporate sectors were restructured. We adopted an expansionary monetary and fiscal stance to prevent further contraction of the Malaysian economy.

Despite the severe criticism leveled at us when we first adopted selective exchange controls, the unorthodox measures have yielded positive results as they provided the stability required for recovery measures to be effective. What is perhaps most significant is that the economic recovery was achieved with minimal social costs to the most vulnerable segments of society. Unemployment remained low, and poverty did not increase significantly. Our experience has shown that the standard Fund policy prescriptions introduced during the earlier part of the crisis did not work for Malaysia.

We are encouraged by the progress that we have made so far. Our GDP grew by 4.1 percent in the second quarter after five consecutive quarters of negative growth. Malaysia's economic recovery reflects broad-based strength and is expected to be sustainable. Key monetary aggregates have improved, and the multiplier effects of a more expansionary stance have begun to manifest themselves more strongly. Economic recovery was also stimulated by the strong export growth that we have enjoyed for eight consecutive quarters. This followed the large monthly trade surpluses we have registered for 21 consecutive months since November 1997. At the same time, there has been a significant revival in private consumption. The fiscal stimulus package further reinforced the expansion in domestic activities. Meanwhile, Malaysia's balance of payments continues to be in substantial surplus, and the external reserves position has improved significantly from 3.8 months of retained imports in August 1998 to 6.8 months at end-August, or $31.3 billion, four times larger than the nation's short-term external debt. The total external debt remained manageable at about 59 percent of GNP. Our debt-servicing ratio remains low at 6 percent.

The return of stability to the financial markets allowed Malaysia to liberalize the exchange controls within six months of its implementation. In February 1999, a graduated exit levy was introduced to allow funds to be repatriated freely. Subsequently on September 21, the two-tier levy system was streamlined. The expiry of the 12-month holding period for portfolio funds on September 1 did not result in a major exodus of foreign funds.

At the onset of the crisis, the Malaysian banking system was at its strongest, with the risk-weighted capital asset ratio at 12 percent, while nonperforming loans (NPLs) were at a low of 3 percent. The financial sector was less affected by the crisis, primarily because a sound and relatively well-developed financial infrastructure was already in place. This reflected the results of earlier comprehensive regulatory changes to restructure the financial system, following the recession in the mid-1980s. Such measures included a new Banking and Financial Institutions Act, with stringent prudential regulations on connected lending. Over the past decade, continuous measures were implemented to keep in line with international banking standards. In addition, Malaysia had in place an adequate bankruptcy legislation and corporate governance structure.

During the crisis, Malaysia adopted a preemptive strategy to address emerging problems in the banking sector, well before they reached serious levels. The institutional framework was established early in the crisis to address the emerging problems of NPLs and recapitalization of affected banking institutions. Because of the preemptive measures,

Malaysia could effectively use the period of stability accorded by the selective exchange controls to accelerate the pace of financial and corporate restructuring, which helped to hasten the economic recovery process.

The asset management corporation, Danaharta, has made significant progress, with its initial acquisition phase completed six months ahead of its target. To date, Danaharta has acquired and managed a total of RM 39 billion worth of NPLs from the financial system. Of these, RM 29 billion were from the banking system, accounting for 35 percent of total nonperforming loans in the banking system. With the carve-out of NPLs by Danaharta, the net nonperforming loans of the banking system had eased to 7.9 percent of total loans (RM 29.7 billion) at end-June 1999, based on the six-month NPL classification period, and (12 percent) on a three-month basis.

With the completion of the purchase of NPLs, Danaharta has embarked on its loan and management process and this is progressing well. To date, Danaharta has met with 1,732 borrowers with NPLs amounting to RM 38 billion. Approximately 2 percent of these accounts have been regularized or fully settled, while 423 borrowers with loans of RM 10.3 billion (representing 27 percent of total loans under management) have submitted their restructuring proposals. These proposals are at various stages of evaluation. In total, Danaharta has initiated recovery with 61 percent of the borrowers.

On asset disposal, Danaharta conducted a restricted open tender on July 5, 1999, to dispose of its foreign loan assets, which comprise non-Ringgit loans and marketable securities extended to or issued by foreign companies amounting to $142.82 million. The recovery rate on this loan was 55.3 percent.

At the same time, Malaysia has recapitalized 10 banking institutions. With the economic recovery, however, the capital position of some of the recapitalized banking institutions has improved and consequently, total investment by Danamodal, the special purpose vehicle set up to recapitalize financial institutions, had declined from RM 6.2 billion to RM 5.9 billion. This amount is substantially lower than the initial estimate made a year ago of RM 16 billion needed to recapitalize banking institutions. With the capital injection from Danamodal, the risk-weighted capital ratio of these banking institutions had strengthened to 13.3 percent at end-July from 9.9 percent at end-September 1998.

The Corporate Debt Restructuring Committee (CDRC) has made good progress in its debt-restructuring exercise for the larger debts. Currently, CDRC is in the process of working out the restructuring schemes of 39 applications involving debts worth RM 20.9 billion, while the debt-restructuring schemes for 10 applications have been completed and are at various stages of implementation. In addition, the restructuring of corporations is also being implemented by merchant banks and Danaharta in the process of managing the NPLs.

While we are heartened by the progress that we have achieved thus far, we are mindful that sound domestic policies alone are not enough. Adverse external factors can negate good domestic policies. It is for this reason that reform of the international financial architecture is of great urgency to reduce the impact or avert future crises.

The globalization of financial markets has been the outcome of concerted efforts to free trade in goods and services. The greater liberalization of trade flows has created much wealth to exporting countries. This has resulted in owners of this wealth seeking to maximize returns on their capital. Unfortunately, the absence of prudential rules to guide the profit-maximizing behavior of owners of capital has significantly negated much of the benefits of free capital flows. In the case of trade, the push toward free trade was matched by adequate rules on market-opening measures and procedures for dispute settlement. In contrast, the push to liberalize capital movements has not been matched by a parallel move to develop rules to safeguard economies from the adverse consequences of market excesses.

In the absence of rules to manage capital flows, small emerging market economies have become extremely vulnerable to volatility. The global financial system clearly does not provide a level playing field, as large players can effectively corner and manipulate small markets with impunity. In our view, reforms are needed to safeguard the interests of small emerging markets so that they will not be subjected to the predatory tendencies of large market players.

It should also be noted that in spite of the best institutional framework, small countries can be completely overwhelmed by a liberalized capital account framework. Without a parallel institution at the international level, countries may be forced to resort to more inward-looking policies in order to protect incomes and employment.

The recent Group of Seven initiatives, particularly the establishment of the Financial Stability Forum and its working groups, represent an important step forward. However, given the restrictive nature of this forum, the concerns and interests of small emerging market economies have not been adequately addressed. This is further aggravated by the exclusion of smaller economies in the Group of Twenty (G-20) that was set up over the weekend. None of the ASEAN countries has been included, although their economies are open and well integrated into the global financial system and have been the major victims of the crisis. We urge for an expanded membership in the Financial Stability Forum and the G-20 to ensure greater acceptance and ownership of the recommendations of both these fora.

Current efforts on the new architecture need to consider options for some form of indirect and direct regulation of highly leveraged institutions, in addition to measures to enhance the transparency of their operations. Given the increasingly important role of the private sector in the global economy, a more balanced approach to the issue of transparency and disclosure by both the public and private sectors is essential. Ongoing efforts to promote greater transparency of government operations must be complemented by a mechanism to strengthen the surveillance and transparency of private sector market participants that are of systemic importance to guard against market failure. Consideration of the issues associated with managing volatile capital flows should include both debt as well as non–debt-related flows. Lest we forget, let me remind you that the Asian crisis was largely due to the non–debt-creating capital flows by the private sector.

In addition to extending disclosure requirements to the private sector, we also need a global mechanism to supervise international financial markets. Such a global regulator would ensure the orderly functioning of the international capital markets and compliance with measures to inhibit cross-border manipulative activities in financial markets and design rules against the cornering of financial markets, circuit breakers, and appropriate international standards for financial institutions.

The experience in the past two years indicates that small countries are most vulnerable to liberalization. It is our view that they should not be coerced into accepting capital account liberalization at any cost. Instead, they should be allowed to liberalize at a pace commensurate with their stage of development. Liberalization of the capital account should not be part of Fund conditionality. Malaysia believes that a more productive approach is to create a conducive environment, which would serve as an incentive for countries to liberalize their capital accounts. This requires stable financial markets that would make it "safe" for countries to open their capital accounts.

In our view, any expansion of the Fund's jurisdiction over the capital account should await the outcome of discussions in various international fora on reform of the international financial architecture. The issue of Fund jurisdiction over capital movements can be revisited at a future date. At this juncture, the priority should be ensuring a sustainable recovery in the crisis-affected countries and on reforming the architecture of the international financial system to restore stability and order in global financial transactions.

While prospects for recovery have improved, indicators show that global poverty continues to worsen. Extreme poverty, as measured by the proportion of the population living on less than $1 a day, has been increasing over the years, and progress in meeting the goals set for poverty reduction and elimination has been limited. Against this background, Malaysia believes that the international community, including the Bank and the Fund, need to reexamine current strategies and policies on poverty redressal.

In this regard, we welcome the ongoing efforts to modify the ESAF and HIPC initiatives through the simplification of its conditionalities as well as enhancing its accessibility to more heavily indebted poor countries. While Malaysia believes that countries should settle their debt obligations, this new ESAF-HIPC Initiative would provide breathing space for them to use their limited resources to undertake social spending to reduce poverty levels.

In concluding, let me reiterate the importance of addressing issues of liberalization and globalization and their impact on small open economies. Given the vulnerability of these economies to the risks arising from globalization, we need to move forward aggressively to achieve better progress in reforming the international financial architecture. In this, the voice of developing countries that are most vulnerable to destabilizing capital flows is important. In pushing for liberalization and globalization, let us not forget the adverse implications of such a policy on small economies. We do not want globalization and liberalization to further aggravate the sufferings of smaller developing economies. We urge the international community to be mindful of the adverse consequences that globalization and liberalization may have on these economies whose success in providing a better life for their citizens has fallen far short of expectations. Let us redirect our efforts to eliminate poverty and humanize globalization.

STATEMENT BY THE GOVERNOR OF THE BANK FOR MALTA

John Dalli

It is a pleasure and an honor for me to address once again the Annual Meetings of the Fund and the World Bank.

We are pleased to note that the outlook for the world economy has improved considerably over the last year. Most of the economies that were seriously affected by the international financial crises are showing strong signs of recovery, while those that emerged relatively unscathed from the crises have managed to maintain a steady rhythm. It is encouraging to observe that forecasts for world economic growth in 1999 have been revised upward, and prospects for the year 2000 are definitely brighter than they were a year ago. The developments over the past year have also demonstrated that governments in major economies were able to respond to the international financial crises in a rapid, concerted, and determined manner. This ensured that a potentially prolonged and severe economic crisis, which could have had serious repercussions on developing countries, was generally averted.

The financial crises in Asia, the Russian Federation, and recently, Brazil have also highlighted the important role that the Fund and the World Bank are playing in strengthening the architecture of the international financial system. We are convinced that the outcome would have been very different today had it not been for the effectiveness of both the Fund and the Bank in tackling the crises. In this regard, we are glad to note that the collaboration between the two institutions has been enhanced, especially where this is related to the monitoring of member countries' financial systems. The Fund has continued to stress the importance of surveillance and transparency in economic policymaking. It is essential that policy processes are as transparent as possible, as greater transparency helps to improve both the quality and the timeliness of decision making by both international institutions and member countries. The development by the Fund of a Code of Good Practices on Transparency in Monetary and Financial Policies is certainly a major step forward, as it promotes more transparent institutional arrangements. We believe that transparency and accountability are the key factors that need to be in place before structural reforms are undertaken. Otherwise any institutional arrangements would tend to lack credibility and, hence, the authority to carry out the necessary changes. My country has adopted a number of measures in recent years to strengthen accountability and transparency in the financial sector. Apart from putting in place various pieces of legislation to ensure high ethical standards as far as financial operators are concerned, we have also strengthened the powers of the government auditor to carry out investigations and the powers of parliament to examine in detail the activities of various public financial agencies.

Malta fully supports the Fund in its efforts to further enhance the standards of economic and financial data published by members. We are monitoring closely developments of both standards for data dissemination established by the Fund. While at present we have decided to participate in the General Data Dissemination System, it is very much our intention to subscribe to the Special Data Dissemination Standard as soon as possible. We are in the process of upgrading our statistical agencies to improve the quality and integrity of our data. In recent months we have set up a number of task forces to enhance the method of statistical compilation where government finance statistics and the balance of payments are concerned. In this regard we are grateful to the Fund's Statistical Department for providing us with technical assistance in both these fields.

We have observed also that the Fund has taken new initiatives to strengthen the transparency of the surveillance process. Members are being encouraged to release more information on the discussions that take place at Executive Board level after Article IV consultations have been conducted by the Fund with member countries. Malta recently agreed to participate in the Fund's pilot project under which member countries voluntarily release the Fund staff report prepared by the Fund at the conclusion of Article IV consultations. As a result, Malta was among the first group of countries to release the staff report to the media in Malta early this summer.

Our policy of openness and transparency is consistent with our overall strategy, which is to modernize and upgrade our economic structures ahead of accession to the European Union. We are taking action on all fronts, particularly in the financial sector, which has been liberalized almost totally. Interest rates now move in line with market forces and the central bank is free to formulate and implement monetary policy. Our banking sector has recently been enhanced by the participation of a large international bank that has purchased one of the largest commercial banks in the country after this was privatized by the government. All financial institutions in Malta are supervised actively by the competent authorities, and it is my government's intention in the near future to consolidate all supervisory functions under a single financial services regulator. An important step over the next three years will be to complete the process of capital control liberalization. This will enable the Maltese financial markets to integrate closely with the large and deep European financial markets, particularly in the light of the rapid developments of these markets following the introduction of the single currency, the euro.

Malta is fully aware of the benefits of having a liberalized capital account and is conscious that such a condition is essential for membership in the European Union. However, having observed the experiences of a number of countries with capital account liberalization, we feel that we should proceed cautiously and not get carried away by the attraction of unlimited capital inflows. The implementation of sound and consistent macroeconomic policies, together with the attainment of a sustainable position on the current account of the balance of payments, are necessary preconditions for full capital convertibility. Thus before capital controls are completely relaxed, we will aim at achieving much more stability in our economy by first addressing the structural imbalances, particularly in the fiscal sector.

Following the revival of its application to join the European Union, Malta is currently undergoing a screening process prior to the commencement of negotiations for membership, which will probably start early next year. Our aim still remains to join the EU as part of its next enlargement process. In this regard, Malta is rigorously pursuing policies aimed at restructuring the economy in line with EU requirements. This includes the reduction of the fiscal deficit, maintaining public debt at a sustainable level, and keeping inflation in line with that of our major European trading partners. As part of an overall strategy, the Maltese government has reformed its tax collection strategies and reintroduced the value-added tax. It has also embarked on a program for the removal of government subsidies, the abrogation of protective levies, and the gradual abolition of monopolies, as well as the privatization of public sector enterprises. Privatization is expected to contribute positively to efficiency in the economy, and so it is the intention of the government to embark on a long-term program of privatization. A strategy document on the privatization process has recently been prepared with the assistance of World Bank experts, and this is expected to be presented for discussion in parliament in the next month.

The small size and vulnerability of our economy necessitates constant vigilance and an effective economic strategy to counter external shocks. We recognize clearly the need to upgrade continuously and strengthen our economic structures in order to compete effectively in the international environment. However, while the main focus of our attention is our own internal development, we are concerned about the plight of the highly indebted developing countries and are willing to support all measures that contribute toward their developments particularly if this takes the form of debt relief or concessional finance.

In this regard we are pleased to observe that the Interim and Development Committees of the Fund endorsed a strengthening of the current framework of the Initiative for Heavily Indebted Poor Countries to provide deeper debt relief in a way that strengthens the incentives to adopt and implement economic and social reform programs, and provides a clear exit from unsustainable debt burdens.

We also noted with satisfaction that this item stood high on the agenda of the Cologne Summit of heads of governments of the Group of Seven countries in June 1999, which pledged their full support to this initiative. On its part, Malta despite its limited resources has agreed to contribute to the HIPC Initiative by contributing the balance held in the second Special Contingent Account, after having made these funds available as an interest-free loan for the past two years.

Malta has always sought to contribute to such Fund assistance programs and, in the past, has granted credit at low interest rates to the ESAF subsidy account. We are also satisfied that the Fund has agreed to provide contingent credit lines as a new instrument of crisis prevention for member countries with strong economic policies, when faced with potential balance of payments problems from international financial contagion.

In conclusion, I would like to thank the managements and staffs of the Fund and Bank for their continued support and wish them all success in their operations. Finally, I would like to express my country's appreciation for the assistance and advice that is provided throughout the year by the Executive Directors who represent Malta on the Boards of the Bank and the Fund.

Statement by the Governor of the Fund for Mauritania

Mahfoudh Ould Mohamed Ali

I am honored to speak today on behalf of the Governors representing the Arab members of the World Bank Group and the International Monetary Fund, and I would like to begin by extending my congratulations on your selection as this year's Chairman of the Boards of Governors.

At our Annual Meetings this year, we are pleased to note the success that the international community has achieved in containing the adverse effects of the series of financial crises that caused great damage to the economies of Southeast Asia, then spread to Russia and a number of Latin American countries, in particular Brazil. The people of these countries witnessed a large reduction in the growth rates of their economies, a significant increase in unemployment, and a sharp decline in their standards of living. Yet despite all these difficulties, the Asian countries affected by the crisis diligently implemented ambitious reform programs aimed at restructuring their economies, and within a relatively short period of time, succeeded in restoring confidence in world financial markets and achieving positive real growth rates. Brazil also implemented a difficult structural reform program, which helped restore stability to its financial markets. As for Russia, we hope that the authorities will proceed quickly to implement the comprehensive reforms necessary to revive the economy. The situation has also improved in other parts of the world, such as Japan, whose economy shows signs of recovering after a long period of stagnation, and Europe, where economic growth rates are expected to increase. In the United States, the economy continues its exceptional performance, accompanied by general price stability.

Yet despite the recent marked improvement in the world economic environment, a number of latent dangers remain that could hinder continued increases in world economic growth in the foreseeable future. These dangers are largely related to an expected slowdown in the American economy. The international community hopes that other regions of the world, particularly Europe and Japan, can achieve sufficient increases in the growth rates of their economies to compensate for the slowdown in growth in the United States and ensure continuation of the current revival of the world economy. At the same time, we are aware that this reform process could also result in great fluctuations in the prices of the principal currencies, which could pose a threat to the soundness and stability of world financial markets. This danger will increase if the expected slowdown in the U.S. economy occurs suddenly, as a result of overly strict monetary policies enforced by the authorities or a sudden correction in the stock market, among numerous other factors that affect the U.S. economy.

It goes without saying that the international community places great importance on the economic policies adopted by the major industrial countries, given their tremendous effect on the degree of stability that will accompany the expected reform of the world economic system. We therefore call upon these nations to adopt appropriate policies to protect the world from the latent dangers currently facing the world economy. We call upon the U.S. monetary authorities to follow closely developments in the stock market and take them into consideration in determining monetary policies. We hope that the European authorities will hasten to intensify structural reforms, especially in their labor markets, to stimulate growth in their economies. In Japan, it is hoped that the authorities will continue their expansionary policies to stimulate growth of the country's economy while continuing to implement important structural reforms in the banking sector, which have recently begun to produce positive results.

I would now like to turn to a discussion of the initiatives proposed to strengthen the international monetary and financial system, in order to control outbreaks of future economic crises and the adverse effects that they produce. We wish to assert first of all that, while we acknowledge the advantages of the globalization of financial markets and its effect on developing countries through the transfer of private capital and support of their development efforts, we must also acknowledge that the recent financial crises warned the international community of the dangers of premature capital account liberalization in developing countries, as well as the importance of strengthening the financial and banking sectors to ensure that they are well established, before proceeding to liberalize the capital account.

We support the efforts of the Fund to assist member countries in controlling short-term capital flows, which we believe played an important role in the outbreaks of recent financial crises. We also support the Fund's efforts to create mechanisms to help reduce dependence on these flows as a source of financing, and to stimulate long-term capital flows, especially those related to foreign direct investment.

We call on the Fund to expand and complete its study concerning systematic capital account liberalization in order to help developing countries determine the appropriate pace for liberalizing their accounts, and to take appropriate measures to maximize the benefits obtained from capital inflows and reduce the possible adverse effects upon their economies. It is important to take the particular circumstances of each country into consideration in determining the appropriate pace and phases for liberalizing their capital accounts.

We welcome the efforts of the Fund and the World Bank to help developing countries strengthen their financial and banking sectors, and we call on them to give greater importance to technical assistance in this area, focusing on the establishment of adequate precautionary measures to help the economies of these countries absorb the shocks that may result from fluctuations in capital flows.

We also welcome the Fund's increased interest in developing and publishing internationally accepted economic regulations and standards, while we stress the importance of taking into consideration the particular circumstances of each member country and how they affect its ability to comply with these standards. Technical assistance from the Fund is necessary to help member nations publish and comply with the standards that are applicable to them, although we have some reservations concerning attempts to make the Fund responsible for monitoring the application of standards not directly related to its area of specialization. We would also like to mention the strong interest of the Arab countries in improving the management methods of their public and private institutions, and in taking the required measures to comply with the principles of transparency and accountability.

We applaud the efforts of the Fund to get the private sector involved in reducing the likelihood of future financial crises and sharing the burden of handling such crises when they occur. It is also important to improve surveillance of the international activities of private financial institutions in the advanced countries, and to require these institutions to publish accurate data on their activities, in particular their high-risk activities.

The Arab countries support international efforts to reduce poverty and improve living standards among the world's poorest. The assistance provided to the poorest countries by the countries and institutions of our region testifies to the importance we attach to this goal.

We support in particular the international initiative to reduce the debt burden of low-income countries, and we welcome the recently proposed measures to increase the amounts of assistance provided and to accelerate the delivery dates, while strengthening the link between debt forgiveness and the requirement that countries take the necessary steps to reduce poverty within their borders. We also support the recommendation of the Group of 24 concerning the future expansion of this initiative to include highly indebted countries with mid-level incomes. We believe that the World Bank should take the leading role in implementing this initiative, as it is the institution with considerable experience in developing and implementing social policies aimed at reducing poverty. Close cooperation between the World Bank and the Fund is essential in order to distribute the tasks appropriately on the basis of each institution's area of specialization, to ensure that the objectives of this initiative are achieved in the optimal manner.

The success of this noble initiative naturally depends on its receiving adequate funding. We support the international financing plan that includes selling a portion of the Fund's gold reserves and investing the proceeds of the sale. A large number of Arab countries, both oil producers and non-oil-producing countries, are willing to help finance this initiative to the extent they are able, while maintaining the financial soundness of the Arab funds and other institutions concerned.

As was the case in other regions of the world, the Arab countries did not escape the adverse effects of the financial crises of 1997 and 1998. The decline in world demand for oil and the sharp fall in prices led to a marked reduction in resources available to the governments of the oil-exporting Arab countries and a corresponding reduction in their economic growth rates, especially in 1999, despite the fact that oil prices began to rise again last March. Although oil prices have risen lately, their actual levels still remain below the average rate over the past 10 years.

The oil-producing Arab countries have confronted this significant decrease in revenues by intensifying their efforts at economic reforms aimed at reducing the deficits in government budgets and the balance of trade, by reducing expenditures, diversifying the sources of government revenue, and privatizing public projects. They have also increased their efforts to diversify the base of economic activities to reduce the effect on their economies of fluctuations in world oil prices. These efforts have included additional structural reforms aimed at encouraging private sector participation in various economic activities, including such infrastructure components as communications, electricity generation projects, water systems, and construction and management of airports and seaports, in addition to attracting foreign investments. At the same time, a number of oil-producing Arab countries are making concentrated efforts to develop financial market systems in order to increase participation by foreign investors.

The adverse effects of the successive world financial crises have not spared the non-oil-producing Arab countries, which have witnessed a general reduction in capital inflows and demand for their exports, along with a significant increase in the size of their imports, owing to the fall in prices of imports from the countries hit by the crisis. These developments have had an adverse effect on the balance of payments in many countries of the region, although the economic reform policies and structural reform programs being implemented in these countries since the beginning of the decade have helped to reduce the severity of the effects of the world financial crisis upon them. These policies and programs, which are currently being intensified, have produced a marked improvement in the investment climate in these countries, which has in turn helped to increase private sector participation in economic activities. Important progress has also been made in privatizing public enterprises in many Arab countries, and private sector participation in various infrastructure projects has increased in a number of sectors. The banking sector in many Arab countries has been developed by strengthening bank supervision systems and updating regulations for trading in the stock market, to achieve the required transparency.

Regional cooperation among the Arab countries was enhanced last year, as a reduction of customs tariffs was implemented within the framework of the Greater Arab Free Trade Zone agreement, starting in January 1998, to stimulate development in the Arab countries. Partnership agreements were also signed between a number of Arab countries and the European Union, which we hope will help attract investments to the region and increase exports from Arab countries to foreign markets.

I would now like to discuss a number of topics that concern the World Bank Group. The past fiscal year was characterized by a continued improvement, both quantitative and qualitative, in the Bank's activities. Loans and credits increased compared to the past year, and a larger percentage of projects achieved their development targets. Agreement was reached last year concerning the twelfth increase in the resources of the International Development Association, and the Bank's net income also increased.

Last year the World Bank Group participated in confronting the current challenges on a number of levels. Loans and credits increased considerably compared to amounts granted during the past two years, and assistance has been focused on promoting policies of reform and open markets, supporting the private sector, and providing relief to the poorest sectors of society. Borrowing countries in our region obtained loans and credits for projects in critical areas including human resource development, management systems, the agricultural sector, social services, and water resources. The Bank also provided technical services and sponsored research aimed at developing various aspects of economic and financial policy and benefiting from the exchange of experiences. The International Finance Corporation and the Multilateral Investment Guarantee Agency also continued their activities focused on supporting the private sector.

We applaud these efforts and call for a continued focus on assistance in priority areas for the borrowing countries, as well as expansion of the World Bank Group's activities to include countries that have not received assistance from the Bank for many years. We also call for continued assistance to the Palestinian Authority to develop its infrastructure and improve the living standard of the Palestinian people, as well as technical assistance to the non-borrowing Arab countries. We hope that the International Finance Corporation and the Multilateral Investment Guarantee Agency will likewise expand their activities to include a wider range of beneficiaries.

With respect to the policies of the World Bank Group in the foreseeable future, we call for increased efforts to reduce poverty, given the limited success that has been achieved to date, and a focus on long-term projects, along with continued efforts to achieve tangible results through development activities and projects. We call for efforts to reduce the debt burden of the largest number possible of low-income countries and assistance to developing countries—including Arab countries—to help improve their position in the upcoming trade negotiations in Seattle. With respect to the Comprehensive Development Framework project, we would like to see a verification of its feasibility at the trial stage, with due consideration given to the particular circumstances and degree of readiness of each country. As for the Bank's financial situation, we commend the negotiations currently being conducted by the Executive Board and the Development Committee, and we look forward to the recommendations they may produce for strengthening the Bank and its financial position.

We applaud all these positive developments and the efforts of the World Bank Group in a period of difficult and complicated world circumstances. At the same time, we wish to emphasize that the principal objective of the Group—the reduction of poverty—remains a distant goal, especially in light of the recent financial crises that have increased the number of the world's poor and greatly reduced economic growth rates in the developing countries, in addition to the destruction caused by armed conflicts and natural disasters. These challenges will require greater efforts and additional resources, directed in particular at the low-income developing countries.

The Arab countries look forward to playing an effective role in helping the international community to confront the many challenges that face it. The Arab countries—like all the developing regions—have met with great difficulties as a result of the financial crises that recently shook the world economy. We are still suffering from weak economic activity, the slow improvement of social conditions, and continually increasing unemployment rates, in addition to the most severe water crisis of any region in the world. Furthermore, the peace process continues to constitute one of the principle obstacles to achieving greater economic development and creating a suitable environment for investment.

In conclusion, I would like to express my appreciation to the Executive Directors of the Fund and the World Bank for deciding to hold the Annual Meetings for 2003 in Dubai, in the United Arab Emirates. These meetings, the first ever to be held in an Arab country, will enhance the position of the Fund and the World Bank in the Arab world, which over the years has demonstrated its commitment to international cooperation in all forms and all fields.

STATEMENT BY THE GOVERNOR OF THE BANK FOR MONGOLIA

Yansanjav Ochirsukh

It is a great privilege and pleasure for me to represent the government of Mongolia at the fifty-fourth Annual Meetings of the Boards of Governors of the World Bank Group and the Fund, here in Washington D.C.

Economic recovery in the transition economies has been mixed during 1999. Most of the countries of the Commonwealth of Independent States and those in southeast Europe have been experiencing a lower economic recovery in relation to the central European and Baltic countries, which clearly demonstrates that growth is achieved when there is progress on structural reforms. Rapid disinflation has been achieved by many of the transition economies, which has been possible because of the timely strong stabilization support package of the international communities. Growth has been generally fastest in the areas where reforms were most far reaching and bolder. The countries in transition had the benefit of a relatively large agricultural sector and rural labor surpluses. There has been a mixed approach on the methods of privatization, but all agree that there is no alternative to privatization. Regarding banking sector reform, transition economies have set a priority for improving corporate governance, prudential regulation, and supervision. Countries have now begun to realize the potential of the underground economy, which in some countries amounts to more than 20 percent of GDP. Excessive regulatory discretion, weak rule of law, and corruption are perhaps common to the transition economies. All the growth witnessed by these countries has been accompanied by an increase in income inequality and social instability. The vital steps needed for the creation and strengthening of legal, fiscal, and regulatory infrastructures are needed for the operation of a market-led economy. Let me now discuss my point on how Mongolia is performing within this framework.

The Economy

For three consecutive years, Mongolia has been experiencing an annual growth of 3–4 percent. The year 1998 was hard on Mongolia because of a steep decline in key export commodity prices and the deepening of the regional financial crisis. Copper prices plunged 42 percent in 1998 and 17 percent in the first quarter of 1999. In addition, the international prices of gold and cashmere dropped, resulting in a terms-of-trade shock of about 9 percent of GDP. This has resulted in a chain of deterioration in other sectors of the economy. External shocks led to a large cut in fiscal revenue and resulted in the widening of the fiscal deficit to over 11 percent of GDP. The adverse external conditions and resulting fiscal stress strained Mongolia's financial system. The increased deficit plus reduced foreign financing sharply increased the domestic bank financing of the budget and put upward pressure on interest rates. The bank loan portfolio performance deteriorated as a result.

Despite all the adversities at the end of 1998 and the beginning of 1999, Mongolia managed to achieve a growth of 3.5 percent and a sharp decline in inflation from over 53 percent in 1995 to single digits in 1998. With little prospect for significant improvements in the terms of trade over the medium term, the government has embarked on a strong adjustment program: to maintain inflation at a low level of below 10 percent, to promote sustained growth of about 4–5 percent, and to strengthen Mongolia's external position with the assistance of the second Fund-supported program under the ESAF. The parliament of Mongolia has approved a fiscal policy package designed to progressively reduce the government deficit through a reduction in the net bank credit to government, a consolidation of price stability, and the freeing of additional resources through the privatization of remaining public assets; the government will thus be better positioned to promote the fragile private sector. The government has also moved to address financial system distress by placing three insolvent banks under conservatorship and taking a whole set of measures aimed at bank restructuring.

Social Issues and Structural Adjustment

Consolidating price stability and achieving economic growth closer to Mongolia's potential will be essential to improving living standards and reducing poverty. For the purposes of improving the social safety net, the government enacted the law on social safety nets early this year. A Mongolian proverb called the plentiful life states, "a country prospers when its citizens prosper." The government recognizes the need for health care reform in order to improve the efficiency of public health services. The introduction of the health insurance system is easing considerably the budgetary burden of health care. Reforms in the pension system are being undertaken as well. It is the aim of the government to improve the financial position in these sectors, first by the introduction of cost recovery measures, and later by putting them on a sounder financial footing.

Governance Reform

A new Public Sector Management and Financial Act awaits parliament decision. The act would introduce a new framework to rationalize government functions and improve the delivery of public services, and is aimed at enhancing the accountability of all budgetary entities while increasing their flexibility. The public sector reform will help significantly in the reengineering of the Mongolian public sector. Over a 10-year period, it is expected that the pilot administrative reforms and the public financial reforms will undoubtedly lead to significant economic and social benefits for the whole country.

Environmental Issues for Sustainable Development

Extensive livestock production supports at least half the population, and since 1990 it has become the social safety net of last resort. Pasture land is now under severe pressure because of overconcentration of herds around urban centers. Effective policy interventions are needed to alleviate rural poverty, tackle pressure on grazing land, and ensure natural resource conservation and sustainable development. It is necessary to develop land management practices, clarify the land law, promote alternative income-generating activity, and rehabilitate the local infrastructure.

Potential for Future Growth

Mongolia has a tremendous growth potential, despite its obvious disadvantages. In many ways, Mongolia has only scratched the bottom of the mountain. Regional integration is in the interest of the whole economy. Beyond better exploiting its comparative advantages, Mongolia needs to invest more resources in its people, as the education of its people is essential in today's high-tech age of globalization.

The years 1999–2002 are crucial to enhancing Mongolia's economic stabilization and establishing a strong foundation for future development. The major economic objectives of the Mongolian government over the medium term are to enhance further macroeconomic stabilization, intensify structural reforms in the economic and social sectors, institute the private sector–led economic structure, and on this basis, rapidly develop export-oriented production and increase domestic savings. With all these challenges ahead, we are approaching the new millennium. Over the past few years, we have learned that a good deal of judgment is involved in preparing monetary and fiscal programs under the ESAF. In rapidly changing economies such as ours, and where the global environment is also rapidly changing, it is impossible to derive truly scientific and precise performance criteria, the lack of which will lead to substantially worse outcomes in terms of inflation, interest rates, exchange rates, and international reserves. Therefore, on the behalf of the government of Mongolia, I would like to ask the senior management of both the Bank and the Fund to be lenient and flexible with Mongolia and not to impose conditions that will be too tough or unnatural to meet. We have noted that the Fund has demonstrated these qualities in the past with Mongolia as well as other countries, and therefore request that the Fund continue to be flexible over the course of the ESAF-supported program, the second year of which commenced in June 1999. Transitional economies, including that of Mongolia, are receiving handsome assistance from the donor countries and multilateral financial institutions. However, the utilization of these funds remains a sensitive issue in these countries. In order to avoid the duplication of funds in the sectors of the economy, we would be encouraged by continuing support from the Bank. In June, Mongolia successfully organized the seventh donor's conference, held for the first time in Ulaanbaatar, the capital of Mongolia. In fact, the successful outcome of the conference, the donors' willingness to assist, and their commitment are based, in part, on the tremendous efforts of the Bank staff. In conclusion, I would like to take this opportunity to record our heartfelt gratitude and appreciation for the willingness of the Bank and the Fund to support Mongolia in its critical period of transition.

STATEMENT BY THE GOVERNOR OF THE BANK FOR MYANMAR

U Khin Maung Thein

On behalf of the Myanmar delegation, I wish to join my fellow Governors in expressing our sincere thanks to the management and all concerned in the Fund and the Bank for their excellent arrangements in convening the Annual Meetings. May I also congratulate you, Mr. Chairman, on your election as Chairman of these important meetings.

First of all, may I touch upon Myanmar initiatives for economic development. As you are aware, since late 1988, after introducing the market-oriented economy, concerted efforts have been made for the development of Myanmar's economy, and achievements have been made in implementing short-term and long-term plans. Necessary fundamental reform measures were instituted in line with the political, economic, and social objectives laid down by the state, and in line with these objectives, with national perspectives, administrative and international relations are embodied in it. Our ultimate goal is to build up a new modern developed nation in accordance with the new State Constitution. While adopting a market-oriented economic system and by undertaking measures systematically for national reconciliation for the emergence of a peaceful and stable nation with disciplined democracy, Myanmar is determined to build a democratic system in accordance with our culture, traditions, and historical background, as well as the desires and aspirations of the entire people. Necessary policy guidelines have been put in place to ensure adequate basic human needs, such as food, clothing, shelter, and to improve the living standards of its entire people. As agriculture is the base in building the national economy, entrepreneurs are encouraged to engage in cultivating vacant, virgin fallow lands and wetlands to increase agricultural production on a commercial scale with the use of their capital, management skills, and technical know-how. They are urged to increase sown acreage, boost per acre yield, upgrade the quality of crops, and double or triple cropping with that momentum. On the other hand, conventional cultivation methods have been substituted with modern scientific techniques, and the state has also been providing the necessary farm implements and machinery. Moreover, dams and reservoirs are being built all over the country with our own financial resources for sufficient water supply in the dry zone area.

Myanmar is striving to develop its national economy not only in the agricultural sector, but also in promoting industrial development by establishing industrial zones throughout the country. Entrepreneurs are encouraged by the government to increase output and improve the quality of products, aiming toward import substitution. We have recognized that the forces of agriculture and industrial sectors should be combined for national development. To meet this harmonious effort for combination of these two sectors, the state has laid down the following objectives for the industrial sector:

- to develop agro-based industries;
- to raise the quality and quantity of industrial products;
- to produce new machinery items;
- to produce machines, parts, and tools for industries; and
- to obtain good foundations for turning the country into an industrialized nation.

Myanmar has been endeavoring to develop her economy in conformity with the market system to meet the basic needs of the people and maintain environmental norms all over the country. A Bank mission visited Myanmar in June, and during its stay, fruitful discussions were made between the Bank mission and responsible officials from respective ministries, and some mission members visited areas related to their assigned duties in the fields of health, education, and infrastructure development in relation to poverty alleviation.

I would like to reiterate that, as you are quite aware, in the past year, I have presented our intention to cooperate with the Bank as before. However, one year has elapsed, and we do not have significant progress toward a normal relationship between us. Myanmar has been a legitimate member of the Bank and the Fund since 1952. As a legitimate member, Myanmar is fully eligible for the Bank's development assistance. However, the Bank has neglected Myanmar's development efforts, and it has failed to assist Myanmar for the past 12 years—even though we have cooperated with the Bank and the Fund and have been servicing our outstanding payments to the Bank regularly, up to the end of 1997. We are still looking forward to having close cooperation and coordination for our mutual benefit. As they are multilateral institutions, we expect them to have a full understanding of our endeavors and achievements, with constructive views and an optimistic outlook for a brighter and better future.

In conclusion, I wish to express our deep appreciation and best wishes to the Boards of Directors, the managements, and the staffs for their valuable contribution to the Annual Meetings. Let us move forward to shape a better future of peace and prosperity in the next millennium.

STATEMENT BY THE ALTERNATE GOVERNOR OF THE BANK FOR NEPAL

Ram Binod Bhattarai

It is indeed a great pleasure and privilege for me to address these Joint Annual Meetings of the Board of Governors of the World Bank and the International Monetary Fund. On behalf of the Nepalese delegation and on my own, I express sincere appreciation to the people and the government of the United States for their hospitality and to the Bank and the Fund for the excellent arrangement made for these meetings. Let me also take this opportunity to congratulate the management and staff of the Bank and the Fund for their able and close partnership in managing the financial turbulence in East Asia and other parts of the world. As a member of these institutions, it is a matter of great satisfaction to note that these institutions have served their members well at the times of greatest need.

The slower growth witnessed in recent years in the world output in general and that in the developing world in particular has become the serious concern of the developing countries, the affected economies and the international community as a whole. However, the growth outlook for 1999 has improved moderately. These outcomes have a direct bearing on the growth and development prospects of developing countries. The hopes that we had while the Uruguay Round Agreements were signed are still to be felt by many of us. Many countries are yet outside the realm of the World Trade Organization. Some industrial countries need to fulfill their global commitments toward easing the constraints of international trade and development. The progress in poverty reduction is not satisfactory to all of us. A lot more needs to be done in safeguarding the acute needs of small and least developing countries like ours. There are, however, some indications of a positive nature. Recent recovery in international commodity prices and of East Asian economies as well as positive growth outlook in industrial countries present some hope for the revival of the global economy and, in turn, increase in development assistance.

We are now at the verge of next millennium, whereby globalization of markets has provided both opportunities and challenges to all of us, for promoting growth, equity, and development. Many small and poor countries have not been able to reap the benefit of globalization. Therefore, greater attention is needed, particularly by industrial countries and international institutions to create an enabling environment that can take care of the interests of the poor and least developed countries.

Our experience has shown that, unlike the developed countries, developing countries need a relatively long transition period to fully realize the benefits of economic liberalization. Developing countries, including Nepal, have a hard time making the process of liberalization a widely beneficial phenomenon to the society as a whole, at a time when we are faced with a huge agenda of institutionalization of the democratic process and heavy burden of external debt servicing.

The transfer of official development assistance to developing countries has not shown any serious move toward the tune of international call and our appeal for many years. The relevance of foreign grants and highly concessional assistance for the growth of developing countries is still very important and appears to remain so for a number of years to come as many of these countries have to develop key sectors of the economy, where the private sector is still shy in making investments.

Having said that let me turn to the Bank- and Fund-related matters. It is very much encouraging to learn about the progress made by the Bank and the Fund in strengthening the international financial structure. We welcome the initiative taken by the Bank and the Fund in reducing the unsustainable debt of heavily indebted poor countries. We note the Bank and the Fund are currently working for an enhanced framework for faster, deeper, and broader debt relief of the poor countries. We support additional financial assistance from the donors toward this framework. Similarly, further considerations should be given to include the poorest countries, which are being presently excluded from these arrangements.

The Bank and IDA deputies deserve our special thanks for the successful conclusion of the twelfth replenishment of IDA. We stress that the Bank Group should focus IDA lending to those countries where the need is greatest to meet the needs of the poor and least developed countries. It should also focus on the environment-related issues, which the private sector is least capable of addressing.

We are encouraged by the Bank's activities focused on flexibility, change, and partnership to serve its clients better in the days to come. In this regard, we believe that the Comprehensive Development Framework would prove to be a vehicle for sustainable growth. We understand that this process is based on a holistic approach to development and recognizes the importance of institutional, structural and social aspects of the development along with macroeconomic fundamentals.

We appreciate the strategy of making ESAF arrangements a central point of the poverty reduction program and the Fund's efforts to help member countries in handling structural and institutional reforms. The role of IMF in strengthening the financial sector and the establishment of the Contingent Credit Line would help attain the objective of a more sustainable growth in member countries.

Now let me turn to my own country, Nepal. Nepal is a landlocked country in South Asia, which has not so far been a party to either any miracle or debacle. The country's per capita income is one of the lowest in the world and more than two-fifths of its population are living in a state of absolute poverty. The average growth rate of GDP during the past two years was estimated at slightly above 3 percent against the target of 6 percent average growth as set forth by the Ninth Plan (1997–2001). The ratio of gross domestic saving and investment of GDP is still very low. The rate of inflation crossed single digit and reached almost 12 percent toward the end of the last fiscal year. The deteriorating performance of the agricultural sector despite the highest priority assigned to it has been the major factor for the grave situation of poverty in Nepal. The unfavorable climate, uncertainties in economic reforms, slowdown in resource utilization, and increased fiscal imbalances are considered as responsible factors for slowing economic activities. The balance of payments situation, however, has improved, basically due to better performance of the export sector and the decline in imports. As a result, the foreign exchange reserve, at present, is at comfortable position.

After the restoration of democracy in 1990, people's expectations rose to a new height. The impressive economic progress made in the first half of the 1990s could not be sustained during the past four and half years due to the political instability that transpired from the nature of the composition of the last Parliament. As a result, considerable slackness surfaced in the economy, and the utilization of resources including external resources slowed down. In the aftermath of general elections held in May 1999, the present government has come to power by holding a comfortable majority in the Parliament. Taking into account the overall performance needs in various fronts of the economy, the new government is committed to creating a strong macroeconomic situation. In this regard, the balance of payments position continues to be strong, inflation appears to be moderate, and economic growth picked up slightly from the last years' depressed level. The actions of the government have been well sequenced to alleviate widespread poverty and unemployment. On the fiscal side, revenue growth has increased in the past few months and the fiscal deficit has been kept within the affordable limit. The government is also fully committed to resume the process of liberalization as was initiated in the beginning of this decade.

Nepal has put a poverty reduction agenda always at the forefront. For this, we have focused on achieving a high economic growth rate, expanding social and safety programs, encouraging participatory development, and ensuring good governance. In order to achieve these, we have adopted strategies of the modernization of agriculture, rural development, community participation, and creation of employment opportunities. Likewise, other strategies have been developed for the development of social and economic infrastructure, better mobilization and use of economic resources including external resources, and promotion of private sector development. This will be achieved through continued persuasion of economic reform programs and the transformation of the development administration into a service- and result-oriented one. Various measures are adopted to strengthen the institutional capacity of project implementation. The civil service reform process is on the way. The government has also adopted various measures to make its affairs more transparent.

Implementation of the 20-year Agriculture Perspective Plan (1997–2016) has been our priority in order to increase economic growth and alleviate poverty. We have emphasized the development of the social sector and increasingly allocated financial resources for education, health, drinking water, and human resource development. The empowerment of women is one of the prominent agenda of our development. The process of privatization of public corporations has been reactivated.

We consider financial resources as the most effective and critical means of development and a major instrument of the success of policy implementation. We are committed to manage public expenditure more efficiently. Prioritization of the development expenditure is being further improved and projects are selected based on cost/benefit analysis, availability of sustainable resources, and implementation capacity. The new financial rules formulated with a view to reduce discretionary power in awarding contracts and ensure transparency of statements and records as well as develop a time-bound decision-making system are already in operation. In order to enhance the effectiveness of overall resources, Aid Receiving Strategy is being formulated and enforced within this fiscal year.

The need for internal resources mobilization is enormous in Nepal. The structure of the tax administration is being reviewed to raise its quality of performance. The value-added tax system has been fully implemented as the main instrument of revenue mobilization. Tax and customs administrations are being made more transparent and supportive. A system of regular and continuous dialogue with the private sector is being developed in order to generate mutual confidence and enhance tax collection. Customs administration are being made more efficient in line with the requirements for membership in the World Trade Organization, the South Asia Preferential Trade Arrangement, and the South Asia Free Trade Arrangement.

Currently, we are actively engaged in the devolution of power to local government bodies. The process of decentralization has achieved its milestone as the Act relating to it has come into effect. The Act provides extensive economic, administrative, and political power to local authorities. The new arrangement would also address issues of governance throughout the country. Similarly, the government has launched several programs for urban sector development. In this regard, our capital city, Katmandu, has been facing an acute shortage of drinking water supply for over a decade. In order to solve this problem, we have proposed the Melamchi Water Supply Project for donors' assistance. I, therefore, take this opportunity to thank the donors for their support and commitment to this project and would appreciate any additional assistance to meet the financial gap and for the speedy implementation of the project.

It is important for us to build on the achievements made in the past and also continue to address necessary issues that stand as hurdles along the path of poverty alleviation and sustainable development. The current year's budget and the Ninth Plan have placed clear directions for reforming policy course. We believe that greater efforts are essential to enhancing domestic resource mobilization and improving public resource management. Another equally important task is to build technical and institutional capability in order to prepare and implement complex and sweeping reforms over a broad front and prevent potential crisis.

It is a matter of common experience of developing countries like Nepal that no matter how important the reform process may be, it invariably encounters a great resistance and the process itself is long and painful. In order to overcome these difficulties while we, as a member of developing countries, have to put all our resources in achieving the development goals, the continued support of bilateral and multilateral agencies would be required more than ever before. I would also like to emphasize the importance of sequencing reforms as a critical factor in making the reform program a success.

The role of the Bank and the Fund in the twenty-first century will be even more challenging. We are confident that the Bretton Woods institutions are better prepared to surmount such challenges and will continue to remain as reliable, flexible, and dynamic development partners for their member countries in the new millennium. We are thankful to the international donor community for its consistent and strong support of Nepal's economic development programs. I would like to mention here that Nepal Aid Group Meeting would be held in March, next year in Paris. As in the past, we are confident of receiving the strong support of the members of the Nepal Aid Group to implement our development programs. Let me express our sincere appreciation to the Bank and the Fund for providing valuable technical and financial cooperation to our development efforts. I look forward to rewarding partnerships with these institutions in the future.

STATEMENT BY THE GOVERNOR OF THE BANK FOR THE NETHERLANDS

Gerrit Zalm

The recent international financial crisis clearly demonstrated that improvements must be made to enhance the effectiveness and the fairness of the international monetary and financial system. Already, the system has been made more open and transparent. The Fund deserves praise for the role it has played in the development of international transparency standards and the promotion of the implementation of these standards. However, I think we should be more ambitious. I have three particular areas in mind in which work remains to be done: the involvement of the private sector in financial crisis prevention and resolution; the strengthening of the Bretton Woods institutions; and the HIPC Initiative and its financing.

Private Sector Involvement

On private sector involvement, in the absence of a set of clear internationally accepted rules on how to promote private sector involvement, the Fund has proceeded on an ad hoc basis. Although this approach succeeded in securing private contributions to the funding of members' financing gaps, the approach carries a number of risks. First, this is not very transparent, making the pricing of debt difficult. Furthermore, considering every case on an ad hoc basis might also lead to unequal treatment of countries as well as of creditors. While recognizing that every crisis situation has its own specific characteristics, I see a clear need for establishing some general principles and instruments for the involvement of the private sector in international financial crises. A key principle is that of equal treatment. Therefore, the following instruments should remain on our agenda: collective action clauses, creditor committees, and the use of rollover options in debt contracts.

The Fora: International Monetary Fund and Interim Committee

I now turn to our institutions. Recent experiences have clearly shown us how important it is to have strong Bretton Woods institutions. The Fund should remain at the heart of the international monetary and financial system. By combining wide membership with well-defined procedures for representation through constituencies, the Fund and its fora are better suited than any informal or ad hoc grouping to discuss and decide on matters relating to the monetary and financial system. The participatory nature of the decision-making process in the Fund guarantees ownership of and accountability for Fund policies with all IMF members. I welcome the fact that the role of the Interim Committee as the preparatory body for the Board of Governors has been reconfirmed. Improving the preparation of the Interim Committee by Interim Committee deputies on an as-needed basis can contribute to this. Further strengthening could take place through the creation of working groups of flexible composition under the Interim Committee, with the appropriate participants being selected on the basis of the topic under consideration.

Capital Adequacy and the World Bank Group

Let me now turn to the World Bank. Unfortunately, progress with respect to strengthening the financial position of the World Bank Group has been limited since the spring meetings. Naturally, the need for an increase in its risk-bearing capacity and its size are directly related to the IBRD's strategy. We are not in favor of a strategy that takes the excessive liquidity support of the past years as a starting point. I would sympathetically consider proposals for additional capital for the World Bank Group, including the IFC, if this is needed for a strategy aimed at long-term structural development and poverty alleviation.

ESAF and HIPC

It is of central importance to develop a concept of economic growth that is centered around durable poverty reduction. In that respect, I warmly welcome the enhanced link between debt relief and poverty reduction as exemplified in the new HIPC Initiative. It should therefore come as no surprise that the Netherlands supports the proposed modifications of the HIPC Initiative with the purpose of providing wider and deeper debt relief while encouraging recipient countries to conduct good policies. We support the idea of using floating completion points, and stress the importance of including key social and economic reforms as conditions for completion. It is of the greatest importance that we maintain the focus on good policies in the modified HIPC Initiative and secure full and equitable financing for debt relief quickly, so that the road to sustained growth and poverty reduction in highly indebted poor nations is cleared. In this respect, I hope that improved cooperation between the Bank and the Fund takes off. Better quality and depth of the Bank's poverty analysis should help the Fund to adequately sequence and fine-tune macroeconomic stabilization policies. In addition, the financing of the self-sustained ESAF deserves the full attention of the international community.

Southeastern Europe

In addition to their tasks in promoting international financial stability and sustainable growth, the Bretton Woods institutions have an important responsibility to help members whose economies have been severely damaged by a war or natural disaster to get back on their feet. I welcome the efforts that have been made by World Bank and the Fund, in good cooperation with the EU, to help southeastern Europe overcome the hardship caused by the crisis in Kosovo. A combination of well-targeted international assistance and sound domestic policies should facilitate a speedy recovery.

Conclusion

The world economy is in far better shape than we could envisage last year. The Fund and the World Bank have played a key role in this improvement. I trust that under the leadership of the President and the Managing Director, the Bank and the Fund will continue their further work on the various issues that I have outlined. Rest assured of the continued support of the Netherlands in doing so.

STATEMENT BY THE GOVERNOR OF THE FUND FOR NEW ZEALAND

Sir William F. Birch, M.P.

I am pleased to be speaking at these Annual Meetings of the World Bank and the Fund in very different circumstances to those of last year. Twelve months ago, this felt like a crisis meeting. It was crucial that we endorsed open market fundamentals and that we resisted the urge to return to protectionism. The international institutions held their nerve, member nations held their focus, and we are better off for it. Last October, consensus forecasts were for New Zealand's top 10 trading partners to grow by only 1.4 percent in 1999. Now, those forecasts are more than double at 3.2 percent. Given that our top four trading partners are the United States, Australia, the European Union, and Japan, that is a good sign that the world economy is improving, and it is definitely good for New Zealand.

The Article IV staff report on New Zealand publicly released on September 16 projects growth of 3.3 percent in our economy for the next two years. We are confident those forecasts can be bettered. New

Zealand is one of a growing number of countries participating in the pilot program where the Fund staff report is made public. The release of staff reports will increase the need to have confidence in, and justification of advice by, the Fund. Similarly, if a country is not following advice recommended by the Fund, the authorities of that country will have to justify their reasoning to the public. The advantages of open disclosure are equally true with respect to World Bank advice. There is the potential for publication to reduce the frankness of discussions and the candor of the staff reports. However, New Zealand's experience with giving policy advice that is subject to the freedom of information laws is that transparency does not substantively alter advice—rather it increases incentives for advice to be of the highest quality. And the sound policies that transparency encourages have real payoffs for people.

Without reform, the impact of the Asian crisis on New Zealand would inevitably have been high interest rates, serious bankruptcy, and massive unemployment. A policy framework of five principles—an open and competitive economy, low inflation, quality fiscal policy, flexible labor markets, and low taxes—has allowed the economy to cope with shocks and to keep making progress. Our own bounce back from the Asian crisis has been rapid and sustainable. Economic reform has made New Zealand the master of its own destiny. Our future is no longer tied to any one market or to surviving any particular shock. Our future is with the world. As a small economy, our domestic market is limited to 3.8 million people. But no matter the size of any economy, the global market is the real prize for us all.

That is why I was so pleased with the outcome of the recent meeting of APEC leaders in Auckland. In New Zealand, APEC leaders reconfirmed their commitment to achieve their goals of free and open trade and investment for the developed APEC economies by 2010 and the developing ones by 2020. Many of those economies, including our own, are already making substantial steps to remove all tariffs. APEC wants to conclude an agreement in the WTO this year on the Accelerated Tariff Liberalization Initiative, which includes fish and forest products, and launch at the Seattle WTO ministerial a new round of multilateral trade negotiations for comprehensive market access, including the abolition of export subsidies. That is to be concluded in three years.

In conclusion, I would like to make the following observations. First, despite the severity and depth of the recent economic crisis, few if any economies resorted to protectionism to try to stave off its impacts. On the contrary, many responded by maintaining, if not advancing, their efforts to reduce barriers to trade and investment flows. Second, it showed the need for greater transparency and openness of markets, of policy settings, of rules and regulations, of standards, and of performance against them—including improved reliability and timeliness of information. Accountability is fundamental. If banks can make bad lending decisions with relative impunity from financial consequences, there will be no end to bad loans they make. The Fund has to be more than a financial bank. It should also be a knowledge bank—a provider and facilitator of surveillance, expert advice, and, even more important, an assurance of transparency. Third, countries faced with economic challenges can accomplish much on their own, but much more in cooperation with their colleagues. The crisis mobilized the international community like never before, and the fruits of that cooperation are already evident in the improved economic performance of many of the most affected countries. But the events of last year and the challenges we face today serve to remind all of us there are no easy answers to sustained economic performance and there will always be risks. Fourth, and finally, for the poorest and most vulnerable in our societies the continuing challenge is to work to ensure that they too benefit from sustained economic growth—in terms of their living standards, health, education, and overall quality of life. Building stronger economies through open and efficient markets is ultimately directed at that goal.

Statement by the Governor of the Fund for Norway

Svein Ingvar Gjedrem

It is my pleasure to address the 1999 joint Annual Meetings on behalf of the Nordic-Baltic constituency consisting of Denmark, Estonia, Finland, Iceland, Latvia, Lithuania, and Sweden, as well as my own country: Norway. The present meeting takes place in a more sanguine atmosphere than last year's. During the year, international financial markets have come closer to a state of normality and the economic outlook appears brighter in several regions. However, these encouraging developments do not leave room for complacency.

The financial crises in Asia, Russia, and Brazil have caused great hardship in the affected countries. Furthermore, a large number of smaller countries have experienced significant economic and financial stress during the last couple of years. Last autumn, the Russian crisis caused serious disruptions to international financial markets, which yet again demonstrated how national financial crises can have far-reaching and even global repercussions.

The Fund has played an important and positive part in the resolution of the recent crises. The fruits of this work can now be seen. The developments in Asia and Latin America are encouraging, although significant problems remain. Developments in Russia have been mixed. We should use the current "breathing space" to learn from the recent crises. We must take steps to reduce the likelihood of new crises, as well as to improve our handling of them. These topics will occupy the main part of my speech.

Crisis Prevention

The Fund's main role is to be the guardian of a stable international monetary and financial system. To this end, the natural starting point is to seek to prevent financial crises from happening or spreading.

The Nordic and Baltic countries fully support the work on a strengthened international financial architecture. We note with satisfaction that the recent crises have not, in general, led to the adoption of exchange restrictions or other steps that prevent efficient resource allocation. Instead, the focus has been on adopting positive rules to enhance the functioning of markets.

Improved statistics and more transparency should have a stabilizing effect on capital markets. Standards for economic policy will draw attention to necessary action for domestic policymakers, and make it easier for international investors to make informed decisions.

We favor a central role for the Fund in helping countries to open up their capital accounts in an orderly and properly sequenced way. The Fund should be given appropriate jurisdiction over the liberalization process. An opening of countries' capital accounts must be preceded by a strengthening of the domestic financial system, for example, through more information and improved regulation and supervision. Furthermore, liberalization must be accompanied by adequate macroeconomic and structural policies. However, liberalization of the capital account should, as far as possible, be synchronized with the liberalization of trade in goods and services. One-sided integration into the world markets may be destabilizing and increase exchange rate volatility. The new multilateral trade round to be launched in December, coupled with a strengthened international financial architecture, is important for the overall stability of the world economy.

International interbank loans with very short maturities played a major role in some of the problems in Asia. On the debtor side, the crises have revealed serious cases of deficient debt management, and we encourage the Fund to work with national authorities to improve debt management policies. The ongoing work on changing the Basle rules on capital ratios is also essential and should encourage more prudence on behalf of creditors.

The recent crises have yet again taught us the importance of solid macroeconomic "fundamentals." Large government deficits and a rapid debt buildup make a country vulnerable to changes in investor sentiments. When seeking to strengthen the budget, it is important to work on the expenditure side as well as the revenue side. With respect to the latter, we support the Fund's work aimed at making countries improve their tax systems.

The most appropriate exchange rate regime depends on the economic circumstances facing the individual country. However, experience reveals the risk of upholding a rigid exchange rate policy when there are underlying pressures in the economy and financial markets are characterized by rapid capital movements. Exchange rate pegs require a high degree of prudence in macroeconomic as well as financial sector policies.

The newly released report on the external evaluation of Fund surveillance is interesting reading. We would like to draw attention to the recommendation that the Fund put more emphasis on identifying macroeconomic vulnerabilities. An important part of the prevention policy is to identify which shocks are likely to arise and analyze how member countries can most effectively absorb these shocks. Moreover, as recommended in the report, it is important that the Fund strengthen its cooperation with other international financial institutions.

The lesson with respect to crisis prevention can be summed up in one sentence: Financial stability requires solid macroeconomic fundamentals and resilient financial markets. This message is not new. On the contrary! What is new is that liberalized capital markets and new information technology have increased the urgency of the message. The financial markets have become less forgiving.

The Fund's Lending Policy

Irrespective of the positive efforts aimed at prevention, the world will experience new financial crises in the future. The Fund is, and will continue to be, the major institution appropriate to address them. Therefore, we find it useful to raise a few key points about the Fund's lending policy.

The catalytic effects of the Fund's programs are of paramount importance. This requires that the credibility of IMF lending must not be undermined. Loans should only be extended to countries undertaking genuine and strong steps to solve their economic problems. The conditionality must not be weakened, even if the consequence, in some cases, may be that loans cannot be extended to countries experiencing serious difficulties.

In general, the Fund should put more emphasis on adjustment requirements. In particular, the Fund should not bail out governments running unsustainable deficits for extended periods of time. Support should be given only when the crisis country undertakes significant adjustment efforts and it is clear that the country has assumed "ownership" of the program. Increased attention should also be given to the use of "prior actions."

As part of a strengthened financial architecture, the Contingent Credit Line initiative should contribute to reducing the spreading of future crises. However, to achieve this, the facility must not create new moral hazard problems. It is important that the eligibility requirements be interpreted very strictly, that the countries involved conduct a firm and credible policy, and that serious steps be taken to involve the private sector. We note that this facility has, so far, not been used.

Moral hazard problems would be reduced if the private sector were involved to a larger extent in crisis resolution. The overriding principle should be that the private sector must be involved primarily on a voluntary basis. However, we believe there is a need to establish a framework that clarifies the roles of the various actors in international financial crises. It is important that transparent ex ante rules are instituted, leading to a strengthening of the pricing mechanism. The Fund has an important role to play in such a framework.

A number of countries have taken steps to stimulate long-term private sector involvement; for example, by establishing private contingency credit lines. The Fund should encourage countries to undertake such initiatives. The ongoing work to promote the establishment of creditor committees and the introduction of collective action clauses in bond contracts should be intensified. We support that the Fund follows a restrictive lending practice with the aim of involving private sector lenders. It is an often-raised concern that such steps would increase the cost of borrowing for emerging markets. We are not entirely convinced by this argument. First, the main aim must be to achieve a better pricing of international loans, reflecting the underlying productivity of capital. Second, if the steps lead to increased financial stability, the risk premium could actually fall. In sum, moral hazard problems and a tendency toward a reduction of the catalytic effects of IMF programs suggest that some adjustment of the Fund's lending policy is warranted. We should seek to tip the balance toward more adjustment and local "ownership" of the programs. Furthermore, we strongly support active steps to involve the private sector in the resolution of crises.

The HIPC Initiative

The Nordic-Baltic constituency supports the enhanced HIPC Initiative, as well as the proposal to put more focus on social reforms in ESAF programs. The ESAF/HIPC arrangement is an important tool for supporting macroeconomic reforms in the poorest member countries. We very much welcome the agreement in the Fund on the financing of the ESAF/HIPC arrangement. We appreciate that the gold sales are envisaged to be a one-time operation of a highly exceptional nature.

Final Comments

In the same way as "ownership" is important in individual programs, it is important that the global community assume "ownership" of the ongoing process in order to strengthen the international financial architecture. The participation of all countries in the work must be assured The constituency structure of the Fund and the World Bank safeguards this. We consider it vital that work on the architecture, to the greatest extent possible, be within the established framework of the Bretton Woods institutions. Furthermore, while preserving the principle of genuine participation of the whole membership, there is a strong need to consider how to strengthen the policymaking bodies of the Fund and improve their working methods. Progress in this area is crucial to ensure the continued leadership of the Fund in international monetary and financial matters.

The increased globalization has brought about a number of benefits but also a range of challenges. Recent years have seen an unprecedented number of countries experiencing economic and financial problems. The relative calm experienced during the past few months should not let us defer the difficult task of devising new and better rules for strengthening the international financial system and stabilizing the world economy. The Fund will play a key role in this endeavor.

It must be underscored, however, that the complexity and composition of the economic problems facing the world are such that increased cooperation is called for. The Fund must work closely with the World Bank, regional development banks, the Bank for International Settlements, and other institutions. The rapid changes in the world around us underscore the need to continue to adopt and reform the Fund. New challenges await us in the next century.

STATEMENT BY THE GOVERNOR OF THE BANK FOR NORWAY

Hilde Frafjord Johnson

It is a pleasure for me to address this forum on behalf of the Nordic countries. Last year I attended my first Annual Meetings as Governor. It was in the midst of the Asian financial crisis, and the meeting was overshadowed by the fear of international contagion. Even though a worldwide recession is no longer imminent, we must not relax our efforts to strengthen the international financial architecture to prevent similar crises in the future.

The international financial crisis opened our eyes. Not only did it illustrate the interdependence between developing and developed countries, it was also clear evidence that development is a multifaceted process, where economic, financial, structural, and social factors form a single, seamless web.

The World Bank President, Mr. Wolfensohn, expressed this eloquently in his address to the Annual Meetings last year, and he reverted to it in more practical terms when launching the CDF early this year. The CDF sums up the experience gained through decades of development efforts. Many have said that the messages of the CDF are not new. This is true. But the momentum, the concept, and acting on them would be. We should note that the CDF initiative came from an institution that for years had the reputation for being concerned primarily with economic issues, for paying too little attention to the social issues related to successful development, and for having a tendency to override local ownership. Now the tide is turning. The Nordic countries welcome the CDF. This initiative puts the country in charge of its own development and presupposes cooperation and coordination with the UN system and other development actors.

I want to give the Bank credit for refocusing its business and for its crucial role in initiatives such as the CDF and the HIPC debt relief mechanism. At the same time, I would urge the Bank management to make sure that new values and priorities are internalized by each and every staff member. It is important to remember that to the various stakeholders in the borrowing countries, it is the individual country director or task manager who *is* the World Bank. Furthermore, the skills mix of the Bank staff and the budget structure must be such that it is possible to deliver quality work on social aspects of development.

Changing an institution like the World Bank takes time. Changing the world is an even greater challenge. But that is really what we are trying to do. The responsibility for making change happen obviously does not rest with the Bank alone—nor with the Fund, or other parts of the multilateral system. These institutions have an important role in facilitating change, and constitute important fora where developing and developed countries can meet. But the prime responsibility lies with us, with the individual members of these institutions.

I dare say there is now fairly broad consensus—at least on a theoretical level—on what it takes to foster development. But what does it take to translate this into real change? This question deserves our full attention. We must get beyond the rhetoric and the good intentions. We must act.

And the climate for concerted action is promising. The international community is now discussing some fundamental issues that continue to hamper change. For a long time some of these issues were taboo, not to be mentioned aloud in international debates on economic development. And some of them are still controversial.

I am talking about issues such as governance, democratization, and respect for universal human rights. I am talking about moral obligations and solidarity between human beings—both at the national and at the international level.

The inequalities between rich and poor countries are paralleled by the inequalities between rich and poor people within a country. I would like to spend the rest of my address talking about the responsibility of the political and economic leadership in the poor countries—and the responsibility of the rich countries—to make the necessary changes happen.

Increased weight has been put on the individual country's own responsibility for its development. And this is crucial. It is basic psychology. We all need to be in charge of our own development. And countries are increasingly ready to take this responsibility. This was evident at a recent workshop in Stockholm a few weeks ago, where participants from Tanzania, Uganda, Vietnam, the Nordic countries, the World Bank, and the UN came together to discuss how to make partnerships work on the ground. However, focus on country responsibility does not mean that the rich countries can mind their own business from now on, and leave the whole process to the poor countries alone.

At the country level, it must be clear that ownership and responsibility do not only mean government ownership and responsibility. The leaders must have the people behind them. Democracy and development are inseparable. Economic reforms are necessary but not sufficient. Unless the political leadership is committed to fighting corruption and putting in place good governance, and unless people feel that their leaders represent them, sustainable development is not going to happen. Developing countries must continue their efforts to promote good governance and ensure respect for human rights.

I think we have made progress in improving our policies and actions when it comes to development assistance. We are concerned with local ownership and donor coordination. We have taken steps toward untying aid. We have come a little further down the road, but we still have a long way to go before what we say matches what we do.

I am referring in particular to the need to see aid policies and trade policies as a coherent whole. A globalized world offers many benefits, but there are also many countries, particularly the poorest ones, that have not yet been able to profit from this process. Unless we cease to treat development and international trade as two separate issues, we will never be able to integrate all the developing countries into the global economic system, and do so in a more just manner.

The marginalization of the poorest countries warrants exceptional treatment. I would like to quote from IMF Managing Director Camdessus' United Nations Economic and Social Council (ECOSOC) address in Geneva on July 5 this year: "The international community can (also) make a major contribution. The industrial countries could open their economies to all exports of the poorest countries, not only encouraging existing primary commodity exports, but—more important for long-term growth—creating the potential for new, more diversified, export production."

This leads us to one of the most difficult and challenging dilemmas of international development. How can we avoid a situation where ministers responsible for development cooperation, like myself, advocate more reasonable distribution of resources in fora like this, while other ministers restrict the import of agricultural products as well as textiles and clothing from developing countries? I am not pointing a finger at anyone in particular. I am afraid almost all of us are faced with dilemmas like this in our respective countries.

We, who are concerned with development assistance, must convince the rest of our constituencies that it is our common responsibility to do away with the injustice and suffering that poverty represents. Closing the gap between the "haves" and the "have-nots" *within* developing countries as well as *between* countries is a question of mindsets, morals, and ethics. It is very much a question of solidarity.

In an ideal world, each and every one of us would be eager to do something about poverty. Our motivation would be that we could no longer endure seeing another human being suffer. But even with a pragmatic and less altruistic view of the world, it is in our own interest to close the gap. The truth is that developing countries represent future growth for us all. And equitable growth means peace and stability for our planet as a whole.

STATEMENT BY THE GOVERNOR OF THE BANK FOR PAKISTAN

M. Ishaq Dar

It is a matter of privilege and pleasure for me to attend the Annual Meetings of the Fund and World Bank Group. This happens to be the last meeting of the present millennium. An eventful century is coming to a close and, in another 14 weeks' time, a new millennium with multiple challenges and immense promise will be ushered in. This meeting provides us with a unique opportunity to reflect back as well as look forward.

Looking back, one notes that despite the Great Depression, two World Wars, natural calamities, and ideological and territorial conflicts, the twentieth century has witnessed tremendous technological and economic advancement. Even the developing countries have experienced substantial economic progress. Notwithstanding these remarkable advances, the fact remains that one-third of the developing world's population is still caught in the web of abject poverty. As a matter of fact, poverty has started rising again in the wake of the East Asian crisis and the outbreak of conflict in many countries. Further, the economic achievements have not been without heavy cost. The pressure on global resources has intensified, reflecting the fourfold increase in the world population and the indiscriminate exploitation of resources, which has endangered the environment. Given these grim realities, there should be no doubt that the task ahead for the world community will be a challenging one, and we have to persist with rapid economic and social advancement while ensuring that the gains are widely and equitably shared and poverty is reduced in a lasting fashion.

We are entering the next millennium with an increasing emphasis on globalism and liberalism. It is no coincidence that the present century also began with similar circumstances: with freer movement of goods and services across national frontiers and economic thought dominated by market-based solutions. The current situation is, however, more complex, as it goes beyond the traditional areas of trade and commerce to new areas of finance, technology, information, communications, and similar fields whose global flows are expanding rapidly.

Most developing countries are responding to the challenges posed by globalization by liberalizing their markets and disengaging their governments from many economic activities. However, the unevenness of the starting point and the backlog of deprivation and inequity of the past decades are significantly constraining the developing world in benefiting from the gains of globalization. In fact, rapid globalization and integration is tending to enlarge the economic and social gap between rich and poor nations and make many economies fragile and susceptible to external shocks. Mr. Camdessus, the Managing Director of the Fund, in his address yesterday had urged that globalization be given a human face and its cost be shared equitably. To translate his hope into reality, the developed countries need to increase the concessional resource transfers to the developing countries, reduce their debt burden, and facilitate their access to the developed markets.

The turmoil in East Asia has taught us important lessons. We are now more aware of the various elements that are needed to reduce the severity of potential risks in the process toward liberalization: consistent macroeconomic policies, a sound and well-regulated domestic financial sector, and an appropriate contingency mechanism to deal with potential threats to sustainability of open regimes. On the latter point, as noted in the communiqué of the the G-24, the limited applicability of the Contingent Credit Line calls for a reexamination of all possible options, including consideration of a global lender-of-last-resort. We would also urge further analysis of the efficacy of specific capital controls and look forward to an early agreement on a comprehensive and structured framework for involving the private sector in crisis resolution. We hope that this will be done in a manner that does not cause widespread disruption, nor raise the cost of capital flows to developing countries. The Fund can play a crucial role in this endeavor as a facilitator of good relations of sovereign debtors with their creditors.

We welcome the new initiatives for strengthening the international financial architecture, especially as it relates to the intensification of work on social sector issues. In this regard, the recently developed proposals by the Bank and the Fund to strengthen the link between debt relief under the HIPC Initiative and poverty reduction, to judiciously blend policies of poverty alleviation with structural adjustment and other reform, and to transform the ESAF so as to give greater emphasis to poverty reduction, are especially noteworthy. We hope that the necessary financing for the enhanced HIPC Initiative will be forthcoming and that the funding embodies genuine additionality and does not come at the expense of non-HIPC developing countries. In this context, we are concerned about using IDA resources in any form to fund the initiative. While these developments are praiseworthy, we should not lose sight of the debt problems of low-income non-HIPC countries.

I also welcome the proposal of Mr. Wolfensohn, the President of the World Bank, for a CDF. This is a timely and useful concept that promises to ensure integrated and coordinated economic and social development policies in developing countries. We are watching with great interest CDF pilot countries and hope that it will be possible to apply the concept widely in the light of experience gained in those countries. It should be ensured that the adoption of this approach does not lead to burdensome conditionalities in program design. I may add that a similar approach has already been taken in Pakistan, where a comprehensive and integrated medium-term development strategy is being followed. The government of Pakistan has recently launched a long-term "Vision 2010" project, which, in addition to sustaining high levels of economic growth and financial stability, emphasizes social and human development, poverty alleviation, and good governance within an integrated and mutually reinforcing framework, with the active involvement of the community and stakeholders.

Let me now briefly comment on the economic situation in Pakistan. The comprehensive program of macroeconomic adjustment and structural reforms that was initiated by our government in February 1997 with the support of the international financial community had started to yield positive results. Economic growth accelerated, and inflation was brought down from double-digit to single-digit levels, against a backdrop of tight macroeconomic policies and the implementation of a number of efficiency-enhancing structural reforms. Unfortunately, the momentum of our efforts was derailed by the unavoidable events of May 1998 and its aftermath. However, I am pleased to note that, since those extraordinarily difficult times, we have been able to consolidate and build on our earlier gains and have succeeded in placing the Pakistan economy on a more sustainable growth path. Financial support from the international financial institutions has been reactivated, and we have reached agreement with the Paris Club and the London Club on rescheduling our external debt-service obligations. Indeed, in the current fiscal year, we have broadened and deepened our adjustment effort and strengthened our focus on poverty alleviation. Concurrently, we have taken steps to improve governance and ensure accountability and transparency. We firmly believe that the challenges of globalization, as well as those arising out of the low stage of economic and social development of the country, can only be met by significant improvements in governance.

STATEMENT BY THE GOVERNOR OF THE BANK FOR PAPUA NEW GUINEA

John R. Kaputin

The core mandates of the World Bank and IMF remain fully relevant and consistent with the objectives and requirements of the Papua New Guinea government. Papua New Guinea's immediate concern is with her macroeconomic stability objectives. Although many of our problems originated from sources beyond our control (the Asian financial crisis and several natural disasters), Papua New Guinea has not been assisted by external donor financing since 1997.

Consistent with the Fund's advocated policy prescriptions—but, I emphasize, prior to any Fund program—Papua New Guinea has set itself firmly back within a prudent macroeconomic policy framework. Fiscal tightening, fiscal expenditure control and monitoring, and the independent conduct of monetary policy have been reestablished since July 1999. In fact, our macroeconomic objectives in 1999 are probably more stringent than those that would have been set by the Fund had it been able to respond to our policy stance with greater speed.

Consistent with both institutions' mandates, we are also embarking on a rejuvenation of the structural reform agenda. For some years, structural adjustment has been progressing at a less than satisfactory pace. The implications of procrastinating with structural reform are evident in so many case studies today. Papua New Guinea does not intend to become one of these case studies.

Transparency of the reform process is a feature of paramount importance. Striving to achieve the control of corruption will allow fuller benefits to be enjoyed. In this regard the Corporate Governance initiatives of the World Bank are very welcome. I point out that the public sector, and in particular its interaction with the private sector, must become an important target area of Corporate Governance reform. Furthermore, while Corporate Governance comprises internal and external architectures, the external aspect has appeared within the practiced policy mandate of the Bank to date.

Capacity building within institutions is crucially important and a vital complement to the reform process if reform is to remain an ongoing string of events. As well, capacity of institutions will impact on the effectiveness of poverty-reduction efforts made by donors and sovereigns alike. Papua New Guinea must ensure that, in reestablishing macroeconomic stability and the process of effective reform, her institutions are less vulnerable to crises and more able to deal with Papua New Guinea's long-term development demands.

Papua New Guinea has a need for capacity strengthening in key institutions and has been lucky enough to receive expressions of interest from more than one donor in some areas. In other areas, such as road maintenance and rural development, Papua New Guinea is fortunate to enjoy the presence of more than one donor's interests. While it may seem desirable to receive such attention, a multiple of donors in one area puts a much greater demand on the capacity of institutions to coordinate and reconcile development effort. The Comprehensive Development Framework instrument would appear to be useful in this regard, and its development and use may hold benefits for many countries. I would like to encourage the ongoing work in refining this development tool.

Papua New Guinea has, relative to many less developed countries, a relatively diverse export product base. Our export range is almost entirely made up of mineral production (oil, gold, and copper) and agricultural commodities (coffee, oil palm, copra, cocoa, and timber). In 1998, agricultural commodities accounted for 28 percent of our export revenues, while 66 percent was accounted for by mineral exports, and the balance by marine products. It is clear then that commodity risk management is of great importance to Papua New Guineans. Much of our rural population relies on the production and sale of these commodities for its livelihood. As such, I am pleased that the President of the World Bank, in his address to the Development Committee, has committed the Bank to developing a framework for the development of a market-based approach to risk management.

Papua New Guinea strongly supports the Fund and Bank's objectives in addressing the debt burdens of heavily indebted poor countries. There are very real human consequences that need to be addressed. However, we do have very strong reservations regarding the possible sale of gold to finance the initiatives. Gold exports made up 33 percent of Papua New Guinea's export revenues in 1998 and were responsible for a significant portion of our fiscal receipts.

STATEMENT BY THE GOVERNOR OF THE BANK FOR PARAGUAY

Federico Antonio Zayas Chirife

It gives me great pleasure to address you on behalf of the Republic of Paraguay at this fifty-fourth Joint Annual Meetings of the World Bank Group and the International Monetary Fund. This is a particularly significant occasion for my country, as we wish to reaffirm here today that the Paraguayan people are committed to defending our republic's democracy and its institutions and are willing to undertake a successful structural transformation of our society and national economy. This will only be possible, however, if we can count on the full cooperation of multilateral organizations and friendly nations around the world. Viable reforms of economic systems require a climate of social, political, economic, and financial stability. Paraguay managed to overcome a difficult challenge to its institutions as recently as six months ago, and must now face another major challenge: the reconstruction of our country, a task that our government of National Unity has been focusing on since it took office. As the President of the Republic of Paraguay said at the recent United Nations General Assembly, "The government of National Unity today faces the dramatic challenge of rescuing Paraguay from its state of chronic economic stagnation and grave social inequality."

To gain a sense of my country's critical economic situation, consider that Paraguay's economy grew by 2.9 percent a year on average between 1990 and 1994, but by only 2.0 percent a year between 1995 and 1998. This clearly illustrates the slowdown in the Paraguayan economy, which is made worse by the natural population growth rate of over 2.5 percent a year on average recorded during the 1990s. We are aware that Paraguay's economy must attain higher growth rates in the years ahead, if it is to meet its social needs while maintaining political, economic, and financial stability.

Empirical evidence shows that those countries that have achieved economic success have done so in the context of free market systems, and, by generating sustained economic growth, have enabled large segments of the population to escape from poverty. We therefore wish to express our support for the poverty reduction and sustained growth initiative. We believe, moreover, that options for reducing or offsetting the effects of barriers to free trade need to be explored, and we wish to voice our disapproval of the use of agricultural subsidies.

Our challenge in this process is to overcome the manifold constraints that are seriously complicating our efforts to improve the welfare of our people. The government of National Unity has taken a historic step by forming a Cabinet representing different political groups and by recently forging a consensus on a medium- and long-term economic program designed with the participation of representatives of the various political parties, thereby ensuring that the members of the National Congress are committed to its implementation. Our government is striving to bring about a consensus on the pathways to reform and has reached agreement with the various political parties and the National Congress on a government program containing a substantial package of structural reform measures, which is in the process of being implemented.

My country's government has launched a frontal attack on corruption, as witnessed by the signing of a cooperation agreement with the World Bank and by tangible measures to combat smuggling and brand piracy, coordinated among the nation's various institutions with the support of the country's grassroots organizations.

A draft government banking reform law has been prepared, with a view to rationalizing the financial public sector and converting it into a unified, streamlined, and efficient entity.

As regards government expenditure administration, and with a view to improving and making efficient use of treasury resources, a draft financial administration law has been prepared, which seeks to modernize the current management of government expenditure and thereby establish more effective quality control over fiscal outlays. Moreover, the financial crises that recently shook world markets have undoubtedly left their mark on our small, open economy. This makes it imperative for us to join in the efforts of the Bretton Woods institutions to design a new international financial architecture that will help developing countries strengthen their financial markets and ensure their proper integration into the globalized world.

Now that 54 years have elapsed since the creation of the Bretton Woods institutions, and as a representative of one of their founding countries, I wish to state my conviction that these institutions must endeavor to maintain their effectiveness and their relevance as they pursue their objectives. We believe it essential that equity be included among the aims of the programs implemented and that the anticipated effects of international cooperation and partnership should materialize in a more favorable climate, so that our people can—in the not-too-distant future—begin reaping the benefits of their efforts. Adjustment programs must show their human face and must contain remedial social policies that mitigate societal differences.

We call for support and cooperation from multilateral organizations, in order to ensure the success of our economic revitalization and antipoverty programs, as such measures will be essential to strengthening our government's effort to sustain democracy.

In this context, we are heartened by the 1998 review of the Concordat, the purpose of which was to reconsider the principles of Bank-Fund cooperation and collaboration with a view to increasing the effectiveness of both institutions. The World Bank should be able to present us with various options for enabling it to maintain its financial capacity, in terms of the specific challenges facing its member countries, while safeguarding its net income.

Paraguay's present government has shouldered an immense historical responsibility, imposed by the heavy costs of the events in our country in March 1999 (*Marzo Paraguayo*). Furthermore, our government is committed to focusing its actions on implementing the structural reforms necessary to achieve sustained and sustainable economic growth through the development of a production framework based on competitiveness, with a view to fostering social progress for the Paraguayan people. The role of the state will be to promote the rationalization and redirection of government expenditure toward social sectors, investment in infrastructure, and the strengthening of the production sector. Also, our government's responsibilities include achieving qualitative improvements in poverty analyses, making it possible to direct government expenditure toward the specific objective of improving the welfare of our people.

In closing, I urge you to appreciate our government's desire to have an open and structurally coherent economy—an economy in which our leadership is committed to facilitating the attainment of economic growth in an environment of freedom and democracy, while advocating the balanced and reciprocal liberalization of trade and finance, so that we can usher in the new millennium with zero-inflation growth, fiscal equilibrium, and a dynamic and competitive private sector that responds innovatively to the challenges of competitiveness, technology, and efficiency, for the sake of all those who inhabit our land and who yearn to live in peace and happiness.

Statement by the Governor of the Bank for Peru

Victor Joy Way

It is a great honor and privilege for me to address this assembly as the representative of Argentina, Bolivia, Brazil, Chile, Colombia, Costa Rica, the Dominican Republic, Ecuador, El Salvador, Guatemala, Guyana, Haiti, Honduras, Mexico, Nicaragua, Panama, Paraguay, Spain, Suriname, Trinidad and Tobago, Uruguay, Venezuela, and my own country, Peru, on the occasion of the fifty-fourth Annual Meetings of the Governors of the World Bank and the International Monetary Fund.

Global and Latin American Economic Development

The countries of the region regard the slow but steady recovery of the global economy with hope and a certain measure of optimism. On the one hand, the United States continues to lead the world in economic growth, at the same time maintaining low inflation and a high level of employment. The European countries are showing signs of increased economic activity, Japan is emerging from recession, and the other Asian countries have succeeded in stabilizing their economies and resuming growth. The resurgence of these economies will contribute to renewed demand for our region's major exports and normalization of their international market prices.

Throughout 1999, the Latin American economies continued to be affected by deteriorating terms of trade and the reduction in capital flows that had begun in 1998. However, thanks to their sustained prudent policies and greater dynamism in the global economy, conditions have been created that can be expected to result in 3.9 percent GDP growth in the region in the year 2000. This achievement goes hand in hand with a continuing decline in the inflation rate. There can be no doubt that these improved prospects are ascribable to some extent to the positive developments in the economy of Brazil, which has managed, after a major effort, to reverse the conditions of uncertainty that prevailed a year ago and achieve a higher level of economic growth than initially projected.

On the other hand, elections are to be held in several countries in the region in 1999 and 2000. However, given the consolidation of our democratic systems and the fact that a consensus has emerged in favor of economic stability, we do not expect this heavy electoral calendar to be a cause of economic disruption. At the same time, we are aware that we are still at risk should there be adverse developments in the global economy—such as an economic slowdown in the United States. On this score, we take a positive view of U.S. preventive monetary policy measures, which will contribute to the stability of international financial markets.

The unforeseen, major shocks that many of our economies have had to contend with since mid-1997, not to mention the rapidity and extent of their contagion, have proved a sharp reminder that the individual countries, as well as the international financial system as a whole, need to strengthen existing preventive mechanisms. The Contingent Credit Line introduced by the Fund in April this year is a valuable tool in this regard, although we believe its design could be improved in certain respects.

This initiative, designed to prevent the contagion effects of international financial crises in countries that are following sound economic policies, is a major element in the new international financial architecture. Nevertheless, there is still no clear view in the markets as to whether a country's access to the Contingent Credit Line should be interpreted as insurance against risk, or, on the contrary, as a factor that increases the perception of risk and so adds to the country's cost of access to capital.

I would now like to review some of the key proposals for strengthening the international financial system and expanding the scope and coverage of the initiative to reduce the debt burden of the heavily indebted poor countries. Strengthening of the links between debt relief and poverty reduction, in the context of the programs the Fund and the World Bank provide for their poorest and most indebted member countries, is of particular importance to several of our countries.

Strengthening the International Financial System

Given the globalization of international capital markets, it is difficult to imagine a system in which private operators would not play an important role not only in the prevention but also in the resolution of financial crises. Our countries support the initiative calling for voluntary participation by the private sector in the resolution of international financial crises, and in doing so wish to reiterate that it is necessary to exercise caution in designing and implementing the arrangements through which such participation would materialize. In our opinion, creditors should participate on a voluntary basis and in their own best interests; steps should be taken to minimize possible adverse effects on the risk premium applied to the developing countries; and the mechanism should be sufficiently flexible to accommodate the varying circumstances surrounding the issue of debt instruments by private entities.

In this process, the Fund must help seek solutions that will be viable for both sides and not impose any one specific solution on private creditors. The proposal by the industrial countries to incorporate provisions in bonds that would facilitate their restructuring is a positive initiative that should first be adopted in the developed countries, in both the public and private sectors, so as to establish a new standard. Nevertheless, until conditions such as these prevail in the market, it is likely that this clause would adversely affect the access of developing countries to the international capital market.

The countries in our region approve of the efforts to strengthen the international financial system by going beyond the Basle standards. Nevertheless, the role to be assigned to risk assessment agencies must be approached with extreme caution, and care should be taken in general to ensure that the measures do not affect our countries' access to international markets or the costs they incur in the process.

On the subject of choice of a particular exchange rate arrangement, our position is that countries are entitled to opt for whatever exchange system they consider best suited to their needs. The experience of our countries has demonstrated that the most important factor is the fit between the country's economic policies and the exchange system that it has chosen.

There is general consensus that the process of capital account liberalization should follow an ordered sequence so as to minimize risks like those stemming from the contagion effect of crises originating outside the particular country. Our countries stand to benefit from the opening up of the capital account, as long as they follow sound macroeconomic policies and move ahead with essential structural reforms, including stronger financial system regulation and supervision. The Bretton Woods institutions should continue assisting those countries that require it to strengthen their public administration and the institutional framework through which such policies and reforms are implemented.

Linking the HIPC Initiative to Poverty Reduction

The countries in the region have consistently supported proposals for providing substantial debt relief for the heavily indebted poor countries. Consequently, we regard as very important the proposal submitted at the G-7 meeting in Cologne, calling for an increase in the scope and coverage of debt reduction for the HIPC countries; it is also essential, therefore, that the necessary financing be provided.

The countries in our region are making considerable efforts to contribute to this financing, not only through the multilateral institutions, but also in some cases by reducing the official debt of countries that have qualified for HIPC assistance—as Brazil has done. Some of the non-HIPC countries in the region should join in a plan to share the cost of such financing equitably.

In this connection, we wish to express our concern regarding the financial stability of the regional multilateral institutions, whose commitment to the HIPC Initiative could jeopardize their continuing role in financing development projects in the countries of the region. There is also some concern regarding the financial position of the World Bank and IDB, which are facing serious problems in financing their participation in the enhanced debt relief framework. In our view, the main source of additional financing should be the bilateral contributions from the countries with the largest economic capacity, particularly those that took the lead in enhancing the HIPC Initiative.

The countries in our region applaud the Fund's efforts to find a creative solution to the problem of selling 14 million ounces of its gold reserves by employing a procedure that takes account of both the legitimate interests of gold-producing developing countries, and also the need to secure adequate resources to enable it to contribute to the enhanced HIPC Initiative. The region welcomes the joint efforts of the Fund and the World Bank to strengthen the links between debt relief and poverty reduction, in the context of the economic programs introduced under the HIPC Initiative. But we wish to emphasize that this is an instance of cooperation between two institutions with different mandates. The Fund should continue to concentrate its experience and expertise on issues relating to the macroeconomic stability of its member countries, while the World Bank should focus on development, including poverty reduction. The countries in our region agree that it would be very difficult in practice to include specific social indicators in the quantitative and structural targets in Fund programs in general, although we acknowledge that, in HIPC countries, substantial progress on social issues and poverty reduction should form part of the final objectives of the Initiative.

The Peruvian Economy

I would now like to refer to the economic situation in Peru. Fiscal stability and monetary prudence, combined with the ambitious program of structural reform that has been implemented over the present decade, have enabled Peru to reduce its inflation rate from 7,600 percent to the level of about 4 percent projected for this year. The stability thus achieved has created favorable conditions for sustained economic growth, spurred by private investment and exports. Over the past five years, annual GDP growth has averaged 6 percent.

This year, despite a continuing deterioration in the terms of trade and reduced capital inflows, we expect increases in output to reach 3 percent, with 5 percent in the year 2000. From 1993 to 1999, exports doubled, thanks to a sound macroeconomic base and maintenance of a floating exchange rate. The current account deficit has been narrowed, and this year it should be reduced by approximately 4 percent of GDP. It has been financed by the long-term private capital associated with investment projects resulting from the government's commitment to macroeconomic stabilization and the adoption of measures to strengthen the existing legal framework, which is clearly favorable to domestic and foreign investment.

We have been able to deal with the adverse external events that have affected our economy since 1998, including El Niño, because of the soundness of the economy and maintenance of both a prudent level of international reserves and a strict framework of regulations and prudential supervision. It must be emphasized that the level of international reserves is more than enough to cover short-term debt and future external debt maturities. However, the shocks we have had to face have resulted in a slowdown in domestic demand and in tax collection. As part of the process of approving the budget for the year 2000, the government has announced austerity measures to improve its fiscal position and foster the necessary conditions for the recovery of private sector activity.

Peru's economic progress has brought about substantial advances in poverty reduction and improvements in the living standards of its people. I must emphasize how important it has been to win a victory over terrorism and finally establish peace with Ecuador. These events have been especially significant in improving the prospects for investors and, above all, in enhancing the welfare of our citizens.

Over the past decade, Peru's achievements have been substantial, consisting of economic stability, domestic and international peace, and integration into the global economy. We have established the basic conditions necessary for Peru's sustained growth over the coming years, providing opportunities for all its citizens within a market economy based on private investment, this being the foundation we are endeavoring to consolidate.

The great challenge of our time, and our principal national objective—the aim upon which a consensus must be reached by all social and productive sectors and all political groups, regardless of any ideological considerations or circumstantial disagreements—is poverty reduction, or, in other words, an increase in wealth through the creation of productive employment throughout the country. All our efforts are directed toward this basic goal and should continue to be directed toward it, with increasing determination.

The challenges facing Peru are to achieve growth, which is first and foremost equitable; to develop a market-based economy; to strengthen democracy and institutions; and to guarantee access to health care and education for all. In Peru, we have taken up these challenges with the same earnestness and conviction that have characterized the country's performance over the past decade.

I wish to express the appreciation of the Peruvian government for the efforts of the Fund, and particularly the work of Michel Camdessus and the President of the World Bank, James Wolfensohn, and for the support that both institutions have provided for the economic and financial policies that the country has pursued since 1991. This year, Peru has signed a new three-year Extended Arrangement with the Fund, a fact that confirms the county's commitment to macroeconomic stabilization, reaching beyond the approaching elections.

The approach of the new millennium, and these Annual Meetings of the Fund and the World Bank, provide an appropriate time for us to renew our faith in a higher destiny for all the men and women on this planet. The twenty-first century will find Peruvians working and helping build a more humane and just world.

Statement by the Governor of the Bank for the Republic of Poland

Hanna Gronkiewicz-Waltz

I am honored to participate in the Annual Meetings of the International Monetary Fund and the World Bank taking place on the eve of the new millennium. The turn of the century is an excellent opportunity to sum up our recent accomplishments and to set clear objectives for the future. After the latest financial crises that so strongly affected many countries of Asia, Latin America, and Europe, the global situation is gradually stabilizing, although its far-reaching effects will persist for a long time. However, that does not mean that the most serious problems faced by an ever-increasing number of the poor of our planet are vanishing. We welcome the fact that international financial institutions attach growing importance to the problem of poverty.

The discussions on the necessity of reforming the international financial system and creating a basis for new international financial architecture are already bringing noticeable effects. Our viewpoint is that capital flow liberalization, in combination with the implementation of adequate and rational fiscal and monetary policies, can contribute to foreign capital inflows—to an increasing extent from private sources—which are essential to achieving fast, sustainable economic growth. However, because of a huge volume of daily capital flows, the question of liberalization needs to be considered with due care, as free capital can be a source of potential turmoil in international financial markets. Poland actively takes part in all discussions on these subjects, taking the view that the most important question is the actual implementation of internationally accepted standards of conduct that may be instrumental in alleviating problems related to the flows. A decision to join the Fund's operational budget on September 1, 1999, was our practical contribution to increasing the Fund's lending capacity.

Within the process of strengthening financial systems, we attach great importance to the analyses and assessments made by the Financial Stability Forum. Its works on capital flows, risk related to excessive short-term debt, and the role played by international financial organizations able to exert political and economic influence will significantly contribute to the implementation of a reasonable policy in all areas relating to a stable financial system. We believe that the forum should take into consideration the opinions of as many countries and international institutions as possible. The first-hand experience of the emerging markets affected by the recent crisis and, to an even greater extent, of the ones that have managed to withstand it can undoubtedly heighten the effects of the actions undertaken by this body.

One of the key elements in the process of strengthening the international financial system and successful carrying out economic reforms is transparency of actions taken by governments and central banks. Disclosure of information related to fiscal and monetary policies enables the public to understand and evaluate financial policy as a whole, thus facilitating the authorities' undertaking actions leading to financial and systemic stabilization. It is obvious to us that only a credible information system can guarantee an effective execution of the economic policy. Since the beginning of the transformation process, Poland has conducted an open information policy, which has contributed to a successful implementation of the economic policy in our country.

For many years, preventing financial crises and alleviating their adverse effects have been the focus of attention of the international financial community and governments, as serious financial difficulties can turn at a fast rate into devastating economic crises. Investors very often include all emerging markets in the same investment risk group. A crisis arising in one country brings about deleterious consequences for others in the region, and owing to the contagion effect, an immediate foreign capital flight follows. We are glad to notice that at present much consideration is given to this question, but we believe that it should remain the center of attention.

We should also aim at increasing the involvement of the private sector in the process of preventing and overcoming a crisis. Cost sharing should be determined on a voluntary rather than obligatory basis. Emerging markets' governments should attach more importance to regular cooperation with the private sector on creating advantageous conditions for long-term foreign investment as well as to maintaining current contacts. The international community—especially international financial institutions and governments of the most developed countries—has a crucial role to play in the fight against poverty and in assisting the countries suffering from the effects of crises. We are satisfied with the fact that the terms of alleviating the poorest countries' debts under the HIPC and ESAF programs have been agreed. It is definitely a desirable step toward improving their situation and beginning the process of an economic revival. To support this valuable initiative, Poland has declared a 20-year interest-free deposit with the Fund and additionally declared 5 million SDRs.

However, it ought to be emphasized that the debt reduction itself, without a tailor-made assistance program for each country, will not yield expected results. Debt reductions should supplement and not replace assistance offered to help achieve economic development. We also need to be aware of a crucial task of determining the size of the necessary assistance and a period of time during which it is supplied. We should consider ways of providing political consulting on the steps that have to be taken by the local authorities toward opening the economy, administering public and assistance funds, and pursuing sound economic policy. Taking into account situations specific to individual beneficiaries, we can learn from the useful experience of the countries that have already gone through this difficult stage of their history. The Comprehensive Development Framework, presented by Mr. Wolfensohn, President of the World Bank, can be instrumental in pursuing this objective.

Another priority we must not fail to recognize is taking up a determined fight against a phenomenon of widespread corruption, which is one of major factors hampering economic and social development. Corruption diminishes the effectiveness of international assistance to the poorest countries, which, in extreme cases, can even be discontinued. However, applying only legal means in this fight is not sufficient. Such actions need to have strong political and social support. Eliminating the adverse effects of corruption on international financial and commercial transactions requires the close cooperation of developed and developing countries. In the ever-changing international situation, defining new forms of corruption as well as increasing pressure on applying effective means, which have already been used in numerous developed countries, of counteracting corruption at any level, should also be taken into consideration.

Poland is ready to combine her efforts with those of all the countries that are represented here today, and with the Fund and the Bank, to find the way out of the difficulties that still lie ahead of us to enter the new millennium with a more stable global situation.

STATEMENT BY THE GOVERNOR OF THE BANK FOR PORTUGAL

Antonio de Sousa Franco

Since our last meeting, global economic prospects and financial markets have improved significantly, mainly in the past few months, largely eliminating earlier concerns of a worldwide economic recession. We are especially happy with the right policies and international solidarity, which made possible the containment of the Brazilian crisis and the quick beginning of recovery in Brazil. However, all over the world, the recovery is uneven across regions and remains unbalanced among industrial countries, while developing countries are growing at a rate that is still insufficient to make a difference in the poverty situation.

You will understand, my fellow Governors, that for my country, the most important event in the past months is the referendum in East Timor and the following massive destructive actions. Let me pay homage to the brave people of East Timor, who in spite of risking their lives, gave to all of us a lesson of their firm commitment to take their future into their hands and pursue an independent democratic state. This was a first step in creating the necessary conditions for peaceful development within the country. Before initiating that process, however, peace, law, and order have yet to be restored and emergency assistance is extremely urgent, with the help of all friendly countries, all East Timor's neighbors, and the international community as a whole.

Looking toward the future, let me stress that, as the sources of financial instability subside and world recovery expands and takes root, it is our obligation to address urgently the needs of the poorest countries. Fighting against poverty is a long-term and complex process, and we can not afford setbacks and further marginalization of countries or groups of people within countries. We warmly support the proposals to enhance the HIPC Initiative and call for its effective implementation. Debt relief is just an instrument for achieving sustainable poverty reduction and development in a broader sense. What is needed is not just growth, but growth that creates jobs; eliminates inequalities of income and gives access to education, health, water, sanitation, and other basic services—in other words, growth that provides opportunity to all people. We have the political commitment, we have closer cooperation between the Bank and the Fund, and we need the means to translate our commitment to debt relief into results on the ground, under the leadership of recipient countries. Portugal has long been granting debt relief; it has already contributed to the HIPC Trust Fund, and my country stands ready to further contribute at a higher level of commitment toward this joint effort.

Development is a long-term, multifaceted, and interrelated process. It will require strong multilateral financial institutions, capable of—along with recipient countries and other partners—assisting countries in this process. The World Bank Group's financial situation has been put under some stress, and we have a responsibility to undertake measures to strengthen its financial capacity. We strongly support having an institution that is able to fulfill its development mandate and serve its members.

Globalization is a fact of life, but not all countries are taking part equally in this irreversible process, and inequality is an undesirable consequence of that. One way to help countries to become more integrated with the world economy is through participation in international trade. We concur with the proposed approach by the Bank to help developing countries to participate in the upcoming round of World Trade Organization negotiations.

It is time to rethink globally, on the other hand, a new financial architecture. Both the Bank and the Fund are moving in the right direction, but we urge all countries—especially the Group of Seven members—to quickly and globally rethink the current situation. Otherwise, new crises will certainly emerge out of the slow pace of reform. Deep and quick reform is not only needed by each one of our countries, it is also needed urgently by international institutions.

Before ending, I would like to return to my first topic: East Timor. We call for the international community to take firm action to restore peace, provide emergency aid, and contribute to the reconstruction needs of this devastated territory and people. We have to focus on immediate humanitarian needs—protecting and feeding displaced people, helping them return safely to what is left of their homes, preventing any recurrence of violence, reconstructing families and communities, and providing basic infrastructures. At the same time, we have the obligation—an obligation of solidarity—to begin the urgent and demanding process of reconstruction, and to help East Timor in building schools, health facilities, starting up economic activities, and setting up institutions and training people for a democratic and self-governed nation. Otherwise, words like democracy, human rights, law and order, social and economic development would become quite empty. As our institutions have shown in the past, and will show again in the future, cooperation for democracy and development shall be the right and urgent medicine for this situation.

STATEMENT BY THE GOVERNOR OF THE BANK FOR THE RUSSIAN FEDERATION

Viktor Khristenko

World Economic Outlook

Since our previous meeting last year, the global economic situation has improved substantially. Economic recovery in the countries hardest hit by the crisis came about faster than previously expected. Projections for growth in the Asian economies in 1999–2000 have been substantially upgraded, the economic downturn in Brazil turned out to be less serious than previously expected, and in Russia a return to economic growth that was interrupted in 1998 is now expected in 1999.

I would also like to mention the signs of economic recovery in Japan, which has been in recession for a long time. The stabilization of world commodity prices, together with increases in world prices for oil, have helped to improve the financial position of commodity exporting countries. The increase in capital flows to emerging market economies creates a background for stable economic growth in these countries over the medium term.

Despite the general improvement, however, the latest edition of the *World Economic Outlook* notes the remaining uncertainties and risks. In an environment where a slowdown in the U.S. economy seems unavoidable and the recovery in Europe and Japan remains problematic, it is not clear who will act as the "engine" for the global economy. Moreover, the long-standing divergence in growth rates among the leading industrial economies has already resulted in serious current account imbalances.

Crisis Resolution in Emerging Market Countries

In the Asian region we see a gradual improvement in the economic situation, which manifests itself in renewed growth and inflow of foreign private capital. This is particularly true of Korea and Thailand, which pursued the most steadfast and consistent policies in the period following the financial crisis. At the same time, these countries have not yet completed the complex structural reforms, especially in the banking and corporate sectors.

Economic contraction in a number of countries of Latin America this year is explained largely by the impact of the financial crisis in Brazil. On the other hand, the decline in output in Brazil itself was not as severe as had been previously expected. This was primarily the result of responsible macroeconomic policy and vigorous structural reforms carried out in the country, which made it possible to restore investor confidence quite rapidly. It is expected that in many Latin American countries there will be a resumption of growth as early as next year.

As far as the Russian Federation is concerned, we can already say today that the worst fears expressed after the severe financial crisis in August 1998 have not materialized. The policies of the government and the central bank largely stabilized the situation. Moreover, the devaluation of the ruble had a positive impact on the real sector. For example, in the first half of this year industrial output grew by 3 percent compared to the same period last year.

A reasonably tight monetary policy helped reduce inflation to 1.2 percent in August 1999, in comparison with double-digit monthly inflation last year. It is expected that this year, as a result of the devaluation of the ruble and higher oil prices, there will be a substantial improvement in Russia's current account (which is expected to reach a surplus of up to 14 percent of GDP). This, in turn, is stabilizing the central bank's foreign exchange reserves and the exchange rate of the ruble.

Noticeable progress has been achieved in the fiscal sector, which has been the weakest point in Russia's economic policy over the recent years. Tax and tariff collection improved significantly; in the first half of this year federal budget revenues exceeded 13 percent of GDP as compared to 11 percent last year. Moreover, all federal budget revenues are being collected in cash, since the practice of mutual offsets has been terminated. It is already clear that the federal budget primary surplus of 2 percent of GDP stipulated for this year will be successfully achieved. The draft federal budget for 2000 calls for an increase in the primary surplus to 3.2 percent of GDP.

Of course, many problems remain, especially on the structural front. We must complete the restructuring of the banking system, which was hard hit by the crisis. Strengthening payment discipline and reducing the degree of "barterization" of the economy continue to be among the most important objectives. The government and the central bank intend to address all these issues in close cooperation with the Fund and the World Bank. Currently, Russia is successfully implementing a Stand-By Arrangement agreed with the Fund.

Strengthening the International Financial Architecture

Increasing globalization of international capital markets is bringing new challenges to exchange rate regimes in emerging market economies. As the recent experience of many countries shows, defending the exchange rate with interventions counter to the market sentiment merely leads to rapid exhaustion of foreign exchange reserves. Many believe nowadays that the only choice for emerging market countries should be either a freely floating system or a currency board arrangement.

It is true that during the recent financial crisis, countries with currency board arrangements successfully defended their national currencies. They paid for this, however, with a loss of competitiveness, and an economic downturn. Meanwhile, some countries that were pursuing a more discretionary exchange rate policy managed to avoid both an economic downturn and a sharp depreciation of the national currency. These countries are known for their healthy macroeconomic situation and stable financial system, and also for a high level of foreign reserves, which significantly exceed their monetary base. It seems that precisely these factors also determine the stability of the currency.

Clearly, exchange rate stability is of great importance for robust development of the economy, since it reduces the degree of uncertainty for all agents. Successful management of the exchange rate, however, requires a whole range of conditions, such as a healthy macroeconomic situation, a strong financial system, and a high level of foreign exchange reserves. For emerging market countries where these conditions do not hold, it is better to adhere to a floating exchange rate policy. This is especially true for countries that are heavily dependent on world commodity prices, since a floating exchange rate makes it easier to absorb terms of trade shocks.

Liberalization of capital flows is useful and beneficial. At the same time, it does entail considerable risks and requires careful preparation. The main condition for success, in addition to general macroeconomic stability, is the need to have strong financial and banking systems backed by independent regulatory bodies. Prudential control of capital flows (especially short-term ones) are permissible, and in certain cases even desirable. The very term "orderly liberalization of capital movements" assumes the sensible use of restrictions and their gradual relaxation in line with the pace of economic reforms. The advisability of employing such restrictions is determined by a whole set of circumstances, such as the overall level of a country's economic development, depth of financial markets, state of the banking system, and so on. As noted in Fund reports, many countries view such restrictions as a useful instrument and their own experience in using these restrictions as an obvious success.

Moreover, interest in the experience of these countries has been growing lately. Therefore, we believe that there is a need to continue the studies of experience with using capital control measures. We are not opposed to amending the Fund Articles of Agreement to add the capital account liberalization to the Fund's objectives. At the same time, capital account liberalization should not become a condition for access to Fund resources.

The question of involving the private sector in forestalling and resolving financial crises is very important for strengthening the global financial architecture. We have no doubt about the need for the private sector to participate in the resolution of financial crises. At the same time, we believe that this is a very complicated task requiring a cautious approach. On the one hand, we understand the desire to work out a set of rules on this issue, which would both help reduce uncertainties on financial markets and provide for a more equitable burden sharing among various groups of creditors. On the other hand, any hasty and unwise steps in this area could lead to a drastic deterioration in borrowing conditions for emerging market countries. We would also note that some useful experience is being gained in this area now.

We also need to maintain an ongoing dialogue with representatives of the private sector. We need to explain that the Fund does not seek to impose specific parameters for restructuring private sector claims, and that the Fund simply evaluates the status of a country's balance of payments, while all decisions should properly be based on the outcome of negotiations between creditors and debtors. It is also important that the private sector not get the wrong idea that some specific decision taken with regard to one country or another will henceforth necessarily become a rule.

We support the transparency and international standards initiatives undertaken by the Fund to increase the degree of openness of its activities, as well as its relations with member countries. Substantial progress has been achieved in the development and implementation of international standards in the areas directly related to the Fund's mandate. We support the strengthening of the SDDS with respect to international reserves and external debt. We also believe that the codes of good practice for fiscal, monetary, and financial policies developed at the Fund will be very useful to countries working to strengthen their budgetary and financial systems. At the same time, we believe that the use of standards in the Fund's activities should be restricted to the analysis of progress achieved by the countries, and recommendations about further improvements; in no way should they be used to categorize countries for whatever purpose.

Cooperation Between the Fund and the World Bank

Successful cooperation between the Bretton Woods institutions is a crucial element of the international financial architecture. This cooperation becomes even more important during major financial crises. The Fund and the Bank are currently faced with a dual task: dealing with the aftermath of the crises and preventing contagion and recurrence. We are pleased to note significant progress achieved in this area. The Interim and Development Committees devoted much attention to the specific aspects of cooperation between the two institutions. This cooperation should be based on two fundamental principles—complementarity and avoiding duplication. On the one hand, each institution should focus on its own area of expertise; on the other, the knowledge and experience should be shared between the two and integrated into respective policies and documents. Contacts should be established at all levels of the hierarchy. In our view, the activities of the Financial Sector Liaison Committee of the Fund and the Bank may be viewed as a model for such cooperation. However, the mandates of the two institutions remain different. Specifically, national fiscal and monetary policies tend to affect the situation in other countries and regions. The Fund is thus charged with a special surveillance mandate. This function is not a part of the World Bank mandate, which is therefore not a standard-setting body. The Bank's role is to provide resources for development and poverty alleviation in developing and transition economies. The Bank's valuable role as a knowledge institution should remain client-driven and advisory only.

Initiative for Heavily Indebted Poor Countries

We support the HIPC Initiative and the reallocation of resources currently going to service external debt toward funding poverty reduction programs. The countries pursuing sound macroeconomic, structural, and social policies should be able to escape from the "debt trap" in the nearest future. The Russian Federation will continue to fully participate in operations to assist individual countries on the basis of the agreed principles of burden sharing. We particularly welcome the new emphasis on poverty reduction in the initiative design, which fits so well the Comprehensive Development Framework. However, our support for the expansion of the initiative is conditioned on its adequate financing. At the same time, we would welcome a compromise solution that takes into account budgetary and domestic political problems of individual donors and creditors. Firm donors' commitments can be combined with a more flexible schedule of actual payments.

STATEMENT BY THE ALTERNATE GOVERNOR OF THE BANK AND THE FUND FOR SRI LANKA

G.L. Peiris

It is a privilege for me to address the fifty-fourth Joint Annual Meetings of the Fund and the Bank on behalf of the government of Sri Lanka. Let me join my fellow Governors in congratulating you on your assumption of the chairmanship of the 1999 Annual Meetings.

World Economy and Policy Challenges

Global economic and financial market conditions have improved since the last Annual Meetings, allaying our earlier fears of a worldwide economic recession. Despite further prospects reflected by some factors, risks, and uncertainties remain high, posing challenges to policymakers. A major concern in this regard arises from the imbalanced growth pattern among major industrial countries, leading to persistence of macroeconomic imbalances and aggravating systemic risks for potential sharp corrections in response to reassessment of market confidence and monetary policy changes. Furthermore, net capital flows into developing countries and transition countries remain low and costly. The continuation of depressed nonfuel commodity prices creates terms-of-trade difficulties for commodity-exporting countries. Furthermore, potential reactions to actual or perceived Y2K compliance in the run-up to the year 2000 may create an additional risk factor.

These concerns underscore the necessity of strengthening macroeconomic policy coordination among the major industrial countries. Such policy coordination is also crucial to minimize sharp exchange rate fluctuations among major international currencies. Meanwhile, strengthening of noninflationary demand in industrial countries and further opening of their markets for developing country exports are necessary to create a conducive external environment for developing countries.

Let me turn now to my own country. Despite the adverse impact of international financial crises, Sri Lanka achieved 4.7 percent economic growth in 1998, reflecting improved resilience in the economy and the benefits of continuing prudent macroeconomic management. The policies in place and new policy responses could not eliminate the completely adverse impact of external shocks, but they mitigated the contagion effect to a large extent. The inflation rate further declined owning to improved supply conditions, lower import prices, and successful monetary management. The rate of unemployment continued its downward trend for the sixth consecutive year, reflecting expansion of job opportunities, mainly in the private sector. Investment has expanded, reflecting improved investor confidence. Domestic savings increased at a faster rate, reducing the investment savings gap. Even though export revenue has been affected during the first half of 1999 on account of depressed commodity prices in the international markets, economic prospects are now improving in the second half as expected.

The government has been actively pursuing its primary objectives, moving toward sustainable high economic growth, and ensuring the fair distribution of benefits of such growth. Improving macroeconomic stability, promoting private investment, strengthening international competitiveness, and addressing directly the problems of poverty and unemployment are the main elements of our strategy. Within this strategy, special emphasis has been placed on structural reforms in order to address deep-rooted growth-hindrance issues. In the political sphere, considerable progress has been made in building consensus among all parties on major issues addressed by the proposed constitutional reform package in order to find a political solution to the ongoing conflict. I greatly appreciate the increasing support of the international community for this difficult but necessary endeavor.

Bretton Woods Institutions

Turning to the Bretton Woods institutions, we commend their efforts to facilitate world economic recovery and to develop crisis-preventive and resolving measures. We appreciate the progress made by the Fund in improving the existing instruments and introducing new instruments, in order to provide faster and adequately necessary resources to crisis-affected countries. We also welcome the introduction of a facility to help members to meet their balance of payments need, related to Y2K compliance problems. My country strongly supports efforts for improving the effectiveness of the ESAF and enhancing the HIPC Initiative to provide deeper, broader, and faster debt relief. I am happy to state that my country has decided to make available its balance in the second Special Contingent Account as an interest-free deposit for the HIPC financing.

While noting recent improvements in the Fund's liquidity position following the quota increase under the Eleventh General Review, we underscore the necessity of early completion of the amendment to Article II for a one-time "selective" SDR allocation. We welcome the appointment of the Quota Formula Review Committee, necessary as it is to improving the quota allocation of the Fund by taking into account developments in the world economy. Given the increasing demand for the Fund's resources, an early resumption of new "general" SDR allocation under the current Articles of Agreement, giving due recognition to increasing the share of developing countries in the world economy, is also an essential step.

We welcome the Fund's efforts in expanding external evaluations to improve its surveillance and research activities. I am confident that implementation of constructive proposals in these evaluations will strengthen the Fund's surveillance activities and its role as policy adviser. While commending the successful accomplishment of IDA-12, I wish to emphasize the necessity of ensuring proper burden sharing in the mobilization of the required resources.

We appreciate the World Bank's efforts in poverty alleviation activities. However, we underscore the necessity of mobilizing a more bilateral contribution for financing the enhanced HIPC Initiative in order to ensure resource availability for the World Bank's normal development credit facilities. Given the increasing demand for World Bank resources, it is essential to explore all equitable options, including a general capital increase. I welcome the World Bank Group's innovative approach to facilitating and encouraging private sector investment in developing countries. We welcome the progress made so far on a number of fronts by the Fund and the World Bank in collaboration with other institutions in their efforts to strengthen the international financial system. However, I wish to reiterate the necessity of adequate and effective involvement of developing countries in this process in order to develop measures acceptable to all of us. We welcome the World Bank's increasing efforts, together with other international organizations, to provide the necessary assistance to strengthen institutional capabilities in developing countries to handle trade-related issues. Developing countries look forward to the outcome of the ongoing work of the task force led by the World Bank to formulate a new initiative for stabilizing and hedging commodity prices.

Statement by the Alternate Governor of the Fund for Switzerland

Kaspar Villiger

A remarkable change has taken place in the global economic situation since our meeting last year. The risk of serious slowdown has receded, and financial markets have calmed down significantly. In my statement last year, I cautioned that we should not overdramatize existing problems, but tackle them. Positive developments over the last year underscore that we have been quite successful. Overall, skillful economic management, implementation of ambitious structural reforms in many crisis-hit countries, as well as some progress in strengthening the international financial system are the main reasons for the improvement of the global situation.

This being said, we have no reason to be complacent. It would be a fundamental mistake to relent on our efforts to tackle the still remaining challenges based on improved circumstances. Developments in recent months have shown that financial markets can become volatile very quickly, given the remaining uncertainties. Abrupt corrections in exchange rates of major currencies cannot be excluded, given existing imbalances between major economies. Furthermore, the uncompleted agendas of structural reform in the banking and corporate sectors in many countries could become a serious source of concern in the event of a deterioration of the global economic picture.

To reduce further the risks of future financial crisis, we must continue with our endeavor to strengthen the international financial system. I am convinced that our efforts to date are beginning to bear fruit.

Significant progress has been achieved in the area of promoting greater transparency of members' policies and IMF advice. Article IV reports are being published by a large number of countries, and most members with IMF-supported programs are publishing their policy documents. Better-informed populations and market participants translate into less uncertainty and strengthened ownership of economic policies. I also commend the Fund for its efforts in establishing international standards and best practices in the areas of its core activities. The next step is to ensure the implementation of these standards and practices and monitor the progress. The Fund plays a key role in this area, given its universal membership and its surveillance mandate. In the context of standards, I also welcome progress made by the World Bank in the areas of corporate governance and social policies. Our experiences in recent crises have demonstrated how macroeconomic difficulties can be exacerbated by weaknesses in corporate governance. Furthermore, we have all witnessed the social hardships associated with economic crises. Therefore, defining and implementing standards and good practices also in these areas is important. A strong cooperation between the Fund and the World Bank will be crucial in this respect. We should continue our endeavor to make full use of the complementary nature of the two institutions and reduce work duplication.

We must continue our efforts to involve the private sector in forestalling and resolving financial crises. Progress has been relatively slow in this area because of the complexity of the issues involved. However, in my view, market participants have received the most important message, namely that private creditors should no longer be bailed out by official resources. Future policies will have to be based on the ongoing experience with specific cases of private sector involvement. This will allow us to develop consistent approaches over time. The private sector is only able to assess the risks of its lending correctly if the rules of the game are clear.

Let me now turn to the HIPC Initiative. Switzerland has strongly supported this joint IMF-World Bank initiative and has contributed generously to its financing. I welcome the proposals to enhance the current HIPC framework. Providing deeper and faster debt relief and strengthening the link to poverty reduction should help ensure that the stated goals of the initiative can effectively be reached. However, increasing the amount of debt relief and providing it faster will not be sufficient to do the job. Debt relief has to be accompanied by sound economic policies and a solid institutional framework that will allow the financial resources to be used effectively. This means an efficient tax system, a transparent budgetary process, and good debt management capacities. The enhancement of the HIPC Initiative has entailed a significant rise in financing costs. I am pleased that after a long period of uncertainty, a satisfactory solution could be found to secure the necessary financing. However, I would have preferred to see a greater share of the costs financed through bilateral contributions. This, particularly, given the forcefulness with which several major donors have pushed for enhancing the HIPC framework. I urge all members to ensure that their current pledges will result in effective payments. The HIPC Initiative is only one element in our endeavor to reduce poverty. I note with satisfaction that poverty reduction has moved to the top of our agenda more generally. I fully support the view that poverty reduction has to be the objective for all of our assistance and of our policy dialogue. I welcome the strengthened cooperation between the Fund and the World Bank to ensure that poverty alleviation is a priority for all the activities of both institutions with regard to developing countries. The proposed new Poverty Reduction Strategy Papers will be a useful instrument to concentrate the minds of the governments, the Fund, and the World Bank on this central challenge and to outline concrete action plans. It will be impossible to reduce poverty in a sustainable way without improving the quality of public governance. Strengthening public institutions and their partnership with civil society has to become an integral part of all World Bank projects and programs. All lending instruments should be analyzed as to their impact on strengthening institutions and as to their contribution to strengthening governance.

We must also continue with our efforts to reduce the scope of corruption. Such behavior has a negative impact on poor people's access to public services and results in an inequitable redistribution of resources. Specific anticorruption programs designed by governments should be fully supported by the Bretton Woods institutions in addition to improving the functioning of the public administration, increasing fiscal transparency, and improving the regulatory framework in general.

Another key element to fight poverty is the strengthening of the private sector in developing countries. It is urgent for the World Bank Group to create synergies in private sector development. A close look must be taken at the respective functions of the Bank, the IFC, and MIGA. The World Bank Group has to become more effective in supporting privatization; small, medium, and microenterprises; private investment in utilities; and linking the productive and the financial sectors. These are all essential elements for the future World Bank Group. They should be implemented urgently.

Let me conclude by thanking the staff and management of both the Fund and the World Bank for their commitment to the work of our institutions. I remain fully convinced that the Bretton Woods institutions with their well-established structures provide the best framework for finding solutions for the multiple challenges we are facing. Therefore, we must be careful not to undermine it by creating parallel structures. I can assure you that the Fund and the World Bank will continue to have Switzerland's full support.

STATEMENT BY THE GOVERNOR OF THE FUND FOR THAILAND

Chatu Mongol Sonakul

It is an honor for me to address the Bank-Fund Annual Meetings, which will be the last in this century. Looking back over the past years, there are many accomplishments that the two Bretton Woods institutions can be proud of. We have gained virtually universal membership. Economic development has kept a strong momentum, although disparity continues to widen between the developed and developing worlds. While we are witnessing many positive trends, large challenges remain for developing and transition economies as they enter the next millennium.

Global Economy

It is worth noting that the global economy is yielding surprises, recovering more rapidly than previously expected from the severe effects of the currency and financial crisis. The net effect of interest rate cuts in the industrial countries, fiscal stimulus in Japan, stabilization and modest growth of Asian imports, and improved financial conditions in emerging markets have been stronger than expected, leading to increased global growth forecasts. These events and trends have been bolstered by a number of positive developments, including the unexpected speed with which some larger developing countries are adjusting to adverse shocks, the stronger-than-expected Asian recovery, the continued strong performance of the U.S. economy despite some signs of slowing, and the strong first-quarter advance in Japan. With the rapid recovery in Asia, world trade has rebounded strongly, stimulating activity around the world. And in Asia itself, strong interregional trade is accelerating the recovery in domestic activity.

Though these are all positive developments, 1999 remains a year of weak growth for developing countries, particularly relative to pre-crisis levels. The overhang of bad debt and troubled banks and other financial institutions will limit our prospects for a rapid growth rate. Not surprisingly, capital flows to developing countries remain disappointing. Spreads remain high, and banks continue to reduce their exposure to emerging markets. Nevertheless, liquidity conditions in emerging markets have loosened considerably this year, with lower domestic interest rates; rising equity prices; and, in some cases, upward pressure on currencies.

The overall outlook remains positive. A stronger and positively reinforcing Asian recovery and a sharper rebound in Europe are both upside possibilities. A stock market correction and hard landing in the United States and a relapse into recession in Japan are the principal downside risks. Nevertheless, the considerable reform efforts undertaken in many developing countries make it unlikely that another currency crisis will trigger the contagion effects of 1997/98. As in Thailand, I hope the global economy continues to surprise on the upside as we put the recent crisis behind us and move into the new millennium.

Thai Economy

I am pleased and encouraged that Thailand, along with many other countries, has turned the corner on the recent crisis. Having bottomed out in the second half of 1998, we expect positive growth of 3–4 percent this year, driven by export growth, increased government expenditure, and private consumption. A stable macroeconomy with inflation of less than 1 percent, a current account surplus of \$11.5 billion and reserves of

$33.5 billion, intensified efforts to resolve financial sector difficulties, and broad-based structural reform will all help to ensure that the recovery is sustainable.

Of course, obstacles remain. Unemployment remains significant. Bank lending remains sluggish in light of remaining problems with risk and nonperforming loans. The latter remain unacceptably high at 47.7 percent and reflect the difficulties many businesses still face in restructuring.

I am confident, however, that Thailand is laying the groundwork for a sustained recovery. Demand, both domestic and export, has picked up. And, on a more fundamental level, we have also seen a positive supply-side adjustment, with a sustainable portion of businesses shifting toward the tradable sector. Foreign direct investment and foreign strategic partnership have strongly supported the adjustment.

Efforts have been intensified to resolve financial sector difficulties. A voluntary market-based approach to corporate debt restructuring has been facilitated. Overall recapitalization has advanced at an impressive rate, with over B 725 billion raised by banks and finance companies since the beginning of 1998. With new strategic partners, banks are acquiring better technology, management, and professional skills—leading to increased strength, transparency, and competitiveness. Recognizing the importance of legal and regulatory reforms as the foundation for sustained recovery, we have intensified the momentum for reform. We are now in the final stages of drafting a new Financial Institution Law and a new Bank of Thailand Law. The Code of Civil and Commercial Procedure Bill on Default Judgment is well on its way to timely passage. The new bankruptcy court is now in session, with more than 100 cases currently under consideration.

To preserve and enhance human resources so as to strengthen the adjustment and consolidate the recovery over the medium term through increased productivity and competitiveness, Thailand is embarking upon broad restructuring in social and public sectors, as well as implementing social and welfare programs, emphasizing training, health care, and job creation. The international community has supported these efforts through structural adjustment lending and social safety net programs.

Macroeconomic policy will continue to support recovery. The latest fiscal package announced in August aims at ensuring a sustained recovery, facilitating the restructuring of the manufacturing sector, and strengthening private sector competitiveness. The package focuses on the small and medium-sized enterprises as a cornerstone for recovery. The government continues to maintain the expansionary fiscal stance to stimulate the economy and alleviate social ills. On the monetary side, policy will continue to accommodate the recovery while remaining vigilant against the buildup of inflationary pressures and excessive exchange rate volatility. In addition, Thailand is moving to adopt flexible inflation targeting as a monetary objective in the medium term, helping to preserve our remarkable record of low inflation, even with the removal of the nominal anchor of the fixed exchange rate.

Thailand's outlook has improved dramatically since last year's meetings and, with continued progress and reform together with favorable external conditions, we fully expect further improvement by next year this time. With macroeconomic stability firmly established and financial and corporate sector adjustments steadily advancing, we will increasingly turn our attention to implementing supply-side policies.

Bank and Fund Matters

Let me now turn to Fund matters; we would like to compliment the Fund on its role in and contribution toward the reform of the international financial architecture. In this area, there are a number of issues on transparency, international standards, and the strengthening of the Interim Committee. The voluntary preparation and publication of transparency reports—focusing on a description of a member country's practice and progress on meeting the standard—is an important step toward strengthening the overall financial system. Many crucial issues, however, still require further work. We urge that concrete mechanisms be established for securing private sector involvement in resolving and forestalling the financial crisis. In this regard, careful consideration should be given to allow the international community to sanction a temporary stay on creditor litigation in extreme circumstances. Regarding the Fund's role in the liberalization of capital movements, we would like to reiterate that the sequence and pace of liberalization should be closely linked to stage of economic development and to a country's individual circumstances, given the complexity of the issues.

On the HIPC Initiative, we welcome the Bank and Fund's efforts in providing faster, deeper, and broader debt relief for the poorest countries, which demonstrate a commitment to reform debt and poverty reduction. We therefore support the off-market gold sale and other initiatives to secure the ESAF and HIPC financing. We, however, share the concerns of other developing countries regarding the financial burden that the enhanced HIPC framework will have on the multilateral development banks. We urge that major industrialized economies take a strong leadership in this important endeavor through bilateral contributions based on a fair burden-sharing principle.

Regarding Bank matters, I believe that the World Bank and the Asian Development Bank have been helpful partners throughout the crisis, supporting our initiatives and complementing the efforts of the Fund. I am gratified by the way the Bank has helped to put together assistance for financial and corporate restructuring and for its role in supporting our social agenda to cushion the impact of the crisis on the poor and vulnerable. The role it plays also reflects very much the approach embodied in the Comprehensive Development Framework, which we fully support. However, strong partnership and ownership of the government must be central to the CDF initiative, and we urge that the Bank must be flexible and mindful of the government's view. The Bank also has a crucial role to play in the new international financial architecture and must go beyond its current role as coordinator and collaborator, and influence the consensus at the international level with the perspective of the developing countries. It also has a key role in the international trade agenda, promoting issues of interest to developing countries. With the resources and knowledge that it has, the Bank can help developing countries to prepare and develop the trade agenda as well as to support their institutional capacity for trade negotiation.

STATEMENT BY THE GOVERNOR OF THE BANK FOR TURKEY

Selcuk Demiralp

It is a great pleasure and honor for me to address the joint Annual Meetings of the Fund and the Bank. I will begin with a few remarks on the current state of the world economy, and then will describe recent economic developments in Turkey following the recent earthquake, which was the worst disaster in the history of the Turkish Republic.

Developments and prospects in the world economy during the past year have generally been satisfactory and encouraging. This is certainly a relief after witnessing the two consecutive crises of 1997 and 1998. The world economy has steadily improved since last year's Annual Meetings. There are signs of a real recovery and revival of activity in many parts of the world, and a general mood of optimism concerning the immediate global outlook.

However, these favorable signs are accompanied by serious challenges that leave no room for complacency. There are risks that must be met with precautionary policy actions. Careful fine-tuning of U.S. policies will be needed to control potential inflationary pressures.

Structural reforms must be completed before Japan's recovery can be considered durable. In Europe, serious efforts must be made to remove the obstacles blocking the reduction of structural unemployment. For the emerging market economies, the picture is mixed. For some Asian countries, the recovery from the crisis has been much faster and stronger than expected, but Latin American growth has never really recovered from the debt crisis of the 1980s. Here, too, further progress with structural reforms is badly needed.

At the present juncture, there is general recognition of the risks in the global financial markets and an international consensus that the time has come to restore the stability of the international financial system. We must now translate that consensus into action. The Fund and the Bank, each preserving its specialized function and nature, must improve the coordination of their responses to countries' financial problems. Enhancing the effectiveness of Fund surveillance will enable it to help its members adjust before market discipline forces adjustment upon them.

In this connection, we join the emerging consensus that private financial institutions must play a more active contribution to the stability of the international financial system by accepting orderly debt workouts based on equitable burden sharing. This appears to be one of the thorniest issues facing the international community today.

Having summarized our thoughts on these agenda items, I would now like to touch on some very serious matters affecting the Turkish economy, particularly the effects of the recent earthquake.

Although extremely serious, and likely to result in missing macroeconomic targets, we do not believe that the economic losses caused by this natural disaster will derail Turkey's structural adjustment process. The solid but resilient structure of the Turkish economy will enable it to limit the effects of the shock to the short term. With support from the international community, the government will be able to fulfill its commitment to finish its program of structural adjustment. In fact, we were in the midst of calibrating our macroeconomic targets for the next stage of our anti-inflationary program when the earthquake struck.

In addition, implementation of the stabilization program monitored by the Fund in the framework of Turkey's "staff-monitored program" has gone fairly smoothly: the program stance has been maintained, and the fiscal targets, in particular, have been met. Progress so far is fairly in line with last July's agreement with the Fund.

Other steps taken in line with this understanding with the Fund include significant progress in the structural area, including increasing the financial system's efficiency and strengthening banking supervision; a constitutional amendment permitting international arbitration for the telecommunications and energy sectors; and reformation of the social security law. All this legislation has been approved by parliament.

These accomplishments will be complemented by the government's firm determination to reduce the budget deficit and impose fiscal discipline on the public sector. These goals will shape Turkey's budgetary and fiscal plans for the year 2000, and Turkey will continue pursuing its anti-inflationary program, working in cooperation with the Fund and Bank to achieve lasting results. We count on the continued support of the international community as we make progress with our program.

Here, on behalf of my country and its people, I wish to pay due tribute to the international community, and particularly the Fund and the Bank, for the immediate and splendid aid and cooperation provided to help us cope with the effects of the earthquake. Now I would like to discuss, briefly, what we have been able to learn so far about the economic effects, immediate and more remote, of this catastrophe. This natural disaster is one of the most serious to occur during the century just ending. Over 15,000 lives have been lost, and there is extensive damage to Turkey's industrial heartland. An estimated half-million people are homeless. As the nation digs out of the rubble, it is clear that a major reconstruction and restoration plan is needed. World Bank studies indicate that direct costs, including material damage and wealth loss, will amount to 1.5 to 3.0 percent of GNP. A detailed survey of capital and inventory losses in the housing and enterprise sectors is not yet complete, but a more or less precise estimate will eventually be available. Preliminary estimates indicate that the earthquake will reduce GNP for 1999 by about 1.0 percent. Employment losses in the affected areas are expected to exceed 20 percent. The disruption of Turkey's economic recovery creates challenges that are enormous, but not insurmountable.

Let me thank the Fund, the Bank, other multilateral institutions, and bilateral donors for their early support in the design of streamlined emergency arrangements for the massive rescue operations. We are confident that this essential cooperation will continue during reconstruction efforts to restore essential facilities and services and reestablish basic economic activities in the disaster zone, so that long-term economic and social disruption can be avoided. We are also grateful to the Fund, the Bank, and other donors for their coordinated assistance within the comprehensive plan toward the effective restoration of normal economic and social conditions.

Let me end by restating our appreciation to the Bank and the Fund for their help with our development efforts. I hope that the 1999 Annual Meeting will lead to a fruitful exchange of views on international economic and financial matters, and I look forward to a closer development partnership in the new millennium.

STATEMENT BY THE GOVERNOR OF THE FUND FOR TURKMENISTAN

Khudaiberdy Orazov

It is a great pleasure and honor for me to address the Annual Meetings of the World Bank Group and the Fund. The continuing efforts of both organizations to implement reforms of the international financial system in order to avoid future global financial crises are well appreciated. Significant financial and technical assistance from these organizations enables developing member countries to implement the reform process and to create a basis for strengthening their economies. However, the global crisis is undermining the efforts of developing countries to achieve economic growth. This is particularly true for Central Asian countries and countries of the former Commonwealth of Independent States that have much work to do to complete the transition process.

The economic development process depends more on factors of regional character, than on existing global problems. Countries whose economies are largely dependent on external trade deserve special attention. Turkmenistan has been particularly affected by the economic crisis in our region with a combination of falling commodity prices, slower growth in trading partner countries, and chronic nonpayment of debts by debtor countries.

I will not try to discuss all the problems of our economy at this time, many of which are within our own capacity to control, but would like to draw the attention of my fellow Governors and the Fund staff to the need to make urgent progress in improving the external payment arrangements in the countries of the former Soviet Union.

A smooth working payment system is vital to the future development of this region. While the region as a whole is likely to run a considerable current account deficit with the rest of the world in the coming future, this should not blind us to the fact that some countries—such as Turkmenistan—are inherently creditor countries within the region and need to be paid in cash on time for their exports if they, in turn, are to meet their trade and debt obligations to the rest of the world.

Resolution of this issue would also assist the Fund's goal to stamp out inefficient and inequitable barter trade. Turkmenistan agrees with this objective and has made considerable strides in reducing barter trade within its own borders. However, in attempting to apply that same principle to trade and payment relations with our neighbors, we find that the system does not work. Therefore, with no basis for enforcing payment for exports, we must often fall back on barter payments as a second-best alternative.

I would like to highlight three areas where urgent action is needed to improve the payments system. First, attention needs to be given to the rules of conduct of intergovernmental trade transactions. In our early period of independence, exports of gas and other commodities within our region were always regarded as being an intergovernmental transaction between sovereign states. Such transactions were given a special status that provided some protection to the exporter, since collection of payments for such exports could be enforced under Fund programs. In a sense, it acted as a substitute for the export insurance facilities available to western countries. While countries in this region may eventually also move in the insurance direction, the stability of intergovernmental arrangements provides important glue for existing trade arrangements.

Unfortunately, we saw a disturbing abrogation of this long-standing principle, when Ukraine declared that its obligations under the agreement on gas supplies signed by the governments of two countries were not the state's obligations, referring to the status of the organizations responsible for the execution of this agreement. In fact, these organizations are operated and managed within the state management system. This has led to the strange outcome whereby the Fund is formally unable to assist the Turkmenistan authorities in collecting vital export payments because of a mere technicality.

Indeed, we now see the hugely inequitable outcome from the fact that high-interest debt owed to international banks—on the assumption that the Fund would always bail them out through its program—is required to be paid back by the Fund, whereas debt owed to an impoverished nation like Turkmenistan is not subject to the same condition.

The need for early action to correct this anomaly should be evident to all, as other countries throughout the region are trying to follow such an example. Already we have been informed by Tajikistan and Kazakhstan that debts formerly conceded as being of an intergovernmental nature were in fact "private sector" transactions even where the entities involved were owned and controlled by the nation concerned.

The second principle relates to the need to provide a mechanism to enforce previously agreed debt payment schedules. In 1996 Turkmenistan bilaterally agreed to reschedule about $400 million of debt owed from Georgia. However, this agreement was not honored. At present, the amount of outstanding arrears has risen to $120 million. This situation does not allow us to address our social and economic development issues and complicates the servicing of our external debt. While larger creditors can afford to adopt a benevolent approach to this issue, Turkmenistan's financial position—worsened by nonpayment for our exports—does not permit such an approach.

In that context, we have welcomed efforts by the Fund to establish an orderly and certain approach to settlement, but are concerned that the Fund will not pay adequate regard to the economic situation of individual creditors. Clearly, it is one thing for the United States, the European Union, or Japan to offer debt relief and restructuring to countries such as Georgia for well-intentioned reasons. However, in the case of Georgia, it is more difficult for us to take such decisions because, being the largest creditor, Turkmenistan has been in fact receiving fewer payments than other creditors. If debt relief is to be provided in such circumstances, we see it as essential that the burden be borne equitably and that the larger nations be asked to make a more than proportionate contribution to the relief provided.

Third, the Fund needs to assist a quick resolution of the correspondent account debts among countries of the former Soviet Union—most of which were incurred before the introduction of independent central banks and currencies in our countries.

The existence of debts is a running sore in country relationships, often impeding more fundamental agreements on what trade and investment arrangements should be in place in the future. In fact, irresponsible approaches to the solution of correspondent account debts, incurred in the early stages of independence, have led to more complex issues of increasing amounts of external debt and outstanding arrears on bilateral and multilateral credits. It would be most useful, therefore, if the Fund could require resolution of these debts in the normal course of program design and implementation.

The Annual Meetings and regular discussions with two major development organizations provide us with an appreciation of the need for unity in the international community and the genuine desire by that community for outcomes that benefit all countries of the world and further strengthen the international financial system. My purpose here today has been to highlight the need to ensure that the financial architecture being put in place takes into account the needs of countries such as Turkmenistan.

STATEMENT BY THE GOVERNOR OF THE BANK FOR THE UNITED ARAB EMIRATES

Mohammed Khalfan bin Khirbash

I am honored to convey the thanks and appreciation of the government of the United Arab Emirates for the Boards of Governors' decision to select the city of Dubai to host the 2003 Annual Meetings. I am also honored to express my thanks to the Boards of Governors for their decision, which embodies the principle of maintaining a geographic balance in selecting the sites for these meetings. Holding the meetings for the first time in an Arab country has great significance in light of recent developments in the international arena, as well as the economic and political stability enjoyed by the United Arab Emirates, along with its particular geographical location and its forward-looking position with respect to the challenges of the new millennium.

The choice of the United Arab Emirates is an affirmation from the international community of the tremendous development and great successes in all areas that have been achieved by our country under the skillful leadership of Shaikh Zayed bin Sultan Al-Nahayan, our President. These successes have allowed the United Arab Emirates to play an effective role in both the international and regional arenas, on the basis of its strong belief in international cooperation and its continued support of the development efforts and economic reforms being carried out by developing countries.

I would like to take this opportunity to commend the efforts of the Fund and the World Bank to confront the challenges resulting from the fundamental changes taking place in the world economy, as well as their valuable contributions to helping member countries meet these challenges by monitoring economic developments and providing financial assistance, including their efforts to reduce the debt burden of the poorest countries and the historical IMF–World Bank initiative to develop a joint strategy for reducing poverty, encompassing the financial, structural, social, and humanitarian aspects of the problem. I would also like to commend the Fund's recent initiative to determine the means for preventing future crises, to improve the performance of world markets, and to encourage private sector participation in this undertaking. In conclusion, I reiterate my thanks and appreciation for your efforts, and look forward to seeing you in Dubai in 2003.

STATEMENT BY THE GOVERNOR OF THE FUND AND ALTERNATE GOVERNOR OF THE BANK FOR THE UNITED KINGDOM

Gordon Brown

Global financial stability depends on individual national governments pursuing strong domestic policies. There are two supremely important tasks that national governments must undertake in order to succeed in the global marketplace: first, building a platform of stability based on openness and transparency in policymaking; and, second, pursuing structural economic reform to promote productivity and employment.

In today's global economy, there is little place for the fine-tuning of the past that tried to exploit a supposed long-term trade-off between inflation and unemployment, which proved elusive. But equally in today's deregulated liberalized financial markets, governments can no longer try to deliver stability through the application of rigid monetary targets.

The answer to the uncertainty and unpredictability of ever more rapid financial flows is, first, clear long-term policy objectives; second, the certainty and predictability of well-understood procedural rules for monetary and fiscal policy; and, third, an openness that keeps markets properly informed and ensures that objectives and institutions are seen to be credible.

On the continent of Europe, where the search for macroeconomic stability is being pursued through monetary union, the same lessons are being learned with a commitment to monetary stability through the creation of an independent European Central bank; a commitment to fiscal sustainability through the stability and growth pact of the European Union; and a system of multilateral surveillance within Europe involving commitment to fiscal targets and rigorous peer review.

As I said in my October 1997 statement to the British Parliament, we are committed to making an economic assessment of the case for British membership. The decisive test as to whether and when we will enter will be based on five economic tests we have set out.

Stability in Britain

- In Britain we have set out clear long-term policy objectives:
- The monetary framework promotes price stability through a pre-announced inflation target of 2.5 percent—a symmetrical target.

Inflation outcomes below target are viewed just as seriously as outcomes above target.

- In fiscal policy, we have set two strict fiscal rules to ensure sustainable public finances: the golden rule requires that over the cycle we balance the current budget, and the sustainable investment rule requires that, as we borrow for investment, debt is set at a prudent and stable level.
- And we have established well-understood procedural rules: setting the inflation target, a clear remit for the Monetary Policy Committee of the Bank of England to meet this target and the open-letter system; and an equivalent and equally important set of fiscal procedures legally enshrined in the Code for Fiscal Stability.

Openness and transparency keep markets properly informed and ensure that objectives and institutions are seen to be credible. We have enhanced the transparency and openness of monetary policy in Britain. And the Code for Fiscal Stability requires the government to conduct fiscal policy in a transparent and responsible way, with key fiscal assumptions independently audited.

Following our own monetary and fiscal reforms I believe that we have now a sound and credible platform for stability for the British economy. Over the past 10 months, inflation has remained within 0.5 percentage points of the government's target. Headline inflation is down to 1.1 percent, and underlying inflation at 2.1 percent—around its lowest level for almost five years, and inflation is expected to remain close to target.

Short-term interest rates peaked at half their early 1990s level and have fallen to 5.25 percent now from 7½ percent in October. Long-term interest rates and mortgage rates are their lowest levels for over 30 years. The 10-year bond differential with Germany has fallen to about 0.7 percentage points now from 1.7 percentage points in April 1997.

Public borrowing has been reduced by £31 billion over the past two years—a cumulative fiscal tightening of 3¼ percent of GDP, the largest fiscal tightening since 1981—and we will continue to lock in that fiscal tightening by keeping the public finances under control, while allowing fiscal policy to continue to support monetary policy in the next stage of the cycle. As a result of our cautious and prudent approach to managing the public finances, we remain on track to meet the fiscal rules while guaranteeing an extra £40 billion for schools and hospitals over the next three years and more than doubling public investment, including in transport and infrastructure.

So, against a difficult world economic background, through early and decisive action on monetary and fiscal policy, both financial markets and the British public see that Britain is delivering—for the first time in this generation—economic stability.

We have brought inflation to its target and the fiscal deficit under control. And, at the same time, the economy has continued to grow and create jobs throughout this year, with the consensus of outside forecasts now predicting growth in 1999 of 1.4 percent—within the government's own budget forecast range of 1 to 1.5 percent. We will publish new economic forecasts next month in our Prebudget Report.

Britain's National Economic Potential

Our task now is to raise our national economic potential. This year's Prebudget Report will focus on the next stage of reforms to labor, capital, and product markets needed to exploit the growth potential of Britain. I believe that the British economy has the potential to reach the upper end of our growth ranges and in a way consistent with meeting our inflation target. But we can only do so if we combine prudence with long-term economic reform and modernization of our economy.

The four conditions for our economy achieving high and stable levels of growth and employment opportunity for all—the modern definition of full employment for the twenty-first century—are therefore:

- first, a proactive monetary policy and prudent fiscal policy;
- second, strengthening the program to move the unemployed from welfare to work;
- third, responsibility and an avoidance of "short-termism" in pay and wage bargaining across the private and public sectors; and
- fourth, a commitment to what matters for higher productivity—namely, high-quality long-term investment in science and innovation, new technology, and skills.

All of these conditions must be met. And if we can achieve these, then I believe Britain can not only continue to steer a course for stability and steady growth, but secure higher prosperity for all.

STATEMENT BY THE GOVERNOR OF THE BANK AND THE FUND FOR VANUATU

Sela Molisa

It gives me great pleasure to address the fifty-fourth Annual Meetings of the Fund and the World Bank Group on behalf of the Pacific Constituency comprising Kiribati, the Marshall Islands, the Federated States of Micronesia, the Republic of Palau, Samoa, the Solomon Islands, and Vanuatu. This year's meeting is unique in that it ends the Annual Meetings of this century as we approach the new millennium. On the threshold of the new century, let us not forget to look back and reflect on the achievements and failures, the lessons from which we may be better equipped to face the challenges ahead.

Our struggle to achieve economic advancement has not always been easy going. The task is even harder for most of the small island nations, some of which I stand here before you to represent. Given the small size of the Pacific Island states and the pursuit to open up our economies, we are becoming more exposed, thus, vulnerable to external shocks. The financial turbulence in Asia, the crisis in the Russian Federation, and the turbulence in Brazil have sent out waves of shocks globally in varying magnitude, impinging upon our economies directly and indirectly, making the years 1998 and 1999 particularly difficult for the Pacific Islands. The deceleration in growth in 1998 affected the Pacific Islands. The economies witnessed lower export earnings and an acceleration of commodity prices' downward trend, compounded by a sharp decline in demand. The situation was aggravated by an increased supply from the emerging countries facing economic difficulties over the period.

The Pacific Islands, although beautiful, are susceptible to natural calamities. We are hit by cyclones every year. We also have droughts and tidal waves, as was the trauma in Papua New Guinea last year, when part of Papua New Guinea was struck by severe tidal waves causing extensive damage and a loss of lives. The future prospects are bleak for the low-lying atolls of the Pacific, particularly those whose quality of life is threatened by the rise in sea level associated with global warming. Much too often, the negative externalities of our economic pursuits are ignored.

We note the signs of recovery in several Asian countries, which would seem to indicate that the worst of the financial crisis is over. Risks remain, however. There is a crucial need, therefore, for industrial countries to implement prudent policies. The improvement in the world economy is expected to have positive effects on the economies of the Pacific

Islands. Nevertheless, the lesson learned is that "globalization" and liberalization have the potential to be disruptive, owing to their close financial and economic ties with other countries.

Some of the problems of the island states are very unique and require special attention. We have come to realize the need to maintain strong economic fundamentals through the pursuit of economic reforms and adjustments. Indeed many of our countries have used this opportunity to push through demanding reform agendas. Some degree of reform to that effect has begun in the region. These reform programs were implemented with assistance from other external sources and supported by the World Bank and the Fund.

Our island economies are small, and one-sidedly structured, and resources are too limited to insulate the economies from the spillover effects of external crises. In spite of these problems, the damage can be minimized by means of appropriate reforms, as are already under way in some countries. It is appreciated that in view of the need to revitalize the global economy, the Fund and the World Bank took the initiative to find ways to finance the ESAF and HIPC Initiatives. Indeed, we are proud to see members of our constituency already indicating their willingness to join the international effort by passing their SCA-2 balances to the HIPC Trust. We understand that the initiative would take into consideration the concerns of the gold-producing countries, some of which pertain to my constituency, especially the idea that the involvement of the Fund's gold be limited to off-market measures.

We are grateful for the services extended to the Pacific by the Bank and the Fund in running seminars as well as providing technical assistance. With regard to technical assistance, we note the review made by the Fund. It is hoped that future Fund technical assistance will be sensitive to the unique needs of small island economies and will be available in appropriate forms. The Pacific Technical Assistance Center based in Suva, Fiji, plays a crucial role in the region and continues to serve its members well. In the monetary field, sustained technical support and advice have been productive, particularly with central banking operations.

We welcome the Fund's intention to establish a new Fund facility for Y2K-related balance of payments difficulties associated with the millennium computer problem. We believe that this facility is an appropriate response by the Fund in the likely event of Y2K-related capital outflows.

We note with appreciation the increasing presence of the World Bank and the potential to increase its services to the region. We believe this to be undoubtedly a worthy endeavor. We welcome the Bank's initiative for small states envisaged under the Comprehensive Development Strategy. We also note the importance of the IFC and, in particular, the presence of the South Pacific Project Facility, both of which have helped sector development in the region.

We are thankful for the IDA resources that have been provided to us on concessional terms. It is hoped that this will continue. We commend the Bank and Fund activities in the region, as they well complement the reforms under way. We understand that special consideration will be given to our environment, given that it so much determines the quality of our lives. Let me conclude by thanking the managements, staffs, and Boards of both the Fund and the Bank for all your assistance, particularly some very constructive advice and assistance.

Statement by the Governor of the Fund for Vietnam

Le Duc Thuy

From the outset, on behalf of the Vietnamese delegation I would like to express our high appreciation to the management of the International Monetary Fund and the World Bank Group, the Joint Secretariat, and the host country for their efforts and assistance in making conditions favorable for delegates from around the world to attend the Annual Meetings, a significant yearly event of the international financial community.

These Annual Meetings take place amid good signals showing that international financial markets have gradually stabilized, economic activity has bottomed out in the developing market economies of Asia, and the impact of this financial crisis on other parts of the world has been effectively checked. We are pleased to note that, according to recent forecasts, the economic growth rate in East Asian economies in 1999 will be higher than expected. However, there remain potential challenges to be overcome with bigger efforts to ensure a vigorous recovery and sustainable growth in the years to come.

Since the last Annual Meetings, these two international financial institutions have done their best to adjust and amend several policies, aimed at strengthening the international financial system and expanding assistance and support to the developing member countries, especially the poor ones and those that have been experiencing the financial crisis. At this forum, I would like to touch upon a number of issues of our deep interest.

Since the late 1980s, the Fund and the Bank have extended many highly concessional loans, in the form of ESAF arrangements and SAC, to more than 50 low-income member countries in support of their medium-term structural adjustment programs. We call upon these two institutions to make greater efforts to ensure adequate financing for this assistance. If one desires to efficiently implement the SAC/ESAF-supported programs, it is necessary to promote the ownership of the program countries. The conditionalities contained in the agreement between the Fund and Bank missions and the authorities should take into full account all the realities and peculiarities of the host countries, since they vary from country to country. In establishing these highly concessional programs, closer coordination between the Fund and the Bank is warranted.

We warmly welcome the Fund and Bank's jointly launched HIPC Initiative to help poor countries toward external exit from the debt burden. However, many analysts have expressed deep concerns about the depth of debt relief and the pace of its implementation, especially the financing of the HIPC funds, and the limited coverage of beneficiary countries. Against this background, we highly value the joint statement of the Bank's President and the Fund's Managing Director, which contains the principles for modifying the original HIPC Initiative. In addition, it is necessary to stress that debt relief should be closely linked to poverty reduction. We would like to take this occasion to call for expedited multilateral and bilateral contributions to the HIPC funds so that this initiative can be delivered more quickly and more extensively.

We would like to warmly welcome the World Bank President's proposal for a Comprehensive Development Framework, in which Vietnam has been chosen as one of a dozen pilot cases. This proposal has been considered a potentially powerful management tool with the capacity of catalyzing a longer term development vision, strengthening country ownership, and providing a vehicle for enhancing partnerships and donor coordination.

Availing myself of this opportunity, allow me on behalf of the government and the people of Vietnam to convey our sincere gratitude to the managements and the staffs of the Fund and the Bank for their cooperation and assistance in the form of financial programs, project loans, and technical assistance programs to our country over the past few years. I sincerely hope for increasingly better relations between Vietnam and the Fund and the Bank.

Given the fact that the economies of many countries in our region have been in the process of recovery and have started to achieve higher than expected growth, the consequences of the financial crisis and economic recession and the complicated situation in the region and elsewhere are causing disadvantages in various sectors of our economy, especially export activity and foreign investment.

At a meeting to review the economic performance of the first half of this year, the Vietnamese government adopted an action plan comprising seven groups of measures that focus on such essential undertakings as promotion of investment and consumer demand to make full use of the internal strength and encouragement of production and business; stimulation of export activity; consolidation of the financial sector; stabilization of the production and investment environment; continued restructuring of the state-owned enterprises; poverty alleviation; and so on and so forth. With these measures, our government hopes to create the necessary preconditions to overcome the temporary difficulties and become prepared to enter into the year 2000, our first successful year of the next millennium.

In conclusion, I would like to express our firm confidence that, thanks to the enormous efforts of the state and people of Vietnam, making the best use of their existing internal strength—and to the important assistance of the international community—our country has been and will be surmounting innumerable difficulties; minimizing the adverse impact of the regional economic crisis; ensuring political, economic, and social stability; and moving forward in many areas.

CONCLUDING REMARKS

STATEMENT BY THE GOVERNOR OF THE BANK FOR SOUTH AFRICA

Trevor Andrew Manuel

On behalf of South Africa and the countries of our region, I wish to express my sincere gratitude at being selected to serve as Chairman of the Boards of Governors of the World Bank Group and the International Monetary Fund for the coming year. In assuming this responsibility, I wish to express my admiration for the manner in which the outgoing chair, the Honorable Mahesh Acharya, has conducted these meetings.

As I assume this responsibility, I am deeply conscious of the many challenges we continue to face as we enter the new millennium. While the worst of the financial crisis is behind us, with growing signs of global economic recovery, no country is in any position to become complacent. Now is the time to enter into a real partnership and embark on a course of action that would see a tangible improvement in the lives of many who currently find themselves in conditions of abject poverty.

Over the past few days, many positive developments have taken place. These range from the endorsement in the Interim and Development Committees of the enhanced HIPC framework to improvements in the gold market. Clearly, these developments and others provide a sound basis for us to enter the new millennium.

Successful poverty reduction efforts, however, require that the operations of the Bank and the Fund, together with donor assistance and other bilateral and multilateral partners, all pull in the same direction. At the same time, governments must develop their own programs and strategies needed to underpin this renewed and committed long-term partnership.

I offer Mr. Wolfensohn, Mr. Camdessus, and the staffs of the two institutions my heartfelt appreciation for the important work they have done and will continue to do in the future. I look forward to a constructive engagement with these two institutions over the next 12 months.

The agendas for these two institutions are full. The challenges are before us. The time for action has arrived. Let us work together for a better life for all. I look forward to seeing you next year in Prague for the year 2000 Annual Meetings.

CONCLUDING REMARKS BY THE CHAIRMAN OF THE BOARDS OF GOVERNORS AND THE GOVERNOR OF THE BANK AND THE FUND FOR NEPAL

Mahesh Acharya

We all understand that the power of time is great. It allows us to measure opportunities and set heavy duties and responsibilities. Our time here together has permitted us to set concrete and important goals. As Chairman of the Boards of Governors, it is now my duty to bring our deliberations to a close.

It has been a great honor for Nepal and also my great privilege to have served as Chairman of the Boards of Governors of the Bank and the Fund. I would like to take this opportunity to thank everyone for the tremendous support extended to me during my tenure here at the Annual Meetings.

On behalf of all Governors, let me first of all thank the President of the United States for his immensely meaningful address. We salute and are moved by his deep understanding and strong commitment toward poverty reduction and debt relief in developing countries. I would also like to take this opportunity to thank the people of Washington, D.C., for their warm hospitality.

As these 1999 Annual Meetings draw to a close, I would like to review briefly some of the major themes that have emerged from our discussions and their implications for our two partner institutions and member countries. Governors have noted that, since our last meeting, global economic prospects and financial markets have improved significantly. Indeed, many developing as well as industrial economies are now experiencing favorable growth trends or are in a recovery phase and the world economy is likely to continue improving during 2000.

However, Governors have also stressed that we cannot afford to be complacent and that it would be a fundamental mistake to relent on our efforts to tackle the major challenges before us. At the opening of these meetings, I spoke about two major challenges that face us at the dawn of the new millennium. One major challenge is to continue our efforts to reform the international financial system to prevent future crises. Governors have commented favorably on the progress that has been achieved over the past year. But you have also noted that much remains to be done. Work needs to continue in a number of areas, including international standards and good practices, financial sector reform, private sector involvement in crisis prevention and resolution, and the liberalization of capital movements. Fellow Governors, these are complex issues that will require our personal attention over the coming year.

The second major challenge is to listen and respond to the "voices of the poor" that Mr. Wolfensohn and Mr. Camdessus described so vividly in their opening remarks. The progress that we have made in the last few days in enhancing the HIPC Initiative, ensuring that it is adequately financed and linking debt relief to poverty reduction should be of great benefit to the poor in heavily indebted countries. But much more needs to be done if we are to meet our objective of reducing by half the level of extreme poverty by the year 2015. At the national level, governments need to bring the social and structural aspects of development together with the macroeconomic and financial side. They need to enhance transparency and improve governance. Institutional capacity must be strengthened and the private sector energized. At the international level, we need to continue improving market access and reducing barriers to trade, especially for the benefit of developing countries. The worrisome decline in international development assistance must be reversed and broad-based support for international development must be built.

In addressing these challenges, Governors have emphasized the crucial importance of successful collaboration between the Bank Group and the Fund, as well as among member countries. Governors thanked the managements and staffs of the two institutions for the tremendous work they continue to do. I welcome the personal commitment of Mr. Wolfensohn and Mr. Camdessus to continue efforts to improve our institutions. Governors welcomed the progress made by both institutions in enhancing the transparency of their operations and encouraged them to continue working together to improve the functioning of the global economy. Governors also welcomed the concept of a Comprehensive Development Framework, the introduction of Poverty Reduction Strategy Papers, and the transformation of the ESAF into the Poverty Reduction and Growth Facility. These are all important steps in concentrating the minds of governments, the Fund, and the Bank on the central challenge of poverty reduction.

My fellow Governors, the message that I will take away from these meetings is that we have recognized the challenges before us in reforming the international financial system and in addressing the needs of the poorest. Our ultimate aim is to make a difference in the lives of our people. As a finance minister from a developing country like Nepal, I am aware that implementing many of the reforms that we have discussed will not be easy. However, with the support of our two institutions, I am confident that we can overcome these difficulties. Indeed, we are reassured that so many of our aspirations are at the core of the work of these two institutions. When we meet again next year in Prague, it is my sincere hope that we can say that we have together moved closer to these important goals. With our renewed commitment to break the shackles of debt and poverty, we can indeed welcome a new international development architecture compatible with the emerging global financial architecture.

Before adjourning these last Annual Meetings of this millennium, I would like to congratulate Mr. Wolfensohn on his reappointment as President of the World Bank. I would also like to express my appreciation to both Mr. Wolfensohn and Mr. Camdessus for their relentless efforts, and I hope they continue to stand together and strengthen our coalition for global progress and prosperity. I also thank the staff of the Joint Secretariat for their hard work and dedication, which have helped make our meetings a success. I would also like to extend my best wishes to the Governor for South Africa, who succeeds me as Chairman of the Boards of Governors.

I conclude by once again thanking everyone and wishing all a safe journey home. The 1999 Annual Meetings of the World Bank Group and the International Monetary Fund are hereby adjourned.

STATEMENT BY THE PRESIDENT OF THE WORLD BANK GROUP

James D. Wolfensohn

Thank you very much indeed, Mr. Chairman, and let me start by expressing my gratitude to you for the way in which you have chaired these meetings and my admiration for the work you have done in this past year. We look forward to our continuing relationship with you.

I am told that the attendance at these meetings was a record—I think we had 19,960 people registered. That strikes me as a quite remarkable number, and I want to particularly thank the staff and the organizers for the remarkable work that they have done in preparing for these meetings and for the way in which they have been conducted.

I think that all of us probably feel that there has been a very good atmosphere at these meetings, of course, framed by the fact that we do not have the crisis that we did last year, but conscious of the fact that the problems are not all over. I think we are also conscious of the fact that this is the last session that we will have in this millennium. So there has been a real acceptance, I believe, of the fact that the main challenge is poverty and that we need to come together to face this. The future is not only full of challenges but also full of hope if we can get together.

You were all pleased, I think, with the development of the new Poverty Reduction Strategy Paper, which will be jointly done between the Fund and the Bank to address the questions of growth and poverty together and come up with a single document that will guide the activities of the Bank in the context of ESAF and IDA. Certainly, on the Bank side, we are very pleased indeed with this new development. We look forward very much to our joint work with our partners not only for poverty reduction and growth but also for the well-being of all who share our world.

There was also quite some interest expressed at these meetings in the Comprehensive Development Framework. I was delighted to have the chance to talk to many of you about this subject, together, not only at this meeting—at which many of the Governors referred to this initiative—but also in meetings that I had directly with the Governors. I found those meetings extraordinarily useful, both in terms of the substance of the observations and also the sense of movement there is for all of us to come together.

This issue of partnership between the participants in the development process: between the two Bretton Woods institutions, of course, but also the bilaterals, the regional banks, civil society, and the private sector—all in the service of your governments—is something that I think has been accepted and agreed to by all of us. I was personally very delighted that this coming together is so apparent.

I talked of the creation of a new development architecture to parallel the financial architecture. That, too, I think, was something that had some resonance in the hallways. We are building coalitions for the improvement of the lot of our people who are less well-off; we are building coalitions for the next century, and it is certainly the position of the Bank that we are very anxious as we move forward to have our doors open to you for any ideas that you can bring to us, and we want to assure you that we are there to serve you and to work with you to achieve the objectives of your countries.

I was glad that there was such a good and interested reaction in the issue of the *Voices of the Poor*. This study we have done was announced here during the course of these meetings, and we will be continuing. I would like to say that, as far as the Bank is concerned, this listening to the voices and acting on the focus of their remarks are going to be central to our work as we move forward. It relates to all countries, really, and I think all of us, as we go into the next millennium, face this challenge to which I referred of both demographic changes and growth, and the notion that within another 25 years we will have another 2 billion people on our planet. This poses us with an extraordinary challenge, a challenge that relates to equity, a challenge that relates to justice, a challenge that relates to the type of world that we are going to leave our children.

So I conclude these meetings with a feeling that we are united to try to deal with this issue. I am glad that we were able to make such good progress on HIPC for debt forgiveness, for that is, indeed, an important element in the process; but what is most needed is for all of us to come together to reconstitute ourselves as a team that is enthusiastic, that is open, and that has as its top priority the establishment of a more just and a more peaceful world.

So I thank you. I thank the Governors for their contributions. I read with care many of the interventions that I did not attend. I look forward very much to the meetings next year in Prague and in the United Arab Emirates in 2003, and I am delighted that that location has been chosen. So, thank you again.

Statement by the Chairman of the Executive Board and Managing Director of the International Monetary Fund

Michel Camdessus

Let me first express my congratulations to Jim Wolfensohn on his reappointment to the Presidency of the World Bank Group, and my pleasure at the prospect of continuing to work with him and his colleagues during his second term. Especially so, in view of the stronger ties that are now being developed in key areas of Bank and Fund operations.

These have been a truly productive few days; indeed some, including the Chairman of the Interim Committee, have referred to the historic nature of the decisions that have been reached. You have conveyed a striking unity in your assessment of the current economic prospects, and of the priorities for economic policy in terms of what needs to be done to strengthen the present recovery. You have offered overwhelming endorsement of our efforts to deal with the crisis of the past two years and for the work that we have been doing with the World Bank and others to strengthen the international monetary and financial system. And above all, the enhancement of the HIPC Initiative, the launching of our Poverty Reduction and Growth Facility, and all that goes with these steps, have created a strong new impetus to the war on poverty. For the staff and management of the Fund the fact that 91 countries, including 58 developing countries, have contributed their money to financing the Fund's share in the HIPC Initiative is the clearest possible vote of confidence.

In our discussions, I have detected three key themes. The first is determination to avoid complacency. Certainly, the atmosphere surrounding these meetings could hardly be more different than one year ago. Many Governors have sounded a note of relief, perhaps even of surprise, that the recovery has become evident so soon. But, almost unanimously, Governors have sounded a cautionary note, no one more clearly than the Governor for Canada in saying that, "We will be making a grave error if we let the return of relative calm in financial markets and the improvement in world growth prospects lead us to believe that further reforms are not necessary." Equally in your assessment of the work that has been done in the area of the financial architecture, I have heard notes of satisfaction, but even more forcefully, the recognition that a tremendous task lies ahead of us.

If more stable global conditions prevail, it has allowed renewed attention to be paid to the huge variety of challenges that confront so many members.

- We were reminded of the tremendous challenges of development around the world. The Governor for Madagascar spoke of the challenge for all Africa of "financing development and poverty reduction in the face of declining resource flows, the high instability of Africa's export earnings, the debt burden, Africa's marginal role in the international financial system, the threat of the HIV/AIDS epidemic, and weak human and institutional capacity."
- We have been reminded of the vulnerability of countries at all levels of development to the natural disasters of the past year: hurricanes in Central America and the Caribbean, and the recent devastating earthquakes in Turkey, Greece, and Taiwan Province of China.
- We have also been reminded of the consequences of military conflicts in many parts of the world, including many that are too often overlooked by the global community. But foremost on the minds of many Governors was the sad situation in East Timor. You can be sure that the Fund is ready to do its part to assist in the urgent, demanding task of reconstruction.

The urgency of the second theme is captured in recurring key words: action and implementation. There is a desire for further progress on what has been initiated, so as to minimize the effects of the lingering risks that we all discern in our current situation. The immediate agenda consists of the two broad areas that have dominated our discussions: the global financial architecture and poverty reduction.

With respect to international monetary and financial reform, I perceived a degree of impatience for advancing reforms that are pending: issues of exchange rate regimes; involving the private sector in preventing and resolving crises; and the liberalization of capital movements. These will be high on the agenda of the Executive Board in the coming months. While your comments continue to reflect a diversity of views, there is no question about the determination to carry forward the debate as quickly as possible.

Increasingly the international institutions and national agencies will be caught up in the implementation of what has already been agreed. Governors have also supported our work in the area of transparency and standards and have warmly welcomed the work the Fund has been doing in the area of financial sector assessments in close collaboration with the World Bank. But as we proceed, we must also heed the note of caution, in this experimental area, as to how far the Fund should itself become engaged in the details of implementation. And one of the most severe constraints may be human resources. Many countries will need technical assistance for many years from many sources—the international standard-setting agencies and the bilateral countries—but there is a risk that these sources may become too stretched to meet the demand in some critical areas. Providing technical assistance in a coordinated and efficient manner will be one of the key issues in the coming months and years.

All of these issues have a bearing on the role of the Fund's surveillance, the review of which will be completed by the Executive Board in the months ahead. Rest assured that the Fund's energies will be primarily and energetically focused on the macroeconomic policies and balance of payments issues that are our traditional mandate. But as so many Governors have pointed out, we live in an era of rapid, often volatile, capital movements and where balance of payments crises may be triggered by factors outside the traditional boundaries of surveillance. Therefore we must try to avoid the effectiveness of early warning signals being eroded by too narrow a focus in our surveillance.

These meetings have resulted in a clear mandate for the Fund to integrate the objectives of poverty reduction and growth more fully into its operations. We will do so through our participation in the enhanced HIPC Initiative, through an ESAF transformed into a Poverty Reduction and Growth Facility, and through a closer link between debt relief and poverty reduction. We will also continue to consider how better to include a social dimension in our policy dialogue with our wider membership. The incidence of poverty extends far beyond the poorest countries. Although we have concentrated at these meetings on the poorest people in the poorest, most debt-ridden countries, the need extends to poor people in all countries. As the Governor for Japan reminded us with reference to East Asia, "Those who had received the smallest fruits of economic growth are now being left behind." The Chairman spoke of his own country Nepal, poor, but not a participant in the HIPC Initiative, yet where the incidence of poverty is pervasive. Our policy dialogue and advice will be attentive to such cases and will continue to be based on the basic premise that the best route out of poverty is strong, sustainable high-quality growth.

All our work in this area hinges critically on our partnership with the World Bank. As the Governor for the Netherlands reminded us, "Better quality and depth of the Bank's poverty analysis should help the Fund to adequately sequence and fine-tune macroeconomic stabilization policies." The challenge that faces both our institutions is how to implement, across a wide range of countries, at ground level, the broad principles that have been agreed between us over the past few weeks and months. And the agenda Jim Wolfensohn mapped out at the opening session points to the enormity of the task that awaits. I am sure that the seven pledges will provide this work with invaluable guideposts.

As we consider the issues that should be high on our agenda for the year ahead, let me reassert the importance for development and for sustainable growth of an open, competitive trading system. To this end I warmly welcome President Clinton's call yesterday for a new trade round, to be launched later this year, that would focus strongly on products of interest to the developing countries. Let us work as hard as possible to complete this round expeditiously.

Finally—I can be very brief—the third theme arises from the expectation that, this time, the international community and national governments will deliver what has been promised. I need not elaborate. In one word: we have an obligation to deliver.

The Governor for Norway, in his remarks, reminded us, "Closing the gap between the 'haves' and 'have-nots' within developing countries as well as between countries is a question of mindsets, morals, and ethics. It is very much a question of solidarity." I believe these meetings have given substance and full recognition to the social pillar as an integral part of the new global architecture.

Specifically, we have firmly established poverty as a permanent, pressingly urgent matter on the agenda of the international financial community, no longer an issue to be consigned to an afterthought in communiqués or policy papers. We have brought these concerns to the heart of our operations. And equally we have recognized that poverty and social justice are key ingredients of the framework for national policy formulation framework.

As the meetings draw to a close, I would like to thank you, Mr. Chairman, for your role in chairing these exciting meetings. I would also like to welcome the Governor for South Africa, as he takes on the mantle of Chairman of the Boards of Governors through our next meeting in Prague. I look forward to those meetings, not least because they will bring into the spotlight the achievements of the transition countries, which, as a group, has received less international attention than other, more troubled regions in the recent past. I am also particularly pleased that the United Arab Emirates has graciously offered to host the 2003 Annual Meetings.

DOCUMENTS AND RESOLUTIONS OF THE BOARD OF GOVERNORS

SCHEDULE OF MEETINGS[1]

Sunday	
September 26	9:00 a.m.—Joint Meeting of Interim and Development Committees
	10:00 a.m.—Interim Committee[2]
	3:00 p.m. —Interim Committee
Monday	
September 27	8:30 a.m.—Joint Development Committee
Tuesday	
September 28	10:00 a.m.—Opening Ceremonies Address by the Chairman Annual Address by President, World Bank Group Annual Address by Managing Director, International Monetary Fund
	3:00 p.m.—Annual Discussion
Wednesday	
September 29	9:30 a.m.—Annual Discussion
	3:00 p.m.—Annual Discussion
	6:15 p.m.—Joint Procedures Committee
	6:30 p.m.—MIGA Procedures Committee
Thursday	
September 30	9:30 a.m.—Annual Discussion
Following the conclusion of the Annual Discussion	Procedures Committees' Reports Comments by Heads of Organizations Adjournment

[1]Meetings of the Joint Development Committee were held jointly with the Board of Governors of the Bank. The sessions of the Annual Meetings were held jointly with the Boards of Governors of the World Bank Group.

[2]Fund only.

PROVISIONS RELATING TO THE CONDUCT OF THE MEETINGS

Admission

1. Sessions of the Boards of Governors of the World Bank Group and the Fund will be joint and shall be open to accredited press, guests, and staff.

2. Meetings of the Joint Procedures Committee shall be open only to Governors who are members of the Committee and their advisers, Executive Directors, and such staff as may be necessary.

Procedures and Records

3. The Chairman of the Boards of Governors will establish the order of speaking at each session. Governors signifying a desire to speak will generally be recognized in the order in which they ask to speak.

4. With the consent of the Chairman, a Governor may extend his statement in the record following advance submission of the text to the Secretaries.

5. The Secretaries will have verbatim transcripts prepared of the proceedings of the Boards of Governors and the Joint Procedures Committee. The transcripts of proceedings of the Joint Procedures Committee will be confidential and available only to the Chairman, the President of the World Bank Group, the Managing Director of the Fund, and the Secretaries.

6. Reports of the Joint Procedures Committee shall be signed by the Committee Chairman and the Reporting Members.

Public Information

7. The Chairman of the Boards of Governors, the President of the World Bank Group, and the Managing Director of the Fund will communicate to the press such information concerning the proceedings of the Annual Meetings as they may deem suitable.

AGENDA

1. 1999 Annual Report
2. Report of the Chairman of the Interim Committee (Fund Document No. 4)
3. Report of the Joint Development Committee (Fund Document No. 5)
4. Financial Statements and Audit Report (Appendix IX of the 1999 Annual Report and Fund Document Nos. 6 and 7)
5. Administrative and Capital Budgets for Financial Year ending April 30, 2000 (Chapter 11 of the 1999 Annual Report and Fund Document Nos. 7 and 8)
6. Amendment of Section 20(b), (c), (d), (e), and (f) of the By-Laws (Fund Document No. 9)
7. Amendment of the Rules and Regulations (Fund Document No. 10)
8. Place and Date of 2001, 2002, and 2003 Annual Meetings (Fund Document No. 11)
9. Transformation of Interim Committee (Fund Document No. 12)
10. Off-Market Transactions in Gold by the Fund (Fund Document No. 13)
11. Selection of Officers and Joint Procedures Committee for 1999/2000

REPORTS OF THE JOINT PROCEDURES COMMITTEE

Chairman—Nepal
Vice Chairmen—Kenya, Philippines
Reporting Member—Dominica

Other Members

People's Republic of China, Dominica, France, Germany, Ghana, Japan, Kenya, Kuwait, Republic of Latvia, Mali, Nepal, New Zealand, Panama, Peru, Saudi Arabia, Spain, Sweden, Turkey, United Kingdom, Republic of Uzbekistan, República Bolivariana de Venezuela, Zimbabwe

Report II[1]

September 30, 1999

Mr. Chairman:

At the meeting of the Joint Procedures Committee held on September 29, 1999, items of business on the agenda of the Board of Governors of the Fund were considered.

The Committee submits the following report and recommendations:

1. 1999 Annual Report

The Committee noted that provision had been made for the annual discussion of the business of the Fund.

2. Report of the Chairman of the Interim Committee[2]

The Committee noted the presentation made by the Chairman of the Interim Committee.

[1]Report I dealt with the business of the Boards of Governors of the Bank, IFC, and IDA. Report II and the recommendations contained therein were adopted by the Board of Governors of the Fund in Joint Session with the Boards of Governors of the Bank, IFC, and IDA on September 30, 1999.

[2]See pages 34–39.

The Committee recommends that the Board of Governors of the Fund thank the Interim Committee for its work.

3. Financial Statements, Report on Audit, and Administrative and Capital Budgets

The Committee considered the Report on Audit for the Financial Year ended April 30, 1999, the Financial Statements contained therein (Fund Document No. 6 and Appendix IX of the *1999 Annual Report*), and the Administrative Budget for the Financial Year ending April 30, 2000 and the Capital Budget for capital projects beginning in Financial Year 2000 (Fund Document No. 8 and Chapter 11 of the *1999 Annual Report*).

The Committee recommends that the Board of Governors of the Fund adopt the draft Resolution set forth in Fund Document No. 7.[3]

4. By-Laws

The Committee considered the recommendation of the Executive Board concerning amendment of Section 20(b), (c), (d), (e), and (f) of the By-Laws and recommends that the Board of Governors adopt the draft Resolution set forth in Fund Document No. 9.[4]

5. Amendments of Rules and Regulations

The Committee has reviewed and noted the letter of the Managing Director and Chairman of the Executive Board to the Chairman of the Board of Governors, dated September 30, 1999, reproduced as Fund Document No. 10, regarding amendments of the Rules and Regulations set forth in Annex I to that document.

The Committee recommends that the Board of Governors of the Fund adopt the draft Resolution set forth in Annex II of Fund Document No. 10.[5]

6. Transformation of Interim Committee

The Committee considered the recommendation of the Executive Board concerning the transformation of the Interim Committee of the Board of Governors on the International Monetary System into the International Monetary and Financial Committee of the Board of

[3]Resolution No. 54-5, page 256.
[4]Resolution No. 54-6, pages 256–9.
[5]Resolution No. 54-7, page 259.

Governors and recommends that the Board of Governors adopt the draft Resolution set forth in Fund Document No. 12.[6]

7. Off-Market Transactions in Gold by Fund

The Committee considered the recommendation of the Executive Board concerning off-market transactions in gold by the Fund and recommends that the Board of Governors adopt the draft Resolution set forth in Fund Document No. 13.[7]

Approved:

/s/ Mahesh Acharya	/s/ Cary A. Harris
Nepal—Chairman	*Dominica—Reporting Member*

Report III[8]

September 30, 1999

Mr. Chairman:

The Joint Procedures Committee met on September 29, 1999 and submits the following report and recommendations:

1. Development Committee

The Committee noted that the Report of the Chairman of the Joint Ministerial Committee of the Boards of Governors of the Fund and the Bank on the Transfer of Real Resources to Developing Countries (Development Committee) has been presented to the Boards of Governors of the Bank and the Fund pursuant to paragraph 5 of Resolutions Nos. 294 and 29-9 of the Bank and Fund, respectively (Bank Document No. 3 and Fund Document No. 5).[9]

The Committee recommends that the Boards of Governors of the Bank and the Fund note the report and thank the Development Committee for its work.

[6]Resolution No. 54-9, pages 260–3.

[7]Resolution No. 54-10, page 263.

[8]Report III and recommendations contained therin were approved by the Board of Governors of the Fund, in joint session with the Boards of Governors of the Bank, IFC, and IDA, on September 30, 1999.

[9]See pages 289–93.

2. *Place and Date of 2001, 2002, and 2003 Annual Meetings*

The Committee considered the recommendation of the Executive Directors of the Bank and the Fund that the 2001 and 2002 Annual Meetings be convened in Washington, D.C., on October 2 and October 1, respectively, and that the 2003 Annual Meetings be convened in Dubai, United Arab Emirates, on September 23, and recommends adoption by the Boards of Governors of the draft Resolutions set forth in Bank Document No. 4 and Fund Document No. 11.[10]

3. *Officers and Joint Procedures Committee for 1999/2000*

The Committee recommends that the Governor for South Africa be Chairman and that the Governors for Estonia and Honduras be Vice Chairmen of the Boards of Governors of the World Bank Group and of the Fund, to hold office until the close of the next Annual Meetings.

It is further recommended that a Joint Procedures Committee be established to be available, after the termination of these meetings and until the close of the next Annual Meetings, for consultation at the discretion of the Chairman, normally by correspondence and, if the occasion requires, by convening; and that this Committee shall consist of the Governors for the following members: Algeria, Angola, Armenia, Australia, Bolivia, Canada, the Dominican Republic, Estonia, France, Germany, Guinea, Honduras, India, Indonesia, Japan, Malta, Nigeria, Saudi Arabia, the Slovak Republic, South Africa, Switzerland, the United Kingdom, and the United States.

It is recommended that the Chairman of the Joint Procedures Committee shall be the Governor for South Africa, and the Vice Chairmen shall be the Governors for Estonia and Honduras, and that the Governor for Saudi Arabia shall serve as Reporting Member.

Approved:

/s/ Mahesh Acharya	/s/ Cary A. Harris
Nepal—Chairman	*Dominica—Reporting Member*

[10]See Resolution No. 54-8, page 260.

RESOLUTIONS

Resolution No. 54-1

Amendment of Section 14(f) of the By-Laws

The Executive Board resolved on April 7, 1999 that action on the amendment should not be postponed until the next regular meeting of the Board of Governors.

In accordance with Section 13 of the By-Laws, the following Resolution was submitted to the Governors on April 9, 1999 for a vote without meeting:

RESOLVED:

That the first sentence of the first paragraph of Section 14(f) of the By-Laws be amended to read as follows:

The Executive Directors and their Alternates are to be reimbursed, in addition, for all reasonable expenses for travel incurred on official Fund business, and for reasonable expenses incurred by them in connection with official Fund business to entertain senior officials of the governments or central banks or relevant persons in the academic, public, or private sectors of the members that appointed, elected or designated them, and relevant members of the media.

The Board of Governors adopted the foregoing Resolution, effective May 10, 1999.

Resolution 54-2

Salary of the Managing Director

The Executive Board resolved on June 16, 1999 to recommend an adjustment in the salary of the Managing Director.

In accordance with Section 13 of the By-Laws, the following Resolution was submitted to the Governors on June 16, 1999 for a vote without meeting:

RESOLVED:

That, effective July 16, 1999, the annual salary of the Managing Director of the Fund shall be two hundred forty-seven thousand, seven hundred and ninety dollars ($247,790).

The Board of Governors adopted the foregoing Resolution, effective July 14, 1999.

Resolution No. 54-3

Direct Remuneration of Executive Directors and Their Alternates

Pursuant to Section 14(e) of the By-Laws, the 1999 Joint Committee on the Remuneration of Executive Directors and Their Alternates on July 23, 1999 directed the Secretary of the Fund to transmit its report and recommendations to the Board of Governors of the Fund. The Committee's report contained the following proposed Resolution for adoption by the Board of Governors.

In accordance with Section 13 of the By-Laws, the following Resolution was submitted to the Governors on July 29, 1999 for a vote without meeting.

RESOLVED:

That, effective July 1, 1999, the annual rates of remuneration of the Executive Directors of the Fund and their Alternates pursuant to Section 14(e) of the By-Laws shall be as follows:

(i) As salary, $151,630 per year for Executive Directors and $130,940 per year for their Alternates;

(ii) As supplemental allowance (for expenses, including housing and entertainment expenses, except those specified in Section 14(f) of the By-Laws), $9,000 per year for Executive Directors and $7,200 per year for their Alternates.

The Board of Governors adopted the foregoing Resolution, effective September 7, 1999.

Resolution No. 54-4

Maternity Leave for Executive Directors and Their Alternates

Pursuant to Section 14(e) of the By-Laws, the 1999 Joint Committee on the Remuneration of Executive Directors and Their Alternates on July 23, 1999 directed the Secretary of the Fund to transmit its report and recommendations to the Board of Governors of the Fund. The Committee's report contained the following proposed Resolution for adoption by the Board of Governors.

In accordance with Section 13 of the By-Laws, the following Resolution was submitted to the Governors on July 29, 1999 for a vote without meeting:

RESOLVED:

That, effective July 1, 1999, as of the effective date of her term of office, each female Executive Director and Alternate of an Executive Director shall be entitled to twelve calendar weeks of leave in conjunction with her pregnancy and the delivery of her child.

The Board of Governors adopted the foregoing Resolution, effective September 7, 1999.

Resolution No. 54-5

Financial Statements, Report on Audit,
and Administrative and Capital Budgets

RESOLVED:

That the Board of Governors of the Fund considers the Report on Audit for the Financial Year ended April 30, 1999, the Financial Statements contained therein, and the Administrative Budget for the Financial Year ending April 30, 2000 and the Capital Budget for capital projects beginning in Financial Year 2000 as fulfilling the requirements of Article XII, Section 7 of the Articles of Agreement and Section 20 of the By-Laws.

The Board of Governors adopted the foregoing Resolution, effective September 30, 1999.

Resolution No. 54-6

Amendment of Section 20(b), (c), (d), (e), and (f) of the By-Laws

WHEREAS, the Executive Board has conducted an outside review of the external audit function of the Fund; and

WHEREAS, the Executive Board has endorsed the changes to the external audit function proposed by the outside review; and

WHEREAS, the Executive Board has approved on May 20, 1999 a report to the Board of Governors on modifications to paragraphs (b), (c), (d), (e), and (f) of Section 20 of the By-Laws to incorporate the proposed changes to the Fund's external audit function,

NOW, THEREFORE, the Board of Governors hereby RESOLVES:

(A) That paragraphs (b), (c), (d), (e) and (f) of Section 20 of the By-Laws are amended to read as follows:

"(b) An external audit of the financial statements of the Fund and of Accounts administered under Article V, Section 2*(b)*, including the financial statements of the Staff Retirement Plan, shall be made annually and such audit shall relate to the period representing the financial year.

(c) An external audit committee shall have general oversight of the annual audit. The audit committee shall consist of three persons who shall be selected by the Executive Board and appointed by the Managing Director. The persons serving on the audit committee must be nationals of different members of the Fund at the time of their appointment; at least one of them shall be a national of one of the six members having the largest quotas. The members of the audit committee must possess the qualifications required to carry out the oversight of the annual audit. They shall be appointed for a period of three years and may be reappointed for a further period of three years. A person appointed to replace a member whose term of office has not expired shall hold office for the remainder of the predecessor's term; any person so appointed may be reappointed for two full three-year terms. In the performance of their functions, the members of the audit committee shall be considered as officers of the Fund for purposes of the Articles of Agreement of the Fund.

Each audit committee shall elect one of its members as chairman, shall determine its own procedure, and shall otherwise be independent of the Management of the Fund in overseeing the annual audit. The Executive Board shall approve the terms of reference of the audit committee. The audit committee may recommend changes to the terms of reference for the approval of the Executive Board.

An external audit firm shall be selected by the Executive Board in consultation with the audit committee and appointed by the Managing Director to conduct the annual audit and issue an audit report. The members of the audit committee and the audit firm, including its partners and personnel, shall respect the confidential nature of their service and the information made available for the purposes of the audit.

(d) The annual audit shall be conducted in accordance with generally accepted auditing standards, and shall include such tests of the accounting records and such auditing procedures as are considered necessary. The audit shall be comprehensive with respect to examination of the financial records of the General Department, the Special Drawing Rights

Department, and Accounts administered under Article V, Section 2(*b*), including the Staff Retirement Plan; shall extend, in so far as practicable, to the ascertainment that the operations and transactions conducted during the period under review are supported by the necessary authority; and shall determine that there is adequate and faithful accounting for the assets and liabilities of the General Department and Accounts administered under Article V, Section 2(*b*), including the Staff Retirement Plan, and for special drawing rights. On the basis of this audit, the audit firm shall state whether the financial statements as presented give a true and fair view of the financial position at the close of the financial year of the General Department, and of Accounts administered under Article V, Section 2(*b*), including the Staff Retirement Plan, and, with respect to the Special Drawing Rights Department, of the allocation and holdings of special drawing rights, and of the result of operations and transactions during that year. For these purposes, the audit committee and the audit firm shall have access to the accounting records of the Fund and other supporting evidence of its operations and transactions, and of its administration of Accounts under Article V, Section 2(*b*), including the Staff Retirement Plan. The Managing Director of the Fund shall furnish the audit committee and the audit firm with such information and representations as may be required in connection with the audit.

(e) The Executive Board shall decide all questions of policy raised by requests of the audit committee or the audit firm for particular information or the inspection of particular records or documents. The refusal of any such requests for reasons of policy shall be explained in the comments of the Executive Board forwarded to the Board of Governors with the audit report.

Any question the audit committee or the audit firm may have concerning interpretation of the Articles of Agreement, the By-Laws, the Rules and Regulations, or the decisions of the Fund shall be discussed with the Managing Director, or officials designated by him, and if the reply is not completely satisfactory to the audit committee or the audit firm, the matter shall be referred to the Executive Board through the Managing Director.

(f) The audit committee shall transmit the report issued by the audit firm to the Board of Governors for consideration by it. Such transmittal shall be made through the Managing Director and the Executive Board which shall forward with the audit report its comments thereon. The audit firm shall afford the

Managing Director an opportunity for explanation to it before deciding that any matter seems to require criticism in the report. The audit report shall be transmitted to the Board of Governors within a reasonable time after its completion.

The audit firm may formally furnish to the audit committee, the Managing Director, and the Executive Board the firm's views and suggestions concerning the system of accounting, internal financial control, and documentary and other procedures which may technically strengthen or improve the administration of the Fund's financial affairs. Such matters need not be dealt with in the audit report unless the audit firm believes they are of such moment as to warrant inclusion.

Except for findings that, in the view of the audit firm concurred in by the audit committee, are considered minor and thus only of interest to the Management of the Fund, all the views and suggestions of the audit firm shall be communicated to the Managing Director and the Executive Board at the same time. The Managing Director's response to the views and suggestions of the audit firm that have been communicated to the Executive Board shall also be communicated to the Executive Board."

(B) That, of the first three appointments made to the committee under the amended paragraph (c) of Section 20 of the By-Laws, one shall be made for one year, one for two years, and one for three years. Any person appointed for a one- or two-year term under this provision may be reappointed for two full three-year terms.

The Board of Governors adopted the foregoing Resolution, effective September 30, 1999.

Resolution No. 54-7

Amendments of the Rules and Regulations

RESOLVED:

That the Board of Governors of the Fund hereby notifies the Executive Board that it has reviewed the amendment of Rules O-1 and T-1(c), which have been made since the 1998 Annual Meeting, and has no changes to suggest.

The Board of Governors adopted the foregoing Resolution, effective September 30, 1999.

Resolution No. 54-8

Forthcoming Annual Meetings

RESOLVED:

That the 2001 and 2002 Annual Meetings shall be convened in Washington, D.C. beginning on October 2, 2001 and October 1, 2002;

That the invitation of the government of the United Arab Emirates to hold the Annual Meetings in Dubai in 2003 be accepted; and

That the 2003 Annual Meetings be convened on Tuesday, September 23, 2003.

The Board of Governors adopted the foregoing Resolution, effective September 30, 1999.

Resolution No. 54-9

International Monetary and Financial Committee of the Board of Governors

WHEREAS, the Board of Governors of the Fund recognizes the need, pending the possible establishment of the Council, to strengthen and transform the Interim Committee of the Board of Governors on the International Monetary System established by Resolution No. 29-8, and

WHEREAS, this strengthening and transformation should be reflected in the name of the Committee and its terms of reference to further its role as an advisory committee of the Board of Governors;

NOW, THEREFORE, the Board of Governors hereby RESOLVES as follows:

1. Composition of the International Monetary and Financial Committee

(a) The Interim Committee shall be transformed into the International Monetary and Financial Committee of the Board of Governors. The members of the Committee shall be governors of the Fund, ministers, or others of comparable rank. Each member of the Fund that appoints an executive director and each member or group of members of the Fund that elected an executive director on or after the date on which the last regular election took place shall appoint:

- (i) one member of the Committee, and not more than
- (ii) seven associates

(b) Members of the Committee, associates, and executive directors or in their absence their alternates, shall be entitled to attend meetings of the Committee, unless the Committee decides to hold a more restricted session. Each member of the Fund that appoints an executive director and each group of members of the Fund referred to in (a) above may designate an alternate to participate in the place of the member of the Committee at any meeting when he is not present. Participation in respect of each item on the agenda of a meeting shall be limited to one person, who shall be a member of the Committee, an associate, or an executive director.

(c) The Committee shall select a Chairman, who shall serve for such period as the Committee determines.

(d) The Managing Director shall be entitled to participate in all meetings of the Committee, and may designate a representative to participate in his place at any meeting when he is not present. The Managing Director or his representative may be accompanied normally by not more than two members of the staff, unless the Committee decides to hold a restricted session.

(e) A member of the Fund whose voting rights are suspended pursuant to Article XXVI, Section 2(b) shall not appoint, or participate in the appointment of, a member of the Committee and his associates. When the voting rights of a member are suspended, the rules in Schedule L, paragraph 3(c) on the termination of office and replacement of executive directors shall apply to the member of the Committee and associates appointed by the member or in whose appointment the member has participated.

2. Representation of Members Not Entitled to Appoint a Member of the Committee

A member of the Fund not entitled to appoint a member of the Committee may send a representative to participate in any meeting of the Committee when a request made by, or a matter particularly affecting, that member is under consideration. The Committee shall determine, upon request by the member, whether a matter under consideration particularly affects the member.

3. Terms of Reference

The Committee shall advise and report to the Board of Governors with respect to the functions of the Board of Governors in:

(i) supervising the management and adaptation of the international monetary and financial system, including the continuing operation of the adjustment process, and in this connection reviewing developments in global liquidity and the transfer of real resources to developing countries;

(ii) considering proposals by the Executive Directors to amend the Articles of Agreement; and

(iii) dealing with sudden disturbances that might threaten the system.

In addition, the Committee shall advise and report to the Board of Governors on any other matters on which the Board of Governors may seek the advice of the Committee.

In performing its duties, the Committee shall take account of the work of other bodies having specialized responsibilities in related fields.

4. Procedures

(a) The Committee shall meet ordinarily *twice* a year. The Chairman may call meetings after consulting the members of the Committee, and shall consult the members of the Committee on calling a meeting if so requested by any member of the Committee. Normally, the Chairman, in consultation with the members of the Committee, will call a preparatory meeting of their representatives ("Deputies").

(b) A quorum for any meeting of the Committee shall be two thirds of the members of the Committee.

(c) Meetings of the Committee shall be held within the metropolitan area in which the Fund has its principal office, or at such other places as the Committee may provide or, in the absence of such provision, as the Chairman shall determine after consulting the members of the Committee.

(d) Appropriate arrangements shall be made for the effective coordination of the work of the Committee and of the Executive Directors. The Secretary of the Fund shall serve as the Secretary of the Committee.

(e) In reporting any recommendations or views of the Committee, the Chairman shall seek to establish a sense of the meeting. In the event of a failure to reach a unanimous view, all views shall be reported, and the members holding such views shall be identified. Reports of the Committee shall be made available to the Executive Directors.

(f) The Committee may invite observers to attend during the discussion of an item on the agenda of a meeting, and may determine any aspect of its procedure that is not established by this Resolution.

5. Termination of Resolution of 29-8

Resolution No. 29-8 adopted October 2, 1974 is hereby repealed.

The Board of Governors adopted the foregoing Resolution, effective September 30, 1999.

Resolution No. 54-10

Off-Market Transactions in Gold by the Fund

WHEREAS, the Executive Board is considering off-market transactions in gold consisting of sales of up to 14 million ounces of fine gold on the basis of prices in the market to cooperating members with repurchase obligations to the Fund falling due, and acceptance of the same amount of gold from those members in payments of their repurchase obligations falling due to the Fund; and

WHEREAS, these off-market transactions will enable the Fund to place an amount of the sales proceeds equivalent to SDR 35 per ounce of fine gold in the General Resources Account and the balance in the Special Disbursement Account for investments for the benefit of the ESAF-HIPC Trust; and

WHEREAS, the Interim Committee has requested the endorsement by the Board of Governors of this approach as a one-time operation of a highly exceptional nature,

NOW, THEREFORE, the Board of Governors hereby RESOLVES that:

The off-market transactions of up to 14 million ounces of fine gold by the Fund that are envisaged will be a one-time operation of a highly exceptional nature that is a part of a broader financing package to allow the Fund to contribute to the resolution of the debt problems of the HIPCs at the turn of the millennium and to the continuation of concessional operations to support countries' efforts to achieve sustained growth and poverty reduction.

The Board of Governors adopted the foregoing Resolution, effective September 30, 1999.

Joint Meeting of the Interim and Development Committees

JOINT STATEMENT BY CO-CHAIRMEN

September 26, 1999

Heavily Indebted Poor Countries Initiative (HIPC) and Enhanced Poverty Focus of IDA and IMF Concessional Programs

1. Ministers of the Development and Interim Committees met jointly for the first time this morning to discuss the enhancement of the HIPC Initiative, which will provide faster, broader, and deeper debt relief with the central goal of reducing poverty in the poorest countries in the world. This joint meeting symbolizes the cooperation and high political commitment of all countries and institutions in this effort, and the new closer relationship between the Bank and Fund which will be crucial in achieving this goal.

2. We focused on three main areas: first, the reforms required to deliver deeper, broader, and faster debt relief; second, strengthening the focus on poverty reduction in Bank and Fund programs; and third, an overview of the financing arrangements that will allow the enhanced HIPC Initiative to start after these Annual Meetings.

3. We endorsed the enhancements and reforms to the HIPC Initiative for those countries pursuing sound policies and committed to reform. We support: lowering the debt sustainability thresholds; providing faster debt relief; shifting the focus of the initiative toward a commitment to, and positive achievements in, poverty reduction; and increasing the number of countries expected to be eligible for debt relief.

4. We stressed the need to ensure that debt relief will result in poverty reduction, though we recognize that debt relief alone is insufficient to achieve this goal. We therefore endorse the framework proposed by the Bank and Fund for strengthening the link between debt relief and poverty reduction. In particular, we welcomed the proposed Poverty Reduction Strategies that countries will prepare in close collaboration with the Bank and Fund. We stressed the need to put in place macroeconomic, structural, and social policies that will generate growth and contribute to poverty reduction. We stressed the crucial role good governance must play in HIPC poverty reduction and implementation of debt relief. We also endorsed the proposals to extend the same approach to strengthen the poverty focus of all IDA and IMF concessional programs.

5. We agree that Poverty Reduction Strategies should be country-driven, and be developed transparently with broad participation of civil society, key donors, and regional development banks. These strategies should be clearly linked with the agreed international development goals, with measurable indicators to monitor progress. We called on the Bank and Fund to give all possible assistance to countries in developing their Poverty Reduction Strategies. These strategies will provide the basis for all IDA and Fund lending to low-income countries and will so assure the close integration of the institutions' work in these areas. We strongly welcomed the commitments of the President and Managing Director to the effective implementation of this approach. We also encouraged regional development banks and donors to use the Poverty Reduction Strategies to guide their support.

6. We reaffirmed the importance of implementing the enhanced HIPC Initiative in accordance with the principles that have guided the Initiative since its inception, including (i) additionality of debt relief, (ii) maintaining the financial integrity of multilateral financial institutions, and (iii) cost sharing on a broad and equitable basis. We agreed financing of debt relief should not compromise the financing made available through concessional windows such as IDA.

7. We expressed appreciation for the many contributions to the HIPC Initiative made thus far, and for the efforts made by multilateral development institutions to provide funding for the Initiative from their own resources. We also welcomed the agreement by the Paris Club to increase its debt relief under the enhanced framework by providing increased debt reduction in net present value (NPV) terms up to 90 percent or more, if needed, on commercial loans as well as additional relief on ODA claims—up to full cancellation—on a bilateral basis.

8. We heard today from Jim Wolfensohn, Michel Camdessus, Omar Kabbaj, and Enrique Iglesias and we have a clear picture of their financing needs. Ministers recognized that there will need to be additional bilateral support in order to meet the financing requirements of the enhanced Initiative. These financing arrangements will need to be considered at the forthcoming Development and Interim Committees. Based on the expressions of goodwill and support that we have heard, we are confident that the political will and commitment is there to allow the Enhanced HIPC Initiative to commence after these meetings so that eligible countries can receive enhanced debt relief within the new poverty reduction framework.

9. We urge the speedy implementation of the enhanced Initiative so that as many countries as possible would qualify for assistance under the Initiative by end-2000.

Interim Committee of the Board of Governors on the International Monetary System

PRESS COMMUNIQUÉ

September 26, 1999

1. The Interim Committee held its fifty-third meeting in Washington, D.C. on September 26, 1999, under the Chairmanship of Mr. Gordon Brown, Chancellor of the Exchequer of the United Kingdom. The Committee expresses its appreciation to the outgoing Chairman, Mr. Carlo Azeglio Ciampi, formerly Minister of the Treasury of Italy and currently President of Italy, for his invaluable contribution to the Committee's work.

Global Economic and Financial Conditions

2. The Committee welcomes the improvement in global economic and financial conditions since the beginning of this year. It has reviewed the challenges required to ensure that the recovery is sustained.

In many emerging market economies and developing countries, raising growth rates on a lasting basis will require not only sustained growth in industrial countries, but also key structural reforms. These include banking reform, corporate restructuring, tax reform and tax administration, establishment of effective legal systems, protection of property rights, and improved governance.

- Recovery is taking hold in crisis-affected countries in Asia, aided by supportive fiscal policies, accommodative monetary policies, and a return of financial market confidence. Financial sector restructuring is generally moving ahead, but further efforts are needed to complete the task. In addition, corporate restructuring and institutional reforms should be accelerated. Indonesia's recovery has been interrupted by structural and political problems that will need to be resolved speedily in order for economic recovery and reform to resume. China and India have weathered the crisis relatively well and economic performance has been sustained, but significant challenges in some areas remain to be addressed.

- In Russia, the Committee welcomes the efforts of the Fund to work with the Russian authorities to encourage macroeconomic stabilization, the continuation of reforms, and the further integration of Russia into the global economy. While acknowledging the recent initial measures to restructure the banking system, strengthen the integrity of financial policies and institutions, and improve governance and transparency, the Committee stresses the urgent need for further progress. It calls on the Fund to work with the Russian authorities to strengthen reforms in these and other areas that are important for economic growth.

- In Brazil, strict implementation of the Fund-supported program has restored confidence, and the outlook for some other countries in Latin America has also improved. In many other countries in this region, adjustment and reform efforts still require further strengthening.

- In the Middle East and Africa, countries that have benefited from the improvement in commodity prices, particularly for oil, have a renewed opportunity to accelerate progress on fiscal consolidation and diversification of their economies.

- Heavily indebted sub-Saharan African countries should take full and prompt advantage of the opportunity offered by debt relief under the enhanced HIPC Initiative to intensify and press ahead with reforms, including allocating additional resources for, and improving the efficiency of, spending aimed at poverty reduction. Outward-oriented strategies and peaceful resolution of armed conflicts are critical for sustaining economic development and higher growth.

- The tragic events that took place in Kosovo this year have had severe negative economic effects on other countries in the region. Coherent stabilization and reform policies supported by the international financial institutions are important for further economic development in the region. Therefore the Committee calls upon the Fund to continue its strengthened support in the form of programs and technical assistance to the countries involved.

A sustained pickup in domestic demand in Europe and Japan, together with medium-term growth in the U.S. in line with potential, will help to achieve a more balanced pattern of growth among the major industrial countries.

- The Committee welcomes the continued strong performance of the U.S. economy that has been critical in supporting global activity. Policies should continue to be directed to sustaining growth on a long-term basis by maintaining a strong fiscal position and increasing national saving.
- The Committee welcomes the growth of the Japanese economy in the first two quarters of 1999, which was supported by a rebound in consumer demand. Given that the prospect for continuing recovery in private demand remains uncertain, however, it urges the authorities to maintain a supportive stance of fiscal and monetary policies through a supplementary budget of appropriate size while, in the context of their zero interest rate policy, providing ample liquidity until deflationary concerns are dispelled. It is also critical to continue efforts to strengthen the banking system and foster corporate restructuring in order to achieve sustained growth in Japan, which should facilitate needed medium-term fiscal consolidation.
- The Committee is also encouraged by the pickup in growth in Europe in the context of price stability. While monetary conditions in the euro area are accommodative and should remain supportive, further efforts toward fiscal consolidation and structural reform, especially regarding the tax system and the labor and product markets, would improve prospects for sustained growth and a further reduction in unemployment.

3. The Committee emphasizes the importance of open and competitive markets as a key component of efforts to sustain growth and stability in the global economy. The proposed launch of new trade negotiations in Seattle later this year is an important opportunity to make further progress in this direction. Further broad-based liberalization in a strengthened rules-based multilateral trading system will help underpin global growth and stability. To ensure that the benefits of liberalized trade and investment are fully realized and shared, the Committee encourages the Fund to work with the Bank and the WTO to strengthen their programs of work to achieve better coherence in global policymaking. It recognizes that coordinated programs of support for developing countries, including targeted technical assistance and policy advice, will support them in meeting WTO commitments and implementing current agreements.

4. The Committee notes that, in fostering economic growth through appropriate macroeconomic policies and structural reforms, the Fund, in close cooperation with the World Bank, and consistent with their mandates, must also take into account the direct social consequences of adjustment and reform efforts as well as the complementarity of

macroeconomic and social policies for long-term growth and improved social indicators.

Poverty Reduction Initiatives

5. The Committee endorses the proposed replacement of the Enhanced Structural Adjustment Facility (ESAF) by the new Poverty Reduction and Growth Facility, which aims at making poverty reduction efforts among low-income members a key and more explicit element of a renewed growth-oriented economic strategy. The cornerstones of the new approach, which should continue to be based on sound macroeconomic policies, are as follows:

- A comprehensive Poverty Reduction Strategy Paper (PRSP) will be prepared by each country, with assistance from the World Bank and the Fund, and with strong country ownership based on public partnership, to guide the design of programs; the PRSP will need the approval of both Bank and Fund Boards.
- Social and sectoral programs aimed at poverty reduction will be taken fully into account in the design of economic policies for promoting faster sustainable growth.
- Greater emphasis will be accorded to good governance, in particular in all government activities, through greater transparency, effective monitoring procedures, anticorruption initiatives, accountability, and the involvement of all sectors of society.
- High priority will be accorded to key reform measures critical to achieving governments' social goals.

6. The Committee takes note of the crucial role to be played by the World Bank and other relevant international organizations in helping governments develop and monitor the implementation of their poverty reduction strategies. It endorses the proposal that PRSPs, as they are developed, provide the basis for all IDA and Poverty Reduction and Growth Facility lending operations and closer Bank-IMF collaboration.

7. The Committee welcomes the joint meeting of the Interim and Development Committees, held earlier today, on the enhanced HIPC Initiative. The proposals made by the Bank and the Fund to this end, which build upon wide-ranging comments from civil society and the international community, are aimed at providing faster, deeper, and broader debt relief and strengthening the link between debt relief and poverty reduction.

8. The Committee welcomes the agreement on the financing of the Fund's participation in the HIPC Initiative and continued concessional

lending by the Fund for growth and poverty reduction in its low-income member countries. It highly appreciates the financial support provided by a wide cross-section of the Fund's membership through bilateral contributions and endorses the decision adopted by the Executive Board for the Fund's participation. The Committee considers that the off-market transactions of up to 14 million ounces of fine gold by the Fund that are envisaged will be a one-time operation of a highly exceptional nature. This is part of a broader financing package to allow the Fund to contribute to the resolution of the debt problems of the HIPCs at the turn of the millennium and to the continuation of concessional operations to support countries' efforts to achieve sustained growth and poverty reduction. The Committee endorses the Executive Board's recommendation that the Board of Governors adopt a Resolution to this effect.

Architecture

9. The Committee welcomes the progressive translation of broad principles into concrete actions in developing and monitoring standards of importance to the international monetary and financial system.

- The Committee encourages the Fund to continue its collaborative efforts with the World Bank and other relevant organizations to complete work on the Financial Stability Forum's compendium of standards.
- The Committee urges all 47 Special Data Dissemination Standard (SDDS) subscribers to continue to enhance their statistical practices, and to report data on international reserves and related liabilities according to the agreed reserves template by March 2000. It encourages further work by the Fund on the SDDS, including on strengthening external debt data and developing macroprudential indicators. It looks forward to the launch of the operational phase of the General Data Dissemination System (GDDS) early next year. The Committee also urges the Fund and member countries to press ahead with efforts to improve the timeliness and comprehensiveness of data on capital flows. The Fund should provide technical assistance to enhance the quality and timeliness of data. Country authorities and relevant international organizations should also take urgent action to improve data on social spending and social indicators.
- The Committee adopts the attached *Code of Good Practices on Transparency in Monetary and Financial Policies: Declaration of Principles* as a guide for members to increase transparency in the conduct of these policies. The Committee urges all members

to implement the new Code as well as the previously agreed *Code of Good Practices on Fiscal Transparency.*

- The Committee welcomes the assessments of the implementation of the Basel Core Principles that have been made in the course of IMF surveillance and technical assistance, and urges that these be embedded into regular surveillance activities. It notes the work under way by the Basel Committee on Banking Supervision to review the 1988 Capital Accord and urges the Basel Committee to complete that review. It encourages the Fund to continue to support this process.

10. The Committee encourages the Fund, in cooperation with other standard-setting bodies, to continue to experiment with assessments of members' observance of international standards and codes of good practice and invites the Executive Board to consider whether to integrate such assessments into the surveillance process.

11. The Committee reiterates the importance of greater transparency in policymaking. With respect to IMF practices and members' policies, it strongly welcomes the steps taken:

- The widespread release of Public Information Notices (PINs), for which there is an agreement on presumption of publication; the public release of many IMF policy papers and the associated summaries of Board discussions; and the release of the external evaluators' reports on IMF surveillance and economic research activities;
- The decisions of 46 countries that have already volunteered to participate in the pilot program for the release of Article IV reports, with 15 reports already available on the Fund Website;
- The agreement to establish a presumption in favor of publication of Letters of Intent, Memoranda of Economic and Financial Policies, and Policy Framework Papers, and the widespread release of documents that has occurred since the policy of greater transparency was adopted; and
- The efforts to ascertain the views of the private sector on the experimental transparency reports.

12. The Committee encourages further actions to make IMF practices and members' policies more transparent without compromising the Fund's role as confidential advisor.

13. Experience in a few cases has highlighted the importance of promoting transparency and accountability especially when IMF resources are being used. In this connection, the Committee notes that the

implications of corruption and money laundering raise important issues for the credibility and effectiveness of IMF programs, and calls on the Fund to perform an authoritative review of its procedures and controls to identify ways to strengthen safeguards on the use of its funds and to report at its next meeting. The Committee considers that further actions for strengthening governance at the national and international levels are crucial. In the financial area, governments must maintain strong internal financial controls and tighten supervision and regulation of domestic financial institutions and offshore banking centers, including measures to deter money laundering. The Committee urges the Fund to enhance its support for members' efforts in these areas, building on its guidelines and other international standards for fostering good governance and transparency in all member countries, including through the application of the codes of good practice that the membership has established in the fiscal and monetary areas.

14. The Committee welcomes the progress made in financial sector reform and banking system restructuring in the context of IMF surveillance, technical assistance, and programs. It looks forward to the continued collaborative work of the Fund, the World Bank, and other institutions, including on the pilot Financial Sector Assessment Program that should facilitate early detection of financial system weaknesses and support a better coordinated dialogue with national authorities. The Committee encourages countries that have not done so to participate in the pilot program.

15. The Committee welcomes the recent independent, external evaluations of IMF surveillance and research activities, and encourages the Executive Board to examine the recommendations of the former further in the context of the next internal review in late 1999. The Committee also reaffirms the importance of independent evaluations of the Fund's operations and policies.

16. The Committee reiterates the importance of ongoing efforts to involve the private sector in forestalling and resolving financial crises, and notes the progress achieved in securing the involvement of the private sector in individual cases. In this connection, the Committee considers that the balance of the various considerations reflected in the report by G-7 Finance Ministers to the Köln Economic Summit provides a helpful framework within which the international community can work to address individual cases that may arise. The Committee asks the Executive Board to build on this framework and to report at the Committee's next meeting on the ways in which the broad principles have been implemented.

17. The Committee considers that increased mobility of capital has raised the requirements, in terms of both policy adaptability and institutional preparedness, for maintaining a fixed exchange rate regime. That said, members should be able to choose a regime that is appropriate to their particular circumstances and longer-term strategy. The choice of exchange rate regime and the implementation of supporting policies are critical for countries' economic development and financial stability, and in some cases potentially for the world economy. In all cases, IMF programs and surveillance should further focus on consistency of macroeconomic and other policies and institutional arrangements with the chosen exchange rate regime. The Fund should assist members to adapt to a world of global financial flows. The Committee encourages the Executive Board to continue to consider these matters, and to report to the Committee on its work.

18. Persistent and sizable capital inflows can be highly destabilizing particularly if they are intermediated by poorly regulated and unsupervised financial institutions. In this context, the Committee welcomes the Fund's recent work on the appropriate pace and sequencing of capital account opening, which has led to a fuller understanding of the conditions for orderly and sustainable liberalization, and has broadly confirmed earlier conclusions that, over the long term, open capital flows accompanied by appropriate prudential measures will benefit the world economy. The Committee encourages the Fund to build on its examination of individual countries' use and liberalization of controls, paying particular attention to the relationship between capital account liberalization and financial sector stability.

19. The Committee calls on the Fund and World Bank to work together, in cooperation with national debt management experts, to develop a set of best practices in public debt management by the spring to assist countries in their efforts to reduce vulnerability.

20. The Committee encourages all members to continue to work on preventive action and to put in place millennium contingency plans, noting that, although business, financial institutions, and government agencies around the world have made considerable progress in preparing computer systems, a risk remains that Y2K problems will be anticipated or will arise, with potential negative consequences for growth, international trade, and international capital flows. To help forestall, and if necessary resolve, possible balance of payments problems related to the Y2K phenomenon, the Committee endorses the Executive Board's decision to introduce a temporary new facility for providing outright short-term access to IMF resources to members facing identifiable Y2K-related balance of payments needs.

21. The Committee endorses the Executive Board's recommendation that the Board of Governors adopt a Resolution transforming the Interim Committee into the International Monetary and Financial Committee and strengthening its role as the advisory committee of the Board of Governors.

22. The next meeting of the Committee will be held in Washington, D.C. on April 16, 2000.

Attachment

CODE OF GOOD PRACTICES ON TRANSPARENCY IN MONETARY AND FINANCIAL POLICIES: DECLARATION OF PRINCIPLES

Introduction

1. In the context of strengthening the architecture of the international monetary and financial system, the Interim Committee in its April and October 1998 Communiqués called on the Fund to develop a code of transparency practices for monetary and financial policies, in cooperation with appropriate institutions. The Fund, working together with the Bank for International Settlements, and in consultation with a representative group of central banks, financial agencies, other relevant international and regional organizations,[1] and selected academic experts, has developed a *Code of Good Practices on Transparency in Monetary and Financial Policies.* The Code parallels the *Code of Good Practices in Fiscal Transparency* developed by the Fund and endorsed by the Interim Committee in April 1998.

2. The *Code of Good Practices on Transparency in Monetary and Financial Policies* identifies desirable transparency practices for central banks in their conduct of monetary policy and for central banks and other financial agencies in their conduct of financial policies. The definitions of "central bank," "financial agencies," "financial policies," and "government" as used in this Code are given in the attached Annex.

[1]In addition to the Bank for International Settlements, the following international and regional organizations and international financial sector groupings were consulted: Basel Committee on Bank Supervision (BCBS), Center for Latin American Monetary Studies (CEMLA), Committee on Payment and Settlement Systems (CPSS), European Central Bank, International Association of Insurance Supervisors (IAIS), International Finance Corporation, International Organization of Securities Commissions (IOSCO), Organization for Economic Cooperation and Development (OECD), and the World Bank.

3. For purposes of the Code, transparency refers to an environment in which the objectives of policy, its legal, institutional, and economic framework, policy decisions and their rationale, data and information related to monetary and financial policies, and the terms of agencies' accountability are provided to the public on an understandable, accessible, and timely basis. Thus, the transparency practices listed in the Code focus on: (1) clarity of roles, responsibilities and objectives of central banks and financial agencies; (2) the processes for formulating and reporting of monetary policy decisions by the central bank and of financial policies by financial agencies; (3) public availability of information on monetary and financial policies; and (4) accountability and assurances of integrity by the central bank and financial agencies.

4. The case for transparency of monetary and financial policies is based on two main premises. First, the effectiveness of monetary and financial policies can be strengthened if the goals and instruments of policy are known to the public and if the authorities can make a credible commitment to meeting them. In making available more information about monetary and financial policies, good transparency practices promote the potential efficiency of markets. Second, good governance calls for central banks and financial agencies to be accountable, particularly where the monetary and financial authorities are granted a high degree of autonomy. In cases when conflicts might arise between or within government units (e.g., if the central bank or a financial agency acts as both owner and financial supervisor of a financial institution or if the responsibilities for monetary and foreign exchange policy are shared), transparency in the mandate and clear rules and procedures in the operations of the agencies can help in their resolution, strengthen governance, and facilitate policy consistency.

5. In making the objectives of monetary policy public, the central bank enhances the public's understanding of what it is seeking to achieve, and provides a context for articulating its own policy choices, thereby contributing to the effectiveness of monetary policy. Further, by providing the private sector with a clear description of the considerations guiding monetary policy decisions, transparency about the policy process makes the monetary policy transmission mechanism generally more effective, in part by ensuring that market expectations can be formed more efficiently. By providing the public with adequate information about its activities, the central bank can establish a mechanism for strengthening its credibility by matching its actions to its public statements.

6. Transparency by financial agencies, particularly in clarifying their objectives, should also contribute to policy effectiveness by enabling financial market participants to assess better the context of finan-

cial policies, thereby reducing uncertainty in the decision-making of market participants. Moreover, by enabling market participants and the general public to understand and evaluate financial policies, transparency is likely to be conducive to good policy-making. This can help to promote financial as well as systemic stability. Transparent descriptions of the policy formulation process provide the public with an understanding of the rules of the game. The release of adequate information to the public on the activities of financial agencies provides an additional mechanism for enhancing the credibility of their actions. There may also be circumstances when public accountability of decisions by financial agencies can reduce the potential for moral hazard.

7. The benefits for countries adopting good transparency practices in monetary and financial policies have to be weighed against the potential costs. In situations where increased transparency in monetary and financial policies could endanger the effectiveness of policies, or be potentially harmful to market stability or the legitimate interests of supervised and other entities, it may be appropriate to limit the extent of such transparency. Limiting transparency in selected areas needs to be seen, however, in the context of a generally transparent environment.

8. In the case of monetary policy, the rationale for limiting some types of disclosure arises because it could adversely affect the decision-making process and the effectiveness of policies. Similarly, exchange rate policy considerations, notably, but not exclusively, in countries with fixed exchange rate regimes, may provide justification for limiting certain disclosure practices. For example, extensive disclosure requirements about internal policy discussion on money and exchange market operations might disrupt markets, constrain the free flow of discussion by policymakers, or prevent the adoption of contingency plans. Thus, it might be inappropriate for central banks to disclose internal deliberations and documentation, and there are circumstances in which it would not be appropriate for central banks to disclose their near-term monetary and exchange rate policy implementation tactics and provide detailed information on foreign exchange operations. Similarly, there may be good reasons for the central bank (and financial agencies) not to make public their contingency plans, including possible emergency lending.

9. Additional concerns could be posed by some aspects of the transparency of financial policies. Moral hazard, market discipline, and financial market stability considerations may justify limiting both the content and timing of the disclosure of some corrective actions and emergency lending decisions, and information pertaining to market and firm-specific conditions. In order to maintain access to sensitive information from market participants, there is also a need to safeguard the confidentiality

and privacy of information on individual firms (commonly referred to as "commercial confidentiality"). Similarly, it may be inappropriate for financial authorities to make public their supervisory deliberations and enforcement actions related to individual financial institutions, markets, and individuals.

10. Transparency practices differ not only in substance, but also in form. With regard to informing the public about monetary and financial institutions and their policies, an important issue concerns the modalities that these public disclosures should take. In particular with regard to monetary policy, should transparency practices have a legislative basis in a central bank law, or be based in other legislation or regulation, or be adopted through other means? The Code takes a pragmatic approach to this issue and recognizes that a variety of arrangements can lead to good transparency practices. On matters pertaining to the roles, responsibilities, and objectives of central banks (and for principal financial regulatory agencies), it recommends that key features be specified in the authorizing legislation (e.g., a central bank law). Specifying some of these practices in legislation gives them particular prominence and avoids ad hoc and frequent changes to these important aspects of the operations of central banks and relevant financial agencies. Information about other transparency aspects, such as how policy is formulated and implemented and the provision of information, can be presented in a more flexible manner. However, it is important that such information be readily accessible, so that the public can with reasonable effort obtain and assimilate the information.

11. In the context of good governance and accountability, as well as the promotion of efficient markets, reference to the public in this code should ideally encompass all interested individuals and institutions. In some cases, particularly for financial policies, it may be expedient for the purposes of administering or implementing certain regulations and policies to define the concept of the public more narrowly to refer only to those individuals and institutions that are most directly affected by the regulations and policies in question.

12. The focus of the Code is on transparency. While good transparency practices for the formulation and reporting of monetary and financial policies help to contribute to the adoption of sound policies, the Code is not designed to offer judgments on the appropriateness or desirability of specific monetary or financial policies or frameworks that countries should adopt. Transparency is not an end in itself, nor is transparency a substitute for pursuing sound policies; rather, transparency and sound policies are better seen as complements. In the realm of financial policies, there are complements to this code that go beyond transparency

to promote good policies, notably the *Core Principles for Effective Banking Supervision* formulated by the Basel Committee for Banking Supervision, the *Objectives and Principles of Securities Regulation* formulated by the International Organization of Securities Commissions (IOSCO), and standards being developed by the Committee on Payment and Settlement Systems (CPSS), the International Association of Insurance Supervisors (IAIS), and the International Accounting Standards Committee (IASC). As these and other financial sector groupings develop and make significant adjustments in their principles and standards as they relate to transparency practices for financial agencies (e.g., in data dissemination requirements for financial agencies), this Code may have to be adjusted accordingly.

13. The Code is directed at the transparency requirements of central banks and financial agencies, not at the transparency procedures relating to firms and individual institutions. However, the benefits of transparency for monetary and financial policies may be fostered by appropriate policies to promote transparency for markets in general, for the institutions that are being supervised, and for self-regulatory organizations.

14. Monetary and financial policies are interrelated and often mutually reinforcing, with the health of the financial system affecting the conduct of monetary policy and vice versa. However, the institutional arrangements for these two types of policies differ considerably, particularly with regard to their roles, responsibilities, and objectives and their policy formulation and implementation processes. To take account of this, the Code is separated into two parts: good transparency practices for monetary policy by central banks; and good transparency practices for financial policies by financial agencies. The basic elements of transparency for both policies are, however, similar. It should be recognized that not all transparency practices are equally applicable to all financial agencies, and the transparency objectives among different financial sectors vary. For some, the emphasis is on market efficiency considerations, for others the focus is on market and systemic stability, while for others the principal consideration is client-asset protection.

15. The operation of a country's payment system affects the conduct of monetary policies and the functioning of the financial system, and the design of payment systems has implications for systemic stability. The institutional structures of the payment system, however, are often significantly more complex than for monetary and other financial policies, and differ considerably across countries. In many instances, the operation of a country's payment system is split between the public and private sectors, including self-regulatory bodies. Nevertheless, most of the transparency practices listed in the Code for financial agencies are applicable for the roles and functions of central banks or other relevant public agencies exer-

cising responsibility for overseeing the nation's payment systems. The coverage of transparency practices for financial policies in the Code includes those for the operation of systemically important components of the nation's payment system, and, where appropriate, makes allowance for the special nature of the payment system's operations (e.g., 5.3).

16. The Code is of sufficient breadth to span and be applied to a wide range of monetary and financial frameworks, and thus to the full range of the Fund membership. Elements of the Code are drawn from a review of good transparency practices used in a number of countries and discussed in the professional literature. The Code thus represents a distillation of concepts and practices that are already in use and for which there is a record of experience. The manner in which transparency is applied and achieved, however, may differ, reflecting different institutional arrangements with respect to monetary and financial policies and legal traditions. The good transparency practices contained in the Code will, therefore, have to be implemented flexibly and over time to take account of a country's particular circumstances. A number of Fund members currently lack sufficient resources and the institutional capacity to implement all of the good transparency practices listed in the Code. These practices are included in the Code in the anticipation that countries would aspire over time to introduce such good practices.

Good Transparency Practices for Monetary Policy by Central Banks

I. Clarity of Roles, Responsibilities, and Objectives of Central Banks for Monetary Policy

1.1 The ultimate objective(s) and institutional framework of monetary policy should be clearly defined in relevant legislation or regulation, including, where appropriate, a central bank law.

1.1.1 The ultimate objective(s) of monetary policy should be specified in legislation and publicly disclosed and explained.

1.1.2 The responsibilities of the central bank should be specified in legislation.

1.1.3 The legislation establishing the central bank should specify that the central bank has the authority to utilize monetary policy instruments to attain the policy objective(s).

1.1.4 Institutional responsibility for foreign exchange policy should be publicly disclosed.

1.1.5 The broad modalities of accountability for the conduct of monetary policy and for any other responsibilities assigned to the central bank should be specified in legislation.

1.1.6 If, in exceptional circumstances, the government has the authority to override central bank policy decisions, the conditions under which this authority may be invoked and the manner in which it is publicly disclosed should be specified in legislation.

1.1.7 The procedures for appointment, terms of office, and any general criteria for removal of the heads and members of the governing body of the central bank should be specified in legislation.

1.2 The institutional relationship between monetary and fiscal operations should be clearly defined.[2]

1.2.1 If credits, advances, or overdrafts to the government by the central bank are permitted, the conditions when they are permitted, and any limits thereof, should be publicly disclosed.

1.2.2 The amounts and terms of credits, advances, or overdrafts to the government by the central bank and those of deposits of the government with the central bank should be publicly disclosed.

1.2.3 The procedures for direct central bank participation in the primary markets for government securities, where permitted, and in the secondary markets, should be publicly disclosed.

1.2.4 Central bank involvement in the rest of the economy (e.g., through equity ownership, membership on governing boards, procurement, or provision of services for fee) should be conducted in an open and public manner on the basis of clear principles and procedures.

1.2.5 The manner in which central bank profits are allocated and how capital is maintained should be publicly disclosed.

1.3 Agency roles performed by the central bank on behalf of the government should be clearly defined.

1.3.1 Responsibilities, if any, of the central bank in (i) the management of domestic and external public debt and foreign exchange reserves, (ii) as banker to the government, (iii) as fiscal agent of the government, and (iv) as advisor on economic and financial policies and in the field of international cooperation, should be publicly disclosed.

1.3.2 The allocation of responsibilities among the central bank, the ministry of finance, or a separate public agency,[3] for the primary debt issues, secondary market arrangements, depository facilities, and clearing and settlement arrangements for trade in government securities, should be publicly disclosed.

[2]The practices in this area should be consistent with the principles of the International Monetary Fund's Code of Good Practices on Fiscal Transparency.

[3]The principles for transparency procedures listed in this Code, where applicable and adjusted as necessary, apply where a separate public agency has been designated to manage the country's public debt.

II. Open Process for Formulating and Reporting Monetary Policy Decisions

2.1 The framework, instruments, and any targets that are used to pursue the objectives of monetary policy should be publicly disclosed and explained. 2.1.1 The procedures and practices governing monetary policy instruments and operations should be publicly disclosed and explained.

2.1.2 The rules and procedures for the central bank's relationships and transactions with counter parties in its monetary operations and in the markets where it operates should be publicly disclosed.

2.2 Where a permanent monetary policy-making body meets to assess underlying economic developments, monitor progress toward achieving its monetary policy objective(s), and formulate policy for the period ahead, information on the composition, structure, and functions of that body should be publicly disclosed.

2.2.1 If the policymaking body has regularly scheduled meetings to assess underlying economic developments, monitor progress toward achieving its monetary policy objective(s), and formulate policy for the period ahead, the advance meeting schedule should be publicly disclosed.

2.3 Changes in the setting of monetary policy instruments (other than fine-tuning measures) should be publicly announced and explained in a timely manner.

2.3.1 The central bank should publicly disclose, with a preannounced maximum delay, the main considerations underlying its monetary policy decisions.

2.4 The central bank should issue periodic public statements on progress toward achieving its monetary policy objective(s) as well as prospects for achieving them. The arrangements could differ depending on the monetary policy framework, including the exchange rate regime.

2.4.1 The central bank should periodically present its monetary policy objectives to the public, specifying, inter alia, their rationale, quantitative targets, and instruments where applicable, and the key underlying assumptions.

2.4.2 The central bank should present to the public on a specified schedule a report on the evolving macroeconomic situation, and their implications for its monetary policy objective(s).

2.5 For proposed substantive technical changes to the structure of monetary regulations, there should be a presumption in favor of public consultations, within an appropriate period.

2.6 The regulations on data reporting by financial institutions to the central bank for monetary policy purposes should be publicly disclosed.

III. Public Availability of Information on Monetary Policy

3.1 Presentations and releases of central bank data should meet the standards related to coverage, periodicity, timeliness of data, and access by the public that are consistent with the Fund's data dissemination standards.

3.2 The central bank should publicly disclose its balance sheet on a preannounced schedule and, after a predetermined interval, publicly disclose selected information on its aggregate market transactions.

3.2.1 Summary central bank balance sheets should be publicly disclosed on a frequent and preannounced schedule. Detailed central bank balance sheets prepared according to appropriate and publicly documented accounting standards should be publicly disclosed at least annually by the central bank.

3.2.2 Information on the central bank's monetary operations, including aggregate amounts and terms of refinance or other facilities (subject to the maintenance of commercial confidentiality) should be publicly disclosed on a preannounced schedule.

3.2.3 Consistent with confidentiality and privacy of information on individual firms, aggregate information on emergency financial support by the central bank should be publicly disclosed through an appropriate central bank statement when such disclosure will not be disruptive to financial stability.

3.2.4 Information about the country's foreign exchange reserve assets, liabilities, and commitments by the monetary authorities should be publicly disclosed on a preannounced schedule, consistent with the Fund's data dissemination standards.

3.3 The central bank should establish and maintain public information services.

3.3.1 The central bank should have a publications program, including an Annual Report.

3.3.2 Senior central bank officials should be ready to explain their institution's objective(s) and performance to the public, and have a presumption in favor of releasing the text of their statements to the public.

3.4 Texts of regulations issued by the central bank should be readily available to the public.

IV. Accountability and Assurances of Integrity by the Central Bank

4.1 Officials of the central bank should be available to appear before a designated public authority to report on the conduct of monetary policy, explain the policy objective(s) of their institution, describe their performance in achieving their objective(s), and, as appropriate, exchange views on the state of the economy and the financial system.

4.2 The central bank should publicly disclose audited financial statements of its operations on a preannounced schedule.

4.2.1 The financial statements should be audited by an independent auditor. Information on accounting policies and any qualification to the statements should be an integral part of the publicly disclosed financial statements.

4.2.2 Internal governance procedures necessary to ensure the integrity of operations, including internal audit arrangements, should be publicly disclosed.

4.3 Information on the expenses and revenues in operating the central bank should be publicly disclosed annually.

4.4 Standards for the conduct of personal financial affairs of officials and staff of the central bank and rules to prevent exploitation of conflicts of interest, including any general fiduciary obligation, should be publicly disclosed.

4.4.1 Information about legal protections for officials and staff of the central bank in the conduct of their official duties should be publicly disclosed.

Good Transparency Practices for Financial Policies by Financial Agencies

V. Clarity of Roles, Responsibilities, and Objectives of Financial Agencies Responsible for Financial Policies[4]

5.1 The broad objective(s) and institutional framework of financial agencies should be clearly defined, preferably in relevant legislation or regulation.

5.1.1 The broad objective(s) of financial agencies should be publicly disclosed and explained.

5.1.2 The responsibilities of the financial agencies and the authority to conduct financial policies should be publicly disclosed.

5.1.3 Where applicable, the broad modalities of accountability for financial agencies should be publicly disclosed.

5.1.4 Where applicable, the procedures for appointment, terms of office, and any general criteria for removal of the heads and members of the governing bodies of financial agencies should be publicly disclosed.

5.2 The relationship between financial agencies should be publicly disclosed.

5.3 The role of oversight agencies with regard to payment systems should be publicly disclosed.

[4]Refer to the Annex for definitions of financial agencies and financial policies.

5.3.1 The agencies overseeing the payment system should promote the timely public disclosure of general policy principles (including risk management policies) that affect the robustness of systemically important payment systems.

5.4 Where financial agencies have oversight responsibilities for self-regulatory organizations (e.g., payment systems), the relationship between them should be publicly disclosed.

5.5 Where self-regulatory organizations are authorized to perform part of the regulatory and supervisory process, they should be guided by the same good transparency practices specified for financial agencies.

VI. Open Process for Formulating and Reporting of Financial Policies

6.1 The conduct of policies by financial agencies should be transparent, compatible with confidentiality considerations and the need to preserve the effectiveness of actions by regulatory and oversight agencies.

6.1.1 The regulatory framework and operating procedures governing the conduct of financial policies should be publicly disclosed and explained.

6.1.2 The regulations for financial reporting by financial institutions to financial agencies should be publicly disclosed.

6.1.3 The regulations for the operation of organized financial markets (including those for issuers of traded financial instruments) should be publicly disclosed.

6.1.4 Where financial agencies charge fees to financial institutions, the structure of such fees should be publicly disclosed.

6.1.5 Where applicable, formal procedures for information sharing and consultation between financial agencies (including central banks), domestic and international, should be publicly disclosed.

6.2 Significant changes in financial policies should be publicly announced and explained in a timely manner.

6.3 Financial agencies should issue periodic public reports on how their overall policy objectives are being pursued.

6.4 For proposed substantive technical changes to the structure of financial regulations, there should be a presumption in favor of public consultations, within an appropriate period.

VII. Public Availability of Information on Financial Policies

7.1 Financial agencies should issue a periodic public report on the major developments of the sector(s) of the financial system for which they carry designated responsibility.

7.2 Financial agencies should seek to ensure that, consistent with confidentiality requirements, there is public reporting of aggregate data related to their jurisdictional responsibilities on a timely and regular basis.

7.3 Where applicable, financial agencies should publicly disclose their balance sheets on a preannounced schedule and, after a predetermined interval, publicly disclose information on aggregate market transactions.

7.3.1 Consistent with confidentiality and privacy of information on individual firms, aggregate information on emergency financial support by financial agencies should be publicly disclosed through an appropriate statement when such disclosure will not be disruptive to financial stability.

7.4 Financial agencies should establish and maintain public information services.

7.4.1 Financial agencies should have a publications program, including a periodic public report on their principal activities issued at least annually.

7.4.2 Senior financial agency officials should be ready to explain their institution's objective(s) and performance to the public, and have a presumption in favor of releasing the text of their statements to the public.

7.5 Texts of regulations and any other generally applicable directives and guidelines issued by financial agencies should be readily available to the public.

7.6 Where there are deposit insurance guarantees, policy-holder guarantees, and any other client asset protection schemes, information on the nature and form of such protections, on the operating procedures, on how the guarantee is financed, and on the performance of the arrangement, should be publicly disclosed.

7.7 Where financial agencies oversee consumer protection arrangements (such as dispute settlement processes), information on such arrangements should be publicly disclosed.

VIII. Accountability and Assurances of Integrity by Financial Agencies

8.1 Officials of financial agencies should be available to appear before a designated public authority to report on the conduct of financial policies, explain the policy objective(s) of their institution, describe their performance in pursuing their objective(s), and, as appropriate, exchange views on the state of the financial system.

8.2 Where applicable, financial agencies should publicly disclose audited financial statements of their operations on a preannounced schedule.

8.2.1 Financial statements, if any, should be audited by an independent auditor. Information on accounting policies and any qualification to the statements should be an integral part of the publicly disclosed financial statements.

8.2.2 Internal governance procedures necessary to ensure the integrity of operations, including internal audit arrangements, should be publicly disclosed.

8.3 Where applicable, information on the operating expenses and revenues of financial agencies should be publicly disclosed annually.

8.4 Standards for the conduct of personal financial affairs of officials and staff of financial agencies and rules to prevent exploitation of conflicts of interest, including any general fiduciary obligation, should be publicly disclosed.

8.4.1 Information about legal protections for officials and staff of financial agencies in the conduct of their official duties should be publicly disclosed.

Annex: Definitions of Certain Terms

To facilitate presentation, certain general terms are used to capture different institutional arrangements in a summary fashion. The following descriptive definitions are used in the Code.

Central Bank

The institutional arrangements for assigning responsibility for the conduct of a country's monetary policy differ among the Fund's membership. For most Fund members, this responsibility is assigned to the central bank or to a system of constituent national central banks in a multinational central bank arrangement. There are a number of countries, however, where this role is designated to a "monetary authority" or to a "currency board." To facilitate presentation, the term "central bank" in the Code refers to the institution responsible for conducting monetary policy, which may or may not be a central bank.

Financial Agencies

A wide range of institutional arrangements prevail among Fund members with regard to which unit of government carries exclusive or primary responsibility for the regulation, supervision, and oversight of the financial and payment systems. In a few countries, an agency has been established with responsibility for regulating and supervising an array of financial institutions (banking, insurance, and securities firms) and markets (securities, derivatives, and commodity futures). For most countries, the oversight responsibility for the financial sector is shared among several agencies. Thus, responsibility for the conduct of bank regulation and supervision or for bank deposit insurance policies in some countries is assigned to the central bank, or to an independent bank supervisory or deposit insurance agency, or split among several units of government. Similarly, responsibility for the conduct of policies related to the oversight of certain categories of financial institutions is assigned to the central bank or to a specialized agency. In some cases (e.g., payment systems) a public agency oversees the activities of private sector self-regulatory bodies. To facilitate presentation, the phrase "financial agencies" is used to refer to the institutional arrangements for the regulation, supervision, and oversight of the financial and payment systems, including markets and institutions, with the view to promoting financial stability, market efficiency, and client-asset and consumer protection. (Where the central bank carries responsibility for financial policies, some of the good transparency practices listed for financial agencies in Sections V-VIII of the Code are already specified in the transparency practices listed for central banks in Sections I-IV of the Code.)

Financial Policies

The term "financial policies" in the Code refers to policies related to the regulation, supervision, and oversight of the financial and payment systems, including markets and institutions, with the view to promoting financial stability, market efficiency, and client-asset and consumer protection.

Government

Unless a particular unit of government is specifically identified in the Code, reference to "government" in the Code refers either to the executive branch of government or to a particular ministry or public agency, depending on the issue at hand or the established tradition of government in particular countries.

Interim Committee Composition

as of September 26, 1999

Gordon Brown, *Chairman*

Ibrahim A. Al-Assaf	Saudi Arabia
Giuliano Amato	Italy
Gordon Brown[1]	United Kingdom
Antonio Casas González	Venezuela
Peter Costello	Australia
Dai Xianglong,	China
Emile Doumba	Gabon
Hans Eichel	Germany
Roque B. Fernández	Argentina
Viktor Gerashchenko	Russian Federation
Marianne Jelved	Denmark
Abdelouahab Keramane	Algeria
Mohammed K. Khirbash[2]	United Arab Emirates
Pedro Sampaio Malan	Brazil
Trevor A. Manuel	South Africa
Paul Martin	Canada
Kiichi Miyazawa	Japan
Didier Reynders	Belgium
Syahril Sabirin	Indonesia
Yashwant Sinha	India
Dominique Strauss-Kahn	France
Lawrence H. Summers	United States
Kaspar Villiger	Switzerland
Gerrit Zalm	Netherlands

Alternate attending for member:
[1]Eddie George
[2]Sultan Bin Nasser Al-Suwaidi

Joint Ministerial Committee of the Boards of Governors of the Bank and the Fund on the Transfer of Real Resources to Developing Countries (Development Committee)

PRESS COMMUNIQUÉ

September 27, 1999

1. The sixtieth meeting of the Development Committee was held in Washington, D.C., on September 27, 1999 under the chairmanship of Mr. Tarrin Nimmanahaeminda, Minister of Finance of Thailand.

2. *Heavily Indebted Poor Countries Debt Initiative (HIPC) and Enhanced Poverty Focus of IDA and ESAF Supported Programs.* Ministers expressed their appreciation to the Bank and the Fund for the transparent and participatory manner in which they conducted the 1999 HIPC Initiative review. They welcomed the important role played by civil society in the development of proposals designed to make the debt relief under the HIPC Initiative deeper, broader, and faster.

3. Ministers endorsed—subject to the availability of funding—the enhancements to the HIPC Initiative framework for countries pursuing sound policies and committed to reform. In this context, they expressed support for: (i) a lowering of the debt sustainability thresholds to provide a greater safety cushion and increased prospects for a permanent exit from unsustainable debt; (ii) the provision of faster debt relief through interim assistance; (iii) the introduction of floating completion points that would shift the focus of assessment toward positive achievements and outcomes rather than the length of track record; and (iv) the resulting increase in the number of countries expected to be eligible for debt relief.

4. Ministers also endorsed the proposed framework for strengthening the link between debt relief and poverty reduction, while recognizing that debt relief alone would be insufficient to achieve this goal. In this context, they welcomed the proposed Poverty Reduction Strategy Papers, to be prepared by national authorities in close collaboration with Bank and Fund staff. They stressed that the Poverty Paper should be in place by the decision point; they recognized, however, that on a transitional basis the decision point could be reached without agreement on a

Poverty Paper, but in all cases demonstrable progress in implementing a poverty reduction strategy would be required by the completion point.

5. Ministers also welcomed and endorsed the proposals developed by the Bank and Fund to extend the same approach to enhance the poverty focus of all IDA and ESAF supported programs, and to strengthen collaboration between the two institutions. The Committee emphasized that the strategies set out in the new Poverty Papers should be country-driven, be developed transparently with broad participation of elected institutions, stakeholders including civil society, key donors, and regional development banks, and have a clear link with the agreed international development goals—principles that are embedded in the Comprehensive Development Framework. They stressed in particular the need to develop macroeconomic, structural, and social policies that will contribute to long-term poverty reduction, and the need to develop measurable intermediate and outcome indicators to monitor progress. Ministers stressed the crucial role good governance plays in HIPC implementation in establishing a framework that discourages corruption and provides more effective monitoring and quality control over fiscal expenditures. Ministers called on the Bank and Fund, in accordance with their respective mandates and expertise, to give all possible assistance to countries in bringing together the necessary social, structural, and macroeconomic policies required in developing poverty reduction strategies, recognizing the countries' capacity constraints. The Poverty Papers would provide the basis for all IDA and Fund lending to low-income countries. Ministers also encouraged regional development banks and donors to use the Poverty Papers to guide their support.

6. Ministers welcomed the proposed reform of the ESAF aimed at giving greater prominence to the goal of supporting countries' poverty reduction efforts and the proposed renaming of the facility as the Poverty Reduction and Growth Facility. Recognizing that the new approach will involve substantial changes in Bank and Fund operations to combat poverty, and the need to tailor the approach to individual country circumstances and to learn quickly from experience in early cases, the Committee strongly welcomed the commitments of the President and Managing Director to its effective implementation. Ministers looked forward to receiving reports on progress achieved.

7. Ministers reaffirmed the importance of implementing the enhanced HIPC Initiative framework in accordance with the principles that have guided the Initiative since its inception, including (i) additionality of debt relief, (ii) the maintenance of the financial integrity of multilateral financial institutions, and (iii) the importance of burden sharing on a fair and equitable basis, including of the costs to multilateral institutions.

They agreed financing of debt relief should not compromise the financing made available through concessional windows such as IDA. Ministers expressed appreciation for the many contributions to the HIPC Initiative made thus far, and for the efforts made by multilateral development institutions to provide funding for the Initiative from their own resources. Ministers recognized that most of these institutions will need bilateral support on an urgent basis in order to meet the additional costs resulting from the proposed enhanced framework and to enable them to implement the Initiative rapidly. The Committee welcomes the agreement on the financing of the Fund's participation in the HIPC Initiative and continued concessional lending by the Fund for growth and poverty reduction in low-income member countries.

8. Ministers also welcomed agreement on the elements of a financing plan for multilateral development banks that respect the above principles. This will permit the Enhanced HIPC Framework to be launched and the delivery of debt relief to begin for those countries requiring retroactive relief and those expected to reach their decision points over the near term. They asked the World Bank to work actively and closely with the whole group of donors and other MDBs to ensure that financing is mobilized to fully fund HIPC debt relief over the longer term.

9. Ministers also welcomed the agreement by the Paris Club to increase its debt relief under the enhanced framework by providing increased debt reduction in NPV terms up to 90 percent or more, if needed, on commercial loans as well as additional relief on ODA claims—up to full cancellation—on a bilateral basis.

10. Ministers welcomed the continuing progress in the implementation of the Initiative, noting that to date 14 countries have been considered under the Initiative—with four brought to their completion points. The Committee urged the speedy implementation of the enhanced Initiative so that as many countries as possible qualify for assistance under the Initiative by end 2000.

11. *IBRD Capital Adequacy.* Ministers reviewed a report from the World Bank that reflected ongoing discussions by the Bank's Executive Board and management on options to maintain and support the IBRD's financial capacity. The Committee agreed with the report's finding that the Bank's finances remain sound. Ministers also recognized that the Bank's financial capacity may limit its ability to respond to future demands, especially when there was a deterioration in the global financial environment. Ministers requested management and the Executive Board to continue their examination of the level of financial capacity needed to preserve the IBRD's financial integrity while permitting it to help meet, within its mandate, the development needs of

borrowing member countries. Ministers requested that the Bank report regularly to the Committee on these issues.

12. *Developing and Transition Countries and the International Trade Agenda.* The Committee noted that effective development and trade policy have become increasingly intertwined. They emphasized the importance of trade to development, poverty alleviation, and sustained global economic recovery. Ministers also emphasized that the next round of trade negotiations needed to deliver early and substantial benefits for developing and transition countries, in particular for the least developed countries. This would require improved market access and further reducing barriers to trade. They stressed that if developing and transition countries are to use the international trading system effectively to promote growth and reduce poverty they will need to become active partners in the next round of trade negotiations. Ministers welcomed the commitment of the new Director-General of the World Trade Organization, Mr. Mike Moore, to achieve this goal and urged the World Bank, the Fund, WTO, UNCTAD, and other agencies to help developing and transition countries build their capacity to participate in further rounds of negotiations. The Committee called on the World Bank, IMF and WTO to cooperate with other parties in developing effective programs of capacity building for trade, including through the Integrated Framework for Trade Related Technical Assistance for the Least Developed Countries. The Bank, in particular, could provide financial and technical support to improve trade-related infrastructure and institutions, helping to build capacity in domestic institutions involved in trade policy and negotiations, and undertaking research on trade barriers to developing countries' exports.

13. *World Bank Support for Strengthening International Financial Architecture.* Ministers welcomed the role the World Bank Group is playing to help strengthen the global financial architecture to reduce the risk and severity of financial crises, and to reduce the vulnerability of developing countries to crises when they occur. The Committee stressed that at the country level the Bank's primary focus, given the objective of preventing crises, should be on assisting developing countries to strengthen their domestic financial markets and their integration with the global financial system. This should be done through helping countries overcome structural and social sources of vulnerability and build the needed policy and institutional capacity. Given the breadth and complexity of the agenda, Ministers encouraged the Bank and the Fund to focus on their areas of comparative strength while developing partnerships with other international institutions. Ministers welcomed progress in the joint Bank/Fund program of financial sector assessments and the Bank's program of Social and Structural Reviews. They also welcomed the pro-

posed enhanced collaboration with the Fund in assisting interested countries to assess their progress in implementing a range of international norms and good practices, with due consideration to differing country conditions. The Committee encouraged the Bank to continue to bring developing country experience and perspectives to the international debate. In this context, they noted the establishment of a global forum on corporate governance, launched in collaboration with the OECD, and the Bank's supportive role for work on insolvency, accounting, and auditing.

14. Ministers welcomed the Bank's help to developing countries on social issues, as well as its report on managing the social dimensions of crises and good practices in social policies. They encouraged the Bank to continue to develop this work and draw on it in supporting countries' poverty reduction efforts. The Bank should accumulate and disseminate knowledge of good practices to help guide countries seeking to create institutions and implement policies that will forestall and mitigate the social costs of economic shocks and protect the most vulnerable.

15. Ministers welcomed the steps being taken to strengthen the work of the Development and Interim Committees, both to better reflect the enhanced level of cooperation between the Bank and the Fund and to reduce duplication in the committees' agendas. They encouraged the Bank and Fund to continue to review experience in this area.

16. *Next Meeting.* The Committee's next meeting is scheduled for April 17, 2000 in Washington, D.C.

DEVELOPMENT COMMITTEE COMPOSITION

as of September 27, 1999

Tarrin Nimmanahaeminda, *Chairman*

Ibrahim A. Al-Assaf	Saudi Arabia
Giuliano Amato[1]	Italy
Eduardo Aninat	Chile
Peter Costello	Australia
Pascal Couchepin	Switzerland
Hilde Frafjord Johnson	Norway
Jose Angel Gurria-Treviño	Mexico
Victor Khristenko	Russian Federation
Pedro Sampaio Malan	Brazil
Kelebone Albert Maope	Lesotho
Paul Martin	Canada
Kiichi Miyazawa[2]	Japan
N'Goran Niamien	Côte d'Ivoire
Fathallah Oualalou	Morocco
Didier Reynders	Belgium
Abdulla Hassan Saif	Bahrain
Clare Short	United Kingdom
Yashwant Sinha	India
Dominique Strauss-Kahn[3, 4]	France
Lawrence H. Summers[5, 6, 7]	United States
Tarrin Nimmanahaeminda[8]	Thailand
Heidemarie Wieczorek-Zeul	Germany
Xiang Huaicheng[9]	China
Gerrit Zalm[10]	Netherlands

Alternate attending for the member:
[1]Antonio Fazio
[2]Haruhiko Kuroda
[3]Charles Josselin
[4]Jean Lemierre
[5]Timothy F. Geithner
[6]Edwin M. Truman
[7]William Schuerch
[8]Suphachai Phisitvanich
[9]Jin Liqun
[10]Eveline Herfkens

ATTENDANCE

MEMBERS OF FUND DELEGATIONS

Albania
Governor
Shkelqim Cani
Alternate Governor
H.E. Anastas Angjeli
Advisors
Milva Dodbiba
Marta Muco
Leon Shestani

Algeria
Governor
Abdelouahab Keramane
Alternate Governor
Mohammed Laksaci
Advisors
Babaammi Hadji
Mourad Belmokhtar
Abdelatif Benachenhou
Karim Djoudi
Tewfik Hadded
Ammar Hiouani
H.E. Ramtane Lamamra
Said Maherzi
Abdelhamid Temmar

Angola
Governor
Aguinaldo Jaime
Temporary Alternate Governor
Marinela Martins Amaral Ribas
Advisors
Maria Luisa Abrantes
Emanuel Maravilhoso Buchartts
Pedro Afonso Cabral
Francisco da Cruz
Agostinho Fernandes
Nazare da Conceicao Ferreira
Joao M. Fortes
Antonio Franca
Antonio da Silva Inacio
Luis Lelis
Camilo Manuel
Laura M.P. de Alcantara Monteiro
Marilia de Fatima T.V. Pocas
Antonio Rafael
Maria Madalena do Rego Ramalho
Amilcar Santos Azevedo da Silva
Irene Beatriz F. Sobrinho
Cristina Van Dunem

Antigua and Barbuda
Governor
Lennox O. Weston
Advisor
Lionel Hurst

Argentina
Governor
Pablo E. Guidotti
Alternate Governor
Miguel Alberto Kiguel
Advisors
H.E. Carlos V. Corach
Eduardo J. Escasany
Edgard Jose Gagliardi
H.E. Diego Ramiro Guelar
Oscar Lamberto
Ana Maria Mosso de Mortarotti
Gilberto Oviedo

Argentina *(continued)*
Horacio Pernasetti
A. Humberto Petrei
Carlos A. Reutemann
Juan Carlos Romero
Osvaldo Sala
Rodolfo Eduardo Vacchiano
Pablo Verani
Carlos Verna
A. Guillermo Zoccali

Armenia
Governor
H.E. Levon V. Barkhoudarian
Alternate Governor
Tigran Sargsyan
Advisors
Stepan Gishyan
Ashot Kirakosyan
Vahram Nersissiantz
H.E. Armen Sarkissian
H.E. Gagik Shahbazian
Bagrat Yengibaryan
Nerses Yeritsyan

Australia
Governor
Hon. Peter Costello
Alternate Governor
Ted Evans
Temporary Alternate Governors
Gary Johnston
Ian J. MacFarlane
Advisors
Mike Callaghan
Michael Dillon
Gary Hobourn
Michael Mugliston
Karen Maree Ongley
R.W. Rankin
Nigel Ray
Nikki Savva
Gregory F. Taylor

Austria
Governor
Klaus Liebscher
Alternate Governor
Gertrude Tumpel-Gugerell
Advisors
Peter Achleitner
Wolfgang Ippisch
Johann Prader
Robert Reinwald

Azerbaijan
Governor
H.E. Avaz Alakbarov
Temporary Alternate Governor
Vakhid D. Akhundov
Advisors
Heidar Babayev
Hafiz Mir Jalal Pashayev
Ulvi Fuad Seyidzade
Samir R. Sharifov

The Bahamas
Governor
Hon. William C. Allen
Alternate Governor
Julian W. Francis
Advisors
H.E. Sir Arlington Butler
Jaunianne Dorsett
Paul Feeney
Therese Turner-Huggins

Bahrain
Governor
H.E. Abdulla Hassan Saif
Temporary Alternate Governor
Naser Mohamed Yusuf Al Belooshi

Bahrain *(continued)*

Advisor

Isa Abdulrahman Al Thawadi

Bangladesh

Governor

Akbar Ali Khan

Alternate Governor

Mohammed Farashuddin

Barbados

Governor

Rt. Hon. Owen S. Arthur

Alternate Governor

Marion V. Williams

Advisors

Myrtle D. Bishop
H.E. Sir Courtney N. Blackman
Daniel Boamah
Kelvin Arthur Dalrymple
Cleviston L. Haynes
Denise Hinds
Grantley Worrell Smith
Philip St. Hill

Belarus

Governor

Petr Petrovich Prokopovich

Alternate Governor

H.E. Nikolai Y. Petrovich Korbut

Advisors

Georgy Egorov
Vadim Sergeevich Misyukovets

Belgium

Governor

Guy Quaden

Alternate Governor

Gregoire Brouhns

Temporary Alternate Governor

Willy Kiekens

Advisors

Gino Pierre Alzetta
Jean-Pierre Arnoldi
Hiliana Coessens
Louis de Montpellier
Bruno Guiot
Pierre-Yves Jeholet
Christian Josz
Marc Marechal
Philippe Peeters
Jean-Jacques Rey
Dominique Servais

Belize

Governors

Hon. Ralph Fonseca

Alternate Governor

Keith A. Arnold

Advisors

Jaime D. Alpuche
Sydney J. Campbell
Hugh J.E. McSweaney
Nestor Mendez
H.E. James Murphy
Joseph D. Waight

Benin

Governor

H.E. Abdoulaye Bio Tchane

Alternate Governor

Idriss L. Daouda

Advisors

Emmanuel Assilamehoo
Paul Derreumaux
Raoul Donge
Ng'andu Peter Magande
Ibrahim Pedro Boni
Libasse Samb
Souleymane Tamboura

Bhutan

Governor

Sonam Wangchuk

Bhutan *(continued)*

Temporary Alternate Governor
Karma Rangdol

Bolivia

Governor
Juan Antonio Morales
Alternate Governor
Ramiro Cavero Uriona
Temporary Alternate Governors
Enrique Ackermann
Jorge Requena
Advisors
Raul Boada Rodriguez
Armando Pinell Siles

Bosnia and Herzegovina

Governor
H.E. Novak Kondic
Alternate Governor
H.E. Jadranko Prlic
Temporary Alternate Governors
Peter William Nicholl
Kasim Omicevic
Advisors
Emir Aganovic
Branko Bokan
Maruf Burnazovic
Damir Fazlic
Niko Grubesic
Sead Tikvina

Botswana

Governor
Baledzi Gaolathe
Alternate Governor
Freddy Modise
Advisors
Pearl M. Keitumetse
S. Kono
Ontefetse Kenneth Matambo
Linah K. Mohohlo

Brazil

Governor
H.E. Pedro Sampaio Malan
Alternate Governor
Daniel Luiz Gleizer
Temporary Alternate Governors
Fabio de Oliveira Barbosa
H.E. Rubens Antonio Barbosa
Amaury Guilherme Bier
Murilo Portugal
Mario Vilalva
Sergio Ribeiro da Costa Werlang
Advisors
Jose Linaldo Gomes de Aguiar
Jose Luiz Osorio de Almeida Filho
Jose Federico Alvares
Paulo Donizeti de Araujo
Patricia Goes Bakaj
Sergio Bath
Carlos Eduardo Dutra
Aurora Maria Paiva de Faria
Marcio Joao de Andrade Fortes
Betty Grosskopf
Joao Batista do Nacimento Magalhaes
Helio Mori
Daniel Andrade Ribeiro de Oliveira
Jose Marcelo Lima Pontes
Byron Costa de Queiroz
Claudia Netto Safatle
Elcior Ferreira de Santana Filho
Rodrigo de Azeredo Santos
Isac Roffe Zagury

Brunei Darussalam

Alternate Governor
Haji Selamat Haji Munap
Temporary Alternate Governor
Chua Pheng Siong
Advisor
Hj Jefri bin Hj Mohd. Salleh

Bulgaria

Governor
Svetoslav Veleslavov Gavriiski
Alternate Governor
Dimitar Borisov Radev
Advisors
Alexander Bozhkov
Nikolay K. Gueorguiev
Bojidar Lubenov Kabaktchiev
Tchavdar Kostov Kantchev
Plamen Vassilev Orecharski
Svetlana Dimitrova Panova
Nikola Tcholakov
Ilian Draganov Vassilev
Petia Pavlova Vassileva
Stilian Petkov Vatev

Burkina Faso

Governor
H.E. Tertius Zongo
Alternate Governor
Lucien Marie Noel Bembamba
Temporary Alternate Governor
Celestin Kouka Zalle

Burundi

Governor
Gregoire Banyiyezako
Alternate Governor
Cyprien Sinzobahamvya
Advisors
H.E. Thomas Ndikumana
Henri Simbakwira

Cambodia

Governor
Chea Chan To
Advisors
Khay Phousnith
Kim Vada
Sum Sannisith
Mrs. Tal Nay Im

Cameroon

Governor
H.E. Edouard Akame Mfoumou
Alternate Governor
Sadou Hayatou
Temporary Alternate Governor
Urbain Olanguena Awono
Advisors
Polycarpe Abah Abah
Aminou Bassoro
Hirceinte Bengono Belinga
Bruno Iboklene
Pierre Kamdem
Rameline Kamga
Rene T. Mbappou Edjenguele
H.E. Jerome Mendouga
Bienvenu Ndzana
Francois Ngoubene
Jean Philippe Njeck
Justin Njomatchoua
Anatole Nkodo Ze
Ibrahim Taiba Malla Oumate
Joseph Tedou
Pierre Titti

Canada

Governor
Hon. Paul Martin
Alternate Governor
Gordon G. Thiessen
Temporary Alternate Governors
Ian Bennett
Thomas A. Bernes
Joy Kane
Terrie O'Leary
James Peterson

Canada *(continued)*

Advisors

Harry Adams
Isabelle Amano
Howard Brown
Tom Bui
Jeffrey Allen Chelsky
Dale Eisler
Paul R. Fenton
Paul Jenkins
Jill E. Johnson
Karl Littler
Stephen Millar
Maria Minna
Bruce Montador
Jeff Nankivell
John G. Nelmes
Scott Reid
Eric Siegel
Bill Singleton
Donald R. Stephenson
Suzanne Szukits

Cape Verde

Governor

Jose Ulisses Correia e Silva

Alternate Governor

Olavo Avelino Garcia Correia

Advisors

Ana Paula Almeida
Gilda Almada Dias
John D.C. Hall
H.E. Amilcar S. Lopes
Ceciliade Oliveira Moreno
Carlos Manuel de Luz Delgado Rocha
Gregorio Semedo

Central African Republic

Governor

H.E. Theodore Dabanga

Alternate Governor

Jonas Yologaza

Advisors

Joseph Agbo
Lazare Dokoula
H.E. Henry Koba
Marcel Nganassem

Chad

Governor

H.E. Bichara Cherif Daoussa

Alternate Governor

Mahamad Amine Ben Barka

Advisors

H.E. Hassaballah Ahmat Soubiane
Aboulaye Beri
Bidjere Bindjaki
Tom Erdimi
Ali Naffa Fadlassid

Chile

Governor

Carlos A. Massad

Temporary Alternate Governor

Guillermo R. Le Fort Varela

Advisors

H.E. Mario Artaza
W. Andreas Bauer
Francisca Castro F.
Nicolas Eyzaguirre
Felipe Morande
Jose Luis Morel
Hon. Jaime Ravinet
Heinz P. Rudolph
Andres Sanfuentes Vergara
Marta Tonda Mitri

China

Governor

Dai Xianglong

Alternate Governor

Li Ruogu

Temporary Alternate Governors

Ge Huayong
Wei Benhua
Fengming Zhang

Advisors

Chen Jing

China *(continued)*

Chen Yonglong
James H. Lau, Jr.
Julia Leung Fung-Yee
Liu Fushou
Zhengming Liu
Ang Lu
Yang Luo
Song Jianqi
Jessica Wing Kwan Szeto
Xiaolei Wang
Wong Alfred Yun Tong
Ms. Yang Fang
Zhang Jian Ping

Colombia

Governor
Miguel Urrutia Montoya
Temporary Alternate Governors
Patricia Correa
Roberto Junguito Bonnet
Salomon Kalmanovitz Krauter
H.E. Luis Alberto Moreno Mejia
Hon. Juan Camilo Restrepo Salazar
Jaime Eduardo Ruiz Llano
Leonardo Villar Gomez
Advisors
Olver Luis Bernal
Martha Isabel Bonilla
Jorge Castellanos Rueda
Sara Ordonez-Noriega
Carolina Renteria

Comoros

Governor
H.E. Assoumany Aboudou
Alternate Governor
Said Ahmed Said Ali
Advisor
Hamada Attoumani

Republic of Congo

Governor
H.E. Mathias Dzon
Alternate Governor
Pacifique Issoibeka
Advisors
Pascal Bobassa-Ebale
Roger Gossaki
Mbouala Kaba
Delphine Birangui Mbouyou
Leon Raphael Mokoko

Costa Rica

Governor
Alberto Dent Zeledon
Alternate Governor
Jose Rafael Brenes Vega
Advisor
Jose Carlos Quirce

Côte d'Ivoire

Governor
H.E. N'Goran Niamien
Alternate Governor
Lansina Bakary
Advisors
Assie Amani
Beatrice Amoakon
Ano Amoa Antoine
Alexandre Assemien
Adon Amedee Assi
Noel Assohoun
Jean Roger Boua
Adamoh Djelhi Yahot Moliere
Namory Karamoko
Koffi Paul Koffi
Yves-Marie T. Koissy
Paul Kouame
Catherine Kouassi
Kouame Kouassi
Honorine Yaoua Kouman

Cote d'Ivoire *(continued)*

Koffi Moise Koumoue
John William Morrisson
Leon Naka
Kouadio N'Da
Sylvain Oka Yao
Tamimou Ousmane
Kouame Espouse Yao Madeleine

Croatia

Governor
Marko Skreb
Alternate Governor
Zdravko Rogic
Advisors
Aleksander Heina
Eugen Leko
Michael Ante Misetic
Tomislav Presecan
Ruzica Vuger

Cyprus

Alternate Governor
H.G. Akhniotis
Temporary Alternate Governor
Leslie G. Manison
Advisor
Iacovos C. Ioannou

Czech Republic

Governor
Josef Tosovsky
Alternate Governor
Jan Mladek
Advisors
Zdenek Hruby
Jiri Jonas
Dimitrij Loula
Ludek Niedermeyer
Pavol Parizek
Petr Prochazka
Vaclav Rombald
Petr Sedlacek
Frantisek Skoda
Jiri Vetrovsky

Denmark

Governor
Marianne Jelved
Alternate Governor
Bodil Nyboe Andersen
Temporary Alternate Governor
Niels Bartholdy
Michael Dithmer
Henrik W. Fugmann
Advisors
Thomas Elkjaer
Niels Peter Hahnemann
Kai Aaen Hansen
Jens Lundager
Mads Toftegaard Madsen
Catherine Skak Nielsen
Thomas Bo Pedersen
Jens Thomsen
H.E. Knud-Erik Tygesen

Djibouti

Governor
Djama Mahamoud Haid
Alternate Governor
Ahmed Osman Ali
Advisors
Mohamed Ahmed Awaleh
Mohamed Sikieh Kayad
H.E. Roble Olhaye
Said Absieh Warsama

Dominica

Governor
Hon. Julius C. Timothy
Alternate Governor
Rosamund J. Edwards
Temporary Alternate Governor
Cary A. Harris
Advisor
E. Eustace Liburd

Dominican Republic

Governor
Hector Manuel Valdez Albizu
Temporary Alternate Governor
Clarissa de la Rocha de Torres
Advisors
Julio C. Estrella
Eduardo Rodriguez

Ecuador

Governor
Hon. Pablo Better
Alternate Governor
Ivan Ayala
Temporary Alternate Governor
Mauricio Pareja Canelos
Advisors
Miguel Babra Lyon
Patricio Beltran
Carlos Carrera
Ramiro Esteban Crespo Fabara
Rafael Cuesta Alvarez
Maria Del Carmen Morla
Jorge Gallardo Zavala
Andres Hidalgo C.
Gonzalo Hidalgo Teran
Pamela Mata
Jose Medina Serrano
Juan Montufar
Eduardo Pozo Caminer
Arturo Valentin Quiroz Martin
Monica M. Salvador
Mauricio Valencia

Egypt

Temporary Alternate Governor
Mahmoud Ibrahim Abul Eyoun
Advisors
Adel Abdel-Salam
Atef M. Hassaan
Hazem H.K. Hassanein
Wael S. Shoaeb

El Salvador

Governor
Rafael Barraza
Temporary Alternate Governor
H.E. Miguel E. Lacayo
Advisors
Nicola Ernesto Angelucci Silva
Guillermo A. Argumedo
Maurico Choussy Rusconi
Yolanda de Gavidia
Claudio Manuel de Rosa Ferreira
Nelly Lacayo Anderson
Craig Leon
Roberto Rivera Campos
Benjamin Vides Deneke

Equatorial Guinea

Governor
H.E. Miguel Abia Biteo Boriko
Alternate Governor
Martin Crisantos Ebe Mba
Advisors
Hermes Ela Mifumu
Baltasar Esono Eworo
Francisca Eyang Ondo
Matias Mba Medja

Eritrea

Governor
Tekie Beyene
Alternate Governor
Woldai Futur
Advisor
Ms. Tsehai Habtemariam

Estonia

Governor
Vahur Kraft
Alternate Governor
Aare Jarvan

Estonia *(continued)*

Advisors
Agate Dalton
Peter Lohmus
Helo Meigas
Marten Ross
Tanel Ross
Jaan Salulaid
Andres Sutt

Ethiopia

Governor
Teklewold Atnafu
Temporary Alternate Governor
Gebreyesus Guntih Hellamo
Advisors
Fisseha Adugna
Girma Negash Damessa
H.E. Philippos Wolde Mariam
Tadelle Teferra
Tilahun Abbay
Michael Yirdaw

Fiji

Governor
Jone Yavala Kubuabola
Alternate Governor
Semesa Ducivaki

Finland

Alternate Governor
Esko Ollila
Temporary Alternate Governor
Kjell Peter Soederlund
Advisors
Markus Fogelholm
Olli-Pekka Lehmussaari

France

Governor
H.E. Dominique Strauss-Kahn
Alternate Governor
Jean-Claude Trichet
Temporary Alternate Governors
Herve Hannoun
Jean-Claude Milleron
Advisors
Patrick Allard
Michele Aubert
Gilles Bauche
H.E. Francois Bujon de l'Estang
Genevieve Chedeville-Murray
Bertrand Couillault
Eric Danon
Philippe de Fontaine Vive
Thierry Dissaux
Jean-Christophe Donnellier
Claude Fandre
Julien Fontaine
Thierry Francq
Pierre Jacquemot
Herve Joly
Stephane Keita
Gerard Kremer
Serge Pascal Le Gal
Isabelle Mateos y Lago
Nina Mitz
Xavier Musca
Gilles Noblet
Danielle Noirclerc-Schoenberg
Dominique Perreau
Jean Pisani-Ferry
Guy Pontet
Luc Remont
Marc-Olivier Strauss-Kahn
Nicolas Thery
Daniel Voizot

Gabon

Governor
H.E. Emile Doumba
Alternate Governor
Jean-Paul Leyimangoye
Advisors
Michael Adande
Faustin Boukamba
Paul Bunduku-Latha
Marie-Louise Enie Kombila

Gabon *(continued)*

Ange Macaire Longho
Ludovic Nah
Fidele Nguembi-Moussavou
Jean-Christian Obame
Lambert Ondo Ndong
Luc Oyoubi

The Gambia

Governor
Momodou Clarke Bajo
Alternate Governor
Momodou A. Ceesay
Advisors
Valdemar Jensen
Abdulrahman Mboob
Grahame J. Nathan
Sidi Sanneh

Georgia

Governor
Irakli Managadze
Alternate Governor
Temur Basilia
Advisors
H.E. Tedo Japaridze
Ioseb Khelashvili
Mamuka Murjikneli
Alexander Sekhniashvili

Germany

Governor
Ernst Welteke
Alternate Governor
H.E. Hans Eichel
Temporary Alternate Governors
Bernd Esdar
Caio K. Koch-Weser
Axel R.K. Nawrath
Hermann Remsperger
Georg Michael Roeskau
Stefan Schoenberg
Juergen Stark
Advisors
Torsten Albig
Joerg Asmussen
Karlheinz Bischofberger
H.E. Juergen Chrobog
Leo Dautzenberg
Wolf-Dieter Donecker
Reinhard Felke
Gisela Frick
Martin Friewald
Doris E. Grimm
Stephanie Hamacher
Dietrich Hartenstein
Barbara Hoell
Dietmar Huesmann-Menge
Elke Kallenbach
Dirk Heiner Kranen
Nicolette Kressl
Frank Merte
Wolfgang Merz
Ulf Meyer-Rix
Claus Moeller
Wolfgang Moerke
Sabine Mondorf
Andrea Neu
Gregor Alexander Pieske
Juergen Pohnert
Adolf Roth
Konrad Scharinger
Hans Peter Schiff
Volker Schlegel
Oliver Schmalzriedt
Klaus-Peter Schmidt-Deguelle
Claus-Peter Schollmeier
Katrin Schroeder
Gerhard Franz Stratthaus
Ruediger Wilhelm von Kleist
Detlev von Larcher
Hans Georg Wagner
Klaus Weise
Matthias Weise
Rolf Wenzel
Eugene Wollfarth
Michaela Zintl

Ghana

Governor
Kwabena Duffuor

Ghana *(continued)*
Temporary Alternate Governor
Kofi Opoku-Manu
Advisors
Fred Apaloo
John Kwabena Kwakye
Emmanuel Korley Martey
Chris Nartey
Kobina Sekyi
Kojo Thompson
Henry A.K. Wampah

Greece
Governor
Lucas D. Papademos
Alternate Governor
Nikolaos C. Garganas
Advisors
Leonidas Ananiadis
Christos Apostolopoulos
Anna Constantinidou
Anastassios Giannitsis
Spyros P. Papanicolaou
Panagiotis A. Pliatsikas
John Spraos
Spyridon Travlos

Grenada
Governor
Dwight Venner

Guatemala
Governor
Edin Homero Velasquez Escobedo
Alternate Governor
Raul Berrios
Temporary Alternate Governors
A. Del Cid-Bonilla
Mario Alberto Garcia Lara
Ana Sophia Garzaro de Rodriguez
Edwin Haroldo Matul Ruano
Lionel Valentin Maza
Manuel Estuardo Roldan
Advisors
Jose Alejandro Arevalo Alburez
Jose Alfredo Blanco Valdes

Guinea
Governor
H.E. Ibrahima Kassory Fofana
Alternate Governor
Ibrahima Cherif Bah
Advisors
Ibrahima Ahmed Barry
Bintou Conde
Mohamed Alkaly Daffe
Alpha Diallo
Fatima Kassory Toure
Sekou Traore

Guinea-Bissau
Governor
Verissimo Paulino Nancassa
Alternate Governor
Boaventura Eutequio Silva
Advisors
Antonio Oscar Barbosa
Henrique Adriano Da Silva
Wouri Diallo
Alfredo Paulo Mendes
Dauda Saw

Guyana
Governor
H.E. Bharrat Jagdeo
Alternate Governor
Gobind Nauth Ganga
Advisors
Winston D. Jordan
Rajendra Rampersaud
Sonya Roopnauth

Haiti
Governor
Fritz Jean
Temporary Alternate Governor
Roland Pierre

Haiti *(continued)*
Advisors
Georgette J.-L. Carisma
Henry Cassion
Ketleen Florestal

Honduras
Governor
Iliana Waleska Pastor Melghem
Temporary Alternate Governor
H.E. Hugo Noe Pino
Advisors
Jacobo Nicolas Atala Zablah
Guillermo Bueso
Marcos Carias
Mauricio Diaz Burdett
Eduardo Facusse Handal
Jorge Alejandro Faraj R.
Irvin Jerez
Jorge Navarro
Mario Rietti
Carlos A. Rivera Xatruch
Manuel Torres

Hungary
Governor
Gyorgy Suranyi
Alternate *Governor*
Peter Adamecz
Advisors
Miklos Blaho
Akos Cseres
Ferenc Szarvas
Bea Szombati
Szilvia Zador

Iceland
Governor
Birgir Isl. Gunnarsson
Alternate *Governor*
Thordur Fridjonsson
Advisors
Bjorn Dagbjartsson
Ingimundur Fridriksson
Olafur Isleifsson
Arni Magnusson
Axel R. Palmason

India
Governor
Hon. Yashwant Sinha
Alternate Governor
Bimal Jalan
Temporary Alternate Governor
Shankar Nath Acharya
Vijay L. Kelkar
Advisors
Sandip Ghose
Narendra Jadhav
Subodh Kumar Keshava
Madhusudan Prasad
Sudhakar Rao
Roshan Sahay
Asuri Vasudevan
Ratan Prakash Watal

Indonesia
Governor
Syahril Sabirin
Alternate Governor
Mochammad Rosul
Advisors
Burhanuddin Abdullah
Rizal Anwar Djaafara
Cyrillus Harinowo
Difi A. Johansyah
Jeffrey Kairupan
Rachmat Saleh
Sugeng
Aslim Tadjuddin
Bambang S. Wahyudi
Prasetijono Widjojo

Islamic Republic of Iran
Governor
H.E. Mohsen Nourbakhsh
Alternate Governor
Mohammad Javad Vahaji

Islamic Republic of Iran *(continued)*

Temporary Alternate Governor
Mohamad Jafar Mojarrad

Advisors
Ahmad Dadfarnia
Abolfazl Gholami
Mohammad Reza Hajian
Bijan Ila
Abbas Mirakhor
Gholam-Reza Nadali Ataabadi
Abbas Shahyar
Mohammad R. Shojaeddini
Saeed Tofangchi
Bahram F. Zaringhalam

Iraq

Governor
Faik Ali Abdul Rasool

Alternate Governor
Abdul Ahad P. Toma

Ireland

Governor
Hon. Charlie McCreevy, T.D.

Alternate Governor
Maurice O'Connell

Temporary Alternate Governors
Peter Charleton
Padraig McGowan
Pol O'Duibhir
H.E. Sean O'Huiginn
George Reynolds
Michael J. Somers

Advisors
Mandy Johnson
Adrian J. Kearns
Aingeal O'Donoghue
Hannah O'Riordan
Kenneth Thompson

Israel

Governor
H.E. Avraham B. Shochat

Alternate Governor
David Klein

Advisors
Eddy Azoulay
Ohad Bar-Efrat
Dan Catarivas
Erez Gilhar
Rachel Hirschler
Ohad Marani
Sylvia Piterman
Joseph Strauss

Italy

Governor
Hon. Giuliano Amato

Alternate Governor
Vincenzo Desario

Advisors
Gastone Alecci
Carlo Baldocci
Fabrizio Befani
Lorenzo Bini-Smaghi
Pier Antonio Ciampicali
Angelo Cicogna
Pierluigi Ciocca
Ruggero Corrias
Guido De Blasio
Raffaella Di Maro
Riccardo Faini
Giannandrea Falchi
Fabio Franceschini
Giorgio Gomel
Vittorio Grilli
Gherardo La Francesca
Vincenzo La Via
Francesca Manno
Giuseppe Maresca
Luigi Efisio Marras
Domenico Nardelli
Enrico Nardi
Franco Passacantando
Fabrizio Saccomanni
Fernando Salleo
Carlo Santini
Giuseppe Schlitzer

Italy *(continued)*

Carlo A.E. Sdralevich
Vittorio Tedeschi
Franco Tempesta
Augusto Zodda

Jamaica

Governor
Hon. Omar Davies
Alternate Governor
Derick Latibeaudiere
Advisors
H.E. Richard Bernal
Winsome J. Leslie
Wayne St.John McCook
Locksley S. Smith

Japan

Governor
H.E. Kiichi Miyazawa
Alternate Governor
Masaru Hayami
Temporary Alternate Governors
Kiyoto Ido
Takatoshi Ito
Tadashi Iwashita
Seiji Kojima
Haruhiko Kuroda
Masayuki Matsushima
Satoru Miyamura
Zembei Mizoguchi
Koji Tanami
Ken Yagi
Yukio Yoshimura
Advisors
Masayoshi Amamiya
Toshiyuki Furui
Mitsuhiro Furusawa
Koichi Hasegawa
Yasuhisa Hashimoto
Tsutomu Himeno
Eiji Hirano
Toshiaki Hiromitsu
Akinari Horii
Yoshio Horimoto
Mitsutaka Inagaki
Hiroaki Isobe
Akira Kamitomai
Hironori Kawauchi
Michio Kitahara
Toru Kodaki
Kazutomi Kurihara
Kiyoto Maeda
Ken Matsushita
Takehiko Nakao
Hideki Nonoguchi
Kentaro Ogata
Toshio Oya
Nobuhisa Sagawa
Tomoyuki Saisu
Tomohiko Sakamoto
Takeo Shikado
Chikahisa Sumi
Masahiko Takeda
Hideki Takezawa
Rintaro Tamaki
Tadashi Uhira
Mamoru Umemoto
Takashi Wada
Hiroshi Watanabe
Katsuki Yamasaki
Mamoru Yanase

Jordan

Governor
Michel Marto
Alternate Governor
Ziad Moh'd Fariz
Temporary Alternate Governor
Ahmad Hasan Mustafa
Advisors
Muhammad M.A. Hamadah Abdallah
Ghassan F. Ifram
Zuhair Khouri
H.E. Marwan Jamil Muasher

Kazakhstan
Governor
Kadyrzhan K. Damitov
Alternate Governor
Zhannat Ertlesova
Advisor
Nadir F. Burnashev

Kenya
Governor
Micah Kiprono Cheserem
Alternate Governor
Maurice John Pette Kanga
Advisors
John Henry Juma
Sally J. Kosgei
Richard Leaky
Mark Letitoiya Lesiit
Paul G. Ngatia
Peter Claver Joseph Otieno Nyakiamo
Anne C.A. Olubendi

Kiribati
Governor
Hon. Beniamina Tinga
Alternate Governor
Reina Timau
Advisors
Haruko Fukuda
Rimeta Tinga

Korea
Governor
Hon. Bong-Kyun Kang
Temporary Alternate Governors
Yong-Duk Kim
Okyu Kwon
Jong Nam Oh
Advisors
Soo-Man Chang
Dong-Soo Chin
In-Kang Cho
Sung Whan Choi
Nam-Duk Heo
Kwang-Woo Jun
Hak-Ryul Kim
Sung-Bae Kim
Yoon-Kyung Kim
Eun Mo Lee
Sangkyu Lee
Jung-Kyu Oh
Chan-Seung Park
Yeung Kyun Rhee
Dong-Kyu Shin
Hyun-Chul Shin
Hyung-Goo Shin

Kuwait
Governors
H.E. Ahmed Abdullah Al-Ahmed Al-Sabah
Alternate Governor
H.E. Sheikh Salem Abdul-Aziz Al-Sabah
Advisors
Sami Husain Alanbaee
Yousef Al-Awadi
Yousef B.Y.H. Al-Roumi
Khalid Sulaiman Al-Ruwaih
Sheikh Salem Abdullah Al-Ahmed Al-Sabah
Nabil Hamoud Al-Saqabi
Ahmad Mohammed Abdulrehman Bastaki

Kyrgyz Republic
Governor
Ulan Sarbanov
Alternate Governor
Sadriddin Jienbekov
Advisors
H.E. Baktybek D. Abdrissaev
Shamshibek Moldokanov
Djoodat Murataliev
Kubanychbek Omuraliev

Lao People's Democratic Republic

Governor
Soukanh Mahalat
Temporary Alternate Governor
Khamsouk Sundara
Advisor
H.E. Vang Rattanavong

Latvia

Governor
H.E. Edmunds Krastins
Alternate Governor
Einars Repse
Advisors
Iveta Bojare
Roberts Latvis Grava
H.E. Ojars Kalnins
Vija Kasakovska
Pauls Puke
Ilmars Rimsevics
Inna Steinbuka
Aivars Veiss
Peteris Vinkelis

Lebanon

Governor
Riad Toufic Salameh
Alternate Governor
Marwan M. Nsouli
Temporary Alternate Governor
Haroutiun Samulian

Lesotho

Governor
Churchill Thabang Thamae
Alternate Governor
Stephen Mustapha Swaray
Advisors
Kekeletso E. Lekaka
Peete Molapo
H.E. Lebohang Kenneth Moleko
Moeketsi Caiphus Moleko
Ben T. Nteso

Liberia

Governor
Hon. John G. Bestman
Temporary Alternate Governor
Sumo G. Kupee
Advisor
Grace B. Yates

Socialist People's Libyan Arab Jamahiriya

Governor
Taher E. Jehaimi
Alternate Governor
Abdallah Ali Khalifa
Advisors
Saleh Ahmed Keshlaf
Bashir Mahmud H. Nahaesi

Lithuania

Governor
Reinoldijus Sarkinas
Alternate Governor
Dainius Grikinis
Advisor
Stasys Kropas

Luxembourg

Governor
H.E. Jean-Claude Juncker
Alternate Governor
Yves Mersch
Advisors
H.E. Arlette Conzemius
Michele Eisenbarth
Jerome Hamilius
Arsene Joseph Jacoby
Emile Jung
Serge Kolb
Carlo Krieger

Former Yugoslav Republic of Macedonia

Governor
Ljube Trpeski

Former Yugoslav Republic of Macedonia *(continued)*

Alternate Governor
A.M. Stavreska
Advisors
H.E. Ljubica Acevska
Bogoliub Jankoski
Oliver Krliu
Igor Popov

Madagascar

Governor
H.E. Tantely R.G. Andrianarivo
Alternate Governor
Gaston Edouard Ravelojaona
Temporary Alternate Governor
H.E. Zina Andrianarivelo-Razafy
Advisors
Jocelyn Andriambahiny
Vonintsalama Andriambololona
Biclair H.G. Andrianantoandro
Mohamed Houssen
Christophe Poulenc
Jocelyn Victor Rafidinarivo
Renaud Rahagafotsy Rajaonah
Faustin Edmond Rajoelison
Robert F. Rakotoarimanga
Jean Joseph Rakotonirina
M. Ramahay-Mandimby
Daniel Ramarokoto
Florence Ramarokoto
Raymond Rasamoelina
Christian Guy Dettriga Rasolomanana
Lea Ravololondratavy
Ferdinand Velomita

Malawi

Governor
M.A.P. Chikaonda
Alternate Governor
Randson Phillimon Mwadiwa
Advisors
Charles S.R. Chuka
Paul Willie Mamba
Alexander Kisa Mkangama
Naphiyo Aloisius Bernard
Kassam Okhai
Patrick F. Zimpita

Malaysia

Governor
H.E. Dato' Mustapa Mohamed
Temporary Alternate Governor
Dato' Zeti Akhtar Aziz
Advisors
Ranjit Ajit Singh
Aman Ahmad
John Patrick Antonysamy
Latifah Merican Cheong
Yvonne Chia
Siti Hadzar Mohd. Ismail
Ms. Halipah Binti Esa
Madeline Loh Kooi Choo
Baharudin Abdul Majid
Siti Mariam Mohd Yusof
Ng Chow Soon
Ruji bin Ubi
Dato' Ismail Shahudin
Ms. Tan Sook Peng
Dato' Tan Teong Hean

Maldives

Governor
Hon. Arif Hilmy
Alternate Governor
Mohamed Jaleel

Mali

Governor
H.E. Soumaila Cisse
Alternate Governor
H.E. Ahmed El Madani Diallo

Mali *(continued)*

Temporary Alternate Governor
Aboubacar Alhousseyni Toure
Advisors
Abdoulaye Daffe
Baba Dagamaissa
H.E. Chieck Oumar Diarrah
Idrissa Traore

Malta

Alternate Governor
David A. Pullicino
Temporary Alternate Governor
Alfred De Marco
Advisors
Michael Debono
Alfred Lupi

Marshall Islands

Governor
David J. Blake
Alternate Governor
Casten Nemra
Advisor
H.E. Banny de Brum

Mauritania

Governor
Mahfoudh Ould Mohamed Ali
Alternate Governor
Sidi Ould Mouhamdi
Advisors
Bass Abal Bass
N'Guissaly Fall
Aly Kane
Haidara Mohamed Cherif
Mohamed Salem Ould Abdessalam
Abdallah Ould Cheikh-Sidia
Mohamed Mahmoud Ould Hamadi
H.E. Ahmed Ould Khalifa Ould Jiddou
Mohamed Lemine Ould Khlil
Abdallahi Ould Sidaty
Bekaye Ould Sidi Mohamed
Kelly Oumar Sada

Mauritius

Governor
Hon. Vasant Kumar Bunwaree
Alternate Governor
Rameswurlall Basant Roi
Advisors
Peter Craig
Krishnanand Guptar
Hemraz Oopuddhye Jankee
H.E. Chitmansing Jesseramsing
K. Saccaram
Somduth Soborun
Ranapartab Tacouri
S. Neysen Udaiyan
Maurice Vigier de La Tour

Mexico

Governor
Guillermo Ortiz Martinez
Alternate Governor
Martin M. Werner Wainfield
Temporary Alternate Governor
H.E. Jesus Reyes Heroles
Advisor
Javier Guzman-Calafell

Federated States of Micronesia

Governor
Hon. John Ehsa
Alternate Governor
Lorin S. Robert
Advisors
Enrico Calderon
James Naich
Samson Pretrick

Moldova

Governor
Leonid Talmaci
Temporary Alternate Governor
Alexandru Muravschi

Moldova *(continued)*

Advisors

Stela Axenti
H.E. Ceslav Ciobanu
Peter Engstrom
Vlad Spanu

Mongolia

Governor

H.E. Amarjargal Rinchinnyam

Alternate Governor

Jigjid Unenbat

Advisors

Ragchaa Baasan
Bavuusuren Bayasgalan
D. Bayasgalan
D. Boldbaatar
H.E. Jalbuu Choinhor
G. Gankhuyag
Damdin Gantugs
Balbaryn Medree

Morocco

Governor

Abdelmalek Ouenniche

Temporary Alternate Governor

Abdeltif Loudyi

Advisors

Omar Alaoui Benhachem
Jamal Chouaibi
Mohammed Dairi
Lahbib El-Idrissi Lalami
Abdallah El Maaroufi
Mohamed El Merghadi
Abdellah El-Ouadrhiri
Mustapha Faris
Youssef Fehry Fassy
H.E. Rachid Filali
Mohamed Ghozlani
Mustapha Lahboubi
Monkid Mestassi
Fouad Samir
Mostafa Terrab
Ali Tricha

Mozambique

Governor

H.E. Tomaz Augusto Salomao

Alternate Governor

Antonio Pinto de Abreu

Advisors

Manuel Chang
Piedade Macamo Matavela
Gamiliel Munguambe
H.E. Marcos G. Namashulua
Mussa Osman

Myanmar

Governor

U Kyaw Kyaw Maung

Alternate Governor

U Nyo Myint

Advisors

Daw Hmway Hmway Khyne
Daw Ommar Sein
U Thaung Tun

Namibia

Governor

Hon. Nangolo Mbumba

Alternate Governor

Thomas K. Alweendo

Advisors

Heinrich Mihe Gaomab
Annah Hange
Immanuel Iyambo
Frans Johan Janson van Rensburg

Nepal

Governor

Hon. Mahesh Acharya

Alternate Governor

Satyendra P. Shrestha

Temporary Alternate Governor

Madhav Prasad Ghimire

Nepal *(continued)*

Advisors

Dinesh Bhattarai
Yuba Raj Khatiwada
Keshab Bahadur Khatry
Prithivi Bahadur Pande
Thakur Nath Pant
Devendra Pratap Shah
Bhabani Devi Sharma

Netherlands

Governor

A.H.E.M. Wellink

Alternate Governor

Jan-Willem Oosterwijk

Temporary Alternate Governors

Age F.P. Bakker
Henk J. Brouwer
Ron Keller
J. Wijnholds

Advisors

Jerrald M. Hasselmeyer
Evert J.P. Houtman
Sjef Ijzermans
Arie Jacobus Kapteijn
Frits Kemperman
Mark A. Roscam Abbing
Johan H. du Marchie Sarvaas
H.E. Valerie Sluijter
Emsley D. Tromp
Erik C.H. van Andel
Jan Willem van den Wall Bake
Alida H. Van Ee
Karel Van Kesteren
Bram van Ojik
H.E. Wilfred Russell Voges

New Zealand

Governor

Rt. Hon. Sir William F. Birch

Temporary Alternate Governor

Alexander J. Wilson

Advisors

H.E. James Bolger
Brendon H. Doyle
Colin Lynch
Richard Ninness
Ian Michael Woolford

Nicaragua

Governor

H.E. Noel J. Sacasa C.

Alternate Governor

Mario J. Flores

Temporary Alternate Governor

Edgard A. Guerra

Advisors

Adolfo Javier Arguello Lacayo
Roberto J. Arguello
Ricardo Manuel Gomez Diaz
Robert J. Zamora Llanes

Niger

Governor

H.E. Saidou Sidibe

Alternate Governor

H.E. Mahamadou Mouctar Sako

Temporary Alternate Governor

Charles Konan Banny

Advisors

Yacouba Abou
Hamidou Boureima
Moussa Dabal
Alain de Suza
H.E. Joseph Diatta
Hamani Harouna
Aissa Miginyaoua
Boubacar Moumouni Saidou
Ibrahim Samaila
Boubacar Sanda
Abdoulaye Soumana
Hassane Taher

Nigeria

Governor

Chief Joseph Sanusi

Alternate Governor

Akinlose Sylvester Arikawe

Nigeria *(continued)*

Temporary Alternate Governors
John O. Aderibigbe
Michael Olufemi Ojo

Advisors
Alhaji M. K. Abdullahi
Justina Ogugua Ashinze
Hon. John Azuta-Mbata
Alhaji Attahiru Bafarawa
Kassim M. Bichi
David Edevbie
George Edokpo
Solomon Ewuga
Kayode Garrick
James Ibori
Benjamin D. Ibe
Ogunyemi Charles Ijaleye
Hamilton Isu
Christopher Osiomha Itsede
Hajia N.A. Jimoh
Abduliahi M. Nyako
Chigozie E. Obi-Nnadozie
Okorie Awa Uchendu
Udoma Udo Udoma
Mohammed Zailani

Norway

Governor
Svein Ingvar Gjedrem

Alternate Governor
Tore Eriksen

Temporary Alternate Governors
Jarle Bergo
Anne Berit Christiansen

Advisors
Sigurd Klakeg
Kristian Odegaard
Enok Olsen
Lene Sauvik
Erik Storm
Paul Winje

Oman

Governor
H.E. Ali Mohamed Moosa

Alternate Governor
H.E. Hamood Sangour Al-Zadjali

Advisor
Jawad Mohammed Jawad Talib

Pakistan

Governor
Muhammad Yaqub

Alternate Governor
Khalid Jawed

Advisors
Meekal A. Ahmed
Mehrunnisa Bashir
H.E. Tariq Fatemi
Agha Ghazanfar
Tariq Hassan
Abdul Ghafoor Mirza
Azizali F. Mohammed
Farrakh Qayyum
M.A. Zuberi

Palau

Governor
Elbuchel Sadang

Alternate Governor
Casmir Esang Remengesau

Advisor
H.E. Hersey Kyota

Panama

Governor
Ricardo Quijano

Alternate Governor
Bolivar Pariente

Papua New Guinea

Governor
Leonard Wilson Kamit

Alternate Governor
Loi Martin Bakani

Advisors
Graham Michael
Simon Tosali

Paraguay
Governor
Samuel Washington Ashwell
Advisors
H.E. Juan Esteban Aguirre
Carlos Gustavo Fernandez Valdovinos
Orlando Ferreira Caballero
Raul Alberto Florentin Antola
H.E. Armando Hermosilla Martinez
Hernan Mejia J.
Ovidio C. Otazu
Monica Perez dos Santos
Enrique Ramirez

Peru
Governor
German Suarez
Temporary Alternate Governor
Guillermo Castaneda-Mungi
Advisors
Luis Baba Nakao
Jorge Francisco Baca Campodonico
H.E. Gustavo Caillaux
Luis J. Carranza
Juan Miguel Cayo
Claudio de la Puente
Roberto Fernandez
Roberto Heimovits
Oscar A. Hendrick
Carlos Herrera
Carlos Adrian Linares Penaloza
Martin A. Naranjo Landerer
Miguel Risco
Alfonso Rivero
Roberto Rodriguez
Renzo Rossini Minan
Carlos Saito Saito
Luis Alberto Sanchez
Edgar Zamalloa

Philippines
Governor
Rafael B. Buenaventura
Temporary Alternate Governor
Benjamin Estoista Diokno
Advisors
Ramon Z. Abad
Carlos A. Arellano
Rodrigo P. Castelo
Edgardo O. Castro
Florido P. Casuela
Hon. Joseph H. Durano
Nestor A. Espenilla, Jr.
Lily Kho Gruba
Rolleo Ignacio
H.E. Ernesto M. Maceda
Wilhelmina Cruz Manalac
Federico C. Pascual
Gabriel C. Singson
Cesar E.A. Virata

Poland
Governor
Krzysztof J. Ners
Temporary Alternate Governor
Jacek Tomorowicz
Advisors
Edward Basinski
Mieczyslaw Kaminski
Jakub Karnowski
Alicia Kornasiewicz
H.E. Jerzy Kozminski
Tomasz Skurzewski
Wieslaw Szczuka
Krzysztof Wybieralski

Portugal
Governor
Antonio Jose Fernandes de Sousa
Alternate Governor
Antonio Manuel Pereira Marta
Temporary Alternate Governors
Maria Helena Cordeiro
Joao Mauricio Fernandes Salgueiro

Portugal *(continued)*

Advisors

Helena Maria Franco Bebiano
Nuno Maria Mariano de Carvalho Jonet
Maria Lucia A. Almeida Leitao
Emilio Aquiles de Oliveira
Antonio Manuel da Silva Osorio
Vitor Manuel da Silva Rodrigues Pessoa
Jose Joaquim Berberan e Santos Ramalho
Joao Santos
Anselmo Teng
Maria Jose Vaz Rocha Vidal

Qatar

Governor

Yousef Hussain Kamal

Alternate Governor

Hussain Al-Abdulla

Advisors

Salah Mohamed Ibrahim Al-Jaidah
Khalaf Ahmed Al-Mannai
Saeed Abdulla Al-Mosnid
Izzat Mohammed Al-Rasheed
Abdulbasit Al-Shaibei
Bashir Issa Al-Shirawi
Khalid bin Ahmed Al-Suwaidi
Kalid Bin Thani Al-Thani
Abdurahman Dashti
John P. Finigan
Maqbool Habib Khalfan
Ahmed Muftah

Romania

Governor

Mugur Isarescu

Alternate Governor

Ionut Mircea Costea

Advisors

Cosmin Dobran
Ion Dragulin
Mircea Dan Geoana
Gabriela Mihailovici
Andreea Moraru
Gheorghita Oprea
Eugen T. Radulescu
Mugur Tolici

Russian Federation

Governor

Viktor Gerashchenko

Temporary Alternate Governors

Andrei Bugrov
Anatoly Chernyshov
Ivan Ivanov
Mikhail Kasyanov
Oleg V. Mozhaiskov
Aleksei V. Mozhin
Tatiana Paramonova
Oleg Vyugin

Advisors

Dmitri Beskurnikov
Dmitri Borisov
Oleg Gavrilov
Grigori Y. Glazkov
Ekaterina O. Kornitch
Andrei Kostin
Mikhail Lopatin
Andrei Lushin
Stanislav Naumov
Sergei Ovseichik
Lev V. Palei
Aleksander E. Polonskiy
Andrei Reus
Sergei Scherbakov
Aleksandr Shamrin
Vladimir Smenkovski
Aleksandr Surikov
Svetlana Vtyurina
Igor A. Zakharchenkov

Rwanda

Governor

Donald Kaberuka

Alternate Governor

Francois Mutemberezi

Rwanda *(continued)*

Advisors
Alfred G. Kalisa
Camille Karamaga
Anastase Munyandamutsa
Prosper Musafiri
Jean-Marie Nyirimihigo
Guido Rurangwa
Jean M. Rutayisire
Richard Sezibera

St. Kitts and Nevis

Governor
Halva Hendrickson
Alternate Governor
Wendell E. Lawrence
Advisors
Kutayba Y. Alghanim
Jasmine Huggins
Osbert Wordsworth Liburd

St. Lucia

Alternate Governor
Claire Zenith James
Advisors
S.C. McHale Andrew
Martha Auguste
James Fleming
Albert Preville

St. Vincent and the Grenadines

Governor
Arnhim Eustace
Alternate Governor
Maurice Edwards
Advisor
Wendell Samuel

Samoa

Governor
Tuilaepa S. Malielegaoi
Alternate Governor
Papali'i Tommy Scanlan
Temporary Alternate Governor
Tauava Lealaitafea Tofa
Advisors
Robert Lyon
Edward Meredith
Michelle Meredith
Mose Sua
Peter Tapsell

San Marino

Governor
Clelio Galassi
Temporary Alternate Governors
Pietro Giacomini
Raffaele Giardi
Advisors
Daniele Bernardi
Milena Gasperoni
Giorgio Lombardi

São Tomé and Príncipe

Governor
Maria C. Pires de Carvalho Silveira
Alternate Governor
Eugenio Lourenco Soares
Advisors
Agapito Mendes Dias
Jose Luis Suarez Losada

Saudi Arabia

Governor
Ibrahim A. Al-Assaf
Alternate Governor
Hamad Al-Sayari
Temporary Alternate Governor
Abdulrahman Al-Tuwaijri
Advisors
Mohammad Abanumay
Abdullah Abu Samh
Haitham Al-Abdullatif
Khaled M. Al-Aboodi
Ahmed Al-Balawie
Abdulrahman Al-Hamidy
Abdullah Al-Hugail
Ibrahim M. Al-Issa

Saudia Arabia *(continued)*

Medlej Al-Medlej
Abdulrahman Mohammed Almofadhi
Ibrahim M. Al-Mofleh
Mohammed Al-Nafie
Suliman Al-Olayan
Ahmed S.M. Alosaimi
Saeed Al-Qahtani
Abdullah Sulaiman Al-Rajhi
Abdulaziz Rashed Al-Rashed
Abdul Monam Rashed Al-Rashed
Rashed Abdulaziz Al-Rashed
Abdul Aziz S. Al-Saghyir
Saud Al-Saleh
Ali Samir Al-Shihabi
Abdulaziz Al-Turki
Sulaiman M. Al-Turki
Abdulaziz Al-Wohayeb
Saud Al-Yemeni
Sami Al-Yousef
Abdullah bin Salem Bahamdan
Jitendra G. Borpujari
Robert Eichfeld
Abdullah I. El-Kuwaiz
Marcos G. Ghattas
Richard R. Herbert
Abdullah Saleh Kamel
Melhem F. Melhem
Abdulaziz A. O'Hali
Nemeh Elias Sabbagh
Abdulhadi Ali Shaiyef

Senegal

Governor
Mouhamed El Moustapha Diagne
Alternate Governor
Aissatou Niang Ndiaye
Advisors
Fatou Diagne
Ousmane Diene
Samcidine Dieng
Adama Dieye
Abdoulaye Diop
Chimere Diop
Seynabou Diop Ly
Mamadou Faye
Moussa Faye
Amadou Kane
Mamadou Diagna N'Diaye
Seyni N'Diaye
Mamadou Mansour Seck
Cheikh Hadjibou Soumare
Oumar Sylla

Seychelles

Governor
Norman J.D. Weber
Temporary Alternate Governor
Francis Chang-Leng

Sierra Leone

Governor
James S. Koroma
Alternate Governor
Edmund Koroma
Advisors
Andrina R. Coker
Abdulai Kakay

Singapore

Governor
Lim Hng Kiang
Alternate Governor
Koh Yong Guan
Temporary Alternate Governor
Khor Hoe Ee
Advisors
Chan Heng Chee
Chen Zhikai
Kok Li Peng
Kathy Lai
Lee Hwee Hong
Thomas Lim Wee Hwe
Kian Heng Peh
Nor Azlina Sulaiman
Teo Swee Lian
Benjamin William

Slovak Republic
Governor
Marian Jusko
Advisors
Ingrid Brockova
Martin Butora
Eva Karasova
Elena Kohutikova
Karol Mrva
Vladimir Rigasz
Juraj Sipko

Slovenia
Governor
France Arhar
Alternate Governor
Samo Nucic
Advisors
Valter Rescic
Ivan Ribnikar
Marjeta Sketa

Solomon Islands
Governor
Rick Nelson Houenipwela
Alternate Governor
George Kiriau

South Africa
Governor
Tito Titus Mboweni
Alternate Governor
Maria Da Conceicao Ramos
Advisors
G.H. Akharwaray
Zingie Dingani
Nomthi Dube
Marlon Philip Geswint
Anthony Frank Julies
Elias Lesetja Kganyago
Qedani Dorothy Mahlangu
Rosalind Colleen Mowatt
Timothy T. Thahane
Danel van Rensburg
Lambertus van Zyl
Logan Wort

Spain
Alternate Governor
Luis Angel Rojo Duque
Temporary Alternate Governor
Gloria Hernandez Garcia
Advisors
Ignacio Alberich Sotomayor
Luis Calvo-Sotelo Rodriguez-Acosta
Ramon Chaves
Inigo Fernandez de Mesa
Maria Fernandez Garcia
Jose Gasset Loring
Leon Herrera
Jose Ignacio Lagartos
Luis Ma. Linde de Castro
Luis Lucena
Pedro Antonio Merino Garcia
Francisco Ochoa Lopez
Jose Luis Pascual
Miguel Angel Sanchez

Sri Lanka
Governor
Chandrika Bandaranaika Kumaratunga
Alternate Governor
A.S. Jayawardena
Temporary Alternate Governor
G.L. Peiris
Advisors
Ibrahim Ansar
Geetha de Silva
Uthuma Lebbe Mohamme Jauhar
P.B. Jayasundera
Rajapakse A. Jayatissa
A.G. Karunasena
Faiz Mohideen
Janadasa Peiris
M.S. Palitha Perera
Warnasena Rasaputram
W.M. Seneviratne
Jayatilleke Silva

Suriname

Governor
Tjandrikapersad Gobardhan
Alternate Governor
Glenn H. Gersie
Advisors
Rudi M.J. Alihusain
Winston Ramon Caldeira
T. Ainsworth Harewood
Rob H. Van den Heuvel
Adelien Wijnerman

Swaziland

Governor
John P. Carmichael
Alternate Governor
Martin G. Dlamini
Advisors
Mary M. Kanya
Winston Lomahoza
Nomalungelo Magagula
Vincent Mawandile Mhlanga
Christopher Morgan

Sweden

Governor
Urban Backstrom
Alternate Governor
Sven Hegelund
Temporary Alternate Governor
Ake Tornqvist
Advisors
Magnus Alvesson
Ingrid Bonde
Erik Martin Carlens
David Farelius
Frida Forsselius
Lars Heikensten
Jens Henriksson
Christine M. Holm
Lars E.R. Mathlein
Christina Nordh Berntsson
Lars Nyberg

Switzerland

Governor
Hans Meyer
Alternate Governor
Kaspar Villiger
Temporary Alternate Governors
Roberto F. Cippa
Ulrich Gygi
Jean-Pierre Roth
Advisors
Giovanni Antonio Colombo
Alfred Defago
Jacques de Watteville
Giorgio Dhima
Christian Etter
Werner Hermann
Alexander Karrer
Thomas Moser
Peter Puntener
Felix Jakob D. Schaad
Raju Jan Singh
Pascal Strupler
Fritz Zurbrugg

Syrian Arab Republic

Governor
Mohammed Imady
Alternate Governor
Mohammad Bachar Kabbarah
Advisors
Georges El-Ouzone
Ali Muhra

Tajikistan

Governor
Gulomzhon Dzhuraevich Babayev
Alternate Governor
Anvarsho Muzafarov
Advisors
Sadriddin Akramov
Svetlana Sharipova

Tanzania
Governor
Daniel A.N. Yona
Alternate Governor
Daudi T.S. Ballali
Advisors
Amina S. Ali
Enos S. Bukuku
Jerome J. Buretta
Hussein S. Khatib
N.N. Kitomari
Joseph Stephen Cecil Mhando
W.A. Mlaki
Anna Muganda
Omar Yussuf Mzee
Peter Efraim Mayunga Noni
Anastase R. Rwegayura
C. Samanyi
Ali Juna Shamuhuna

Thailand
Governor
Chatu Mongol Sonakul
Temporary Alternate Governors
Aroonsri Tivakul
Paiboon Kittisrikangwan
Advisors
Buncha Manoonkunchai
Kleo-Thong Hetrakul
Namtip Sakornratanakul
Orasa Vongthieres

Togo
Governor
A-H. S.B. Tidjani-Dourodjaye
Alternate Governor
Mongo Aharh-Kpessou
Advisors
Kuaku Richard Attipoe
Essivi Yona Djokpe
Ayewanou Agetoho Gbeasor
Frederic Hegbe
Djovi Tchedjiton Kenou
Lorempo Tchabre Landjergue
Mensavi Lulu Mensah
Kossi Nambea
Nonon Saa
Semodji Mawussi Djossou

Tonga
Governor
Siosiua T.T. 'Utoikamanu
Alternate Governor
Marieta Tukuafu
Temporary Alternate Governor
'Aisake V. Eke
Advisors
'Ofa A. Ketu'u
Sione Ngongo Kioa

Trinidad and Tobago
Governor
Morgan Owen Job
Alternate Governor
Winston C. Dookeran
Advisors
Penelope Forde
Beverly Khan
Victoria Mendez-Charles
Joaquin P. Pujol

Tunisia
Governor
Mohamed Daouas
Temporary Alternate Governor
Hamed Gaddour
Advisors
Faycal Gouia
Nejmeddine Lakhal
Noureddine Mejdoub
Sadok Rouai
Habib Sfar

Turkey
Governor
Recep Onal
Alternate Governor
Gazi Ercel

Turkey *(continued)*

Advisors

B. Sen Akman
Omer Altay
Ugur Bayar
Hasan Sukru Binay
Tekin Cotuk
Emin Dedeoglu
Ozgur Demirkol
Ayse Donmezer
Ali Umit Gonulal
Akif Hamzacebi
Aydin Karaoz
Kursat Kunter
Vural Kural
Melih Nemli
Durmus Oztek
Sureyya Serdengecti
Cihan Terzi
Okan Ucanok
Zafer Yukseler

Turkmenistan

Governor

Khudaiberdy Orazov

Temporary Alternate Governor

Kurban Kurbanov

Advisors

Chary Annaberdiev
Halil Ugur

Uganda

Governor

Gerald M. Ssendaula

Alternate Governor

Charles N. Kikonyogo

Advisors

Richard Kabonero
Louis Austin Kasekende
Keith Muhakanizi
Edith Ssempala
Longino Kigambo Tisasirana

Ukraine

Governor

Victor Youshchenko

Alternate Governor

Igor Oleksandrovych Mityukov

Advisors

Valeriy B. Alioshyn
Olexii Berezhnyi
Anton Buteyko
Vladyslav Chemerys
Valentyna Demchenko
Ihor Hryhorovych Gayduchok
Nataliia Hrebenyk
Volodymyr Grygorovych Khrebet
Tymur Khromayev
Vyacheslav Kozak
Sergiy Kruhlyk
Olena Kucherenko
Valeriy Oleksiyovych Lytvytskiy
Petro Mikheyev
Mykola Pasko
Sergiy Piven
Oleh Polishchuk
Vasyl Rohovyi
Olexandr Shapovalov
Borys Sobolyev
Olexandr Mykolayovych Sorokin
Valentin P. Terpilo
Ihor Umanskyi
Yaroslav Voitko
Vadym V'Yun
Yuriy G. Yakusha
Sergey A. Yaremenko
Yuriy I. Yekhanurov
Sergiy Yermilov

United Arab Emirates

Governor

Sultan Bin Nasser Al-Suwaidi

Alternate Governor

Mohamed Obaid Al-Mazrooei

United Arab Emirates *(continued)*

Advisors

Fadhel Saeed Al Darmaki
Humaid Darwish Al-Katbi
Saleh Al-Khatib
Aajlan Ahmad Al-Qubaisi
Sultan Rashed Ebrahim Saif Al-Sakeb
R. Douglas Dowie
Elfatih Eldkihairiyi
Khalifa Mohammed Hassan
Joyshil Mitter
Charles Neil
Abdulla Mohamed Saleh

United Kingdom

Governor

Gordon Brown

Alternate Governor

Edward A.J. George

Temporary Alternate Governors

Stephen P. Collins
Stephen John Pickford
Nigel Wicks

Advisors

Ed Balls
Robert Mark Burgess
Creon Butler
David Clementi
Jon Cunliffe
Howard Davies
John Drage
Alex Gibbs
Fiona Hamilton
Pam Keenan
Ben Kelmanson
Mervyn King
John Kingman
Ed Milliband
Gus O'Donnell
Oliver Page
Clare Roberts
Peter D. Rodgers
Tom Scholar
Shriti Vadera
Mark Walsh
Nicholas Westcott

United States

Governor Designate

Lawrence H. Summers

Alternate Governor

Alan Greenspan

Temporary Alternate Governors

Caroline Atkinson
Timothy F. Geithner
Alan P. Larson
Karin Lissakers
Michael Marek
Barry S. Newman
Jan Piercy
William Schuerch
Edwin M. Truman

Advisors

John M. Abbott
Andrea Adelman
Spencer T. Bachus
Andrew Baukol
Alan Steele Bowser
Colin I. Bradford
Terrence J. Checki
Michael J. Copps
Alice Marie Dear
Vivian Lowery Derryck
Cinnamon Dornsife
Joseph B. Eichenberger
James H. Fall, III
Roger W. Ferguson
Nathaniel Fields
Stephanie Flanders
William R. Ford
Michele S. Godfrey
Maureen Grewe
Milton Gwirtzman
Robert L. Harlow
James A. Harmon
Mark Jaskowiak
Karen H. Johnson
Melinda Kimble

United States *(continued)*

James M. Lister
Ken Ludden
Meg Lundsager
William J. McDonough
Mark C. Medish
G. William Miller
Holly Toye Moore
Norman K. Nicholson
Daniel A. O'Brien
Clyde Robinson
Nouriel Roubini
Karen Shepherd
Todd Stern
Linda Tsao Yang
Theresa A. Wagoner
Maxine Waters
Mary A. Wileden

Uruguay

Governor
Humberto Capote Lopez
Alternate Governor
Aureliano Berro
Advisors
Javier Bonilla Saus
Walter Calcagno
Ariel Fernandez Cova
Carlos Mora

Uzbekistan

Governor
Mullajonov Faizulla Makhsudjanovich
Temporary Alternate Governor
Zainutdin Mirkhodjaev
Advisors
Rashid Adilov
Murod Askarov
Sherzod A. Guzairov
Shavkat Inamov
Muzaffar Madrakhimov
Sadiq S. Safaev
Murat Yakubjanov

Vanuatu

Governor
Sela Molisa
Alternate Governor
Andrew Kausiama
Advisor
Michael S. Hililan

República Bolivariana de Venezuela

Governor
Antonio Casas Gonzalez
Temporary Alternate Governors
Manuel Lago Rodriguez
Angel Ruocco S.
German Utreras
Advisors
Pilar Alvarez
Beatriz Grando de Araujo
Jesus Rodolfo Bermudez Acosta
Jesus Centeno
Indira Rosalba Garrido Perez
William Larralde Paez
Angelo Lucenti
Hernan Oyarzabal
Oscar Rodriguez
Jose Sifontes
Alfredo Toro Hardy

Vietnam

Governor
Le Duc Thuy
Alternate Governor
Phan Manh Hung
Advisors
Nguyen Quang Thep
Nguyen Van Binh
Nguyen Van Du

Republic of Yemen

Governor
Alawi Saleh Al-Salami
Alternate Governor
Ahmed Abdul Rahman Al-Samawi

Republic of Yemen *(continued)*
Advisors
Faisal Amin Abo-Rass
Abdulwahab Al-Hajjri
Mutahar Al-Saidi
Ali Lutf Al Thor
Omar Salim Bazara
Ahmed A. Ghaleb Saeed
Boniface Nonde
Collins Shamutete

Zambia

Governor
Katele Kalumba
Alternate Governor
Jacob Mumbi Mwanza
Advisors
Donald Chanda
Nathan Chishimba
Denny H. Kalyalya
Dunstan W. Kamana
Deepak Malik
Norman Mbazima
Nawa Musiwa Muyatwa
Benjamin Mweene

Zimbabwe

Governor
Leonard Ladislas Tsumba
Temporary Alternate Governor
Edward Mashiringwani
Advisors
Sign Chabvonga
Olindah Chawora
Fortune Chidavaenzi
Fredrick Ephraim Moffat Chihwai
Mutasa Dzinotizei
Rudo Mavis Faranisi
Remi G. Mushambi Kahari
E.C. Kaunga
Anthony Mothae Maruping
Obert Matshalaga
Anna Mathias Msutze
Simbi Mubako
Henry Mukonoweshuro

Observers, Representatives of International Organizations, and Special Invitees

Abu Dhabi Fund for Development

Ahmed Hussein Baqer
Mohammed Saif Al-Suwaidi Bani Yas

African Development Bank

Omar Kabbaj
Ahmed M.F. Bahgat
Thierry De Longuemar
Theodore Nkodo
Dorte Kabell
Selamawit Yemaneberhan N'diaye

African Export-Import Bank

Christopher Chuka Edordu
Benedict Okechukwu Oramah

Andean Development Corporation

L. Enrique Garcia Rodriguez
Hugo Sarmiento K.
Ana Mercedes Botero
Fidel Jaramillo B.
Carolina Espana

Arab Bank for Economic Development in Africa

Medhat Sami Lotfy
Kamal Mahmoud Abdellatif
Ebe Ould Ebe

Arab Fund for Economic and Social Development

Abdulatif Yousef Al-Hamad
Ismail Tawfiq El-Zabri
Mervat Wahba Badawi
Husam Omar Khalil

Arab Monetary Fund

Jassim Al-Mannai
Samir Abiad

Asian Development Bank

Tadao Chino
John Lintjer
B.N. Lohani
Shinji Ichishima
Christine I. Wallich
Louis Wong
Peter Mccawley
Yoshihiro Iwasaki
Masaru Yoshitomi
Shamshad Akhtar
Hisashi Ono
Wong Ching Hoe
Patricia Moser
Eva L. Relova
Arvind Mathur
Richard A. Claudet

Association of African Development Finance Institutions

Magatte Wade

Bank for International Settlements

Andrew D. Crockett
Andre Icard
William R. White
John G. Heimann
Svein Andresen
T.R.G. Bingham
Pierre Cardon De Lichtbuer
Daniele Nouy
Josef Van't Dack

Bank of Central African States

Jean-Felix Mamalepot
Antoine Nkodia
Serge-Blaise Zoniaba
Joseph Nyonuchi Maison
Adam Madji
Aime D. Bida-Kolika

Caribbean Community

Maurice Odle
Evelyn Wayne

Caribbean Development Bank

Neville L. Grainger
Dorla Humes

Center for Latin American Monetary Studies

Juan Manuel Rodriguez Sierra

Central African States Development Bank

Emmanuel Dokouna
Paul-Gilles Nanda

Central American Bank for Economic Integration

Pedro Specia Garcia
Jorge Rodriguez Mancera
Luis Ernesto Santamaria Agudelo
Alejandro Jose Rodriguez Zamora
Maria del Pilar Escobar Pacas
Eduardo Membreno

Central American Monetary Council

Edgard Martinez
Miguel Antonio Chorro Serpas
Roberto Incer

Central Bank of West African States

Michel Komlanvi Klousseh
Emmanuel-Marie Nana
Mamadou Diop
Pascal-Irenee Koupaki
Alain G. Komaclo
Bolo Sanou
Sogue Diarisso
Ismaila Dem

Common Fund for Commodities

Rolf W. Boehnke

Common Market for Eastern and Southern Africa

Nicholas K.N.K. Biwott, Egh, Mp
Erastus J.O. Mwencha
Martin Ogang
Issa Lukwago
M. Serunjogi
Mark Pearson
Hardwork N. Pemhiwa
Azhari Gasim Ahmed

Commonwealth Secretariat

Chief Emeka Anyaoku
Sir Humphrey Maud, Kcmg
Dame Veronica Sutherland
Stuart Mole
Kaye Whiteman
Rumman Ahmad Faruqi
Indrajit Coomaraswamy

Cooperation Council for the Arab States of the Gulf

Ajlan A. Al-Kuwari
Nasser I. Al-Kaud

Council of Europe Social Development Fund

Raphael Alomar
Kari Nars
Ignacio Garrido Sanchez
Martin M. Murtfeld
Rainer B. Steckhan

East African Development Bank

Fabian R. Tibeita
Protase T. Tehingisa
Joram Kariisa-Kasa
Mahesh K. Kotecha

Economic Community of West African States

Lansana Kouyate
D. Barthelemy Drabo
Thierno Bocar Tall
Yaya Sow
Rebily David Asante

European Bank for Reconstruction and Development

Horst Koehler
Charles R. Frank, Jr.
Steven D.F. Kaempfer
Nicholas H. Stern
Noreen Doyle
Marcus J. Fedder
Barbara Ann Clay
Ullrich H. Kiermayr
Ricardo Lago
Olivier Descamps
Ayesha Shah
Kurt Geiger
Axel Bertuch-Samuels
Thomas Moser
Jill Williams
Teresa De Barcenas

European Central Bank

Willem F. Duisenberg
Otmar Issing
Tommaso Padoa-Schioppa
Pierre Van Der Haegen
Manfred J. Koerber
Michele Kirstetter

European Free Trade Association

Kjartan Johannsson

European Investment Bank

Sir Brian Unwin
Wolfgang Roth
Ariane Obolensky
Rudolf De Korte
Ewald Nowotny
Friedolin Weber-Krebs
Jean-Louis Biancarelli
Walter Cernoia
Claudio Cortese
Martin Curwen
Rene Karsenti
Jean-Claude Bresson
Jean-Jacques Schul
Christopher Bearne
Fiona Turner

European Investment Fund

Gerbrand G. Hop
Michel Berthezene
Elena Rotondi

European Union

Poul Nielson
Pedro Solbes Mira
Luis Planas
Giovanni Ravasio
Herve Carre
Joly Dixon
Guenter Grosche
Paul N. Goldschmidt
Philippe Petit-Laurent
Vassili Lelakis
Michael Green
Peter Bekx
Christian Ghymers
Barbara Kauffmann
Hugo Paemen
Werner Schuele
Willy Helin
Anne Vorce
Vlassia Vassikeri

Food and Agriculture Organization of the United Nations

Charles H. Riemenschneider

Inter-American Development Bank

Enrique V. Iglesias
K. Burke Dillon
Charles O. Sethness
Carlos Ferdinand
Ricardo Hausmann
Euric Allan Bobb
Carlos Santistevan
Gabriela Sotela

Inter-American Investment Corporation

John C. Rahming
Raul R. Herrera
Jacques Rogozinski
Roldan Trujillo

International Fund for Agricultural Development

Fawzi Hamad Al-Sultan
Vera P. Weill-Halle
Nikolaus Schultze
Fawzi H. Rihane
Robert Cassani
Jessica Simmons

International Labor Organization

Juan Somavia
Maria Angelica Ducci de Santa Cruz
Eddy Lee
Stanley G. Taylor
Guy Ryder
Anthony G. Freeman
Mary W. Covington

International Telecommunications Union

Walter Richter

Islamic Development Bank

Ahmad Mohamed Ali
Tarik Kivanc
Bader-Eddine Nouioua
Suleiman Ahmad Salem
Amadou Moustapha Diouf
Aftab A. Cheema
Mohameden Mohamed Sidiya

Kuwait Fund for Arab Economic Development

Waleed Al-Bahar

Latin American Economic System

Eduardo Mayobre

Latin American Reserve Fund

Roberto Guarnieri Cammilli
Andres Gamarra
Silvio Javier Comboni Salinas

Nordic Development Fund

Jens Lund Sorensen
Jesper Andersen
Stella Eckert

Nordic Investment Bank

Jon Sigurdsson
Erkki A.O. Karmila
Bo Heide-Ottosen
Eivind Dingstad
Oddvar Sten Ronsen
Heidi Syrjanen

OPEC Fund for International Development

Y. Seyyid Abdulai
Saleh Al-Omair
Said Aissi
Jumana A.W. Dejany
Anajulia Tarter
Nelly Ruiz

Organization for Economic Cooperation and Development
Donald J. Johnston
Ignazio Visco
Richard Carey
Fritz Meijndert
Paul Mylonas

Development Assistance Committee
Jean-Claude H. Faure

Organization of African Unity
Frederick Yao Alipui
Omotayo Olaniyan

Organization of American States
John Christopher Wood

P. L. O.
Mohammad Zuhdi Nashashibi
Fouad H. Sh. Beseiso
Amin M.A. Haddad
Samih Abed
Abla M.Z. Nashashibi
Aziz M. Abu-Dagga
Khalid S.K. Kayed

Saudi Fund for Development
Abdulaziz A. Al-Sehail

United Nations
Kofi Annan
Shashi Tharoor
Ian Kinniburgh
Oscar De Rojas

UN Children's Fund
Natalie Hahn

UN Conference on Trade and Development
John Toye
Yilmaz Akyuz
Karl P. Sauvant
Philip Straatman

UN Development Programme
Mark Malloch Brown
Roy D. Morey
Mounir Tabet

UN Economic Commission for Africa
Kingsley Y. Amoako
Elene Makonnen

UN Economic Commission for Europe
Dieter Hesse
Virginia Cram-Martos

UN Economic Commission for Latin America and the Caribbean
Ines Bustillo
Helvia Velloso
Rex Garcia

UN Educational, Scientific, and Cultural Organization
Frank Method

UN Industrial Development Organization
Judith Evans
George B. Assaf
Jette Jensen

Universal Postal Union
Juan B. Ianni
Heli Heikkila

West African Development Bank
Boni Yayi
Yao Agbo N'de Hounouvi
M'baye Thiam

West African Economic and Monetary Union

Moussa Toure
Younoussi Toure
Kalou Doua Bi
Frederic Assomption Korsaga
Adele Congo-Kabore

World Health Organization

Bernard P. Kean

World Trade Organization

Michael Moore
Richard Eglin
John Hancock
Keith M. Rockwell
Patrick Low

EXECUTIVE DIRECTORS, ALTERNATES, AND ADVISORS

Executive Directors	*Alternate Executive Directors*	*Advisors to Executive Directors*
Abdulrahman Al-Tuwaijri	Sulaiman M. Al-Turki	Melhem F. Melhem
Alex Barro Chambrier	Damian Ondo Mane	Abdel Rehman Ismael
		Bernard Konan
		Joseph Ntamatungiro
		Samba Thiam
Thomas A. Bernes	Peter Charleton	Jeffrey Allen Chelsky
		Paul R. Fenton
		Therese Turner-Huggins
Agustin Carstens	Hernan Oyarzabal	A. Del Cid-Bonilla
		Jose Luis Pascual
Roberto F. Cippa	Wieslaw Szczuka	Fritz Zurbrugg
Bernd Esdar	Wolf-Dieter Donecker	Wolfgang Merz
Nicolas Eyzaguirre	A. Guillermo Zoccali	Jose Antonio Costa
		Oscar A. Hendrick
Riccardo Faini	John Spraos	Joao Santos
		Giuseppe Schlitzer
Kai Aaen Hansen	Olli-Pekka Lehmussaari	Axel R. Palmason
		Inna Steinbuka
Kleo-Thong Hetrakul	Cyrillus Harinowo	Nguyen Quang Thep
Vijay L. Kelkar	A.G. Karunasena	Narendra Jadhav
Willy Kiekens	Johann Prader	Jiri Jonas
		Szilvia Zador
Karin Lissakers	Barry S. Newman	Mark Sobel
Jean-Claude Milleron	Gilles Bauche	Bertrand Couillault
Abbas Mirakhor	Mohammed Dairi	Meekal A. Ahmed
		Mohammad R. Shojaeddini
Jose Pedro de Morais, Jr.	Cyrus D.R. Rustomjee	Patrick A. Akatu
		Lodewyk J.F. Erasmus
		J. Mills Jones
		Yasmin Patel
Aleksei V. Mozhin	Andrei Lushin	Lev V. Palei
Stephen John Pickford		Stephen P. Collins
Murilo Portugal	Olver Luis Bernal	Julio C. Estrella
		Helio Mori
A. Shakour Shaalan	Abdelrazaq F. Al-Faris	Samia S. Farid
		Oussama A. Himani
		Magda Elsayed Kandil
Gregory F. Taylor	Jong Nam Oh	Ian Michael Woolford
Wei Benhua	Fengming Zhang	Yang Luo
J. Wijnholds	Yuriy G. Yakusha	Ion Dragulin
		Evert J.P. Houtman
Yukio Yoshimura	Masahiko Takeda	Mamoru Yanase

LIST OF ABBREVIATIONS

ACP	African, Caribbean, and Pacific Group
AFTA	ASEAN Free Trade Area
APEC	Asia-Pacific Economic Cooperation
ASEAN	Association of South East Asian Nations
BIS	Bank for International Settlements
CCFF	Compensatory and Contingency Financing Facility
CCL	Contingent Credit Line
CDF	Comprehensive Development Framework
CDRC	Corporate Debt Restructuring Committee
CEFTA	Central European Free Trade Agreement
CIS	Commonwealth of Independent States
CPSS	Committee on Payment and Settlement Systems
DAC	Development Assistance Committee
ECOSOC	United Nations Economic and Social Council
EDC	Export Development Corporation
ESAF	Enhanced Structural Adjustment Facility
EU	European Union
FDI	foreign direct investment
FSF	Financial Stability Forum
G-7	Group of Seven
G-20	Group of Twenty
G-24	Group of Twenty-Four
GDDS	General Data Dissemination System
GDP	gross domestic product
GNP	gross national product
GSP	Generalized System of Preferences
HIPC	heavily indebted poor country
HLI	highly leveraged institution
IAIS	International Association of Insurance Supervisors
IASC	International Accounting Standards Committee
IBRD	International Bank for Reconstruction and Development
IDA	International Development Association
IDA-12	twelfth replenishment of IDA
IFC	International Finance Corportation
IMF	International Monetary Fund
IOSCO	International Organization of Securities Commissiond
MDB	multilateral development bank
MIGA	Multilateral Investment Guarantee Agency
NPL	nonperforming loan

NPV	net present value
ODA	official development assistance
OECD	Organization for Economic Cooperation and Development
PACT	Partnership for Capacity Building in Africa
PIN	Public Information Notice
PKSF	Palli Karma Shahayak Foundation
PRSP	Poverty Reduction Strategy Papers
SAARC	South Asian Association for Regional Cooperation
SAC	Structural Adjustment Credit
SCA-2	Second Special Contingent Account
SDDS	Special Data Dissemination Standard
SDR	special drawing right
SRF	Supplemental Reserve Facility
UN	United Nations
UNCTAD	United Nations Conference on Trade and Development
UNDP	United Nations Development Program
WTO	World Trade Organization
Y2K	Year 2000